RESEARCH HANDBOOK ON THE POLITICS OF INTERNATIONAL LAW

RESEARCH HANDBOOK ON THE POLITICS OF INTERNATIONAL LAW

Editor

Garrick Elwin

Socialy PRESS
AN IMPRINT OF SCITUS ACADEMICS

Research Handbook on the Politics of International Law

Edited by **Garrick Elwin**

This Book is Printed on Acid-Free Paper. ♾

ISBN: 978-1-68117-798-4

Library of Congress Control Number: 2017938826

Socialy Press

(An Imprint of Scitus Academics),

616, Corporate Way, Suite 2, 4766,

Valley Cottage, NY 10989

www.scitusacademics.com

Notice

Printed in United States of America.

Preface

Law and politics are deeply entwined. Law is a vital tool of government action, an instrument with which government tries to influence society. Law is also the means by which government itself is structured, regulated and controlled. It is no surprise, then, that law is an important prize in the political struggle and that law shapes how politics is conducted. The scholarly study of law and politics is a growing and assorted field. The range of scholarship in the area reflects the wide scope of issues and questions that are relevant to the field of law and politics and that invite new and further study. Law and politics create their own particular pictures of reality. Sometimes those pictures overlap, sometimes they differ. Yet, there is something that the law should never include in its sphere; namely, the differentiation of adversaries according to a purely political criterion. This leads to a strict separation between "ours" and "yours", or, in its most radical expression, to a strict separation between friend and enemy. When the latter occurs, politics inevitably prevails over the law, and reduces or damages the autonomy of the rule of law. The diversity of scholarly interest in law and politics also reflects the interdisciplinary conversation that the field invites.

Research Handbook on the Politics of International Law presents the studies for comparative analysis of politics and international law at different stages of governance and in different governance systems. It examines some basic characteristics of the relationship between national and international law and politics. The text introduces the theoretical frameworks, empirical cases, policy instruments, and cutting-edge discussions in the field of international law from an International Relations perspective. It will examine the interrelationships between international politics and international law in several specialized areas of international law, such as human rights, the environment, international criminal justice, trade, and/or the use of force.

Table of Contents

1

CHAPTER

Political Modernisation: The Rule of Law Perspective on Good Governance

Jan-Erik Lane

Charles Humbert, Geneva, Switzerland

ABSTRACT

The United Nations, the WB as well as the IMF speak much of "good governance", but what is the meaning and reference of this elusive expression? In this paper, I will link it with the concept(s) of rule of law. Rule of law notions are spreading around the globe, being relevant for the transformation of monarchies and one-party states. Thus, world media are now reporting that for instance China's leadership is seriously debating making state reforms that would be conducive to more of the rule of law in the country. This is not be interpreted as a push towards western democracy. To clarify the relation between rule of law and competitive party democracy, this paper presents an enquiry into rule of law I and rule of law II. This distinction has a long history in political thought and constitutional developments. Data from the encompassing World Bank Governance project is used to validate these concepts referentially.

Keywords: Good Governance, Constitutional Law, Principal-Agent Model, Dimensions of Rule of Law: Rule of Law I, Rule of Law II, Democracy, World

Bank Governance Project, Dimensions of Good Governance, Principal-Agent Theory of Politics and the State, Measuring Rule of Law von Mohl

1. INTRODUCTION

The rationale of constitutional rules or institutions is to be found in the restraining of political leaders in so- called principal-agent games that unfold constantly in politics and public administration. Constitutions are best viewed as institutional mechanisms, devised to constrain the behaviour of political elites. These mechanisms are man or woman made devices of rules that are put in place, and hopefully enforced to constrain activities, i.e. institutions. A mechanism consists of a combination of institutions that are constructed or evolve over time for the purpose of directing human actors towards outcomes. The mechanisms channel the behaviour of men and women, affecting their preferences, objectives and interests.

The essence of rule of law institutions is to constrain the political agents—politicians at various levels of governments, political parties, rulers, bureaucrats, agencies, etc. —to the advantage of the demos, i.e. the population in a country. Only rule of law institutions can restrain political agents from engaging in opportunistic behaviour, like e.g. corruption, favouritism, embezzlement or patronage or the employment of excessive force like torture and sudden disappearances or seizures.

2. CONSTITUTIONAL PRINCIPLES

The doctrine of constitutionalism entails the idea of limited government. Moreover, limited government in relation to civil society implies a state that operates under certain key rules (Brazier, 1990 ; Bradley & Ewing, 2010):

1) Legality: government is exercised by means of laws, enforced ultimately by an independent judiciary;
2) Lex superior: there is a higher law—the constitution—that guarantees certain rights for the citizens, like e.g. equality under the law, due process of law and habeas corpus;
3) Triaspolitica: executive, legislative and judicial powers are to be separated;
4) Accountability: governments can be held responsible for their actions and non-actions through various established procedures of criticism and complaint, enquiry and removal from office as well as redress;

5) Representation: the people have a SAY somehow in government through representative institutions.

These principles above emerged hundreds of years ago, long before democracy was introduced in many countries at the end of the First World War in Europe and America (Lloyd, 1991a; Lloyd, 1991b ; McIlwain, 1958 ; Neumann, 1986). Today all existing democracies endorse these constitutional principles: constitutional democracies. But several non-democratic countries honour principles of the rule of law without accepting Western style democracy. Thus, rule of law is relevant to both democratic and non-democratic regimes.

One encounters the principles of rule of law above in various forms through history, either a few of them or all five (Burns & Goldie, 1991 ; Wormuth, 1949 ; Pennock & Chapman, 1979 ; Jowell, 1994; Jowell & Oliver, 1994). They are to be found long before the democratic regime was theorized thoroughly by Spinoza and Rousseau and it was practised in some countries with Common Law without democracy and in other countries in the form of the German Rechtsstaat (Reiss, 1970 ;Riley, 1983). Kant (1974) advocated rule of law, but he was not a democrat, endorsing constitutional monarchy, underling legality and due process of law more that representation and popular accountability. The political scientist von Mohl (1832) was an exception in Germany, combining all five principles above. Today, the rule of law principles 1 - 5 are relevant to all kinds of political regimes in the world.

Constitutional government embodies institutions or rules that constrain those active in domestic or international politics today. Thus, the meaning of "constitution" is a set of principles or rules that constrain rulers, politicians, governments or states. But there can be constitutional government without Western democracy, based upon competitive elections among political parties. Let me explain the distinction between two key concepts in good governance: rule of law I (legal integrity, judicial autonomy) and rule of law II (competitive party government), as they refer to good governance, according to the World Bank approach in its Governance project.

3. RULE OF LAW I AND II

The concept of good governance has no standard definition in the dictionaries. Instead, I will rely upon the approach of the World Bank project to governance. The World Bank (WB) states:

"Governance consists of the traditions and institutions by which authority in a country is exercised. This includes the process by which governments are selected, monitored and replaced; the capacity of the government to effectively formulate and implement sound policies; and the respect of citizens and the state for the institutions that govern economic and social interactions among them". http://info.worldbank.org/governance/wgi/index.asp

The World Bank's Worldwide Governance project, mapping good or bad governance around the globe during the last decade, identifies six dimensions in of the concept introduced in the quotation above.

In the World Bank Governance project, one encounters the following definition of "rule of law":

Rule of law (RL) = capturing perceptions of the extent to which agents have confidence in and abide by the rules of society, and in particular the quality of contract enforcement, property rights, the police, and the courts, as well as the likelihood of crime and violence (Kaufmann, Kraay, & Mastruzzi, 2010: p. 4).

Rule of law (RL) is explicitly separated from voice and accountability (VA), which is defined as follows in the World Bank project thusly:

Voice and Accountability (VA) = capturing perceptions of the extent to which a country's citizens are able to participate in selecting their government, as well as freedom of expression, freedom of association, and a free media (Kaufmann, Kraay, & Mastruzzi, 2010: p. 4).

The World Bank Governance project suggests four additional dimensions of good governance (political stability, government effectiveness, regulatory quality, and the control of corruption). The World Bank Governance project employs a host of indicators in order to measure the occurrence of rule of law RL around the globe, which results in a scale from −3 to +3.

In a constitutional democracy, there is a combination of both rule of law (RL) and voice and accountability (VA). But rule of law was conceived already in the Ancient and medieval periods, whereas Western type democracy belongs to the 20th century. Thus, I will separate between a narrow concept of role of law I, corresponding to the World Bank's terminology, and rule of law in a broad concept, as including voice and accountability (VA). Several countries have or may introduce rule of law I without accepting rule of law II, i.e. party competitive democracy.

Rule of law principles offer mechanisms that restrain behaviour. We distinguish between rule of law in a narrow sense (legality, due process) —rule of law I—and in a broad sense—rule of law II (constitutional democracy). Some countries practice only rule of law I, whereas other countries harbour both mechanisms. A few countries have neither rule of law I or rule of law II, especially failed or rogue states or states in anarchy or anomie. Let us consider how China is ranked in the World Bank Governance project.

Figure 1 shows the overall country picture with rule of Law II on the x-axis (voice and accountability) and rule of Law I on the y-axis (legality and judicial autonomy).

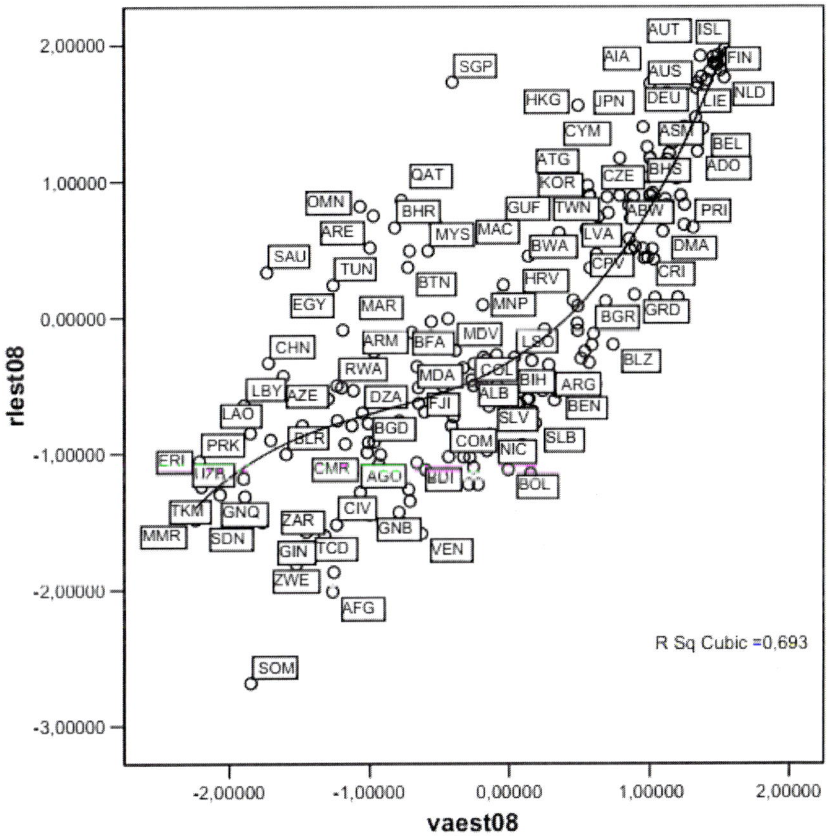

Source: Governance Matters 2009. Worldwide Governance Indicators 1996-2008: vaest08, rlest08.

Figure 1. Rule of law I (rlest08) and rule of law II (vaest08).

In general, the occurrence of rule of law II is a sufficient condition for the existence of rule of law I. But rule of law I—legality and judicial independence—is only a necessary condition for rule of law II—constitutionalism as voice and accountability, according to Figure 1. The largest state on the Earth—China (CHN)—scores low on rule of law II and 0 on rule of law I, whereas the tiny city-state of Singapore (SNG) ranks high on rule of law I and medium on rule of law II. Why, then, would reforms in China towards better rule of law I be important for both the people of the country and international relation?

Figure 1 calls attention to the relevance of the distinction between rule of law I and rule of law II. Several countries in the world satisfy rule of law I requirements without scoring high on the rule of law II requirements. Improving rule of law I with for instance the Ombudsman Office would matter much in many countries, even though they are not democracies, according to rule of law II criteria.

4. WHY RULE OF LAW I OR II: WHAT IS THE BASIC RATIONALE?

There is a form of interaction that tends to be long-term between individuals, which involves a hiatus between the agreement about what is to be done against remuneration (ex ante) and the later in time fulfillment of this contract (ex post). This time interval, lasting often more than several months or years, sets up the monitoring problem: Has the agreement been fulfilled in accordance with the considerations when the contract was made? This type of interaction does not take place in the various market forms, but constitutes a problem of analysis in itself (Arrow, 1985). The more this special type of contracting was analysed, between a principal asking for a service or job on the one hand and a set of knowable agents delivering this service or job on a long-term contract, the more often it was found in various important sectors (Ross, 1973 ; Grossman & Hart, 1983 ;Sappington, 1991 ; White, 1992 ; Ackere, 1993 ; Althaus, 1997). What came to the known as "the principal's problem" was found in lengthy interactions within legal affairs, psychiatry, sock-market trading and agricultural production (sharecropping).

Two basic aspects of long-term contracting are transaction costs and asymmetric information, which never entered in the standard assumptions of the neo-classical decision model in mainstream economics. Since the agent(s) is supposed have much more knowledge about the service or job to be done, the principal needs to diminish this advantage, but without running up too heavy transaction costs, through costly monitoring or litigation. The agent(s) wants remuneration, which has to come from the value of the service or job delivered. Thus, there is both cooperation and conflict. In politics, one may model two principal-agent games, one game for moral hazard focusing upon good or bad performance after the election and another game for adverse selection or the choice of good or bad politicians before the election.

The theory of transaction costs stimulated this way of looking at long-term contracting (Rao, 2002). It was also furthered by insights into the nature of institutions, where rules could be employed to prop up the position of the principal (Furubotn & Richter, 2005 ; Weingast, 1989 ; Persson & Tabellini, 2003). However, the public choice school contributed little to the theory) of principal and agents (Breton, 2007; Mueller, 2003), focusing almost exclusively on rent-seeking. Now, rule of law is nothing less than the regime that hands down institutions that counter-act agent opportunism, bolstering the principal.

5. PRINCIPAL-AGENT INTERACTION IN POLITICS

In well-ordered societies, the political agents in government operate the set of governance mechanisms that we call "state" (Kelsen, 1961; 1967). It claims sovereignty over its country, but it enters into a web of relationships with other states, governed by the rule of law principles of the international society, namely the so-called public international law (Schwöbel, 2011) .

A state or government may be seen as flowing from an agreement among the members about helping each other in securing peace and stability. A body of rules would codify this mutual agreement. A political club quickly develops a division of labour between leaders and followers, the subgroup who implements the rules and the subgroup who follow the rules in their behaviour. I will call the followers the "principal" of the political club and the leaders the "agents". Thus, the political club will be modelled as confronted by the principal-agent problematic, comprising inter alia:

- Who are the political agents?
- How are these agents selected?
- Can agent power be laid down formally?
- Are there restraints on the power of the agents?

The principal-agent framework has enjoyed farreaching success in modelling interaction between persons where one works for the other. This interaction is to be found in many settings, such as agriculture, health care, insurance and client-lawyer (Rees, 1985 ; Laffont & Martimort, 2002). As a matter of fact, the principal-agent problematic is inherent in any employment relationship where one person works for another, who pays this person by means of the value of the output.

Whenever people contract with others about getting something done, there arise the typical principal-agent questions:

1. What is the quid pro quo between the principal and the agent?

2. How can the principal check the agent with regard to their agreement?
3. Who benefits the most from the interaction between principal and agent?

These questions concerning principal-agent interacting arise whenever there is a long-term contract between two groups of people, involving the delivery of an output against remuneration as well as a time span between the making of the contract and the ending of the relationship with the delivery of the output. One finds this type of interaction in the client-lawyer relationship in the legal context, in the owner-tenant interaction in sharecropping as well as in the asset holder-broker relation in financial markets.

In politics, transaction costs are minimised by handing over the responsibility for the tasks of the political club to a set of people, called the leaders. I will employ the word: "agents". The agents provide the members of the political system—the principal—with the chief goods and services of this type of community, when they are successful that is.

The agents and the principal are the two key components of political interaction that run through all political systems, whatever their nature may be. The problem of institutionalising the polity originates in this opposition between agents and the principal.

When governance is modelled as a principal-agent game, then it is not merely a matter of the interaction between two or more persons. The agent(s) is hired to accomplish an output or outcome, to be paid for his/her effort to do so. Here we have the two key foci in a principal-agent evaluation of governance: 1) the achievements—good or bad performance; 2) the remuneration—high or low.

In the literature, these two aspects—performance and remuneration—are not always kept separate. Thus, one speaks of bad performances when there is only high remuneration like in "corruption" or "rent-seeking". Moreover, bad performance is sometimes equated merely with a failure to live up to promises made. The principal- agent framework is applicable to governance even when there is no form of embezzlement by the agent or merely reneging on lofty promises.

6. AGENTS' OPPORTUNISM

Political agents are no different from any other human beings. They are driven by the same mixture of egoism and altruism as the average person. Sometimes political agents may be completely obsessed by protecting their own self-interests, as with cruel personalities like Genghis-Khan, Tamerlane, Hitler and Stalin. Sometimes political agents display great generosity and forgiveness towards their opponents, like Gandhi and Mandela. But on average political agents would be self-seeking, often with guile—the opportunism assumption.

The implications of assuming opportunism on the part of agents are strengthened in terms of importance when one adds the basic fact about long-term interaction of the principal-agent type, namely asymmetric information. It is the agent who delivers the output who knows the most about all things relevant to the interaction. And the agent will use this information advantage to capture a rent, or a set of benefits.

Strategy is a pervasive trait of human interaction, both in the micro setting and in the macro setting. Taking strategic considerations into account goes well in hand with opportunism and asymmetric information. The same applies to tactics. What, then, is the basic issue of contention in the principal-agent interaction? Answer: the division of advantages, given a certain size of the mutual gains to be had.

6.1. The Production of Value and Its Distribution

Political clubs help the population produce an output, a set of goods and services, to be denoted here with "V", meaning value. By providing peace and stability, the population may engage in productive labour, resulting in an output of increasing value year after year. The political agents will claim a part of this value V for their contributions. It is the principal who ultimately has to pay the agents out of the total value V in society.

The agreement about what the agents are to contribute with as well as what they are to be paid may be only a tacit one. It may not even be a voluntary one, as the political agents may force the principal to accept an agreement by the employment of force.

Two things are of major concern to the principal:

1) The maximisation of V: If the political agents act in such a manner as to reduce V, then this is not in the interest of the principal;
2) Reasonable agent remuneration R: If the agents manage to capture a considerable portion of V for themselves, then that would be counterproductive to the principal.

It follows from these two principles that principals would be very unhappy with a situation where their political agents contribute to a low output V, while at the same time providing them with a considerable share of V by maximising R.

What is included in the output V? One may offer a most comprehensive definition of V, denoting both tangible assets and intangible ones? V includes all things that are valuable government and its members: goods, premises, services, assets, perks, prestige, esteem, etc. Or one may confine V to the set of public or semi-public goods. The political club contracts with a set of agents in order to protect V, but the principal must remunerate the agents (R) from V. How can the principal select and monitor its agents so that V is maximised, given the constraint that the set of agents must be compensated for their effort from V?

The interaction between political leaders and the population is omnipresent. Whatever the leaders are called and whichever rules apply for their behaviour, human societies have not been leaderless. Even among groups with a highly egalitarian culture, political leaders somehow emerge. This sets up the principal-agent problematic inherent in government. It is to be found in all levels of goernment whatever the form of institutionalisation.

When two people or sets of people interact, they may arrive at a mutual understanding of the terms of interaction. These expectations may be enshrined in a contract, written or verbal. Yet, even when the expectations governing the interaction between the political agents and the principal are not codified somehow, there is still consideration.

Consideration is at the core of human exchange and contracting: Something of value is given for getting something from another person. Consideration is the inducement, price or motive that causes a party to enter into an agreement or contract. In politics, the leaders receive ample consideration for governing the country. They take a part of total value V for their needs. And they are expected to deliver services to the political club, first and foremost maintain the peace.

The concept of consideration is a broad one, covering any compensation paid, or all inconvenience suffered by the party from whom it proceeds. A consideration of some sort or other is essential to the forming a reasonable contract. A nudumpactum would be an agreement to do or to pay anything on one side without any compensation to the other. In ordinary law no one can be compelled to fulfil a nudumpactum, but in politics absolutist rulerships and dictatorships are essentially just that.

Since the consideration must be some benefit to the party by whom the promise is made, or to a third person at his instance, or some detriment sustained at the instance of the party promising by the party in whose favour the promise is made, politics is replete with consideration. The agents of the political clubs employ a variety of techniques to raise value to themselves as consideration for their governance activities.

In respect of time, a consideration may be executed, or something done before the making of the obligor's promise. In modern law, an executed consideration is insufficient to support a contract but an executed consideration on request or by some previous duty is sufficient to maintain an action. In politics, consideration is omnipresent, although institutionalised to various degrees. The principal holds the agents responsible for the major developments, and it furnishes the agents with the resources necessary to direct government, whether voluntarily or involuntarily.

6.2. Key Forms of Consideration in Political Contracts

In government, the interaction between the agents and the principal varies depending upon the consideration implicit in the contract between them. It is an open question who prevails of the two parties. Thus, logically one may separate between two alternative considerations, or ideal-type structures at the extreme poles:

Subjugation of the principal: In this extreme principal-agent relationship, the principal is reduced to slavery or serfdom, the agents exercising total domination—oriental despotism, totalitarian state. Yet, there is still consideration, as the enslaved population handles in a huge part of the yearly production to the agents, to be employed for governance. Typically, when the grip of the agents over the population slips, then there may occur rebellions, the principal searching for new agents.

Rule of law constraint over the agents: In the opposite extreme type, the political agents are checked by a variety of mechanisms so that they cannot accede to a position of dominance over the principal, like in intense direct democracy plus the popular initiative (Swiss democracy) as well as the recall of agents and imperative mandate (trade union democracy).

6.3. On the Risk of Political Monopoly and Looting

The external costs to principal may be very high, if there is political monopoly. What the principal would not want to have, all other tings equal, is a situation where the political agents not only take a huge remuneration R for their work but also accomplish mediocre or straightforward disastrous outcomes, reducing the value of society V. In the principal-agent literature, excessive remuneration on the part of the agent is referred to as "rent- seeking", whereas the failure of the agents to deliver on what they have promised is called "dissonant" actions. The important point here is that political agents may disappoint their principal on two grounds: 1)

Dissipation of value V, meaning underperformance as measured by outcomes; 2) Looting, i.e. engaging in excessive remuneration R.

A virtue of the principal-agent perspective is that it alerts people to the possibility of large-scale looting in politics. The worst case scenario for the principal is the combination of bad outcomes in politics and excessive remuneration for agents responsible for the results. This happens often when there is looting.

"Looting" refers to any form of taking of value that amounts to an un-proportional compensation in relation to the effort exerted. It may be illegal, as when soldiers go on a rampage. But political looting is often more refined than populist looting when law and order breaks down. The appropriation of the resources of the administrative apparatus ("slack") is a typical form of political looting, much emphasized by Weber for his comparative institutional analyses (Weber, 1978). The concept of political looting is broader than the notion of corruption or embezzlement, which are strictly illegal phenomena.

Looting may occur with or without value dissipation. Political agents may successfully claim a huge portion of the value in society without at the same time reducing the total size of value. In many Third World countries, political looting goes hand in hand with value dissipation though. An extreme case is that of present day Zimbabwe, which country according to its president "is mine".

During known human history, there have occurred a wide variety of forms of looting. One may mention the Pharaohs, who treated the entire country as their "oikos" or household. Mohammed sanctioned looting with a religious argument in order to favour a rapid expansion of the Arab Empire. Looting constituted a key issue in Western feudalism, as the lord and the vassal focused upon how the fruits from the various benefices and fiefs were to be divided, both in the short-run and the long-run perspective. Finally, massive looting occurred in the authoritarian regimes of the 20th century, where both fascist and communist leaders looked upon politics as bo- oty, covering embezzlement, patronage and favouritism.

Sophisticated forms of looting may occur in constitutional democracy, as when the executive allows itself to be surrounded by vast staff of advisors, experts and the like. Or political agents in the legislature manage to provide themselves with excessive budgets and perks. The fact that corruption allegation is an almost constant theme in public debate indicates how sensitive the principal is to the risk of looting. One form of political looting is of course nepotism or favouritism with regard to family members or cliques of friends when conducted by a president or premier for instance. Petty forms of looting involve negligence about the line of separation between private and public expenditures.

The rule of law regime is highly aware of the risk of looting, offering restraining rules about taxation, budgeting and financial accountability. It also aims at counteracting the dissipation of social value through representation, election and re-election. The dissipation of value is a problem of aggregation in society (size of the cake), whereas the risk of political looting presents a distributional problem (who gets what).

6.4. On the Risk of Value Dissipation

The constant focus of policy-makers upon economic growth shows how aware the principal is today about the risk of value dissipation. The population worries not only about various forms of looting but also about the risk of unfortunate or disastrous policy-making that reduce aggregate income or wealth. A set of political agents may be extremely costly to the country because they are incompetent although honest. Political consideration as defining the quid pro quo relation underneath political leadership would comprise some mechanism for replacing one set of agents with another, especially in a rule of law regime.

There is the possibility of a dramatic effect from the combination of looting and dissipation of value, like for instance as matters now stand in countries like Myanmar, Zimbabwe and North Korea. One should not, however, assume that the risk of value dissipation is unique to Third World countries. On the contrary, value dissipation occurs also in First World countries, where the 2003 American led invasion of Iraq offers a telling example, resulting in so huge costs—human and economic—and so little value. And even a country like the UK with its rule of law tradition does not appear to be immune from various looting strategies on the part of parliamentarians, definitely immoral but not always illegal.

6.5. Variety of Principal-Agent Models in Politics

Whether in models of private companies or of the bureaucracy, principal-agent interaction harbours games between two or more players that involve both cooperation and conflict. Generally speaking, the principal may pay high or low remuneration for the effort of the agent(s). And the agent(s) may deliver high or low effort. Thus arise the problematic of offering and monitoring a contract with the agent(s) that elicits the best outcome for the principal, meaning high effort and reasonable remuneration to the agent(s) (Rasmusen, 2006).

The basic principal-agent model above has been developed in various elaborate ways in order to account for elections and re-elections in democracies (Barro, 1973 ; Besley, 2006 ; Helland & Sörensen, 2009). In a general analysis of politics in well-ordered societies or in countries with kleptocracy, the principal-agent approach high lightens two problematic in governance: 1) value dissipation (poor performance); 2) looting (excessive remuneration).

Political agency of whatever kind it may be is fundamentally a job that has to get done against remuneration. This approach to political agency underlines its costs in the quid pro quo: What is the agent to do against what pay? Political agency is heavily institutionalized, as the population as principal wishes to restrict the behaviour of the agents—politicians, bureaucrats, legislators and judges. However, the institutions define the degrees of freedom, but they do not solve the incentive problem: How to motivate the agents to try hard to promote the interests of the principal?

Political costs arise with any form of political agency, as the politicians or political parties will not simply implement the policies the electorate wants without remuneration. The question of the size and nature of this remuneration has become a key issue in the post-modern society where political ideologies motivate less. There are a few key models of this effort—remuneration problematic in politics, stated in terms of the principal-agent approach. Let me briefly mention them in order to pinpoint these model differences concerning how agency costs are conceived:

1) Costs as embezzlement (Helland & Sörensen, 2009);
2) Costs as campaign funds (PAC:s) (Barro, 1973);
3) Costs as pursuing agent's own preferences (Besley, 2006);
4) Costs as bad performance like real policy failure (Ferejohn, 1986 ; Ferejohn & Shipa, 1990).

Groups in the electorate vote for a political party—a set of politicians with a common strategy—in order to have them promote a set of policies by means of outcomes—good performance. Due to the gap between election dates—normally four years, the relationship between the principal and the politicians he/she elects becomes one of asymmetric information, where effort is non-observable and non-verifiable. The politicians have normal incentives, meaning they wish to get paid somehow—maximum perquisites or at least much of them.

Political agency is a game with two rounds of play: election and re-election. Only re-election offers a strong restraint upon the agents not to "shirk", meaning renege upon the effort to promote the interests of the principal. Only re-election gives the principal the opportunity to get rid of an agent who really was not a good one from the beginning (a "lemon").

The theory of political agency as embezzlement is not really a success. Although corruption may be rampant in several Third World countries and flare up in spectacular cases in a few well-ordered societies like e.g. the UK, political agents do not employ such blunt tactics as stealing public money. Helland and Sorensen claim that the threat of embezzlement is a most powerful one, forcing the principal to pay a rent to the agents. This is wrong. Bad agents who embezzle cannot survive the re-election stage, when asymmetric information is corrected.

The theory about agency costs as the extra campaign funds besides normal politician salary fits US democracy well. It models a structural weakness in the US political system, because these extra payments from pressure groups will only be forthcoming when politicians deliver policies, regulations or contracts as reciprocity. This always comes with an extra cost to the economy, involving the risk for social inefficiencies and massive rent seeking costs depleting the rents acquired. However, in other democracies the system of PAC:s is not allowed. In addition, the Barro model presents the difficulty of one agent serving two principals with opposite interests to some extent.

The Besley model is more applicable onto European democracies. It posits a radical separation between good and bad politicians, the latter being leaders or parties that promote their own policy agenda at the detriment of their policy promises to their principals. Given replay, the principal can eliminate bad politicians in the re-elec- tion. But under what conditions will a bad politician push his/her agenda already in the first round of play? Bad politicians could mimic good politicians in at least two rounds of play, surviving the re-election test. Under the Besley model, a lame duck politician would always push his/her policy agenda because there are no more rounds of play. Pushing one's own agenda is lick scoring a rent. Thus, also good politicians will be tempted.

The distinction between good and bad politicians has a moralistic ring to it, which makes it less useful in scientific research. Is a bad politician an embezzler, a lackey of pressure groups or merely an idealistic loner who pushes his/her own convictions? Political agents tend to have their own agendas and the institution of representative democracy places few restrictions upon the mandate. Why would the principal not re-elect an agent who accomplishes positive outcomes by following his/her own agenda?

One may conceptualise the difficulties in governing as two games of principal-agent interaction, comprising two different forms of asymmetric information. In politics, the principal is confronted with the problem of voting for politicians or political parties agents at one election e1. But the voter as principal does not know whether the agents will really deliver—*ex* post the election—high performance although promising to do so (moral hazard). The voter dos not even have—*ex ante* the election—full information whether the agents are capable of high performance (adverse selection). When the voter is not pleased with his/her agent, then he or she can decide to vote for another agent in the next coming election e2. Thus, the principal-agent games in politics have two rounds of play.

The principal would be willing to re-elect an agent who delivers high performance but reject the agent who delivers low performance (incentive compatibility). The risk in politics is that the agents promise one thing but delivers the opposite. Only eternal vigilance on the part of the principal in checking the political agents can improve upon the probability of the best outcome for the principal, given that few agents are benevolent saints. The worst outcome conceivable is that the agents deliver poor results but demands excessive remuneration. In the worst-case scenario, the agent appropriates much value produced in a country, or at least a considerable part of it (looting). In any case, the principal must pay the agent a level of remuneration that he/she could receive elsewhere (participation constraint).

To sum up: It appears from Figure 2 that a majority of the population on the Earth do not enjoy the combined benefits of rule of law I and rule of law II. Actually, large portions of the peoples of the world do not even live under rule of law I in their daily lives, like mainland China.

Figure 2 shows clearly that there is ample room for improvements in rule of law I in several populous states, even if they for various reasons do not endorse rule of law II, or Western democracy.

7. GOOD GOVERNANCE: TRANSPARENCY AND EFFECTIVENESS

It has been pointed out that the expression "goog governance" has received numerous of definitions, some focusing upon the processes of decision-making whereas others have targeted outcomes or results, such as happiness or well-being. When one is confronted by semantic ambiguity or multiplicity of meanings, one research strategy is to enquire into how various concepts linked with the term or expression relate to each other referentially. This is often a more informative strategy that attempting to find the common core in all the various definition, or declare a new stipulative definition like good governance as impartiality (what is an impartial policy mix by government).

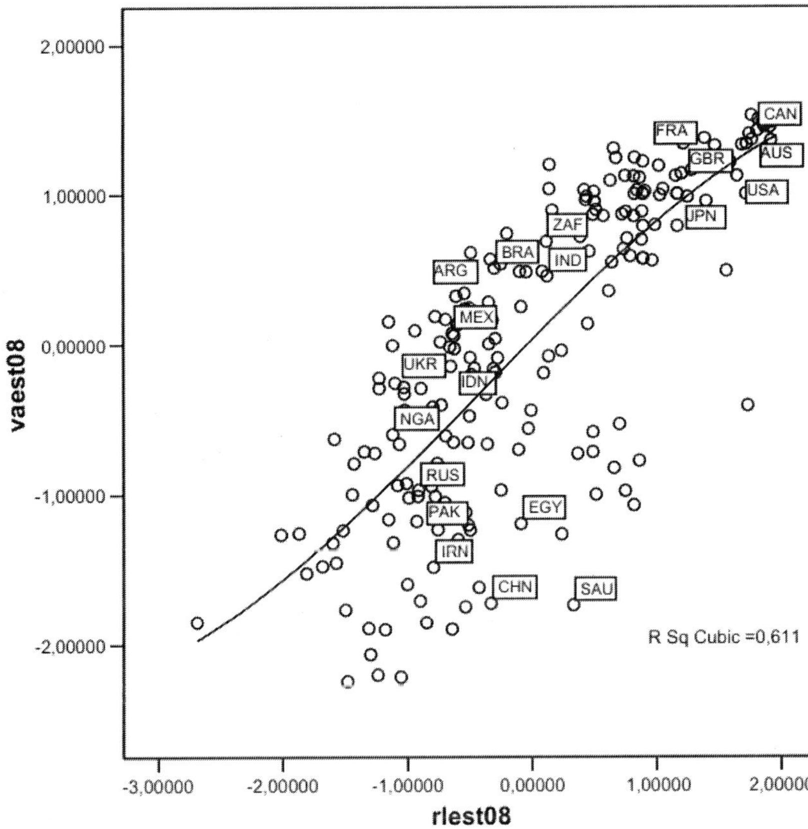

Source: Governance Matters 2009. Worldwide Governance Indicators 1996-2008: vaest08, rlest08.

Figure 2. Rule of law I and II in big states (>10 million inhabitants).

Thus, Figure 3 looks at the relationship between rule of law I and the absence of corruption as transparency in the World Bank Governance project.

Figure 3 provides strong evidence that the institutionalisation or legal integrity and judicial autonomy is conducive to the control of corrupt behaviour or practices. China actually scores better on both indices than Russia or Nigeria, but far from the scores of UAE, Japan and Singapore. Rule of law I is clearly relevant for good governance in countries that have other political systems that Western democracy.

Governmental effectiveness is considered by the World Bank Governance Project as a vital aspect of good governance. Figure 4 shows again that countries may score high on this aspect of good governance without scoring high on rule of law II.

The general trend is though those countries with rule of law II tend to score high on the index of governmental effectiveness.

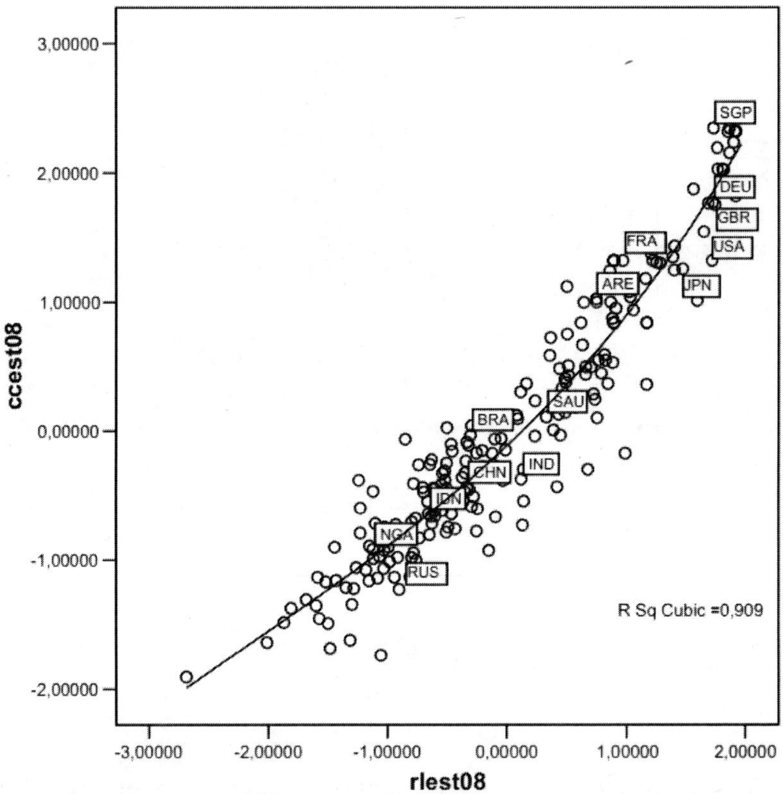

Source: Governance Matters 2009. Worldwide Governance Indicators 1996-2008: rlest08, ccest08.

Figure 3. Rule of law I and transparency (control of corruption).

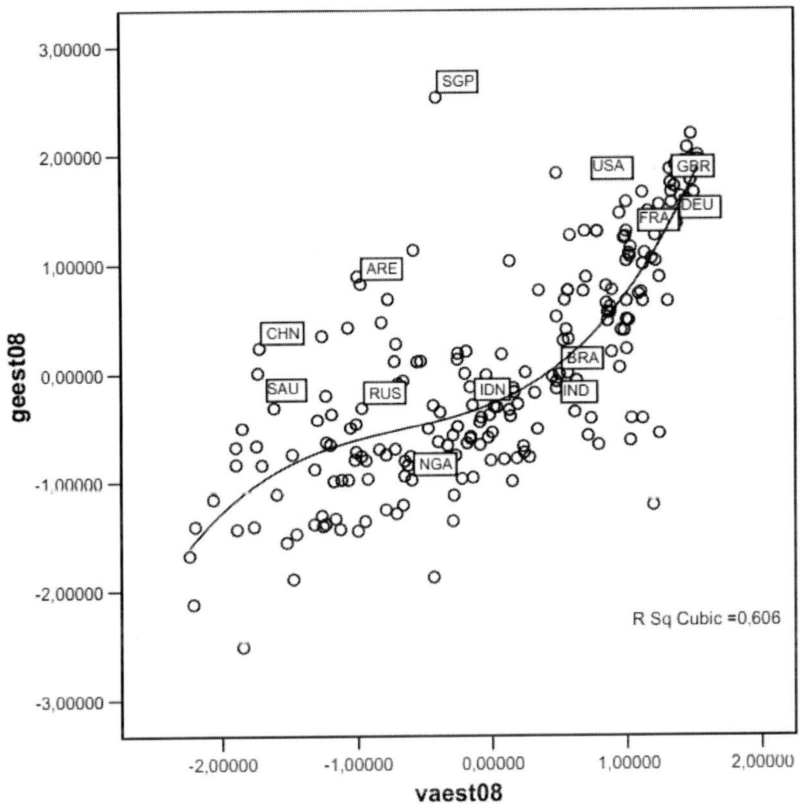

Source: Governance Matters 2009. Worldwide Governance Indicators 1996-2008: vaest08, geest08.

Figure 4. Rule of law II and government effectiveness.

8. CONCLUSION

A political regime that runs according to rule of law would satisfy a few conditions that constrain the exercise of political power (Vile, 1967; Tierney, 1982). Rule of law entails that power is be exercised according to the following precepts concerning due legal process and judicial accountability:

1) Legality (nullum crimen sine lege);
2) Constitutionality (lex superior);

3) Rights and duties: negative human rights (habeas corpus);
4) Judicial independence: complaint, appeal and compensation.

The theory of good governance entails that a government adhering to these precepts will be more successful in enhancing socio-economic development than a government that fails to respect these principles. Thus, economic activity will be stimulated by legal predictability, the protection of property and the autonomy of judges when testing cases for assumed violations of legality or constitutionality (Cooter & Ulen, 2011).

From the rule of law perspective, two unresolved questions are central in political agency, whatever the political regime may be:

1) What is the proper remuneration of the agents, both salary and perks?
2) Do agents really deliver, i.e. how can agent performance be evaluated systematically in terms of outcome data?

The remuneration of political agents, whether in legal or illegal forms, has not been much researched, not even in democracies where information is in principle available. For countries where the state controls such information not much is known, for instance about China. However, it is a well-known fact that political agents information not much is known, for instance about China. However, it is a well-known fact that political agents in some countries engage in comprehensive looting, for instance in Myanmar. The theme of corruption is a most important aspect in a principal-agent model of the interaction between people and political agents. Yet, there are several forms of corruption that need to be studied separately. Somehow the perspective of corruption does not offer a broad enough view of the entire remuneration question. See Meredith (1997) Jan-Erik Lane (1997) for an inventory of all forms of opportunism by politicians and officials in Africa to capture a rent or dissipate value.

REFERENCES

1. Ackere, A. (1993) The Principal/Agent Paradigm: Its Relevance to Various Functional Fields. European Journal of Operational Research, 70, 83-103.

2. Althaus, C. (1997) The Application of Agency Theory to Public Sector Management. In G. Davis, B. Sullivan, & A. Yeatman (Eds.), The New Contractualism (pp. 137-153). Melbourne: Macmillan.

3. Arrow, K. (1985) The Economics of Agency. In J. Pratt, & R. Zeckhauser (Eds.), Principals and Agents: The Structure of Business (pp. 37-51). Cambridge, MASS: Harvard University Press.

4. Barro, R. J. (1973) The Control of Politicians: An Economic Model. Public Choice, 14, 19-42.

5. Besley, T. (2006) Principled Agents? The Political Economy of Good Government. Oxford: Oxford U.P.

6. Brazier, R. (1990) Constitutional and Administrative Law. London: Penguin Books.

7. Burns, J. H., & Goldie, M. (Eds.) (1991) The Cambridge History of Political Thought (pp.1450-1700). New York: Cambridge University Press.

8. Cooter, R. D., & Ulen, T. (2011) Law and Economics. New York: Pearson.

9. Ferejohn, J. (1986) Incumbent Performance and Electoral Control. Public Choice, 30, 5-25.

10. Ferejohn, J., & Shipa, C. (1990) Congressional Influence on Bureaucracy. Journal of Law, Economics, and Organization 6, 1-20.

11. Furubotn, E. G., & Richter, R. (2005). Institutions and Economic Theory: The Contribution of the New Institutional Economics. Ann Arbor, MI: The University of Michigan Press.

12. Grossman, S. J., & Hart, O. D. (1983). An Analysis of the Principal-Agent Problem. Econometrica, 51, 7-46. http://dx.doi.org/10.2307/1912246

13. Helland, L., & Sörensen, R. J. (2009). Hvorforoverleverpolitiskkorrupsjon i representative demokratier. Norsk Statsvitenskapelig Tidsskrift, 25, 219-236.

14. Jowell, J. (1994). The Rule of Law Today. In Jowell and Oliver, op.cit., 57-78.

15. Jowell, J., & Oliver, D. (Eds.) (1994). The Changing Constitution. Oxford: Clarendon Press.

16. Kant, I. (1974). The Philosophy of Law. Clifton, NJ: Augustus M. Kelley.

17. Kaufmann, D., Kraay, A., & Mastruzzi, M. (2010). The Worldwide Governance Indicators: Methodology and Analytical Issues. World Bank Policy Working Paper No. 5430.

18. Kelsen, H. (1961). General Theory of Law and State. New York: Russell & Russell.

19. Kelsen, H. (1967). Pure Theory of Law. Berkeley, CA: University of California Press.

20. Laffont, J. J., & Martimort, D. (2002). The Theory of Incentives: The Principal-Agent Model. Princeton, NJ: Princeton University Press.

21. Lloyd, D. (1991a). The Idea of Law. London: Penguin Books.

22. Lloyd, H. A. (1991b). "Constitutionalism". In Burns and Goldie. op.cit., 254-297.

23. McIlwain, C. H. (1958). Constitutionalism, Ancient and Modern. Ithaca: Cornell University Press.

24. Meredith, M. (1997). The State of Africa. London: Free Press.

25. Neumann, F. L. (1986). The Rule of Law: Political Theory and the Legal System in Modern Society. Berg: Leamington Spa.

26. Pennock, J. R. ,& Chapman, J. W. (Eds.) (1979). Constitutionalism. New York: New York University Press.

27. Persson, T., & Tabellini, G. (2003). The Economic Effects of Constitutions. Cambridge, MA: MIT Press.

28. Rao, P. K. (2002). The Economics of Transaction Costs. Basingstoke: Palgrave/Macmillan.http://dx.doi.org/10.1057/9780230597686

29. Rasmusen, E. (2006). Games and Information: An Introduction to Game Theory. Oxford: Blackwell.

30. Rees, R. (1985). The Theory of Principal and Agent. Bulletin of Economic Research, 37, 3-26. http://dx.doi.org/10.1111/j.1467-8586.1985.tb00179.x

31. Reiss, H. (Ed.) (1970). Kant's Political Writings. Cambridge: Cambridge University Press.

32. Riley, P. (1983). Kant's Political Philosophy. Totowa, NJ: Rowman & Allanheld Publishers.

33. Ross, S. A. (1973). The Economic Theory of Agency: The Principal's Problem. American Economic Review, 63, 134-139.

34. Sappington, D. (1991). Incentives in Principal Agent Relationships. Journal of Economic Perspectives, 3, 45-66. http://dx.doi.org/10.1257/jep.5.2.45

35. Schwöbel, C. E. J. (2011). Global Constitutionalism in International Legal Perspective. Leiden: MartinusNijhoff. http://dx.doi.org/10.1163/ej.9789004191150.i-205

36. Tierney, B. (1982). Religion, Law, and the Growth of Constitutional Thought 1150-1650. Cambridge: Cambridge University Press. http://dx.doi.org/10.1017/CBO9780511558627

37. Vile, M. J. C. (1967). Constitutionalism and the Separation of Powers. Oxford: Oxford University Press.

38. von Mohl, R. (1832). Die Polizei-Wissenschaftnach den Grundsatzen des Rechtstaates. Zweiteumgearbeitete Auflage. German Edition by British Library, Historical Print Editions (2011).

39. Weber, M. (1978). Economy and Society. Berkeley, CA: University of California Press.

40. Weingast, B. (1989). The Political Institutions of Representative Government: Legislatures. Journal of Institutional and Theoretical Economics, 145, 693-703. Reprinted In E. Furubotn, & R. Richter (Eds.), The New Institutional Economics. Tübingen: J.C.B. Mokr (Paul Siebeck) and College Station: Texas A&M Press, 1991.

41. White, W. D. (1992). Information and the Control of Agents. Journal of Economic Behavior and Organization, 18, 111-117. http://dx.doi.org/10.1016/0167-2681(92)90056-H

42. World Bank (2012). Governance Project. http://info.worldbank.org/governance/wgi/

43. Wormuth, F. D. (1949). The Origins of Modern Constitutionalism. New York: Harper.

2

CHAPTER

Managing Fragmentation in Global Environmental Governance: The REDD+ Partnership as Bridge Organization

Aarti Gupta[1], Till Pistorius[2], Marjanneke J. Vijge[1]

[1]Environmental Policy Group, Department of Social Sciences, Wageningen University, Wageningen, The Netherlands

[2]UNIQUE Forestry and Land Use GmbH, Schnewlinstraße 10, 79098 Freiburg, Germany

ABSTRACT

This article analyzes the increasing institutional and organizational complexity and fragmentation surrounding the international financing mechanism REDD+ (reducing emissions from deforestation and forest degradation in developing countries and related forest activities), now being negotiated within the UNFCCC. We focus, in particular, on critically assessing the prospects of managing such fragmentation. We do so by analyzing whether and how (what we conceptualize here as) a "bridge organization"—the voluntary, multi-stakeholder REDD+ Partnership bringing together state and non-state actors from global to local scales—has aided in managing fragmentation in this realm, through exercising four enabling functions (enhancing transparency, participation, knowledge sharing, and coordination). Our analysis shows that the REDD+ Partnership has partially succeeded in furthering such procedural aims, but that this has not resulted in a "scaling up of REDD+ action and finance," its overarching substantive aim. In contrast to dominant views of a bridge organization's modus operandi, we conclude, based on our analysis, that its value lies not in overcoming persisting geopolitical conflicts around climate mitigation and providing a "depoliticized" context within which to manage fragmentation. Instead, its success lies in permitting dialogue and exchange even in the face of persisting political conflicts over its raison d'être and functions. In making these arguments, the article extends recent debates on the prospects to manage fragmentation in global environmental governance and provides a critical assessment of the role therein for bridge organizations.

Keywords: Fragmentation, Climate governance, Global environmental governance, Forests, REDD+ Partnership, Bridge organization, Interaction management, Institutional interplay, Regime complexes

1 INTRODUCTION

Increasing fragmentation of the sites and sources of governance authority is now a pervasive phenomenon in the global environmental realm (Biermann et al. 2009; Zelli and Van Asselt 2013). Yet the *consequences* of fragmentation, and the prospects to *manage* fragmentation to further specified governance ends, still remain theoretically and empirically under-examined. In this article, we analyze the growing fragmentation around the issue-area of REDD+,[1] an international financing mechanism currently being negotiated under the United Nations Framework Convention on Climate Change (UNFCCC). REDD+ is intended to compensate developing countries for reducing forest-related greenhouse gas emissions or sequestering carbon through forest and land-use management strategies.

The idea for such a mechanism was first introduced into UNFCCC negotiations in 2005 by Costa Rica and Papua New Guinea (for a detailed history of its evolution, see Pistorius 2012). Since then, the scope of forest-related activities to be encapsulated within it has continually expanded within the UNFCCC. It is expected that a final agreement on REDD+ will come as part of a broader global climate agreement in 2015. In the interim, debates about, and experiments relating to what REDD+ is, or should be, are underway at multiple levels of governance, driven by an ever-widening array of actors operating in varied institutional and organizational arenas.

In this article, we describe this growing institutional and organizational complexity (i.e., fragmentation) of the REDD+ issue-domain. We then analyze the extent to which the Interim REDD+ Partnership—a voluntary multi-stakeholder initiative set up by REDD+ donor and recipient countries in 2010 to "scale up action and finance"—has aided in *managing* fragmentation in this realm. We do so by conceptualizing the Partnership as a "bridge" organization, given its mandate to bring together, in an informal setting, the key actors, initiatives, and organizations engaged in REDD+ from global to local levels. In conceptualizing it as such, we assess what bridging functions, if any, the Partnership has exercised to date and whether, in so doing, it has succeeded in facilitating a scaling up of REDD+ action and finance. The Partnership was set up, initially, for a three-year period from 2010 to 2012, but was extended at the climate meeting in Doha in 2012 until the end of 2014.[2] Our analysis thus covers the entire period of its existence.

The REDD+ Partnership has been little analyzed in scholarly literature to date (for a few exceptions, see Reinecke et al. 2012; Pistorius and Reinecke 2013). In conceptualizing the Partnership as a bridge organization in a fragmented REDD+ landscape here, our analysis is timely, insofar as it critically engages with the notion of fragmentation *management* now gaining currency in scholarly analyses and because it does so for the empirical issue-area of REDD+, widely seen as one of the farthest advanced climate mitigation options now being negotiated within the UNFCCC, thus eliciting widespread interest and engagement. Our analysis draws on both primary and secondary sources, including REDD+ Partnership primary documents, and participant observation of multiple UNFCCC negotiating sessions and Partnership meetings between 2010 and 2014. We also draw on 15 semi-structured interviews with both state and non-state Partnership participants over this period.

In the next section, we present relevant theoretical propositions about fragmentation in global environmental governance and the prospects to manage such fragmentation. In Sect. 3, we describe how an expanding scope of REDD+ within the UNFCCC has resulted in growing fragmentation around it, with the aim to identify the need for, and functions of, a prospective bridge organization. In Sect. 4, we analyze what bridge functions the REDD+ Partnership has executed and with what consequences for scaling up REDD+ action and finance. In conclusion, we draw out implications of our analysis for the prospects to manage fragmentation in furthering desired ends in global environmental governance.

2 MANAGING FRAGMENTATION IN GLOBAL ENVIRONMENTAL GOVERNANCE

Debates within international relations have evolved in the last decades from analyzing individual "regimes" (i.e., rules, norms, and expectations guiding behavior in a specific issue-area) to focus on "inter-linkages" between two or more regimes (Young 1996; Gehring and Oberthür 2004; Gupta 2008). In recent years, attention has focused as well on broader regime "complexes" (Raustiala and Victor 2004; Keohane and Victor 2011; Abbott 2012) and a growing "fragmentation" in global governance architectures (Biermann et al. 2009; Zelli and van Asselt 2013). These shifting debates reflect scholarly recognition of the changing nature of global (environmental) governance, with multiple arenas for public and private rulemaking, norm setting and knowledge sharing now co-existing in diverse issue-areas. Scholars are now expending much effort on mapping, and developing typologies of, such regime complexes or fragmented governance architectures, in order to further conceptual clarity and advance this research agenda (e.g., Alter and Meunier 2009; Drezner 2009; Betts 2013; Van Asselt and Zelli 2012; Orsini et al. 2013).

A prominent early definition of a regime complex was to conceptualize it as "an array of partially overlapping and non-hierarchical institutions governing a particular issue-area" (Raustiala and Victor 2004, 279). This broad definition was useful in highlighting various constitutive elements of such a complex, including "partially overlapping institutions," the need for delineation of an "issue-area," and the stipulation of "non-hierarchical" relations between constituent parts. Subsequent definitions have sought to add to, or modify, this definition. Keohane and Victor (2011, 8), for example, conceptualize regime complexes as "non-hierarchical but loosely coupled systems of institutions." In offering a contrasting view, Orsini et al. (2013, 29) suggest that the requirement of "non-hierarchical" relations is "an ambiguous and unnecessary feature" of such earlier conceptualizations and that the focus therein on "institutions" is too broad. They propose, instead, to define a regime complex as containing "three or more international regimes" with "overlapping membership" and "potentially problematic interactions." *Non-problematic* interactions between component parts would signal, in their view, the existence of one internally coherent regime, rather than a regime complex.

Our aim here is not to weigh in on, or seek to resolve, such definitional differences, nor to embrace or argue for a specific terminology. Instead, we view such discussions as useful in highlighting a set of analytical concerns relating to the nature and consequences of regime complexity and fragmentation in global environmental governance.[3] These analytical concerns include, inter alia, delineating boundaries around a fragmented issue-area; the need (or not) for a core within such fragmented regime complexes; and the density or number of component elements in such complexes (which could be nested, parallel or overlapping; for a detailed discussion, see Aggarwal 2005; Alter and Meunier 2006; Abbott and Snidal 2006).

As our point of departure, we view the act of drawing boundaries around an issue-area as a fundamentally political one, contingent on (contested) framings of a problem that determine what is included or excluded within a regime complex. Hence, our aim in describing growing REDD+ fragmentation in this paper is not to argue for or against a specific demarcation of this issue-area, but rather to ascertain the governance consequences of having an ever-broadening array of organizations, institutions, and actors engaged in conceptualizing and implementing REDD+ at multiple levels. This approach is aligned with calls in recent literature to move *beyond* debating the merits or demerits of (different types and degrees of) complexity or fragmentation in normative terms, to analyzing its consequences for governance (e.g., Alter and Meunier 2009; Van Asselt and Zelli 2012; Zelli and Van Asselt 2013; see also Zelli et al. 2013).

Our primary interest, moreover, is in assessing the prospects to *manage* fragmentation to deliver on specific governance aims, an aspect that has been the least extensively studied thus far. In focusing on this, we also interrogate the very notion of "managing" fragmentation and thus contribute to discussions on what such management might entail and to what end. In available studies on so-called interaction management in global environmental governance, a few analysts have explored whether and how specific institutional or organizational arrangements (whether public, private or hybrid) can serve as interaction managers between component elements of a regime complex or fragmented governance architectures (e.g., Visseren-Hamakers et al. 2011; Visseren-Hamakers and Verkooijen 2013).

We extend such lines of thinking here in critically assessing the prospects for, and means of, managing fragmentation in the REDD+ arena, through the Interim REDD+ Partnership. In so doing, we draw on and adapt to our case a useful typology of (institutional) interplay management developed by Oberthür (2009). In this typology, Oberthür distinguishes between *levels* and *modes* of interplay management. According to him, the first, highest, level of interplay management is through an *overarching institution,* whereby "... a new specialized overarching institution ... engage[s] in decision-making beyond the interacting institutions" (pp. 375–376). A second level is *joint interplay management* through "active targeted efforts to coordinate activities of the interacting institutions [and] conscious creation of horizontal structures for coordination" between two or more interaction institutions (p. 376). A third, lowest level consists of *unilateral management* by individual institutions through "independent collective action and decision-making within one or more of the interacting institutions without coordination between them" (p. 376).

Added to these three levels are two *modes* of interaction management: *regulatory* and *enabling*. Regulatory interplay management, according to Oberthür, focuses on "prescribing, proscribing or permitting certain behavior" with the possibility to also implement and enforce such prescriptions. Such an interaction management mode resonates with "hierarchical, regulatory, top-down, coercive, and command-and-control approaches" to global environmental governance (Oberthür 2009, 377). A second mode is *enabling* interaction management, which works through learning and capacity building, and focuses not on prescribing behavior, but on communication and knowledge brokering as a way to persuade, and enhance capacities to negotiate and implement (shared) governance goals. This latter mode of interaction management resonates with "non-hierarchical, communicative, voluntary and capacitating/enabling governance approaches" (p. 377).

The above typology provides us with a starting point from which to characterize the level and mode of fragmentation management likely to be at play in our case. First, since the REDD+ Partnership was explicitly intended to play a facilitative and knowledge-brokering role, we assume that it functions in an *enabling* rather than regulatory mode of interaction management, as per the typology above. In terms of *levels* of interaction management, however, our case does not fit any of the three identified by Oberthür. The REDD+ Partnership is not envisioned to function as an *overarching* institution (or organization) above relevant others, nor one that *jointly* with another co-coordinates horizontally across an institutional landscape. Nor is it an *individual* entity exercising decision-making authority by itself, without coordination with relevant others. Instead, we conceptualize the REDD+ Partnership here rather as a *bridge* organization, linking across actors and levels, one that is hierarchically sub-ordinate to the UNFCCC, but links UNFCCC policymakers to sub-national and local (public and private) actors active in REDD+.

Conceptualized as such, we view the Partnership as a site of interaction between *global and local* scales and *state and non-state* actors engaged in REDD+ debates and actions. Our characterization of the Partnership as a "bridging" entity intended to manage fragmentation is, to our knowledge, novel within global environmental governance literatures. In developing our conceptualization further, we thus also draw here briefly on writings within organizational and environmental management, adaptive governance, and social learning, where the notion of a "bridge organization" has been more extensively discussed (e.g., Cash et al. 2006; Crona and Parker 2012; McMullen and Adobor 2011). A bridge organization is generally understood in such writings as, inter alia, "a forum for the interaction of...different kinds of knowledge and the coordination of ...tasks that enable cooperation: accessing resources, bringing together different actors, building trust, resolving conflict, and networking..." (Berkes 2009, 1692). Such organizations can "respond to opportunities, [and] serve as catalysts and facilitators between different levels of governance and across resource and knowledge systems" (Berkes 2009, 1695; see also Folke et al. 2005). Our conceptualization of the Partnership, as serving as a bridging entity in a fragmented REDD+ governance landscape, is akin to such a view of a bridge organization.

In characterizing the Partnership as such, however, our intent is also to subject the very notion of such bridging to critical scrutiny. As a recent analysis of bridging organizations in adaptive resource governance emphasizes, "...little is known about the conditions that foster learning ...and how, specifically, bridging organizations facilitate this process. One reason is that the concept of bridging organizations, as well as the actors, social groups, and collaborative processes involved in them, remains poorly articulated" (Crona and Parker 2012, 32). Our aim is thus to further understanding of such processes, as well as their role in global environmental governance. We do so by analyzing whether the REDD+ Partnership has exercised a variety of enabling, bridging functions as a means to manage fragmentation in this realm *and* if its enabling mode of fragmentation management has helped to further its substantive aim of scaling up REDD+ action and finance.

We turn next to describing how the scope of REDD+ has expanded within the UNFCCC, and the growing institutional and organizational fragmentation resulting from this.

3 INCREASING REDD+ FRAGMENTATION: ROLE FOR A BRIDGE ORGANIZATION?

The UNFCCC acknowledged the role of forests as sinks and sources for greenhouse gas emissions early on, yet its Kyoto Protocol focused only on mitigation options relating to forest carbon stocks in *developed* countries. Reducing emissions from deforestation in *developing countries* came to the fore only in 2003, when Brazilian scientists introduced the concept of "compensated reduction" of deforestation into UNFCCC debates. This had coalesced by 2005 into negotiating a financial mechanism to compensate developing countries for "reducing emissions from deforestation" (RED), and by 2007 into REDD (reducing emissions from deforestation and forest degradation). By 2009, a "+" was added to REDD, to include conservation of forest carbon stocks, sustainable management of forests, and enhancement of forest carbon stocks in developing countries. This expanded scope was pushed for by those countries (such as India and China) that had increasing rather than decreasing forest cover, yet also wanted to participate in this mechanism (for a history of REDD+ negotiations within the UNFCCC, see Pistorius 2012).

This continually expanding scope of forest-related activities under REDD+ has significantly increased the political and technical challenges inherent in converting it into a workable reality. These challenges include, inter alia, the need to develop adequate monitoring, measuring, reporting, and verification (MRV) systems to document forest carbon changes across such a diverse range of activities (Herold and Skutsch 2011; Visseren-Hamakers et al. 2012a; see also Gupta et al. 2012, 2014), as well as the need to ensure that an expanded REDD+ delivers not only carbon, but also "non-carbon" benefits (relating to biodiversity and social aspects) (McDermott et al. 2012; Visseren-Hamakers et al. 2012b). UNFCCC decisions on these and other aspects of operationalizing REDD+ are contained in the 2013 "Warsaw Framework on REDD+" (UNFCCC 2013). Further agreements include a three-phased approach to REDD+ implementation: a first "readiness" phase (including developing national REDD+ strategies); a second demonstration phase; and a third results-based financing phase.

A growing institutional and organizational complexity around REDD+ has accompanied these policy developments within the UNFCCC, as we sketch briefly below, relating to REDD+ readiness and financing, as well as non-carbon benefits or safeguards.

3.1 REDD+ readiness and finance

Being ready for REDD+ requires countries to develop national REDD+ strategies, as well as forest monitoring and MRV systems. Such readiness activities have thus been underway in many developing countries over the last half decade, accompanied as well by extensive experimentation with REDD+ pilot projects on the ground. All of these elements have required capacity building and financial support, and such support has come, increasingly, from a proliferating variety of multilateral, bilateral, and public–private sources, operating at multiple scales. The multilateral initiatives offering such support include, most prominently, the World Bank Forest Carbon Partnership Facility (FCPF) and Forest Investment Program (FIP), as well as the UN-REDD Programme, established jointly by FAO, UNEP, and UNDP. Also active here is the Global Environment Facility (GEF). The FCPF and UN-REDD have each disbursed significant multilateral funding for REDD+ readiness activities, including for capacity building and design of national REDD+ strategies, as well as development of national forest monitoring and MRV systems. Bilateral support for such activities has been forthcoming from, among others, the Norwegian Agency for Development Cooperation (NORAD) Climate and Forest Initiative, and the German International Climate Initiative (Cerbu et al. 2011; Davis and Daviet 2010).

With regard to MRV systems, guidelines for these were initially negotiated within the UNFCCC's Subsidiary Body for Scientific and Technological Advice, which in turn drew upon the Intergovernmental Panel on Climate Change (IPCC)'s good practice guidelines for forest carbon emissions relating to land use and land-use changes (IPCC 2003). The REDD+ Warsaw Framework now provides guidance on establishing such systems, yet allows countries considerable freedom to (differently) interpret and apply its general provisions. As such, multilateral organizations and bilateral agencies have adopted sometimes similar and sometimes diverging approaches to providing support for these activities, ensuring a growing need for coordination among such sources of support (Davis and Daviet 2010). Furthermore, the REDD+ MRV systems to be developed have themselves become ever more complex, given the expanded scope of forest-related activities now covered by this mechanism. This also suggests a need to identify and share information about best practices relating to developing and implementing such systems in diverse national contexts.

Such readiness activities have also been accompanied by extensive experimentation with REDD+ pilot projects on the ground (Wertz-Kanounnikoff and Kongphan-Apirak 2009; Cerbu et al. 2011). Again, multilateral and bilateral donors, as well as an array of public–private initiatives, are now involved in supporting such pilot projects. The latter include non-governmental organizations, such as the World Wildlife Fund (WWF), as well as companies seeking to offset their carbon emissions or invest in such projects for reasons of corporate social responsibility (Streck 2012).

These developments have proceeded, furthermore, in a context where contentious debates are still underway (within the UNFCCC and beyond) on whether REDD+ is to be supported by fund- or market-based financing, as well as what the modalities and disbursement options for such financing should be. REDD+ financing discussions within the UNFCCC have progressed more slowly than have debates on "technical" components of operationalizing REDD+ (relating to forest monitoring and MRV systems, and safeguards) (Streck 2012). In this context, current financing for the different phases of REDD+ is coming from a plethora of actors and organizations. While the bulk of REDD+ financing to date consists of bilateral and multilateral support for the first phase of REDD+ "readiness," market-based funders of the various REDD+ phases and activities have also rapidly emerged. These include, for example, regional and sub-national carbon market initiatives exploring options to include REDD+ credits as offsets in voluntary carbon markets (Streck 2012; Visseren-Hamakers et al. 2012b). Many of these initiatives have also taken the lead in developing standards for *accrediting* carbon credits generated by REDD+ pilot projects. These include, inter alia, the Verified Carbon Standard (VCS), Plan Vivo, and the Gold Standard. These standards are, however, now in fierce competition, due to their considerable overlap (Moss et al. 2011).

3.2 Non-carbon benefits and safeguards

The above developments are related, as well, to another key element of REDD+ implementation: the links between carbon and non-carbon benefits (including biodiversity and social aspects) to be secured through REDD+. This link has brought a whole slew of new actors, from the biodiversity and nature conservation communities, but also from local community groups, into the REDD+ institutional and governance landscape. With regard to climate–biodiversity links, the Convention on Biological Diversity (CBD) has set up, for example, an Ad Hoc Technical Expert Group on biodiversity and climate change to assess potential impacts of REDD+ on its own objectives. The CBD secretariat has also made several submissions and facilitated side-events at UNFCCC meetings on the issue of biodiversity co-benefits under REDD+ (Pistorius 2012; CBD 2015). At the CBD meeting in Hyderabad in 2012, countries agreed on voluntary guidance to monitor the impacts of REDD+ on biodiversity. Although these CBD initiatives have progressed with clear recognition of the UNFCCC as the hierarchical node in an expanding REDD+ governance landscape, the very different governance objectives of each regime makes collaboration between them a contested issue, one on which there is very little consensus.

The UNFCCC's own discussions on non-carbon benefits or REDD+ "safeguards" have meanwhile also yielded general guidelines on the need for countries to develop so-called safeguard information systems, as part of the 2013 Warsaw Framework. However, countries can interpret what such safeguard information systems should look like, in line with their national priorities (McDermott et al. 2012; Visseren-Hamakers et al. 2012b). As such, multiple organizations and actors are now also weighing in to interpret, or give substance to, the notion of safeguards. For example, a number of private (and potentially competing) REDD+ environmental and social safeguard *certification* schemes now exist, with various organizations also helping to establish systems to measure, report and verify non-carbon benefits of REDD+ activities (in addition to carbon-related outcomes). Such initiatives include the REDD+ Social and Environmental Standards, developed by a public–private initiative that includes the Climate, Community and Biodiversity Alliance (CCBA), CARE International, and some REDD+ governments, and the World Bank's Strategic Environmental and Social Assessment (McDermott et al. 2012).

In sum, the growing institutional and organizational complexity around REDD+ is linked to its ever-increasing scope within the UNFCCC. Such fragmentation is reflected in the multiple interpreters of UNFCCC REDD+ rules and guidelines for its component elements, operating at multiple levels. This is evident in the proliferating sources of support, including capacity building and funding, for REDD+ readiness and demonstration activities; in the potentially competing interpretations of certification standards for assessing (carbon and non-carbon) results; and, more broadly, in the growing number of public and private actors at multiple levels jostling to define, operationalize and experiment with REDD+. While the core impetus for such activities is still anchored firmly within the UNFCCC, a multiplicity of actors and organizations now seek to support, interpret, and implement the policy decisions relating to REDD+ within the UNFCCC.

With regard to "scaling up action and finance" for REDD+ then, we can surmise that this growing complexity offers both challenges and opportunities, thereby ostensibly opening up space for a potential bridge organization to leverage opportunities and help mitigate the challenges. The potential opportunities include generating (desirable) competition, and a race to the top for best practices, as well as incentivizing innovative approaches and experimentation on all elements, and in all phases, of operationalizing REDD+. Challenges, on the other hand, include potential inefficiencies or duplicative use of scarce resources, high transaction costs, or confusion regarding the plethora of approaches to MRV and certification standards now available.

As such, a fragmented REDD+ governance arena provides fertile ground for a bridge organization to serve as a site for multi-stakeholder interactions across vertical and horizontal scales, and to exercise a variety of enabling functions. We turn next to analyzing whether and how, and with what consequences, the REDD+ Partnership has played such a role.

4 MANAGING FRAGMENTATION THROUGH THE REDD+ PARTNERSHIP?

As one reaction to the widely perceived "failure" of the 2009 climate meeting in Copenhagen to agree to a successor climate agreement to the Kyoto Protocol, several Parties to the UNFCCC sought ways to at least advance the REDD+ agenda globally. In line with this, 50 countries met in March 2010 in Norway to establish the (Interim) REDD+ Partnership. The Partnership was explicitly designed to be inclusive of all interested countries (both potential REDD+ donors and recipients, called Partners), as well as non-state stakeholders, with the overarching aim to scale up action and finance (REDD+ Partnership 2010a; Reinecke et al. 2012).

The declared core objective of the REDD+ Partnership was:

> *"...to contribute to the global battle against climate change by serving as an interim platform for the Partners to scale up REDD+ actions and finance, and to that end take immediate action, including improving the effectiveness, efficiency, transparency and coordination of REDD+ initiatives and financial instruments..." (REDD+ Partnership 2010a, 1).*

In so doing, the Partnership stated also its aim to be "inclusive of all committed countries as well as representatives of relevant stakeholders including indigenous peoples, local communities, civil society and the private sector" (Partnership 2010a, 2).

Given these objectives, and drawing on our discussion of a bridge organization in Sect. 2, we distill here four bridging, enabling functions that the Partnership has sought to exercise, as a way to manage fragmentation in this realm and meet its substantive aim of scaling up REDD+ action and finance. These functions include, first, *enhancing transparency* around REDD+ actions and finance, as a way to understand who is supporting what and what (unmet) needs exist; second, *enhancingparticipation*, i.e., multi-stakeholder engagement and input into REDD+ discussions; third, *building trust* and *enhancingknowledgesharing*, as a means to identify best practices, and thereby help facilitate a scaling up of such practices; and fourth, *enhancing coordination*, both vertical and horizontal, of REDD+ actions and finance, in order to leverage synergies and avoid duplication in this realm.

In exercising such bridging functions, the Partnership explicitly subordinated itself to the UNFCCC in its founding documents. Except for issue-specific workshops held irregularly, the main Partnership meetings (at least two per year) have been organized back-to-back with UNFCCC meetings, given that most Partners are also UNFCCC REDD+ negotiators. Two co-chairs are selected from the 75 Partner countries (one each from a developed and developing country) to chair the Partnership for non-renewable terms of 6 months each. The co-chairs are responsible for proposing an agenda and activities for their term. UN-REDD and the World Bank's FCPF jointly host the Partnership Secretariat, which is responsible for organizing Partnership meetings, and helping to execute its multiyear work program.

We turn next to assessing whether and how the Partnership has exercised the four bridging, enabling functions of enhancing transparency, participation, knowledge sharing/trust building, and coordination identified above, and whether and how such functions have contributed to meeting the overarching aim of "scaling up REDD+ action and finance."

4.1 Managing fragmentation: Enhancing transparency?

Perhaps most directly related to the Partnership's substantive objective of "scaling up action and finance" is a focus on enhancing *transparency* about such actions and finance. In order to fulfill this aim, the Partnership created two instruments to share and disseminate information about REDD+ actions and financing: the Partnership website and the so-called Voluntary REDD+ Database (VRD). The VRD, in particular, has been one of the most visible and concrete outputs of the REDD+ Partnership. It consists of a database of REDD+ financial flows and relies upon a so-called dual-input procedure by which to gather information, whereby donors report on the REDD+ funding amounts disbursed (and to whom) and beneficiary countries report on funding received. Countries submit information to the Partnership Secretariat, which inputs it into, and maintains, the VRD.

One of the most noteworthy results of this exercise has been a *striking discrepancy* between the funding amounts reported by donors and recipients. At the time of writing, donor countries reported that they have disbursed US$ 7.59 billion in bilateral and multilateral funding for REDD+, of which US$ 5.98 billion has been transferred, or pledged, to specific REDD+ countries. Recipient countries reported, however, a total sum of US$ 4.68 billion, of which US$ 2.25 billion has been transferred or pledged to specific countries (see Fig. 1).

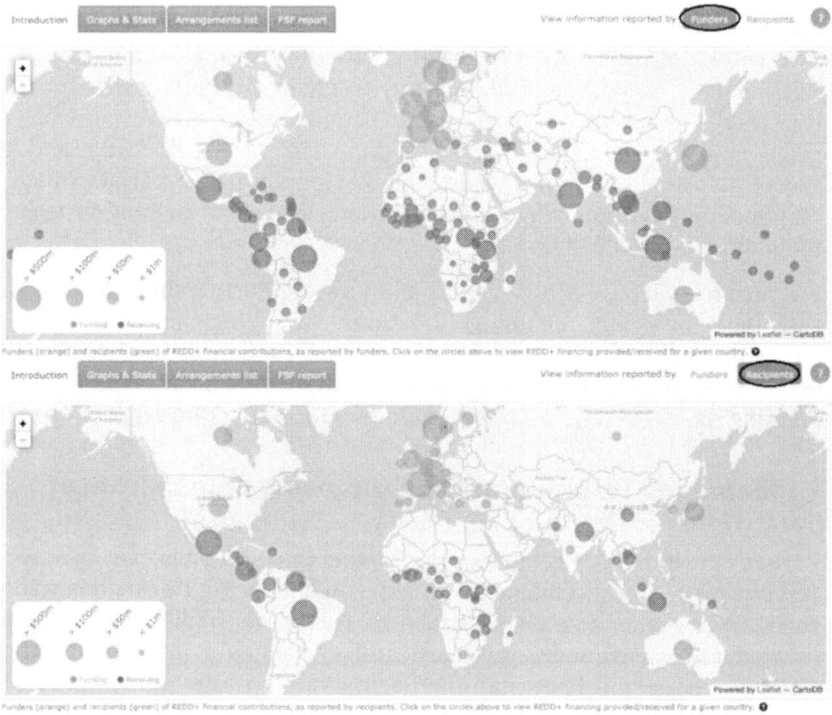

Fig. 1 Transparency about REDD+ financing as reported by funders (*above*) and recipients (*below*). Size of *circles* indicates the amount of funding (retrieved from http://www.fao.org/forestry/vrd/, March 25, 2015)

These discrepancies have led to some heated discussions in Partnership meetings between donor and recipient countries, with regard to explanations for the mismatch. These explanations include, inter alia, that donor amounts include both disbursed and *pledged* funds, while recipient countries report only what they have actually received. More importantly, some donor figures include broad forestry-related development aid funding, rendering the boundaries around what constitutes "REDD+ finance" (and, related to that, "REDD+ actions") fuzzy. On the recipient side, the discrepancy is also explainable by the fact that those required to provide information to the VRD (usually UNFCCC REDD+ focal points within a specific country) may not be aware of funds received by other arms of the government or may not have the resources or capacity to collate and report on received funding or to distinguish between general forestry versus REDD+ specific funding.[4]

Notwithstanding ongoing efforts by Partners and the Secretariat to understand the causes for, and take steps to reduce, the mismatch in reported donor and recipient amounts, this exercise has arguably yielded one of the most valuable outputs of the REDD+ Partnership's bridging efforts to date. It has clearly highlighted that the aim of objectively laying bare, or making transparent, what has been disbursed, by whom, to whom, and for what purpose, is much more complex than assumed. The discrepancy in donor and recipient reporting reveals, instead, that there are very diverse perspectives on *what constitutes* REDD+ actions and finance in the first place and who (should) determine this. The VRD has thus made clear that the nature and sources of REDD+ financing (and related to that, REDD+ actions) are neither clear, nor widely shared, among countries.

It is unlikely, furthermore, that these inherently political issues can be fully resolved through providing "more and better" information to the VRD (as very often called for in this context), since different interpretations of what is "more and better" information, and whose information is valid, persist, regardless of enhanced national capacities to gather data, or technical improvements in inputting data. While such improvements can certainly be sought, the discrepancies suggest that in such contested areas of global environmental governance, transparency itself is often a site of political conflict (Gupta 2010a, b) and can be *constitutive* of that which it seeks to make transparent.[5] This is in contrast to a dominant view of transparency as a value-neutral means by which to reveal an objective "reality" (in this case, about REDD+ financing), in order to facilitate more rational decisions.

The consequences of the enhanced transparency provided by the VRD for the Partnership's substantive aim of "scaling up action and finance" remain to be seen and are linked to a broader question about whether consensual understandings of what constitutes REDD+ (or REDD+ finance) are even necessary for such a scaling up to occur. Meanwhile, at the final meeting of the Partnership in November 2014 in Lima, the Partners agreed to continue the VRD for another 2 years beyond the end of the Partnership itself. This signaled that its dual-input approach to reporting on REDD+ financial flows was acknowledged to be useful by all, even as it revealed conflicting rather than consensual views on the first-order question of what constitutes REDD+ action and finance.

4.2 Managing fragmentation: Enhancing multi-stakeholder participation?

In addition to fostering transparency about REDD+ actions and finance, the Partnership also aimed to be inclusive of a wide array of relevant stakeholders. Again, as with enhancing transparency, the Partnership has provided a valuable experimental setting in which to ascertain the possibilities and challenges of securing enhanced and meaningful multi-stakeholder participation in contested areas of global environmental governance. The experiment has highlighted at least three challenges. These include: first, whether *any stakeholders* are at the table (and the political and logistical constraints that might incentivize or disincentivize this); second, *whose voices* are present and being heard; and third, *how representative* these voices are, i.e., who speaks for whom. All of these aspects shape the nature and significance of multi-stakeholder involvement in this setting, and its contribution, if any, to the Partnership's overall aim of scaling up action and finance.

With regard to whether any stakeholders were engaged at all, the early meetings of the Partnership in 2010 were overshadowed by major disputes about how inclusive it should be (Davis and Daviet 2010). As a result of such disputes, initial Partnership meetings were closed to stakeholders, even though a broad array of civil society groups and private actors active in REDD+ had enthusiastically welcomed the Partnership's establishment, and the opportunity to engage in an informal setting with REDD+ negotiators. While most REDD+ Partner countries pushed for the multi-stakeholder character of the Partnership to be reinstated in these early months, a few countries blocked this, ostensibly, as some have speculated, because of concern that multi-stakeholder presence could result in a shift of the Partnership's focus from a scaling up of finance to issues such as safeguards (e.g., Lang 2010a).

Following an inability to effectively participate in the Partnership in its initial discussions, 35 non-governmental organizations wrote a letter to the co-chairs in September 2010 to "reiterate [their] disappointment with the protracted lack of political will to ensure proper participation of civil society and indigenous peoples' organisations in the processes of the Interim REDD+ Partnership" (Lang 2010b). The issue was only resolved with a change in Partnership co-chairs after the first 6 months (REDD+ Partnership 2010b).[6] Meetings since then have been multi-stakeholder as intended, and the input of stakeholders and experts at technical workshops has been particularly welcomed. However, criticism and debate about whether such interaction is adequate, meaningful, and representative remains. A key indicator for the possibility of meaningful engagement is the timeliness with which information about meeting dates, agendas, and draft work programs is provided to stakeholders. This has proven to be a consistent challenge and source of complaints from stakeholders. During development of the most recent (2013/2014) Partnership work program, for example, stakeholders were only belatedly given an opportunity to comment, but with lack of time and conflicts over the meeting agenda, their possibilities for input were negligible. Such experiences led some to question the added value of continued participation in the Partnership, with interest in doing so declining over time (Lang 2010a, b, 2014).

Additional challenges included a lack of resources to travel to meetings, especially when these were not held back-to-back with the UNFCCC. In response to a significant decline of stakeholder participation in meetings by 2012, the Partnership agreed to finance two non-state representatives from each region (one civil society, one indigenous community representative) to attend its meetings.[7] While this did secure some additional stakeholder participation, it raised issues of representation: whether the right person was at the table, and whom they purported to speak for. Such issues of inclusion and representation constitute long-standing debates in multilevel environmental governance, yet the Partnership experience reiterates that simply securing a seat at the table does not necessarily constitute meaningful engagement.

Where stakeholder engagement *has* been seen as very valuable is in furthering the third Partnership enabling function of enhancing knowledge sharing, to which we turn next.

4.3 Managing fragmentation: Enhancing knowledge (and trust)?

In addition to enhancing transparency and participation, *knowledge and experience sharing* was widely seen as another crucial enabling function, with the aim to facilitate collective learning, enhance trust, and thereby facilitate the scaling up of REDD+ action and finance. Such a knowledge sharing function was explicitly intended to build capacity among REDD+ negotiators to discuss complex and interlinked REDD+ issues under negotiation within the UNFCCC, as well as to share best practices in operationalizing REDD+ in national and local contexts on the ground.

To execute this latter knowledge sharing and collective learning function, the Partnership relied upon a series of thematic, so-called technical workshops, organized during regular Partnership meetings. Topics covered at these sessions included MRV systems; development of "forest emission reference levels," i.e., benchmarks against which REDD+ emission reductions/savings are to be assessed; sources and modes of financing; or development and assessment of non-carbon benefits. Participants in these workshops included Partner countries and other stakeholders, as well as invited external experts.

One interesting dynamic from such activities was to trigger, in some instances, a "race to the top" in experimenting with innovative approaches to operationalizing REDD+ in diverse national contexts. Oft-noted examples include a wide sharing of Guyana's approach to institutionalizing and reporting on safeguards, or Indonesia's readiness efforts and governance reforms (Reinecke et al. 2012), whereby a sharing of experiences helped to stimulate the dissemination of such "best practices" to other contexts (Pistorius and Reinecke 2013, see also La Viña and Lee 2014). Knowledge sharing thus enabled the Partnership to function as a "competitive REDD+ marketplace," whereby REDD+ countries could assess interest and alignment of priorities with specific donors, while displaying innovative approaches. As such, the Partnership's knowledge sharing function has been unanimously seen as helpful. In this, it has indeed served as a bridging entity, bringing actors in a fragmented governance landscape together to enhance collective learning. In acknowledging its utility, the final Partnership meeting in November 2014 in Lima reiterated the need to identify other fora for knowledge exchange, particularly focusing on national-level REDD+ implementation (REDD+ Partnership 2014).

Regarding the related aim of enhancing trust and facilitating progress in UNFCCC negotiations, the extent to which the Partnership has facilitated this remains contested. As one interviewee put it, the Partnership helps to build "trust and understanding... At least... [for] agreeing on the terminology around REDD+ and also kicking around new concepts, I think it's useful."[8]Another stated that "the longer and the more you...share information and ... understand the positions of others, the ... closer we may come to a final breakthrough [in the UNFCCC]."[9]

A key advantage offered by the Partnership setting in this regard was its exclusive focus on REDD+, with participation *limited* to those with a stake in this issue, or as an interviewee put it, for the "coalition of the willing"[10] to engage. This is in contrast to REDD+ discussions within the UNFCCC, where 195 countries negotiate a plethora of partly linked agenda items under extreme time pressure, with REDD+ sometimes becoming a bargaining chip to secure other desired outcomes for countries with little or no interest in it. The Partnership meetings brought together instead those UNFCCC representatives negotiating specifically on REDD+, yet in a setting widely proclaimed to be "not a negotiation body" but rather "a platform where people can... talk openly, freely... without any limitations."[11]

The Partnership was also described as not "clouded by diplomacy"[12] but able to operate "in isolation of" the UNFCCC negotiations.[13] For some, this did indeed serve to enhance trust among Partners, since negotiators could "share in a more frank way their views,...[and] try to come up with solutions that can be satisfactory for all..., [as a way] to simply speed up..."

the UNFCCC negotiations.[14] Others noted, however, that countries that most often dominated discussions and outcomes in the UNFCCC were also shaping discussions in the Partnership. One interviewee argued, for example, that there was "way too much...overlap between the regular negotiators at the UNFCCC and the people sitting at the REDD+ Partnership" causing people to "automatically jump back to negotiation mode."[15] Such a negotiation mode hindered, according to some, the open and free exchange of ideas, and enhancing of trust.

Yet others noted, however, that the desired informal, "non-political" mode of the Partnership was unrealistic from the start. As a Greenpeace representative put it, "...politics, it seemed, was ostensibly to be left outside, so REDD+ could be reduced to a seemingly technocratic and harmonious discussion among family and friends" (Ritter 2012). This mirrors a conclusion we draw from this and other aspects of the Partnership's functioning, that a bridge organization's enabling functions cannot (and indeed, should not seek to) be executed in a "depolicitized" manner, as many continue to call for (e.g., La Viña and Lee 2014), in order to provide value in a contested global environmental governance context.

4.4 **Managing fragmentation: Enhancing coordination?**

Finally, the REDD+ Partnership aimed not only to enhance transparency, participation, knowledge sharing, and trust, but also greater *coordination* (both vertical and horizontal) between REDD+ actors, institutional and organizational entities active at different levels. A few examples of such potential coordination are briefly discussed here. First, and in a horizontal context, there were initial hopes that the Partnership would facilitate discussions between the UNFCCC and the CBD on REDD+ safeguards. Second, through the sharing of experiences and emerging best practices mentioned above, the Partnership also aimed to encourage South–South partnerships and private–public partnerships to facilitate REDD+ implementation on the ground. Third, in requiring the Partnership Secretariat to be jointly managed by the two main REDD+ multilateral financing bodies, the World Bank's FCPF and UN-REDD, the Partnership early on signaled the importance of greater coordination between these entities, as one way to counteract visible fragmentation in the REDD+ issue-domain.

While closer engagement with the CBD did not materialize to the extent that some may have hoped, given conflicts over priorities and primary objectives of the biodiversity and climate regimes,[16] increased South–South partnerships *have* been fostered (La Viña and Lee 2014). With regard to coordination of REDD+ multilateral funding entities, while the joint Secretariat has been important, coordination between the UN-REDD

Programme and the World Bank's FCPF is already underway in other settings, including through joint meetings of the two initiatives, suggesting that the Partnership alone is not instrumental here (see footnote 16). An area where understandings (between donor and recipient countries) on coordination continue to diverge, furthermore, is whether such coordination is most needed at the *multilateral (donor) level or at the national level within* REDD+ recipient countries, with donors arguing for the latter as the most pressing need.

Thus, while enhancing coordination between actors, organizations, and institutions engaged with REDD+ at multiple levels has been sought through the Partnership, such coordination has been difficult to foster in practice, making this one of the hardest bridging aims to fulfill. This is linked to a well-known lack of incentives to coordinate and be coordinated, and lack of clarity regarding who benefits from (what kind of) coordination in global environmental governance. In the REDD+ context, how enhanced coordination at various scales may (or may not) contribute to scaling up of REDD+ action and finance is now a topic under intense discussion within the UNFCCC itself, under its agenda item on coordination of support and (new) institutional arrangements for REDD+.

5 CONCLUSION

We have argued in this paper that the institutional and organizational complexity (i.e., fragmentation) around REDD+ is rapidly increasing, stimulated in part by its expanding scope within the UNFCCC. The UNFCCC remains the (hierarchical) core in a fragmented REDD+ governance architecture, insofar as it establishes the normative and regulatory framework with which all other actors, institutions, and organizations have to contend. Nonetheless, there are large degrees of freedom in doing so, given the general nature of its guidelines and provisions. As a result, there is a potential to produce diverging REDD+ realities in different contexts, with implications for a coordinated scaling up of REDD+ action and finance.

Our analysis hence considered whether and how the REDD+ Partnership, established to fulfill a variety of enabling, bridging functions in this fragmented landscape, has functioned to date and whether it can be said to have "managed" fragmentation, in order to further specified governance aims. We focused, in particular, on its functions relating to enhancing transparency, participation, knowledge sharing and coordination and assessed whether these have facilitated the "scaling up of REDD+ action and finance."

As outlined in the previous section, the Partnership has *partially* fulfilled each of these four enabling, bridging functions, with implications for its overall impact.

With regard to enhancing transparency, the Partnership's efforts have revealed discrepancies in understandings between donor and recipient countries regarding what constitutes REDD+ actions and finance. Countries have decided, nonetheless, that the VRD will continue beyond the lifetime of the Partnership, implying that it may become an important input into future UNFCCC deliberations on REDD+ financing. If so, our findings in this regard are important: they imply that the utility of enhancing transparency does not (solely or necessarily) lie in securing an "objective" reporting of "facts" that will reveal the uncontested "reality" of REDD+ financing and thereby facilitate more rational decisions, as is often assumed. Instead, the VRD's case shows, as do other examples of "governance by disclosure" in the global environmental realm, that *whose* information counts (and *what* is to be made transparent) is often a site of political conflict.

With regard to enhancing participation, our analysis revealed that securing meaningful multi-stakeholder engagement is essentially, and inevitably, a political process. Many stakeholders have become disillusioned in their attempts to participate in the Partnership, because of a realization that, despite its informal voluntary setting, meaningful impact is only marginally more feasible here, as compared to the UNFCCC. As with enhanced transparency, enhancing meaningful multi-stakeholder engagement, as another bridging function, thus remains subject to the broader geopolitical conflicts around REDD+.

With regard to enhancing knowledge and trust, our analysis suggests that many have seen the Partnership as a useful forum to enhance knowledge sharing about REDD+ and thereby also facilitate UNFCCC deliberations. Others have viewed the hierarchical ties between the UNFCCC and the Partnership as too strong to prevent a spillover of the interests and practices from the UNFCCC to the Partnership. This notwithstanding, our analysis implies generally that knowledge sharing and collective learning can be enabled even in the *absence* of trust. If collective learning is occurring, it is occurring in the face of persisting political contestation and potentially divergent interpretations of what is being learned. Yet this renders such learning potentially even more valuable.

With regard to enhancing coordination, the Partnership has been credited with facilitating South–South collaborations in REDD+, yet coordination between diverse multilateral regimes, such as the UNFCCC and the CBD, or between multilateral funding entities, has been harder to incentivize.

More broadly, we conclude from the partial fulfillment of the four bridging functions analyzed here that each is subject to the same political conflicts and dynamics that shape REDD+ deliberations in any other setting. Having an ostensibly informal, voluntary, enabling and bridge-building setting does not, and cannot, transcend the structural dynamics and geopolitics underpinning collective attempts to tackle climate change, wherever these occur.

This is most clearly reflected, perhaps, in the persisting conflicts over how to interpret the Partnership's overarching objective to "scale up actions and finance." In the debate on extending the Partnership during the 2012 climate conference in Doha, the Coalition of Rainforest Nations (CfRN) consisting of approximately 70 tropical countries that negotiate as a block within the UNFCCC, argued that scaling up REDD+ actions and finance meant that the Partnership activities should *directly* result in increased flows of funding. They called for reaffirmation of this primary objective of the Partnership for the period 2013–2014 and voiced their disappointment about the Partnership's achievements to date in this regard.[17]

Others, in particular donor countries, reiterated their understanding that the Partnership's aim to scale up action and finance was to be understood as *enhancing transparency* about existing actions and finances, as a means to assess gaps and identify needs, which could then trigger additional action (including funding), also in other settings. As a recently concluded assessment of the Partnership notes, "Assessing this goal [of scaling up action and finance] was challenging due to lack of shared understanding, or interpretation, of what the objective meant and entailed" (La Viña and Lee 2014, 2, see also Lang 2014).

With regard, then, to our theoretical interest in fragmentation and its management, and the role of bridge organizations therein, our analysis suggests that the overarching normative structures and political dynamics shaping global (environmental) governance not only shape the nature and consequences of fragmentation, but also any attempts to *manage* it. As we have shown, the goals of fragmentation management, and hence the functions of bridge organizations, remain subject to political contestation, multiple interpretations and negotiation. The differences in understandings of the core objective of the REDD+ Partnership to "scale up action and finance" that persisted until its closure are exemplary of this. Such disagreements are unlikely to be resolved through a technocratic, managerial approach to bridging fragmentation, as current understandings of bridge organizations in the literature may imply.

We would argue, instead, that securing a "depoliticized" setting should not be the overarching aim (and measure of success) of a bridge organization.

Based on our analysis, we conclude that the Partnership has indeed functioned as a valuable enabling organization, one that has partially succeeded in operationalizing a set of enabling, bridging functions in managing a fragmented REDD+ governance landscape. However, its value (and success) derives *not,* in our view, from having yielded objective information, non-politicized participation, value-free sharing of knowledge, or rational coordination, as a means to generate consensual, technically sound, and apolitical understandings of REDD+. Instead, the very success of a bridge organization such as the Partnership lies in bringing together key actors with divergent notions of what it should achieve. In active engagement with these diverse interpretations, we would argue, lies the transformative potential of such enabling, bridging entities seeking to manage fragmentation in global environmental governance.

FOOTNOTES

1. REDD+ is the UNFCCC acronym for reducing *e*missions from *d*eforestation and forest *d*egradation in developing countries; and the role of conservation, sustainable management of forests and enhancement of forest carbon stocks in developing countries.
2. For Partnership establishment documents and mandate, see http://reddpluspartnership.org/73943/en/.
3. We use the terms "regime complex" and "fragmentation" interchangeably here.
4. Participant observation during REDD+ Partnership meeting, June 9, 2014, Bonn; Interview with a programme officer at the UN-REDD Programme, 2-12-2014.
5. For a detailed analysis of the politics of making REDD+ transparent, see Gupta et al. (2012, 2014).
6. Interview with representative of DG Climate, European Commission, November 2012, Doha.
7. Interview with a member of the UN-REDD Secretariat staff, December 2, 2014.
8. Interview with representative of DG Climate, European Commission, November 2012, Doha.

9. Interview with first representative of WWF international, 2011.
10. Interview with representative of CfRN, 12 June 2014, Bonn.
11. Interview with representative of German Ministry of the Environment, 2011.
12. Interview with programme officer at the UN-REDD Programme, 2-12-2014, via Skype.
13. Interview with representative of DG Climate, European Commission, November 2012, Doha.
14. Interview with first representative of WWF international, 2011.
15. Interview with observer of the Partnership, 8-02-2012.
16. Interview with member of UN-REDD/Partnership Secretariat, December 2, 2014.
17. Interview with representative of CfRN, 12 June 2014, Bonn.

ACKNOWLEDGMENTS

Earlier versions of this article were presented at the 2013 International Studies Association Annual Meeting, Panel on Institutional Complexity in Global Environmental Governance; and at the 2013 Workshop on Fragmentation in Global Environmental Law and Governance, organized by the VU-University Amsterdam and Stockholm Environment Institute. We would like to thank David Victor and Lukas Giessen for their detailed commentary on our paper at each event, and Kenneth Abbott, Harro van Asselt, Frank Biermann, Peter Glasbergen, Jessica F. Green, Robert O. Keohane, Philipp Pattberg, Oscar Widerberg, and Fariborz Zelli for useful comments. Special thanks goes to Sabine Reinecke for helpful feedback on earlier drafts of this article. We also thank our interviewees in the UNFCCC and REDD+ Partnership processes for the time taken to respond to our queries, and to Wahida Patwa-Shah of the REDD+ Partnership Secretariat for reading an earlier version of the paper. Finally, we are very grateful to the two anonymous INEA reviewers of our article, whose feedback helped us to strengthen our argument.

REFERENCES

1. Abbott, K. (2012). The transnational regime complex for climate change. *Environmental Policy and Planning C: Government and Policy, 30*(4), 571–590.

2. Abbott, K., & Snidal, D. (2006). Nesting, overlap and parallelism: Governance schemes for international production standards. Memo for Alter-Meunier, Princeton Nesting Conference, February 2006. http://www.princeton.edu/~smeunier/Abbott%20Snidal%20memo.pdf. Accessed October 24, 2013.

3. Aggarwal, V. K. (2005). Reconciling institutions: Nested, horizontal, overlapping, and independent institutions. http://www.princeton.edu/~smeunier/Aggarwal%20memo.pdf. Accessed October 24, 2013.

4. Alter, K. J., & Meunier, S. (2006). Nested and overlapping regimes in the transatlantic banana trade dispute. *Journal of European Public Policy, 13*(3), 362–382.

5. Alter, K. J., & Meunier, S. (2009). The politics of international regime complexity. *Perspectives on Politics, 7*(1), 13–24.

6. Berkes, F. (2009). Evolution of co-management: Role of knowledge generation, bridging organizations and social learning. *Journal of Environmental Management, 90*, 1692–1702.

7. Betts, A. (2013). Regime complexity and international organizations: UNHCR as a challenged institution. *Global Governance, 19*, 69–81.

8. Biermann, F., Pattberg, P., Van Asselt, H., & Zelli, F. (2009). The fragmentation of global governance architectures: A framework for analysis. *Global Environmental Politics, 9*(4), 14–40.

9. Cash, D., Adger, N. W., Berkes, F., Garden, P., Lebel, L., Olsson, P., et al. (2006). Scale and cross-scale dynamics: Governance and information in a multilevel World. *Ecology and Society,11*(2), 8–18.

10. Cerbu, G. A., Swallow, B. M., & Thomson, D. Y. (2011). Locating REDD: A global survey and analysis of REDD readiness and demonstration activities. *Environmental Science & Policy,4*(2), 168–180.

11. Convention on Biological Diversity, (CBD). (2015). http://www.cbd.int/. Accessed March 9, 2015.

12. Crona, B. I., & Parker, J. N. (2012). Learning in support of governance: Theories, methods and a framework to assess how bridging organizations contribute to adaptive resource governance. *Ecology and Society, 17*(1), 32.

13. Davis, C., & Daviet, F. (2010). Investing in results: enhancing coordination for more effective interim REDD+ financing. WRI Working Paper. World Resource Institute, Washington DC. http://www.wri.org/publication/investing-in-results. Accessed May 12, 2013.

14. Drezner, D. W. (2009). The power and peril of international regime complexity. *Perspectives on Politics, 7*(1), 65–70.

15. Folke, C., Hahn, T., Olsson, P., & Norberg, J. (2005). Adaptive governance of social-ecological systems. *Annual Review of Environment and Resources, 30*, 441–473.

16. Gehring, T., & Oberthür, S. (2004). Exploring regime interaction: A framework of analysis. In A. Underdal & O. R. Young (Eds.), *Regime consequences: Methodological challenges and research strategies*. The Netherlands: Springer.

17. Gupta, A. (2008). Transparency under scrutiny: Information disclosure in global environmental governance. *Global Environmental Politics, 8*(2), 1–7.

18. Gupta, A. (2010a). Transparency to what end? Governing by disclosure through the biosafety clearing house. *Environment and Planning C: Government and Policy, 28*(1), 128–144.

19. Gupta, A. (2010b). Transparency in global environmental governance: A coming of age? *Global Environmental Politics, 10*(3), 1–9.

20. Gupta, A., Lövbrand, E., Turnhout, E., & Vijge, M. J. (2012). In pursuit of carbon accountability: The politics of REDD+ measuring, reporting and verification systems. *Current Opinion on Environmental Sustainability, 4*(6), 726–731.

21. Gupta, A., Vijge, M. J., Turnhout, E., & Pistorius, T. (2014). Making REDD+ transparent: The politics of measuring, reporting and verification systems. In A. Gupta & M. Mason (Eds.), *Transparency in global environmental governance*. Cambridge: MIT press.

22. Herold, M., & Skutsch, M. (2011). Monitoring, reporting and verification for national REDD+ programmes: Two proposals. *Environmental Research Letters, 6*, 1–10.

23. IPCC. (2003). Good practice guidance for land use, land-use change and forestry. www.ipcc-nggip.iges.or.jp/public/gpglulucf /gpglulucf.htm. Accessed 3 July 2013.

24. Keohane, R., & Victor, D. (2011). The regime complex for climate change. *Perspectives on Politics, 9*(1), 7–23.

25. La Viña, T., & Lee, D. (2014). Assessment of the results of the REDD+ Partnership. http://www.fao.org/partnerships/redd-plus-partnership/en/. Accessed March 9, 2015.

26. Lang, C. (2010a). How the REDD+ Partnership unraveled in Tianjin. http://www.redd-monitor.org/2010/10/12/how-the-redd-partnership-unravelled-in-tianjin/. Accessed November 24, 2014.

27. Lang, C. (2010b). NGO letter to the Interim REDD+ Partnership raises fundamental questions. http://www.redd-monitor.org/2010 /09/10/ngo-letter-to-the-interim-redd-partnership-raises-fundamental-questions/. Accessed December 8, 2010.

28. Lang, C. (2014). The dismal failure of the REDD+ Partnership. http://www.redd-monitor.org/2014/11/20/the-dismal-failure-of-the-redd-partnership/. Accessed November 24, 2014.

29. McDermott, C. L., Coad, L., Helfgott, A., & Schroeder, H. (2012). Operationalizing social safeguards in REDD+: Actors, interests and ideas. *Environmental Science & Policy, 21*, 63–72.

30. McMullen, R. S., & Adobor, H. (2011). Bridge leadership: A case study of leadership in a bridging organization. *Leadership & Organization Development Journal, 32*(7), 715–735.

31. Moss, N., Nussbaum, R., Muchemi, J., & Halverson, E. (2011). A review of three REDD+ safeguard initiatives. UN-REDD Programme & Forest Carbon Partnership Facility. http://www.un-redd.org/PublicationsResources/tabid/587/Default.aspx#joint_publications

32. Oberthür, S. (2009). Interplay management: Enhancing environmental policy integration among international institutions. *International Environmental Agreements, 9*, 371–391.

33. Orsini, A., Morin, J.-F., & Young, O. (2013). Regime complexes: A buzz, a boom or a boost for global governance? *Global Governance, 19*, 27–39.

34. Pistorius, T. (2012). From RED to REDD+: The evolution of a forest-based mitigation approach for developing countries. *Current Opinion in Environmental Sustainability, 4*(6), 638–645.

35. Pistorius, T., & Reinecke, S. (2013). The interim REDD+ Partnership: Boost for biodiversity safeguards? *Forest Policy and Economics, 36*, 80–86.

36. Raustiala, K., & Victor, D. G. (2004). The regime complex for plant genetic resources. *International Organization, 58*(2), 277–309.

37. REDD+ Partnership (2010a). Founding document. http://www.oslocfc2010.no/pop.cfm?FuseAction=Doc&pAction=View&pDocumentId=25019. Accessed October 22, 2013.

38. REDD+ Partnership (2010b). Interim REDD+ Partnership. Modalities of Stakeholder Participation. Tianjin, October. http://reddpluspartnership.org/23477-072817a5ccf72c2071aa1da88ca5a294e.pdf. Accessed October 24, 2013.

39. REDD+ Partnership (2014). Meeting and workshop, 27–28 November, 2014, Peru, Lima. http://reddpluspartnership.org/73943/en/. Accessed December 11, 2014.

40. Reinecke, S., Pistorius, T., & Pregernig, M. (2012). UNFCCC and the REDD+ Partnership from a networked governance perspective. *Environmental Science & Policy*,.doi:10.1016/j.envsci.2012.09.015.

41. Ritter, D. (2012). Whatever happened to the REDD+ Partnership? Global Policy blog. http://www.globalpolicyjournal.com/blog/01/03/2012/whatever-happened-redd-partnership. Accessed December 3, 2014.

42. Streck, C. (2012). Financing REDD+: Matching needs and ends. *Current Opinion in Environmental Sustainability, 4*(6), 628–637.

43. UNFCCC (2013). Report of the Conference of the Parties on its nineteenth session, held in Warsaw from 11 to 23 November 2013. Addendum. Part two: Action taken by the Conference of the Parties at its nineteenth session. Contents. Decisions adopted by the Conference of the Parties. FCCC/CP/2013/10/Add.1.

44. Van Asselt, H., & Zelli, F. (2012). *Connect the dots: Managing the fragmentation of global climate governance.* Earth System Governance Working Paper no. 25. Lund and Amsterdam: Earth System Governance Project.

45. Visseren-Hamakers, I. J., Arts, B., & Glasbergen, P. (2011). Interaction management by partnerships: The case of biodiversity and climate change. *Global Environmental Politics,11*(4), 89–107.

46. Visseren-Hamakers, I. J., Gupta, A., Herold, M., Peña-Claros, M., & Vijge, M. J. (2012a). Will REDD+ work? The need for interdisciplinary science to address key challenges. *Current Opinion in Environmental Sustainability, 4*(6), 646–653.

47. Visseren-Hamakers, I. J., McDermott, C., Vijge, M. J., & Cashore, B. (2012b). Trade-offs, co-benefits and safeguards: Current debates on the breadth of REDD+. *Current Opinion in Environmental Sustainability, 4*(6), 590–596.

48. Visseren-Hamakers, I. J., & Verkooijen, P. (2013). The practice of interaction management: Enhancing synergies among multilateral REDD+ institutions. *Forest and Nature Governance World Forests, 14*, 133–149.

49. Wertz-Kanounnikoff, S., & Kongphan-Apirak, M. (2009). *Emerging REDD+: A preliminary survey of demonstration and readiness activities.* Working Paper 46. Bogor: CIFOR.

50. Young, O. R. (1996). Institutional linkages in international society: Polar perspectives. *Global Governance, 2*(1), 1–24.

51. Zelli, F., Gupta, A., & Van Asselt, H. (2013). Institutional interactions at the crossroads of trade and environment: The dominance of liberal environmentalism? *Global Governance, 19*, 105–118.

52. Zelli, F., & Van Asselt, H. (2013). Introduction: The institutional fragmentation of global environmental governance: Causes, consequences, and responses. *Global Environmental Politics, 13*(3), 1–13.

3

CHAPTER

Governing by Targets: Reductio AD Unum and Evolution of the two-Degree Climate Target

Piero Morseletto[1], Frank Biermann[2], Philipp Pattberg[1]

[1] *Institute for Environmental Studies (IVM), Faculty of Earth and Life Sciences, VU University Amsterdam, 1081 HV Amsterdam, The Netherlands*

[2] *Copernicus Institute of Sustainable Development, Faculty of Geosciences, Utrecht University, 3508 TC Utrecht, The Netherlands*

ABSTRACT

Targets are widely employed in environmental governance. In this paper, we investigate the construction of the 2 °C climate target, one of the best known targets in global environmental governance. Our paper examines this target through a historical reconstruction that identifies four different phases: framing, consolidation and diffusion, adoption, and disembeddedness. Our analysis shows that, initially, the target was science-driven and predominantly EU-based; it then became progressively accepted at the international level, despite a lack of broader debate among governments on the policy implications and required measures for implementation. Once the 2 °C target was endorsed at the level of the United Nations, the nature of the target changed from being policy-prescriptive to being largely symbolic. In this phase, the target became a disembedded object in global governance not linked to a shared agenda nor to coordinated and mutually binding mitigation efforts. The 2015 Paris Agreement marks the last stage in this development and may have further solidified the target as a disembedded object. In the final part of the paper, we suggest ways to overcome the current situation and to develop the 2 °C target into a fully fledged global environmental governance target.

Keywords: 2 °C target, Global environmental governance, Climate governance, International relations and politics, Governing by targets

1 INTRODUCTION

Targets have become an increasingly important tool of environmental governance, from national environmental targets to targets within broader global goals such as the Sustainable Development Goals (Kanie and Biermann 2017; Bergh and Couturier 2013). In governing by targets, we refer to the tendency to rely on these instruments for framing responses to environmental problems. Such a theoretical perspective suggests the importance of investigating how targets are formed, stipulated and employed. This paper analyses the 2 °C target—the envisaged maximum mean temperature increase above pre-industrial levels—that governments agreed upon to be the target of the UN Framework Convention on Climate Change. The 2 °C target aims at pulling together countries' efforts to avoid the dangerous impacts of climate change. As such, it arguably is one of the most prominent targets in global environmental governance. However, the choice of a single figure represents a reductio ad unum, that is, bringing multiple issues down to a single element. Our analysis investigates the process that led to the 2 °C figure and addresses three main research questions: (1) What factors shaped the emergence and development of the 2 °C target over time? (2) What functions does the target perform in the political arena? (3) In how far does the target fulfil the scope for which it was created?

To answer these questions, we identify and examine different phases in the evolution of the target. This includes considering the actors, approaches and institutional contexts that marked the progression of the target. Moreover, the phase-approach makes it easier to confront the target with key concepts from the fields of environmental governance as well as science and technology studies (notably on the interplay between scientists and policymakers, the interests of political actors and on strategic approaches in negotiations).

In the scholarly literature, environmental governance targets have been addressed by a variety of disciplinary approaches in the context of regime theory (Young and Levy 1999; Mitchell et al. 2006; Haas et al. 1993), scientific assessments (Cash 2000; Watson 2005), environmental diplomacy (Barrett 2003; Grubb 1990) and international policy-making (Dietrich 1995). These studies suggest that governing by targets is a key element of the structure and dynamics of environmental governance. Our paper contributes further to the understanding of the role and construction of environmental targets by offering a detailed historical reconstruction of the emergence of the 2 °C target from a governance perspective. Our work draws on extensive document analysis of reports, scientific literature, official documents, as well as on a series of in-depth interviews[1] with individuals who were involved with the formulation of the 2 °C target at various decision-making levels and in different roles.[2]

The paper is organised as follows. Section 2 introduces the concept of (environmental) targets, while Sect. 3 examines the evolution of the 2 °C target over different periods. Subsequently, we discuss the implications of the 2015 Paris Agreement (Sect. 4) and suggest ways to further operationalise the target and make it a fully fledged global environmental governance target (Sect. 5). The final section summarises the key findings.

2 TARGETS, THEIR MECHANICS AND BOUNDARY OBJECTS

Before we engage in a reconstruction of the 2 °C target in climate policy, we first discuss in more detail the general concept of targets. Targets can be defined as a meaningful reference value that expresses a desired operational policy outcome in a synthetic (often numerical) manner. Targets differ from goals and indicators. Goals are non operational overarching objectives that usually require targets in order to achieve them. Indicators are parameters signalling a state or a condition and they are generally used to measure targets. Measurability is indeed a powerful and attractive attribute of targets: it increases the sense of governability, allows monitoring of advancements or deviations and favours the application of economic tools and techniques (Asdal 2008; Miller 2005).

Setting targets entails several steps: identification, discussion, negotiation, agreement, implementation, evaluation and—if required—modification or revision. This process can involve numerous stakeholders at multiple levels of governance, from local to international (Mitchell 2003; Jänicke and Jörgens 2006; Hák et al. 2007; Lester and Neuhoff 2009). Targets rely mainly on scientific knowledge, but science and policy interact in their construction and stipulation, illustrating the dynamic interactions among knowledge-producers, knowledge-users and intermediaries in decision-making (Sarewitz and Pielke 2007; Pierson 2000).

In the definition of targets, different interpretations can arise regarding the metrics to choose, the data classification and standardisation procedures or the quantitative/qualitative value of a target (Bowker and Star 1996, 1999; Turnhout et al. 2007; Davis et al. 2012). Discussions also occur on the suitability and feasibility of a target, as well as on the ways to produce substantive policy responses to reach the desired outcomes. The reference value that emerges is a synthesis of scientific contents, strategic views and problem-solving attitudes and it is proportional to the level of ambition. Moreover, selected targets tend to be simple, because simplification may facilitate managing complex systems (Turnhout et al. 2007). Moreover, simpler targets are easier to use, understand and communicate.

A target is therefore a hybrid. It is neither purely scientific nor political; rather, it is a nested concept that helps to make things work together (Bowker and Star 1996). This includes conflicting interests, worldviews, expectations, commitments, societal needs, scientific understandings, political intentions or organisational programmes. Accordingly, a target is a unifying element, which works as boundary object, i.e. a set of arrangements that allow different actors to cooperate on a basic common understanding while keeping the diversity of their views (Star 2010; Star and Griesemer 1989). Still, a target is usually presented as cohesive, objective and scientifically proven (Porter 1995; Asdal 2008). These aspects strengthen its normative façade: a target affirms what is legitimate to reach, indicates the direction to be taken and provides the common language to translate priorities and programmes into a policy outcome.

The concept of a boundary object is then useful to navigate the construction and evolution of a target. It offers an analytical angle to look at all the elements coalescing into a target: concerns and hopes, problems and solutions, scientific knowledge and political views, promises and results.

3 CLIMATE CHANGE AND THE 2 °C TARGET

The origins of the 2 °C target in climate governance go back almost half a century. This target was first mentioned, to our knowledge, in a paper by Manabe and Wetherald (1967), who estimated a temperature response to doubling carbon dioxide concentrations by approximately 2 °C (Randalls 2010). Since then, the 2 °C figure has been discussed in various studies, including in relation to climate governance (Bodansky 2010, 2011; Dimitrov 2010), the science–policy nexus and the diffusion mechanism in climate diplomacy (Gippner 2014), its implications and policy options (Geden 2010; van Vliet et al. 2012; Höhne and den Elzen 2013) and conceptual or critical aspects of the target (Tol 2007; Shaw 2010; Boykoff 2011; Lenton 2011b; Jordan et al. 2013). Other authors followed the chronology of events for investigating the multifaceted characteristics of the 2 °C target: to consider different interpretations of the target (Jaeger and Jaeger 2010; Knopf et al. 2012), to explore its strengths and weaknesses (Randalls 2010) and to examine its role as an intertwined element of science and policy (Oppenheimer and Petsonk 2005; Cointe et al. 2011). In the following sections, we discuss the development of the 2 °C climate target over four distinct phases: framing, consolidation and diffusion, adoption and disembeddedness.

3.1 **Framing (1988–1996)**

The 2 °C climate target had rarely appeared in scientific literature before the late 1980 s and was used as a heuristic rather than as normative policy-guidance (Randalls 2010). For this reason, we consider the *political history* of the 2 °C target as starting in 1988 with the World Meteorological Organization report *Developing Policies for Responding to Climatic Change* (WMO 1988). The report summarised the findings of two meetings in 1987 (in Villach, Austria, and Bellagio, Italy) of the Advisory Group on Greenhouse Gases, a small advisory body of highly reputed international experts that was created by the World Meteorological Organization, the International Council for Science and the United Nations Environment Programme. This report was intended to offer recommendations for the development of a climate convention by examining the underlying science and its implications for policy (Torrance 2006). In Bellagio, the 2 °C target emerged together with a target of a 0.1 °C temperature increase per decade as the maximum acceptable limit. According to anecdotal evidence, these concrete targets were first debated at a dinner conversation and then formally discussed the day after (Tol 2007; Randalls 2010).

Following these initial discussions, the scientific rationale for the target was strengthened. In July 1988, the Advisory Group on Greenhouse Gases established three working groups, all coordinated by the Stockholm Environment Institute. The report of the working group on "Targets and Indicators of Climate Change"—chaired by scientists Pier Vellinga and Peter Gleick—considered a 0.1 °C increase per decade and a 1° or 2 °C increase as temperature targets, reflecting lower or higher risks of severe damage to ecosystems and nonlinear responses (Rijsberman and Swart 1990). Later on, the 0.1 °C target faded away. One reason for this is that decadal scales have greater natural variability, which makes such a target less useful in practice (Tol 2007).

Around this time, the debate on quantitative maximum targets for global warming entered the political arena. Oppenheimer and Petsonk (2005), for example, underline the interest of the Netherlands in informing policymakers about the impact of climate change. The Netherlands was well placed for being influential in this framing phase of the target. It had wide-ranging climate change research together with dedicated political institutions (van Eijndhoven et al. 2001; Rotmans 1990; Pettenger 2007).

In 1989, the Dutch government assigned Pier Vellinga to organise the Noordwijk Ministerial Conference, which was eventually attended by 67 ministers of both developed and developing countries. This important political venue proved to be relevant for setting fundamental principles such as the notion of climate change as a common concern of humankind (Biermann 1997) and—following a Dutch proposal—the concept of tolerable limits of climate change. However, the conference was unable to reach an agreement on temperature limits. A step in this direction was possible only 1 year later with the 1990 Second World Climate Conference, when the Dutch and Austrian delegations were decisive in supporting the idea of a long-term objective (Oppenheimer and Petsonk 2005).

A further step was the publication in the journal *Climatic Change* of the editorial entitled "The Greenhouse Marathon: A Proposal for a Global Strategy" by Vellinga and Swart in 1991. Here the 2 °C figure first appeared in a climate change context as a clear-cut threshold (Cointe et al. 2011) and as a "means of normatively framing a target-based approach to global climate policy" (Mahony and Hulme 2012: 78). The article gained political significance as it proposed an advanced visual explanation based on a traffic light representation that supported the necessity of the 2 °C increase as a temperature limit. The proposal stated, "In absolute terms we are in the red zone when the increase in global mean temperature is 2° or more above preindustrial levels" (Vellinga and Swart 1991: VII). The 2 °C target was then authoritatively framed, but it needed to be further discussed in the political arena.

In 1992, article 2 of the climate convention stipulated as the "ultimate objective" the "stabilisation of greenhouse gas concentrations in the atmosphere at a level that would prevent dangerous anthropogenic interference with the climate system" (UNFCCC 1992). The treaty did not, however, provide a numeric value. It is important to record that this text combined elements of the statements of both the Noordwijk and the Second World Climate Conference (Oppenheimer and Petsonk 2005). Moreover, the long-term target approach was adopted from the similar approaches in European governance of long-range transboundary air pollution and water quality (Swart and Vellinga 1994).

Shortly before the first conference of the parties in Berlin in 1995, the German Advisory Council on Global Change proposed an innovative approach to climate change mitigation based on temperature ranges and emission quotas. The so-called tolerable windows approach recommended limiting a global mean temperature rise to less than 2 °C (WBGU 1995). Jaeger and Jaeger (2010) underline the importance of this German institute, especially of its chairman Hans Joachim Schellnhuber, in convincing Angela Merkel—then Germany's Minister of the Environment—about the relevance of the 2 °C target.

During Merkel's term as environment minister (1994–1998), the Council of the European Union (EU) stated that "given the serious risk of such an increase [in temperature] ... the Council believes that global average temperatures should not exceed 2 degrees above pre-industrial level" (Council of the European Union 1996: item no 6 of Community Strategy on Climate Change). The limit was derived from the evidence available at the time, mostly from impact studies that were considered in the 1995 Intergovernmental Panel on Climate Change's Second Assessment Report (Metz 2010). This political act can be considered the last and most relevant step of the framing phase of the 2 °C target.

Regarding this early stage of the 2 °C target's political development, some important points should be emphasised. First, some scholars see the emergence of the target as being biased by value judgements of scientists who defined what limits they considered dangerous (Metz 2010). The 2 °C value falls into the consensus estimate of 1.5–4.5 °C with regard to climate sensitivity (van der Sluijs et al. 1998). Among the scientific community, this concept proved to be complex because of the estimated variables and the related uncertainties (Shaw 2010). Those include the equilibrium global mean surface temperature change following a doubling of the atmospheric carbon dioxide concentration relative to the pre-industrial period (van der Sluijs et al. 1998). A target like the 2 °C increase was a suitable simplification for non-specialists as a much handier and more easily understandable concept. However, this scientific simplification was never proposed in absolute terms for policy. The related uncertainty was constantly highlighted. Equally, the role of policymakers in deciding what is dangerous for society was always recognised. For instance, the 1988 Targets and Indicators working group stated that the choice of target "will be a product of the political process of negotiations" (Rijsberman and Swart 1990: X). Still, in climate science "some form of value judgement is inevitable" (Gupta and Van Asselt, 2006: 84), as experts' activity is "a hybrid activity that combines elements of scientific evidence and reasoning with large doses of social and political judgement" (Jasanoff 1990: 229).

Second, it is important to note that, at the beginning, only a few activist and pioneering countries, notably the Netherlands and Germany, promoted the target in both the scientific and political domains. Their action helped to spread the idea of the target while giving it stronger political roots (Jordan and Huitema 2014). The Netherlands made scientists and experts available for the definition of a target, together with crucial support by environment ministers (Interviewee 6; Interviewee 7). In any case, climate change was a theme of special political relevance for the Dutch population familiar with environmental risk (Pettenger 2007). Germany embraced the scientific and political process towards the 2 °C increase slightly later (Interviewee 6; Interviewee 8), then it flexed its political muscles in the process by including the participation of their top politicians and scientists. In Germany, social awareness of climate change was strong. It was home to a robust environmental movement, political parties which included environmental matters in their programmes, and influential environmental non-governmental organisations (Cavender-Bares et al. 2001). Moreover, the organisation of the first conference of parties to the climate convention, which took place in Berlin, underpinned the leadership role of Germany (Yamin 2000).

Third, these pioneering countries also marked the prominence of Europe in giving stability and political substance to the target. This prominence can also be understood in comparison with the USA. While the US government was formally in favour of stabilising greenhouse gas concentrations (Oppenheimer and Petsonk 2005), it opposed accepting any clear target at that time (Randalls 2010). Instead, Randalls (2010) explains that the USA favoured the rise of IPCC as a means to prevent the Advisory Group on Greenhouse Gases, which was perceived as being too politically oriented, from advancing an agenda ahead of scientific and governmental review of climate change science. Consequently, a first instability at the political level emerged, with two powerful actors in the climate process having different positions, with Europe strongly believing in the target approach and the US remaining reluctant to engage with it.

In the political domain, there was another notable instability, i.e. the lack of debate among decision-makers about the implications of the target and about the most effective means of implementation. From interviews and document analysis, it can be inferred that the 2 °C target materialised in Europe as an easy and useful guidance for policy and a way for policymakers to construct climate change as a problem for the future (Shaw 2010). This explains why EU policymakers accepted the target in such a smooth manner. The absence of intense debate about the meaning and implications characterised the target as a particularly consensual boundary object, in which policymakers showed (at least tacit) trust in the underlying scientific content. European decision-makers at that time did not request further scientific scrutiny and did not challenge the idea of a limit (Interviewee 2; Interviewee 3; Interviewee 8). The ease in reaching a political decision was related to both the quality of the documentation presented and the clarity of the proposal. This is an example where trust is a key component in the science–policy relationship (Whyte and Crease 2010; Hunt and Shackley 1999). In environmental risk communication, trust and credibility are determined by factors like the perceived competence and objectivity of the source (Peters et al. 1997; Renn and Levine 1991). Trust might be also attributed to opportunism of policymakers in placing responsibility for action onto the scientists (Grundmann 2006) or on misinterpretation by policymakers of the meaning and implications of the 2 °C target. In this regard, trust can be considered as intertwined with a pragmatic calculation by policymakers in balancing what looked reasonable and politically/economically feasible, but also responding to societal concerns and requests of environmental movements (Randalls 2010, 2011). The target offered a unifying element for policy engagement to lock-in multiple actors into a long-term commitment (Boykoff et al. 2010). Yet, the target was simple, appealing and based on allegedly best available science. These elements eased its consensual acceptance. Decision-makers therefore accepted the level of risk presented by scientists, translating it into the level of risk that a society would take, but without a thorough inquiry into its societal implications.

In sum, this first framing phase showed a 2 °C target that was science-driven (quantified as a possible target for climate change), EU-led (mainly prompted by north-western European countries and their policy-making experiences, with only marginal resistance from the USA and limited involvement of developing countries), trust-based (easily accepted without further investigation by policymakers), but lacking debate and contestation (with a substantial absence of a thorough debate by decision-makers about political and practical implications of the target). Nonetheless, different actors—including scientists, advisory bodies, policymakers, as well as national and international civil servants—were involved in the process. Many events took place to mark the institutionalisation of the 2 °C target science–policy nexus, with policymakers recognising and accepting the scientific content of the target and making it a guiding objective for policy (Underdal 2000).

3.2 Consolidation and diffusion (1997–2009)

The 1997–2009 period led to the further consolidation and diffusion of the 2 °C target. In 1997, the Kyoto Protocol was adopted, including, for the first time, quantitative emission-reduction targets for industrialised countries. Besides the effort of the EU to establish a long-term temperature target (Metz 2010), Kyoto did not prompt any evolution in terms of further political decisions. After Kyoto, the 2 °C target nearly disappeared from mainstream political debate. Ultimately, the Kyoto Protocol, a cornerstone of the climate change regime, required great adjustment efforts to make it possible for it to enter into force in 2005 (Oberthür and Ott 2010).

In 2005, however, the 2 °C target strongly came back into political discourse through a dense sequence of events. In January 2005, a report by the International Climate Change Taskforce—an alliance of the Institute for Public Policy Research in the UK, the Center for American Progress in the USA and the Australia Institute—recommended "a long-term objective of preventing average global surface temperature from rising by more than 2 °C" (ICCT 2005: 3). In February 2005, the Exeter Conference—a preparation event for the G8 summit in the UK—explored temperature thresholds that could trigger irreversible catastrophic events. These scientific findings were collected in a book (Schellnhuber et al. 2006), in which the 2 °C target was analysed, alongside other limits, and evaluated in terms of emissions pathways.

Within a few days after the Exeter Conference, a European Commission communication stated that "scientific evidence indicates that even meeting the 2 °C target will require significant preventive and remedial adaptation efforts around the globe" (Commission of the European Communities 2005: 7). In March, the Presidency Conclusions of the Council of the European Union stated: "The European Council [...] confirmed that, with a view to achieving the ultimate objective of the UNFCCC, the global annual mean surface temperature increase should not exceed 2 °C above pre-industrial levels" (Council of the European Union 2005: 15). In mid-2005, the governments of the Group of Eight (G8) convened in Gleneagles (UK), with climate change being a key topic on the agenda. Governments held the first G8 Climate Change Roundtable, which was constituted in January at the World Economic Forum in Davos. In 2008, the 2 °C target appeared in the Breaking the Climate Deadlock Initiative, led by former British Prime Minister Tony Blair and presented at the G8 summit held in Japan in 2008 (Climate Group 2008).

Before the conference of the parties to the climate convention in 2009, further relevant events occurred. First, there was the publication of a report by the German Advisory Council (WBGU 2009) which provided a better scientific foundation for the target. This study proposed a new budget approach—based on the calculated budget of carbon dioxide emissions still available worldwide—for countries' commitments to global/national decarbonisation trajectories necessary to hold the 2 °C line (Schellnhuber 2010).

Second, the declarations in 2009 by the G8 and by the Major Economies Forum on Energy and Climate (a dialogue forum of 17 large economies that brought together the Group of Eight with Australia, Brazil, China, India, Indonesia, Korea, Mexico, Russia and South Africa) recognised the scientific view that global temperatures should not to exceed a 2 °C increase (G8 2009; MEF 2009). These declarations show how the target found increasing international support beyond Europe, especially among major developing countries.

This sequence of events in the 2005–2009 period underlines the increasing global acceptance of the target and allows for some reflections on its political development. First, Europe remained the main force behind the political consolidation of the target, creating a strong linkage among international actors, while giving impulse to the target's acceptance. European countries organised the major international rallies of this phase and EU political action remained visible in terms of declarations and outputs. The 2 °C target was an already established strategic objective in the EU, which tried to promote the diffusion of the target internationally (Jordan and Huitema 2014; Finnemore and Sikkink 1998).

Second, the target proved to be stable in the international scene. It kept together a variety of actors, while maintaining its significance and force as a proposal. In these terms, the target served as an anchoring device (van der Sluijs et al. 1998), a highly stable boundary object between science and policy, acting as the scientific basis for the political debate. The political events that marked this phase created a path-dependency (Pierson 2000) that consolidated the temperature limit internationally. Here path-dependency was triggered by a cascade of events and outcomes that progressively endorsed the globalisation of the 2 °C target with consequent worldwide reverberation (see Boykoff 2011; Shaw 2013; Cointe et al. 2011). The 2 °C target was able to catalyse interest and broader consent of decision-makers by being easy, broadly appealing and memorisable. The target continued to be appealing as in the framing phase. Through policy, the 2 °C target was acknowledged as being clear and easily conveyable to the public, but also as "the vaguest and the least directly binding" target (Cointe et al. 2011: 1).

Importantly, the consolidation and diffusion phase occurred under the impulse of political leaders. At the same time, it received increasing consideration by non-governmental organisations and growing attention by public opinion (Shaw 2010; Death 2011). Political leaders saw the necessity in having a target vague enough to avoid the perils of policy implications. Nonetheless, the support of political leaders gave further notoriety and legitimacy to the target.

Consolidation and diffusion ensued through what we term as eventification. This is the organisation of prestigious meetings that provided a spotlight on the target. Through statements and announcements, these events created deepened path-dependency for the future of the target. Yet, the lack of a thorough debate among policymakers on the political and practical implications of 2 °C target still persisted in this phase, although the 2005–2009 period was characterised by an intense consensus-seeking and consensus-making activity and the alignment of a few top decision-makers.

The 2 °C target was then accepted and approved in different contexts, including the most relevant economic forums. However, approval and consensus remained at the surface and the 2 °C continued to be regarded as a prescription by science which society had to follow, but without considering how. Even if one accepts this explanation, it is difficult to understand the limited reaction of policymakers and the lack of discussion about concrete proposals. It can be argued that in that period, because of events like the non-ratification of the Kyoto Protocol by the United States Senate, the main actors supporting the 2 °C target focused more on building the largest consensus around the target, than on avoiding discord.

In sum, the 1997–2009 period marked the consolidation and diffusion of the 2 °C target, with Europe remaining at the forefront but now accompanied by the endorsement of other relevant states. Some inconsistencies persisted in this phase and policymakers still avoided engaging in a debate on the implications of the targets with regard to possible actions for its implementation. Nonetheless, the idea that the target was ready for approval at the highest international political level had finally been established.

3.3 Adoption (2009–2010)

This phase encompasses the 15th and 16th conferences of the parties to the climate convention in Copenhagen (2009) and Cancun (2010), in which the 2 °C target was recognised by a majority of countries (Decision 2/CP.15, UNFCCC 2009) and later formally agreed upon (Decision 1/CP.16, UNFCCC 2010). At the Copenhagen Conference, the target discussion had a favourable start. In the opening ceremony, a high number of influential countries[3] explicitly declared their support for an agreement that would include it. The target was formalised on the final day with the support of 141 countries. Moreover, the accord also suggested the consideration of a more ambitious target of 1.5 °C for the future.

This snapshot might signify a diplomatic success, but for the target itself it was instead a "tragic triumph" (Schellnhuber 2010: 229), as problems and instabilities had emerged before and during the conference. In the conference preparation, the two Ad Hoc Working Groups under the climate convention met five times, but no progress was made in terms of agreements (Bodansky 2011; Dimitrov 2010). Negotiations in Copenhagen were thus slow and the impossibility of making the 2 °C target obligatory was confirmed. At the same time, no global emissions reduction was specified, nor was a timeline defined, depriving the target of both a specific context and instruments for its concrete fulfilment. Some scholars, including Christoff (2010), Hulme (2010) and Bodansky (2011), attribute the lack of such a solution to the difficulties in offsetting differences among contracting parties. In particular, the USA and China remained uncooperative with the EU, while other countries remained substantially stuck in their positions (Barresi 2011; Hare et al. 2010).

The EU made a great effort to make the Copenhagen Conference a turning point in climate governance, while extending its own vision of 2 °C target as an accepted global climate system boundary. As previously discussed, the EU remained the main force behind the 2 °C target, using scientific and diplomatic efforts to extend its acceptance (Gippner 2014). In this way, it "succeeded in getting all relevant partners in the negotiations—including even China and the USA—to commit to the two-degree target" (Geden 2010: 2). Nonetheless, though Europe entered the negotiations with a firm idea of the target (Haug and Berkhout 2010), it was unable to shape the course of events with the USA refusing legally binding accords (Hare et al. 2010) which could challenge its wealth and economic structure. At the same time, China, Brazil, South Africa and many other developing countries remained focused on economic growth (Christoff 2010). Small Island Developing States, however, called for a target of no more than a 1.5 °C increase in global temperature, supported by other countries that are particularly vulnerable to climate change. Competing interests, however, blocked a shared understanding on specific political solutions and coordinated measures to comply with the target.

After the framing and consolidation and diffusion phases, the debate on the target opened up at the UN. Having not been discussed in depth by international policymakers, the endorsements of the target—particularly in the consolidation and diffusion phase up to the opening statements of the Copenhagen Conference—collided with diverging interests and worldviews. In short, the target was thriving with no debate, but was weakened once brought to a global arena.

This result can be attributed to the concentration of high-level decision-makers—almost 120 state leaders—attending the final segment of the Copenhagen Conference (Dimitrov 2010) and by high public expectations and extensive media coverage (Boykoff 2011).[4] Yet without a genuine overall consensus, a political accord of merely twelve paragraphs was reached, but only noted rather than adopted (Christoff 2010; Eckersley 2012). The direct involvement of heads of state and government, however, was particularly relevant for the 2 °C target, as the function and nature of the target radically changed. The Copenhagen accord transformed the target into a last resort commitment since the digit was the only quantitative element which proved consensual, as long as no measures or prescriptions were attached to it.

While compromises and mediations are common in international relations as well as in target setting (Turnhout et al. 2007), there was something more in this case. With the impending need for success and the public expectations for a tipping point after Kyoto, the best possible result was a target coated in vagueness, purposely formulated with constructed ambiguity and in sufficiently generic terms that it could be widely agreed upon by everybody. This gave form—rather than substance—to the 2 °C target, but gave no indications for how it would be operationalised and implemented, as also confirmed by the conference of parties in Cancun that formally accepted the content of the Copenhagen Accord (Sepibus and Holzer 2014).

In sum, this phase, in which the target was approved at the highest political level, is marked by the reduced influence of Europe, the emergence of new political powers and the opening up of the debate over the consequences of the target. The presence of political leaders in Copenhagen was decisive for the outcome of negotiations. This favoured a target which was symbolic but nonetheless proved to be resilient. It survived to become an interpretation of article 2 of the 1992 climate convention, i.e. the objective of "stabilization of greenhouse gas concentrations in the atmosphere at a level that would prevent dangerous anthropogenic interference with the climate system" (UNFCCC 1992). The target thus succeeded in making an important step towards this common goal, yet political circumstances were not favourable for defining concrete actions.

3.4 Disembeddedness (2011–2015)

The conferences of Copenhagen and Cancun inscribed the 2 °C target on the international agenda. The conferences of the parties that followed—in Durban (2011), Doha (2012), Warsaw (2013) and Lima (2014)—revived international negotiations. However, in terms of the 2 °C target specifically, they did not lead to more ambitious policy responses (Blok et al. 2012), nor did they provide any substantial addition to the 2 °C target in terms of fulfilment (Bodansky and Diringer 2014; Pandey 2014). While these conferences marked some important innovation and advancement towards the global climate agreement expected to be reached by 2015 in Paris, the negotiating parties were still unable to define a common climate agenda, despite the agreement they reached with the Bali Action Plan[5] in 2007. As such, the 2 °C target evolved into a stable and solid element but without a mobilising role at a more general level. This new phase was marked by a lack of specifications to make the 2 °C target more effective and by the inability to compel near-term political action (Lenton 2011a). Moreover, the target continued to fulfil a symbolic and declarative function, but did not offer political guidance for problem-solving (Geden 2013).

Reflecting on these processes, we characterise this phase as disembedded. Borrowing from the neologism "disembedded" coined by Polany (1944) as opposite to the adjective embedded,[6] we argue that, after Copenhagen, the 2 °C had become a disembedded object. Officially, it is a global target. However, there is no established method for its successful implementation, and it is politically inert and unable to effectively limit the temperature increase.

The fact that the 2 °C is a disembedded object is indirectly confirmed by some academic and political positions that invoke the revision, reinterpretation, replacement or removal of the target from the international climate regime (Geden and Beck 2014; Jordan et al. 2013; Knopf et al. 2012; New et al. 2011). These positions evidence how the target, in its current state, needs stronger interlinkages, renewed commitments and a more robust entrenchment in international environmental governance in order to be purposefully achieved.

In our view, the disembedded characterisation can be explained from three points of view: science and policy, domestic governance and international governance. In terms of science and policy, temperature is an ideal concept to connect scientists, policymakers and the general public. The 2 °C target is a global value for all, but temperature is a local variable that fluctuates significantly (Thornton et al. 2014). A temperature increase implies different risks and impacts at the local level that need to be aggregated and considered globally (Knutti et al. 2016). Moreover, a global mean temperature change is just one metric to reach a climate stabilisation goal. Emissions, cumulative concentration and radiative forces are metrics more related to human activities (Knopf et al. 2012) and need to be strongly combined to the 2 °C target to increase effectiveness and consistency of policy deliberations. Finally, temperature is both a cause and a consequence of environmental change and, because of the functional interdependence of natural sub-systems, it is connected to many transformative processes in the earth system (Biermann 2014). In the current configuration, the 2 °C target has no link to other critical thresholds in the earth system, such as country-level or local sub-targets (Philibert and Pershing 2001) or planetary limits (Rockström et al. 2009).

In terms of national policies, the absence of a coordinated agenda for implementing the 2 °C target and the lack of connected mitigation programmes inevitably disaggregates countries' actions making the global effort to stay within the 2 °C limit inconsistent (Raupach et al. 2014). Countries have now independently determined their climate mitigation goals—and possibly their adaptation plans—and presented their pledges that are now called, after the Warsaw Conference, Intended Nationally Determined Contributions (Decision 1/CP.19, UNFCCC 2013). Apart from the fact that the current aggregated contributions are most likely not sufficient to stay within the 2 °C temperature increase (Roelfsema et al. 2014; CAT 2015), the accounting mechanisms and the procedures for measurement, reporting and verification remain central in the negotiations. Nonetheless, they need substantial upgrading in accountability and transparency to promote trust among parties and to support a virtuous cycle of improvement (Dagnet et al. 2014).

The common goal defined by the target remains expressed in global terms but is difficult to operationalise globally and fine-tune locally because of different national capacities and priorities. In addition, in the current framing of the 2 °C target, the involvement of civil society is still limited, while transition and transformational change are hardly taken into account (Wise et al. 2012; Park et al. 2012). In fact, even if commendable initiatives have been launched (Blok et al. 2012) and voluntary arrangements with great potential like the International Cooperative Initiatives have been acknowledged by the Durban Platform for Enhanced Action (Widerberg and Pattberg 2014), these projects are still not representative of a true engagement of society as a whole to reach the target globally. Furthermore, the range of stakeholders involved in policy spaces remains marginal (Sepibus and Holzer 2014).

In terms of international governance, the 2 °C target poses problems of coordination among institutions. The role of international organisations is unclear, nor which would or could be in a position of leadership to stimulate nations to comply with the 2 °C limit. In an extremely fragmented global environmental governance setting (Biermann et al. 2009) with organisations having different mandates, approaches and structures, the 2 °C target proves difficult to be governed in a global architecture that does not clarify roles and functions for achieving it. In this context, detailed sub-targets related to the 2 °C and mandatory commitments prove to be politically infeasible. Instead, national voluntary contributions to stay within the target rely more on countries' individual reputation; they might weaken international institutions in their central role to guide and pursue collectively global goals.

Concurrently, the identification of national contributions and the absence of an operational accounting system open the door to ambiguity and uncertainty. These can be attractive for countries that are unsure about adopting hard targets.

In sum, the 2 °C target evolved into a powerful and evocative reference for climate policy, but it remains incapable of promoting effective coordination among relevant actors. A global mean temperature seems to be a too vague attribution to make the target a focal point for policy intervention across multiple levels. As a consequence, the 2 °C target became a disembedded object, too weak and isolated to give strength and direction to coordinated actions in climate governance.

4 THE PARIS AGREEMENT

A major development—the impact of which is still difficult to evaluate—is the Paris Agreement reached in December 2015 by the conference of the parties to the climate convention. This Agreement stipulates to keep global temperature levels "well below 2 °C", along with the further intention of "pursuing efforts to limit the temperature increase to 1.5 °C" (UNFCCC 2015: 2). The additional line referring to the 1.5 °C does not fundamentally change the overall target from 2 °C, however. The notion of "well below 2 °C" does not indicate a precise level but reflects a further aspiration that emphasises the urgency of even stronger efforts in the coming years. As indicated in the Paris Agreement, in 2018 the Intergovernmental Panel on Climate Change will produce a special report on the 1.5 °C, but the current gap between aggregated countries pledges and the objective to stay within the 2 °C limit is significant, as also recognised in Paris. The 2 °C target thus continues to be the reference value in climate governance for the time being.

However, the Intended Nationally Determined Contributions will continue guiding country efforts on a self-determined basis. No coordinating mechanism or burden-sharing agreement is envisaged. There is also no binding requirement to implement existing pledges, nor to review or upgrade them, respectively, before 2020 and 2025. Starting in 2023, countries will re-evaluate their commitments every 5 years, with the option to strengthen their ambition level.

Furthermore, the 2015 Agreement notes the link between the temperature target and the global peaking of greenhouse gas emissions. This has to be reached "as soon as possible", with the aim of achieving "a balance between anthropogenic emissions by sources and removals by sinks of greenhouse gases in the second half of this century"

(UNFCCC 2015: 21). This represents a step forward, even though the text does not specify a precise date for peaking and does not employ terms like climate or emissions neutrality for which some environmentalists had pushed. Overall, the Paris Agreement spells out robust global ambitions and proposes a mobilising vision for the future. Nonetheless, strict deadlines and commitments are absent from the agreement.

In terms of the 2 °C target, besides the major advancements in negotiations, the target remains a disembedded object in global environmental governance, as the main reasons for this condition endure. These are the lack of interlinkages with other relevant targets in the environmental and human domains; the lack of fine-tuning of the 2 °C target at different scales of governance and with the enlargement of the stakeholders involved; and the lack of adjustments in the institutional architecture combined with a robust monitoring and reporting system on the achievements. Even so, after Paris, many changes seem to be possible and achievable. Countries, together with the newly established Ad Hoc Working Group on the Paris Agreement and the Paris Committee on capacity-building, as well as with the two permanent subsidiary bodies[7] established by the climate convention, have great potential to write a new phase of the 2 °C target.

5 THE WAY FORWARD

In the vein of the renewed interest on the 2 °C target and of the clear signal sent by the Paris Agreement to the international community, we discuss the way forward with regard to overcoming the weaknesses of the target that we summarised with the term disembeddedness. In order to address this challenge, we consider the approach proposed by Young et al. (2014) for the sustainable development goals. We believe this approach is equally suitable for the 2 °C target and useful for creating a consistent and effective framework to implement the target within an earth system governance perspective.

Young et al. (2014) envisage a multi-layered approach to achieve the sustainable development goals encompassing four tiers: (1) global goals that safeguard the human needs and earth life support systems; (2) individual goals and targets framed in such a way that they can serve as focal points for a wide range of stakeholders; (3) targets framed in global terms but—where possible and relevant—tailored at regional, national, local or corporate/organisational levels; (4) to define indicators and promote monitoring capabilities with the capacity to track change and report on progress.

This scheme, if applied to the 2 °C target, would have several implications. First, it would frame the temperature target within a wide system of other global goals for the sustainability of socio-ecological systems, such as the SDGs. This would better relate the target to anthropogenic drivers, earth transformation indicators, as well as environmental and human development targets, which all affect and are affected by temperature increases. In fact, "in the interlinked social and ecological systems of planet earth, nothing remains independent, and complexities and interconnections abound" (Biermann 2012: 7). Policymakers need access to a wider range of planetary indications to understand the full range of consequences of climate change (Briggs et al. 2015). Therefore, a systemic and comprehensive framework of interlinked targets and indicators, such as the SDGs, if shared and applied universally, would make the 2 °C target more meaningful and coherent with the operational context in which it should be accomplished. The approach by Young and colleagues could for instance favour iterative sets of science–policy dialogues within and between countries, as also proposed by Gupta and van Asselt (2006). This work suggests focusing on indicators of dangerous climate impacts, short-listing and grouping these indicators in a way to identify threshold levels of unacceptable impacts. As a consequence, the 2 °C target could be linked to these indicators and help define suitable countermeasures.

Second, the multi-layered approach would allow considering horizontal and vertical interactions while bridging levels of governance from global to local (Biermann and Pattberg 2012; Gupta et al. 2007). The explicit entrenchment of global commitments with national or sub-national priorities and actions would also foster knowledge production and transfer, while easing the identification of new policy options. This can define a strategy that integrates best available science, policy needs and "policy goals that reflect what policymakers actually control—and thus what they can manage" (Briggs et al. 2015: 969). In this way, coordination and convergence of measures might increase. The more coherent governance system that might derive from better coordination should facilitate achieving the 2 °C more efficiently on the basis of the capabilities of each country. At the same time, this approach would foster participation and support as the target becomes a focal point for multiple and interacting actors, network and institutions. Governments, international organisations, civil society, the private sector and individuals would be collectively involved in actions for staying within the 2 °C boundary.

Third, the approach can be employed to consistently adjust and enforce the global governance architecture in a way that defines comprehensive international programmes, institutional arrangements and practical commitments to comply with the 2 °C target. This requires the clarification of roles and mandates of international institutions. In these terms, the scheme would bridge the gap among sectoral silos by formulating the temperature target within crosscutting programmes and promoting a better articulation and integration in global governance. To complement and enforce these achievements, it is necessary to devise effective and universally applied procedures to track progress and provide indications for corrections or prescriptions to act in accordance with the 2 °C target.

The approach by Young and colleagues (2014) is inherently political as it requires the approval by policymakers. However, in such a scheme, the contentious issue of uncertainty does not disappear. Uncertainties are integral to human knowledge (Gramelsberger and Feichter 2011) and inextricable to complex systems. Staying within the 2 °C target asks for an unprecedented common vision combined with a proactive attitude to overcome contingency and vested interests. If so, a scheme like the one described can help frame the 2 °C target in how it becomes an earth system governance target. This would be a critical node to address multiple issues and an operational element to steer institutions at local and global levels towards mitigating and adapting to earth system transformations. A target so conceived can become a linchpin in global environmental governance, which coherently connects significant targets, fosters incisive measures and promotes coordination among different actors.

6 CONCLUSIONS

The reconstructed history of the 2 °C target presented in this paper has highlighted key features characterising its political dynamic (summarised in Fig. 1).

In the early phase, the target was science-driven and EU-based, that is, promoted by a group of European countries with soft resistance by the USA. The prominence of Europe persisted in the following phase, gaining, since 2005, the support of a larger number of countries, through a path-dependency of events that consolidated the target in the international arena. The adoption at the highest international level occurred at the Copenhagen Conference of the parties in 2009.

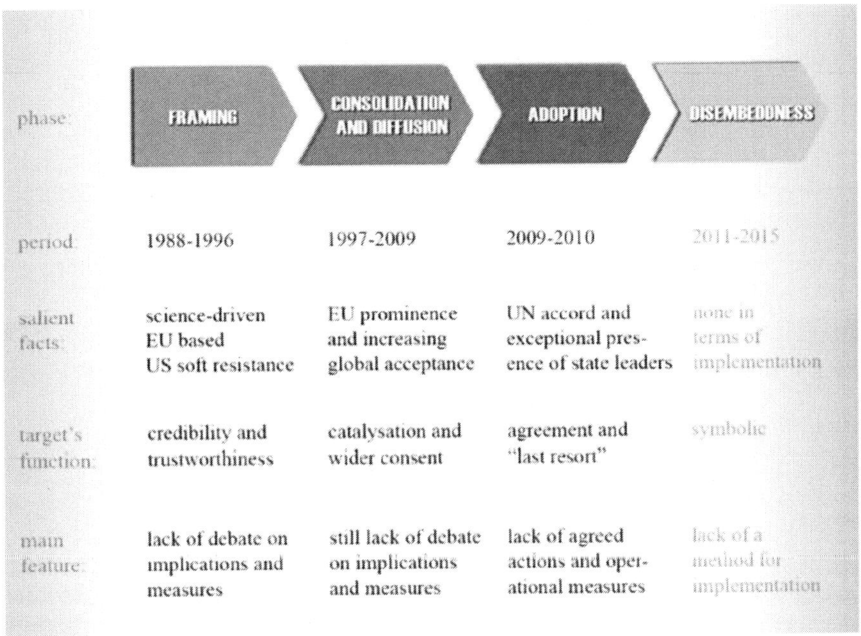

Fig. 1 The 2 °C target's phases

During the various phases the target confirmed the complex dynamics that characterised the target construction and stipulation with the involvement of several actors and institutions (Mitchell 2003; Turnhout et al. 2007; Lester and Neuhoff 2009; Sarewitz and Pielke 2007). The boundary object concept (Star 2010; Star and Griesemer 1989) helped to explore the different functions and contexts in which the target served policy. In the first phase, the target was a credible element in the science–policy interface, then turned to be a catalytic factor around which to build consent, to finally become a last resort element in the Copenhagen accord to ensure an outcome from the conference. Among governments and international decision-makers, a thorough political debate on engaging effectively with the target was absent during the first two phases; when this debate finally emerged in Copenhagen, it became evident that it was impossible to agree on the far-reaching commitments to stay within the limit. The new agreement in Paris 2015 might represent a watershed in climate negotiations, but perhaps now it is too soon to tell.

The reductio ad unum, reducing a complex issue to a single element—specifically, having a single-figure target for climate—was produced by events and circumstances. As every simplification, it brought ease in acceptance and difficulties in fulfilment. The selection of an absolute target with no articulation of its concrete implementation and a lack of shared global and local actions attached to it has transformed the 2 °C target from a boundary object to a disembedded object. Yet, this condition can be changed opting for a more complex, adaptive approach as the one by Young and colleagues (2014). For this, a true engagement by states, international organisations, civil society and the business community is needed to make the 2 °C more tangible and practical, possibly within a conceptual framework that facilitates real and global commitments. If this happens, the 2 °C target can become a fully fledged global environmental governance target and a powerful example of governing by targets.

FOOTNOTES

1. The analysed documents were collected from libraries, data banks and online platforms. Some documents were requested from the responsible organisations, consulted in situ or provided by the authors. For data collection, 10 in-depth interviews were arranged. The interview format was based on a protocol structured around 12 main questions, with multiple sub-questions, all identical for each interviewee: Marcel Berk (Netherlands Ministry of Infrastructure and the Environment), Kornelis Blok (Ecofys; Utrecht University), Michel Den Elzen (PBL—The Netherlands Environmental Assessment Agency), Niklas Höhne (Ecofys), Jip Lenstra (ECN—Netherlands Energy Research Centre), Henk Merkus (Netherlands Ministry of Infrastructure and the Environment), Leo Mayer (PBL—The Netherlands Environmental Assessment Agency), Bert Metz (European Climate Foundation), Robert Swart (Wageningen University and Research Centre) and Pier Vellinga (VU University Amsterdam and Wageningen University and Research Centre). All interviews except one were conducted in August 2012. Eight interviews were conducted in direct meetings, and two over the telephone. The interview format was based on an interview protocol structured around 12 main questions, with multiple sub-questions, all identical for each interviewee. All interviews were recorded with permission of the interviewees and transcribed verbatim. Anonymity of interview content was agreed upon by each respondent to protect confidentiality, and quotations are reproduced with permission of the interviewee.

2. Most interviewers are Dutch or worked for Dutch institutions. The interviews were intended to be instrumental to get insights into specific historical events and on contextual conditions in

which these occurred. The diversity of sources of information—interviews, secondary and primary data—for the current study allows for triangulation to increase the reliability of findings.

3. Notably, Australia for the Umbrella Group (formed by Australia, New Zealand, Iceland, Russian Federation, Japan, Norway, Ukraine, Canada and the USA), Switzerland for the Environmental Integrity Group (formed by Mexico, Republic of Korea and Switzerland), Sweden for the EU (formed by 27 countries).

4. In particular, see the diagrams on pages 25–7, 38, 90 and 110.

5. "A shared vision for long-term cooperative action, including a long-term global goal for emission reductions, to achieve the ultimate objective of the Convention" (Decision 1/CP.13 in FCCC/CP/2007/6/Add.1).

6. The term disembedded, is used here neutrally, because of its lexical meaning. There is no reference to Polany's work, nor to other usages of the term in domains like economics, psychology, pedagogy, sociology. Here a "disembedded object" can be thought of as opposite to a "boundary object" (Star and Griesemer 1989).

7. The two permanent subsidiary bodies are the Subsidiary Body for Scientific and Technological Advice and the Subsidiary Body for Implementation.

ACKNOWLEDGEMENT

We are grateful to the three anonymous reviewers whose contribution highly improved the content of our manuscript. In this regard, we would also like to thank Jon Marco Church, Courtney Vegelin and Salvatore Aricò. Furthermore, we are grateful to Michael Oppenheimer and the many interviewees for their kindness and availability. A special thank you goes to Pier Vellinga for his help and support. Besides our gratitude to all these scholars, all opinions and errors are ours alone. Finally, we wish to thank Eleftheria Vasileiadou and Arthur Petersen for their collaboration in the earlier stages of this research. Eleftheria prematurely died this year. With this paper, we would like to remember her dedication and generosity.

REFERENCES

1. Asdal, K. (2008). Enacting things through numbers: Taking nature into account/ing. *Geoforum, 39*(1), 123–132.
2. Barresi, P. (2011). US-China relations and the fate of the UN Framework Convention on Climate Change: Traditional conservatism as an ideological and cultural constraint on US participation in a successor to the Kyoto protocol on Chinese terms. *Chinese Journal of International Law, 10*, 609–649.
3. Barrett, S. (2003). *Environment and statecraft: The strategy of environmental treaty-making*. Oxford: Oxford University Press.
4. Bergh, G., & Couturier, J. (2013). *A rough guide to emerging consensus and divergence in post-2015 goal areas*. London: Overseas Development Institute.
5. Biermann, F. (1997). "Common Concern of Humankind": The emergence of a new concept of International Environmental Law. *Archiv des Völkerrechts, 34*(4), 426–481.
6. Biermann, F. (2012). Planetary boundaries and earth system governance: Exploring the links. *Ecological Economics, 81*, 4–9.
7. Biermann, F. (2014). *Earth system governance. World politics in the anthropocene*. Cambridge, MA: MIT Press.
8. Biermann, F., & Pattberg, P. (2012). Global environmental governance—conclusion. In F. Biermann & P. Pattberg (Eds.), *Global environmental governance reconsidered* (pp. 265–280). Cambridge, MA: MIT Press.
9. Biermann, F., Pattberg, P., van Asselt, H., & Zelli, F. (2009). The fragmentation of global governance architectures: A framework for analysis. *Global Environmental Politics, 9*(4), 14–40.
10. Blok, K., Höhne, N., van der Leun, K., & Harrison, N. (2012). Bridging the greenhouse-gas emissions gap. *Nature Climate Change, 2*, 471–474.
11. Bodansky, D. (2010). The Copenhagen climate change conference: A post-mortem. *American Journal of International Law, 104*, 230–240.

12. Bodansky, D. (2011). A tale of two architectures: The once and future UN climate change regime. *Arizona State Law Journal, 43*, 697–712.

13. Bodansky, D., & Diringer, E. (2014). *Building flexibility and ambition into a 2015 climate agreement*. Arlington, VA: Center for Climate and Energy Solutions.

14. Bowker, G. C., & Star, S. L. (1996). How things (actor-net) work: Classification, magic and the ubiquity of standards. *Philosophia, 25*(3–4), 195–220.

15. Bowker, G. C., & Star, S. L. (1999). *Sorting things out: Classification and its consequences*. Cambridge, MA: The MIT Press.

16. Boykoff, M. T. (2011). *Who speaks for the climate? Making sense of media reporting on climate change*. Cambridge: Cambridge University Press.

17. Boykoff, M. T., Frame, D., & Randalls, S. (2010). Discursive stability meets climate instability: A critical exploration of the concept of 'climate stabilization' in contemporary climate policy. *Global Environmental Change, 20*(1), 53–64.

18. Briggs, S., Kennel, C. F., & Victor, D. G. (2015). Planetary vital signs. *Nature Climate Change,5*(11), 969–970.

19. Cash, D. W. (2000). *Distributed assessment systems: An emerging paradigm of research, assessment and decision-making for environmental change*. Discussion Paper 2000–2006. Cambridge, MA: Belfer Center for Science and International Affairs (BCSIA).

20. CAT—Climate Action Tracker (2015). 2.7 °C is not enough—we can get lower. Climate Action Tracker Update. 8 Dec 2015. http://climateactiontracker.org/assets/publications/briefing_papers/CAT_Temp_Update_COP21.pdf. Accessed 26 Jan 2015.

21. Cavender-Bares, J., Jager, J., & Ell, R. (2001). Developing a precautionary approach: Global environmental risk management in Germany. In W. C. Clark, J. Jäger, J. van Eijndhoven, & N. Dickson (Eds.), *Learning to manage global environmental risks: A comparative history of social responses to climate change, ozone depletion, and acid rain* (Vol. 1, pp. 61–92). Cambridge, MA: MIT Press.

22. Christoff, P. (2010). Cold climate in Copenhagen: China and the United States at COP15. *Environmental Politics, 19*(4), 637–656.

23. Climate Group. (2008). *Breaking the climate deadlock. A global deal for our low-carbon*

future. http://www.theclimategroup.org/_assets/files/Global-Deal-for-our-Low-Carbon-Futrue-Exec-Summ.pdf. Accessed 29 Oct 2015.

24. Cointe, B., Ravon, P. A., & Guèrin, E. (2011). *2 °C: The history of a policy-science nexus*. Working papers No. 19. Paris: IDDRI.

25. Commission of the European Communities (2005). Communication from the Commission to the Council, the European Parliament, the European Economic and Social Committee and the Committee of the Regions, Winning the Battle Against Global Climate Change. COM(2005) 35 final, 9 Feb 2005, Brussels, Belgium. http://eur-lex.europa.eu/legal-content/EN/TXT/PDF/?uri=CELEX:52005DC0035&from=bg. Accessed 29 Oct 2015.

26. Council of the European Union (1996). 1939th Council Meeting, Luxembourg, 25 June 1996. http://europa.eu/rapid/press-release_PRES-96-188_en.htm?locale=en. Accessed 29 Oct 2015.

27. Council of the European Union. (2005). Presidency conclusions—Brussels, 22 and 23 March 2005—IV. Climate change, 7619/1/05 REV 1 CONCL 1, Brussels, Belgium. http://www.consilium.europa.eu/uedocs/cms_data/docs/pressdata/en/ec/84335.pdf. Accessed 29 Oct 2015.

28. Dagnet, Y., Fei, T. , Elliott, C., & Qiu, Y. (2014). *Improving transparency and accountability in the post-2020 climate regime: A fair way forward*. Working Paper. Washington, DC: Agreement for Climate Transformation 2015 (ACT 2015).

29. Davis, K. E., Kingsbury, B., & Merry, S. E. (2012). Indicators as a technology of global governance. *Law and Society Review, 46*(1), 71–104.

30. Death, C. (2011). Summit theatre: Exemplary governmentality and environmental diplomacy in Johannesburg and Copenhagen. *Environmental Politics, 20*(1), 1–19.

31. Dietrich, W. (1995). *The challenge of selecting goals: Case studies regarding the use of critical levels*. CSIA Discussion Paper 95-05. Cambridge, MA: Kennedy School of Government.

32. Dimitrov, R. S. (2010). Inside Copenhagen: The state of climate. *Global Environmental Politics, 10*(2), 18–24.

33. Eckersley, R. (2012). Moving forward in the climate negotiations: Multilateralism or minilateralism? *Global Environmental Politics, 12*(2), 24–42.

34. Finnemore, M., & Sikkink, K. (1998). International norm dynamics and political change. *International Organization, 52*(4), 887–917.

35. G8. (2003). *Science and technology for sustainable development. A G8 action plan.* Resource document. G8 France. http://www.g8.utoronto.ca/summit/2003evian/sustainable_development_en.html. Accessed 29 Oct 2015.

36. G8. (2005). *Gleneagles communiqué. Resource document.* G8 Information centre. www.g8.utoronto.ca/summit/2005gleneagles/communique.pdf. Accessed 29 Oct 2015.

37. G8. (2009). *G8 leaders declaration: Responsible leadership for a sustainable future, 8.-10.7.09.* Resource document. G8 Italy. http://www.g8italia2009.it/static/G8_Allegato/G8_Declaration_08_07_09_final,0.pdf. Accessed 29 Oct 2015.

38. Geden, O. (2010). *What comes after the two-degree target? The EU's climate policy should advocate for flexible benchmarks.* SWP Comments. Berlin: German Institute for International and Security Affairs.

39. Geden, O. (2013). *Modifying the 2C target: Climate policy objectives in the contested terrain of scientific policy advice, political preferences, and rising emissions.* SWP Research Paper Berlin: German Institute for International and Security Affairs.

40. Geden, O., & Beck, S. (2014). Renegotiating the global climate stabilization target. *Nature Climate Change, 4*, 747–748.

41. Gippner, O. (2014). The 2 °C target: A European norm enters the international stage—following the process to adoption in China. *International Environmental Agreements, 15*(1), 1–17.

42. Gramelsberger, G., & Feichter, J. (2011). Introduction to the Volume. In G. Gramelsberger & J. Feichter (Eds.), *Climate change and policy: The calculability of climate change and the challenge of uncertainty* (pp. 1–8). Berlin: Springer.

43. Grubb, M. (1990). The greenhouse effect: Negotiating targets, vol. 66, no. 1. *International Affairs (Royal Institute of International Affairs 1944)* pp. 67–89.

44. Grundmann, R. (2006). Ozone and climate scientific consensus and leadership. *Science Technology Human Values, 31*, 73–101.

45. Gupta, J., & van Asselt, H. (2006). Helping operationalise article 2: A transdisciplinary methodological tool for evaluating when climate change is dangerous. *Global Environmental Change, 16*, 83–94.

46. Gupta, J., Van Der Leeuw, K., & De Moel, H. (2007). Climate change: A 'glocal' problem requiring 'glocal' action. *Environmental Sciences, 4*(3), 139–148.

47. Haas, P. M., Keohane, R. O., & Levy, M. A. (Eds.). (1993). *Institutions for the earth: Sources of effective international environmental protection*. Cambridge, MA: MIT Press.

48. Hák, T., Moldan, B., & Dahl, A. L. (Eds.). (2007). *Sustainability indicators. A scientific assessment*. Washington, DC: Island Press.

49. Hare, W., Stockwell, C., Flachsland, C., & Oberthür, S. (2010). The architecture of the global climate regime: A top–down perspective. *Climate Policy, 10*(6), 600–614.

50. Haug, C., & Berkhout, F. (2010). Learning the hard way? European climate policy after Copenhagen. *Environment: Science and Policy for Sustainable Development, 52*(3), 20–27.

51. Höhne, N., & den Elzen, M. (2013). The gap between the pledges and emissions needed for 2 °C. In K. H. Olsen, J. Fenhann, & S. Lütken (Eds.), *Elements of a new climate agreement by 2015* (pp. 9–20). Roskilde: UNEP Risø Centre.

52. Hulme, M. (2010). Moving beyond climate change. *Environment: Science and Policy for Sustainable Development, 52*(3), 15–19.

53. Hunt, J., & Shackley, S. (1999). Reconceiving science and policy: Academic, fiducial and bureaucratic knowledge. *Minerva, 37*(2), 141–164.

54. ICCT. (2005). *Meeting the climate challenge, recommendations of the international climate change taskforce*. Washington, D.C.: Institute for Public Policy Research, Center for American Progress, and Australia Institute.

55. International Scientific Steering Committee. (2005). *avoiding dangerous climate change: International symposium on the stabilization of greenhouse gas concentrations. London: department for environment, food and rural affairs*. http://eeg.tuwien.ac.at/eeg.tuwien.ac.at_pages/publications/pdf/NAK_BOO_2006_01_summary.pdf. Accessed 29 Oct 2015.

56. Jaeger, C., & Jaeger, J. (2010). Three views of two degrees. *Climate Change Economics, 1*(3), 145–166.

57. Jänicke, M., & Jörgens, H. (Eds.). (2006). New approaches to environmental governance. In *Environmental governance in global perspective. New approaches to ecological and political modernisation* (pp. 167–209). Berlin: Freie Universität Berlin.

58. Jasanoff, S. (1990). *The fifth branch, science advisers as policymakers*. Cambridge, MA: Harvard University Press.

59. Jordan, A., & Huitema, D. (2014). Innovations in climate policy: The politics of invention, diffusion, and evaluation. *Environmental Politics, 23*(5), 715–734.

60. Jordan, A., Rayner, T., Schroeder, H., Adger, N., Anderson, K., Bows, A., et al. (2013). Going beyond two degrees? The risks and opportunities of alternative options. *Climate Policy, 13*(6), 751–769.

61. Kanie, N., & Biermann, F. (Eds.). (2017). *Governance through Goals: New strategies for sustainable development*. Cambridge, MA: MIT Press.

62. Knopf, B., Kowarsch, M., Flachsland, C., & Edenhofer, O. (2012). The 2 °C target reconsidered. In O. Edenhofer, J. Wallacher, H. Lotze-Campen, M. Reder, B. Knopf, & J. Müller (Eds.), *Climate change, justice and sustainability: Linking climate and development policy* (pp. 122–125). Dordrecht: Springer.

63. Knutti, R., Rogelj, J., Sedláček, J., & Fischer, E. M. (2016). A scientific critique of the two-degree climate change target. *Nature Geoscience, 9*(1), 13–18.

64. Lenton, T. (2011a). Beyond 2 °C: Redefining dangerous climate change for physical systems. *Wiley Interdisciplinary Reviews: Climate Change, 2*, 451–461.

65. Lenton, T. (2011b). 2 °C or not 2 °C? That is the climate question. *Nature, 473*, 7.

66. Lester, S., & Neuhoff, K. (2009). *Understanding the role of policy targets in National and International Governance*. EPRG Working Paper 0909. Cambridge: University of Cambridge.

67. Mahony, M., & Hulme, M. (2012). The colour of risk: an exploration of the IPCC's "burning embers" diagram. *Spontaneous Generations: A Journal for the History and Philosophy of Science, 6*(1), 75–89.

68. Manabe, S., & Wetherald, R. T. (1967). Thermal equilibrium of the atmosphere with a given distribution of relative humidity. *Journal of the Atmospheric Sciences, 24*(3), 241–259.

69. MEF (2009). *Major economies forum declaration of the leaders. The Major economics forum on energy and climate, 9.7.09*. https://www.whitehouse.gov/the-press-office/declaration-leaders-major-economies-forum-energy-and-climate. Accessed 29 Oct 2015.

70. Metz, B. (2010). *Controlling Climate change*. Cambridge: Cambridge University Press.

71. Miller, C. A. (2005). New civic epistemologies of quantification: Making sense of indicators of local and global sustainability. *Science, Technology and Human Values, 30*(3), 403–432.

72. Mitchell, R. B. (2003). International environmental agreements: A survey of their features, formation, and effects. *Annual Review of Environment and Resources, 28*, 429–461.

73. Mitchell, R. B., Clark, W. C., Cash, D. W., & Dickson, N. M. (Eds.). (2006). *Global environmental assessments: Information and influence*. Cambridge, MA: MIT Press.

74. New, M., Liverman, D., Schroeder, H., & Anderson, K. (2011). Four degrees and beyond: The potential for a global temperature increase of four degrees and its implications. *Philosophical Transactions of the Royal Society of London A: Mathematical, Physical and Engineering Sciences, 369*(1934), 6–19.

75. Oberthür, S., & Ott, H. E. (Eds.). (2010). *The Kyoto Protocol: International climate policy for the 21st century*. Berlin: Springer.

76. Oppenheimer, M., & Petsonk, A. (2005). Article 2 of the UNFCCC: Historical origins, recent interpretations. *Climatic Change, 73*, 195–226.

77. Pandey, C. L. (2014). The limits of climate change agreements: From past to present. *International Journal of Climate Change Strategies and Management, 6*(4), 376–390.

78. Park, S. E., Marshall, N. A., Jakku, E., Dowdd, A. M., Howden, S. M., Mendhamf, E., et al. (2012). Informing adaptation responses to climate change through theories of transformation. *Global Environmental Change, 22*, 115–126.

79. Peters, R. G., Covello, V. T., & McCallum, D. B. (1997). The determinants of trust and credibility in environmental risk communication: An empirical study. *Risk Analysis, 17*(1), 43–54.

80. Pettenger, M. E. (2007). The Netherlands' climate change policy: Constructing themselves/constructing climate change. In M. E. Pettenger (Ed.), *The social construction of climate change. Power, knowledge, norms, discours* (pp. 51–73). Aldershot: Ashgate.

81. Philibert, C., & Pershing, J. (2001). Considering the options: Climate targets for all countries. *Climate Policy, 1*, 211–227.

82. Pierson, P. (2000). Increasing returns, path dependence, and the study of politics. *The American Political Science Review, 94*(2), 251–267.

83. Polany, K. (1944). *The great transformation, the political and economic origins of our time*. Boston, MA: Beacon Press.

84. Porter, T. M. (1995). *Trust in numbers. The Pursuit of objectivity in science and public life*. Princeton, NJ: Princeton University Press.

85. Randalls, S. (2010). History of the 2 °C climate target. *Wiley Interdisciplinary Reviews: Climate Change, 1*, 598–605.

86. Randalls, S. (2011). Optimal climate change: Economics and climate science policy histories (from heuristic to normative). *Osiris, 26*(1), 224–242.

87. Raupach, M. R., Davis, S. J., Peters, G. P., Andrew, R. M., Canadell, J. G., Ciais, P., et al. (2014). Sharing a quota on cumulative carbon emissions. *Nature Climate Change, 4*(10), 873–879.

88. Renn, O., & Levine, D. (1991). Credibility and trust in risk communication. In R. E. Kasperson & P. J. M. Stallen (Eds.), *Communicating risks to the public: International perspectives* (Vol. 4, pp. 175–217). Dordrecht: Springer.

89. Rijsberman, F., & Swart, R. (Eds.). (1990). *Targets and indicators of climate change: Report of working group ii of the advisory group on greenhouse gases*. Stockholm: The Stockholm Environment Institute.

90. RIVM. (1988). *Concern for tomorrow: A national environmental survey 1985–2010*; RIVM Rapport 010198901. Bilthoven: Rijksinstituut voor Volksgezondheid en Milieu.

91. Rockström, J., Steffen, W., Noone, K., Persson, Å., Chapin, S. F., Lambin, E. F., et al. (2009). Planetary boundaries: Exploring the safe operating space for humanity. *Ecology and Society,14*, 32.

92. Roelfsema, M., den Elzen, M., Höhne, N., Hof, A. F., Braun, N., Fekete, H., et al. (2014). Are major economies on track to achieve their pledges for 2020? An assessment of domestic climate and energy policies. *Energy Policy, 67*, 781–796.

93. Rotmans, J. (1990). *IMAGE. An integrated model to assess the greenhouse effect*. Dordrecht: Kluwer Academic Publishers.

94. Sarewitz, D., & Pielke, R. A. (2007). The neglected heart of science policy: Reconciling supply of and demand for science. *Environmental Science and Policy, 10*(1), 5–16.

95. Schellnhuber, H. J. (2010). Tragic triumph. *Climatic Change, 100*, 229–238.

96. Schellnhuber, H. J., Cramer, W., Nakicenovic, N., Wigley, T., & Yone, G. (2006). *Avoiding Dangerous climate change*. Cambridge: Cambridge University Press.

97. Sepibus, J. D., & Holzer, K. (2014). UNFCCC at a crossroads. *Carbon and Climate Law Review,1*, 23–34.

98. Shaw, C. (2010). The dangerous limits of dangerous limits: Climate change and the precautionary principle. In B. Carter & N. Charles (Eds.), *Nature, society and environmental crisis* (pp. 103–123). Oxford: Wiley.

99. Shaw, C. (2013). Choosing a dangerous limit for climate change: Public representations of the decision making process. *Global Environmental Change, 23*(2), 563–571.

100. Star, S. L. (2010). This is not a boundary object: Reflections on the origin of a concept. *Science, Technology and Human Values, 35*(5), 601–617.

101. Star, S. L., & Griesemer, J. R. (1989). Institutional ecology, translations' and boundary objects: Amateurs and professionals in Berkeley's Museum of Vertebrate Zoology, 1907–39. *Social Studies of Science, 19*(3), 387–420.

102. Swart, R. J., & Vellinga, P. (1994). The 'ultimate objective' of the framework convention on climate change requires a new approach in climate change research. *Climatic Change, 26*, 343–349.

103. SWCC. (1990) Declaration of the second world climate conference. In Jager, J., & Ferguson, H. L. (Eds.) (1991), *Climate change: Science, impacts and policy—Proceedings of the second world climate conference*. Cambridge: Cambridge University Press.

104. Thornton, P. K., Ericksen, P. J., Herrero, M., & Challinor, A. J. (2014). Climate variability and vulnerability to climate change: A review. *Global Change Biology, 20*(11), 3313–3328.

105. Tol, R. S. J. (2007). Europe's long-term climate target: A critical evaluation. *Energy Policy, 35*, 424–432.

106. Torrance, W. E. F. (2006). Science or salience: Building an agenda for climate change. In R. B. Mitchell, W. C. Clark, D. W. Cash, & N. M. Dickson (Eds.), *Global environmental assessments. Information and influence*. Cambridge, MA: MIT Press.

107. Turnhout, E., Hisschemöller, M., & Eijsackers, H. (2007). Ecological indicators: Between the two fires of science and policy. *Ecological Indicators, 7*(2), 215–228.

108. Underdal, A. (2000). Science and politics: The anatomy of an uneasy partnership. In S. Andresen, T. Skodvin, A. Underdal, & J. Wettestad (Eds.), *Science and politics in international environmental regimes* (pp. 1–21). Manchester: Manchester University Press.

109. UNEP. (2013). *The emissions gap report 2013.*

110. UNFCCC. (1992). *The United Nations framework convention on climate change.* 1992 FCCC/INFORMAL/84 GE.05-62220 (E) 200705.

111. UNFCCC. (2007). *Report of the conference of the parties at its thirteenth session, held in Bali from 3 to 15 December 2007, Addendum, part two: Actions taken by the conference of the parties at its thirteenth session.* FCCC/CP/2007/6/Add.1.

112. UNFCCC. (2009). *Report of the conference of the parties on its fifteenth session, held in Copenhagen from 7 to 19 December 2009 Addendum part two: Action taken by the conference of the parties at its fifteenth session.* FCCC/CP/2009/11/Add.1.

113. UNFCCC. (2009). *Draft decision -/CP.15 proposal by the president Copenhagen Accord.* FCCC/CP/2009/L.7.

114. UNFCCC. (2010). *The Cancun agreements: Outcome of the work of the Ad Hoc Working Group on Long-term Cooperative Action under the Convention.* FCCC/CP/2010/7/Add.1.

115. UNFCCC. (2013). *Further advancing the Durban platform.* FCCC/CP/2013/10/Add.1.

116. UNFCCC. (2015). Adoption of the Paris agreement. Proposal by the president. Draft decision-/CP.21. FCCC/CP/2015/L.9/Rev.1.

117. van der Sluijs, J., van Eijndhoven, J., Shackley, S., & Wynne, B. (1998). Anchoring devices in science for policy: The case of consensus around climate Sensitivity. *Social Studies of Science,28,* 291–323.

118. van Eijndhoven, J., Dinkelman, G., van der Sluijs, J., Pleune, R., & Worrell, C. (2001). Finding your place: A history of the management of global environmental risks in the Netherlands, Vol. 1. A comparative history of social responses to climate change, ozone depletion, and acid rain. In *Social learning group. Learning to manage global environmental risks. 2. A functional analysis of social*

responses to climate change, ozone depletion, and acid rain. Vol. 2 (pp. 115—138). Cambridge, MA: MIT Press.

119. van Vliet, J., van den Berg, M., Schaeffer, M., van Vuuren, D. P., den Elzen, M., Hof, A. F., et al. (2012). Copenhagen Accord Pledges imply higher costs for staying below 2 °C warming. *Climatic Change, 113*, 551–561.

120. Vellinga, P., & Swart, R. J. (1991). The greenhouse marathon: A proposal for a global strategy. *Climatic Change, 18*, 7–12.

121. Watson, R. T. (2005). Turning science into policy: Challenges and experiences from the science-policy interface. *Philosophical Transactions of the Royal Society of London B: Biological Sciences, 360*(1454), 471–477.

122. WBGU. (1995). *Scenario for the derivation of global CO2 reduction targets and implementation strategies. Statement on the occasion of the first conference of the parties to the framework convention on climate change in Berlin.* Berlin: Wissenschaftlicher Beirat der Bundesregierung Globale Umweltveränderungen, WBGU.

123. WBGU. (1996). *World in transition: Ways towards global environmental solutions.* Berlin: Wissenschaftlicher Beirat der Bundesregierung Globale Umweltveränderungen, WBGU.

124. WBGU. (2009). *Special Report, Solving the climate dilemma: The budget approach.* Berlin: Wissenschaftlicher Beirat der Bundesregierung Globale Umweltveränderungen, WBGU.

125. Whyte, K. P., & Crease, R. P. (2010). Trust, expertise, and the philosophy of science. *Synthese,177*, 411–425.

126. Widerberg, O., & Pattberg, P. (2014). International cooperative initiatives in global climate governance: Raising the ambition level or delegitimizing the UNFCCC? *Global Policy, 6*(1), 45–56.

127. Wise, R. M., Fazey, I., Stafford Smith, M., Park, S. E., Eakin, H. C., Archer Van Garderen, E. R. M., et al. (2012). Reconceptualising adaptation to climate change as part of pathways of change and response. *Global Environmental Change, 28*, 325–336.

128. WMO. (1988). *Developing policies for responding to climatic change, A summary of the discussions and recommendations of the workshops held in Villach (28 September to 2 October 1987) and Bellagio (9–13 November 1987) under the Auspices of the Beijer Institute. Stockholm, World Climate Impact studies Program, World Meteorological Organization.* WCIP-1 WMO/TD-No. 225.

129. Yamin, F. (2000). The role of the EU in climate negotiations. In J. Gupta & M. Grubb (Eds.), *Climate change and European leadership* (pp. 47–66). Dordrecht: Springer.

130. Young, O. R., & Levy, M. A. (1999). The effectiveness of international environmental regimes. In O. R. Young (Ed.), *The effectiveness of international environmental regimes: Causal connections and behavioral mechanisms* (pp. 1–32). Cambridge, MA: MIT Press.

131. Young, O., Underdal, A., Kanie, N., Andresen, S., Bernstein, S., & Biermann, F., et al. (2014). *Earth system challenges and a multi-layered approach for the sustainable development goals*. Post2015/UNU-IAS Policy Brief #1. Tokyo: United Nations Institute for Advanced Study of Sustainability.

4
CHAPTER

Trends of Development of International Water Law

Paulo Canelas de Castro

Faculty of Law, University of Macau, Macau, China

ABSTRACT

International water law has been witnessing profound changes in the latter twenty years. These changes denote certain cardinal options for new goals and values that the newer international water law is seeking to embrace. Amongst these new goals and values, the ones of environmentalization, humanisation, economicisation stand out as attempts at bringing efficient response to the challenges set by the current global water crisis and the more complex expectations of the international community. They amount to an innovative normative message and even true paradigm- shifts in the understanding of international water law. These trends of development of international water law set this legal field in line with other chapters of contemporary international law and derive in part from the cross-fertilisation of normative ideas and principles between these chapters of international law.

Keywords: Economicisation, Environmentalization, Global Water Crisis, Humanisation, Human Right to Water, International Water Law, Paradigm Changes, Trade in Water, Water Protection, Water Services

1. INTRODUCTION

After a few decades of a rather lethargic state, corresponding to the attempt at codifying it—undertaken, particularly, by the International Law Commission[1,2], and marked by a rather schizophrenic debate over the prevalence of two water sharing principles[3], simplistically seen as competing: those of the equitable and reasonable use of international watercourses and the obligation not to cause damage, also known as the no harm principle-International Water Law has been witnessing a considerable normative development in the latter two decades.

This normative development may be detected in multiple signs. Foremost, in the frantic law-making endeavors permeating international life: most noticeably, those translated in the adoption of numerous treaties at the different ambits of the international society[4]; but also in, the not less significant, soft law[5], undertaken in particular by manifold international organizations or conferences, which, in the period, have brought water issues to the forefront of the global international agenda. Additionally, also in the several international disputes where water is invoked as the main subject-matter and the unprecedented swathe of decisions which take water and international water law as their casus decidendi and rationale[6].

This hectic normative development is, moreover, of a much diversified character. Mirroring trends which had already been at the origin of the formidable development of International law at large, more broadly over the last seven decades, and which had led a leading scholar to adroitly proclaim the post-ontological hour of international law (Franck, 1995) , it seems arguable that this progress has in general been happening by cross-fertilizing the traditionally rather impermeable body of international water law with other fields of international law[7]. This global trend towards the corpus iuris of international water law building bridges with other fields of international law—and namely, international environmental law, international law of human rights and international economic law—may therefore be summarily apprehended in three main substantive "friendships" or "leanings" of international water law, its newer value or teleological choices: A choice towards "naturalizing", "environmentalising" or "greening" international water law; a trend towards "humanizing" international water law or, more broadly, rendering it more inclusive; and, more recently, a leaning towards looking more attentively at water, and the international law which is related to it, through a more consciously economic angle.

2. THE ENVIRONMENTALIZATION OF INTERNATIONAL WATER LAW

The environmentalization of International Water Law passes firstly through the normative apprehension of the reality of water bodies as it really happens: in its multiple interconnections and unitary complexity—of (non-confined) groundwater with surface water[8], of the watercourses with other biota and ecosystems[9], with the land mass[10] as well as with marine waters[11]. Several legal documents advocate that catchment areas or other analogous integrating concepts be used as the water management units[12]. This then permits and facilitates a more realistic or effective legal discipline: one where development of water is not any longer the sole goal pursued, but where instead development becomes integrated with the goal of protection of water[13]; one where, therefore, only sustainable development is lawful. Protecting the environment or ecosystems of watercourses, water quality, as well as the fight against diverse forms of pollution, thus become main concerns and normative areas of the newer international water legal disciplines[14]. Correspondingly, the scope of the obligations comprehended is equally enlarged: beyond obligations of mitigation and minimization or reduction and control of harm[15]—of risks[16], even—there are now obligations of prevention of impacts, of precaution[17]. They all explain the consecration of procedural duties, ranging from notification of planned measures to consultations and negotiation[18], from simple obligations of access to information to a general duty to perform environmental[19] and strategic impact assessments, sometimes ex post even[20]. This wider approach becomes the more necessary as one acknowledges the crucial relevance of water in the ongoing conditions of scarcity[21]and climate change[22]. Both realisations call for actions and measures[23] that have a broader and cyclical time reference. These developments are in line with the concept of integrated water resources management as defined by the Global Water Partnership and based on the 1992 Dublin Statement on Water and Sustainable Development.

3. THE HUMANIZATION OF INTERNATIONAL WATER LAW

International Water Law has equally been witnessing a move towards including more legal personae within the remit of participating legal subjects.

This move concerns its traditional legal subjects, first: the States, the riparian States. Increasingly, the new international water law advocates that all those States, riparian to a particular shared watercourse, participate in the corresponding legal discipline[24], thus matching at this level an effort at ensuring that the said legal discipline corresponds to reality, and that it therefore may prove more efficient. Moreover, in a few instances, international law equally calls on the participation of coastal States adjacent to the riparian ones[25], in a legal development which again evidences an attention to natural reality and the real dynamics of impacts.

Secondly, the newer international water law equally concerns intergovernmental organizations and institutions of very different structures and functions[26,27]. Their establishment or revival[28] reflects the perceived need of States to enhance cooperation to manage shared water resources over several territories[29]. Their existence facilitates the recurring dialogue between the riparian States as to the activities that each of them purports to promote within its jurisdiction, particularly with regard to the sharing of rights and benefits deriving from the development of the waters as well as the prevention, reduction and control of risks of damages. They especially allow for an institutional process of communication, made of different procedural acts which permit the assessment of the effects of planned or existing measures or projects[30]. Finally, they also enable the carrying out of joint activities.

Most noticeably, different legal instruments[31] recommend that river/watercourse commissions be set up or that their experience is used[32] in the daily effort of implementing but also developing primary regimes[33]. In some cases, international organizations or international commissions are equally called to complement the action of the States (by providing financial and technical assistance[34], or working as instances for the prevention and settlement of disputes[35])[36].

Additionally, these organisations and institutions are sometimes also the platform for other non-governmental actors to intervene; like environmental, human rights' or governance NGOs, as well as epistemic communities, companies and individuals. All of them, thus thereby find their way to voice their concerns, grievances, interests, information, expertise[37]. Simultaneously, they obtain some legal status in the processes of decision-making or adjudicating the manifold issues of water management[38,39].

The whole movement reaches its climax once international law engages into its humanization—firstly, by recognizing procedural rights of access to information[40], participation in decision-making and in administrative decisions relating to the environment as well as the judicial appeal against such decisions, and rights of participation in impact assessments as well as in the aforementioned institutional water platforms. The 1998 Aarhus Convention on access to information, public participation in decision-making and access to justice in environmental matters[41], in the UNECE universe, stands out in such context as a prominent illustration[42,43].

The humanization of international water law is evidenced then, in the adoption of a human right to water and sanitation[44], which corresponds to the satisfaction of the most basic human needs[45,46] and overcomes a blatant *lacuna* of the International Bill of Human Rights. Initiated with General Comment n° 15 of the Economic and Social Council[47], the process of consolidation[48] of such double right gained momentum in 2010, by the adoption of corresponding resolutions by the General Assembly of the United Nations[49] and the Human Rights Council[50]. These documents[51] mainly anchor such right[52]of multifaceted content[53] in the remit of economic, social and cultural rights—a qualification, which renders these rights, ones of a progressive realization[54]. Be as it may, it equally implies a certain number of consequential obligations for the States, namely obligations to respect, protect and fulfill[55]. Amongst other duties, they call for the States' supplementary regulatory working. It is equally certain that the human right to water does not hinder the State to perceive payment for the services rendered. This applies, moreover, to not only the State but also other actors, which may, in particular, intervene in the provision of water services or waste treatment services[56]. This intervention seems justifiable: not only because the right is neutral as to the economic model adopted by the State as to such vital public services, but also because momentous investments seem indeed to be in order for rendering this proclaimed right a true reality. In any event, the interface between this right and a kind of water management more economically-driven is, doubtlessly, one of the areas where international water law may need further development and clarification.

4. THE ECONOMICISATION OF INTERNATIONAL WATER LAW

The third vector of renewal of international water law contends with the integration of the economy and its international legal disciplines. The departing point is parallel to the ones seen in regard to the aforementioned strands of evolution of this body of rules: besides being taken as an environmental good, and a pole for legally empowering a diverse host of actors, and particularly for accrediting human rights, water is also more and more apprehended as a commodity, as an economic good[57].

This development is propitiated by several factors: the widespread awareness of water scarcity and unequal distribution[58], leading to a mounting demand for the resource as well as a rising capacity to dispose thereof over time and space[59].

Such developments then lead to elucubrations whether water or the service of its provision gains in being set in a market context[60], attached a "rationalizing" price tag[61]. It is equally questioned whether there is merit in trading bulk water[62] besides increasingly conveying it across space from "water-rich" to "water-poor" areas[63], as well as collecting it from the natural milieu, bottling it and selling it in a growing market of water "products"[64]. This approach is epitomized in some policy documents from the nineties of last century, like the Agenda 21[65], the Dublin Declaration[66] or the World Water Vision of the World Water Council[67].

Similarly, an apparently growing stream of legal thinking seems to be devoted to wondering whether there may be merit in applying international trade law (and the WTO agreements, GATT and GATS foremost)[68] as well as international investment law (the myriad of regional agreements and BITs)[69], as well as the corresponding institutions, to relevant water operations and what may be the consequences of such course of action.

More specifically, this rather creative or "outside-the-box" legal thinking is concerned, firstly, in regard to the trading of bulk water products, whether water may be treated as a "good"[70], a "product"[71,72]. It wonders, next, whether there is anything specific to water[73], justifying, if not imposing, that these principles governing international trade be derogated (the principles of most favored nation, of non-discrimination) or instead that it compels certain water-rich countries to envisage exporting water resources in abundance[74]. Were the GATT disciplines deemed to be applicable[75], another line of enquiry is what would the margin of maneuver for an exporting State mindful of the necessity to follow a precautionary approach in the management of its water resources be[76], so as to avoid violating GATT obligations aiming both at reducing tariff barriers and quantitative restrictions on trade as well as to remove any national measure that discriminates against domestic products vis-à-vis imported products[77]; whether in its managerial policies of environmental protection or driven by social considerations, such State could be comforted in the excepting clauses of Article XI. 2(a) and, particularly, Article XX of GATT[78]. Equally, it is asked whether it would be sensible to depend on the adjudicatory mechanisms of the WTO dispute settlement system for pursuing such policies[79].

In regard to water and wastewater services and the applicability of GATS, the main queries regard, besides classification issues[80], the possibility of carving out water public services in case of opening up the market to other foreign or domestic service providers[81]. Alternatively, it seems important to assess the usefulness of the reasons that article XIV of GATS provides, permitting derogations from the State's specific commitments, and, more largely, the extent of regulatory powers, which the host State may safeguard in the name of the pursuance of the public interest. Another provision with relevance is Article XIII of GATS, which sets out that the obligations of most favored nation treatment, market access and national treatment do not apply to "laws, regulations or requirements governing the procurement by governmental agencies of services purchased for governmental purposes and not with a view to commercial resale or with a view to use in the supply of services for commercial sale". If the contracts between public authorities and private water companies can be characterized as "government procurement", then the GATS regime (the obligations of most favored-nation, market access and national treatment) does not apply either[82]. It does not seem, however, that the concession contracts or build-operate-transfer contracts that are frequently used for ensuring water services should be considered public procurement[83].

In substantive connection to such debate, albeit not in terms of the legal instruments at stake, appear the discussions on investment solutions in the water sector. They derive from the apparent growing recognition of the financial crisis of the State. This financial crisis leads the State to rethink the priorities and engagement in the economic sector and, in particular, in the water area, towards catering technical expertise and financial assets through multiple forms of privatization of services which had previously axiomatically been seen as public— namely by engaging sometimes very powerful multinational enterprises willing to offer such services on an economic profit logics; as it drives the State to opening up to foreign direct investment, usually protected by the body of rules of international investment law and its mechanisms of dispute settlement, often relying on international arbitration. In spite of its close proximity, whereas the former debate on market liberalization systematically pertains to WTO law instruments and the GATS regime in particular[84], this latter one, for the lack of an investment dimension in the WTO agreements, rather has its systemic legal "seat" in the area related to the hundreds of regional and bilateral investment treaties.

The main issue debated relates to the host State's regulatory powers in view of the obligations to protect international investment and the mechanisms for the State to protect public interest in regard to private sector participation in the economic management of water. The effort is at striking the right balance between the powers seeking the protection of public interest and serving corresponding obligations like those correspective of a human right to water or those related to the protection of the environment, on the one hand, and those directed at the protection of international investments, on the other hand. A number of awards through ICSID dispute settlement[85] may be viewed as indicative of progress in such direction[86].

5. CONCLUDING REMARKS

The protrayed newer leanings or trends of development of international water law reveal an effort at holistically apprehending and giving normative response to a more complex reality of problems and social expectations than those that used to be addressed by the old international water law, centered on the pure regulation of the uses of water. The changes involved are diverse and numerous. It seems however possible to identify some common threads underlying all the changes and trends identified. A first one is the move towards establishing a creative interface between the traditional core of this body of principles and rules dedicated to water and those other disciplines of international law which more directly address the concerns with the protection of the environment, social equity, and a sensible weighing of the economic values. Internormativity is thus one of the keys for understanding the evolution of international water law and the vigor thereof; the normative dialogue generates cross-fertilisation and renovation of international water law. Another one is the implicit sense of urgency that these proposed changes and trends carry, corresponding only to the magnitude of the global water crisis. These changes are definitely momentous, as the newer law became much more complex in the normative responses pursued. They are not however deprived of an underlying vision: on the contrary, the newer international water law announces decisive cardinal options, pursues shared goals, honours certain values, follows principles which lend heuristic and interpretative sense to the reconstruction of this legal field. In the whole, the changes thus amount to true paradigm-shifts (Kuhn, 1962) . But this realisation also alerts us to the uncertainties that are still involved in the progress of international water law. It is of the very nature of paradigm-shifts themselves that they comprehend ambiguities and even elicit resistance. The uncertain harmonisation of the trends for environmentalisation and humanisation of water, on the one hand, and its economicisation, on the other, is in this regard telling. To this, one should add the realisation that these developments are an ongoing process: new problems seem already perceptible in the horizon—"climatising" international water law, adapting it to the challenges of climate change seems to be one of them. Another one is the struggle to render the whole movement of "legalisation" or more and newer law-making, a living reality: ensuring that the newer normative messages are complied with, should also become one of the major tenets of the evolution of international water law. Assessing the past but also looking ahead, one can not but be reminded of the works of Sisyphus.

NOTES

1. See Tanzi & Arcari, 2001 , and McCaffrey, 2007 . The Law of International Watercourses—Non-navigational Uses, Oxford: Oxford University Press, 2nd ed., 2007.

2. Prior to the International Law Commission's effort, the same concern had already led the International Law Association to adopt in 1966 the Rules on the Uses of the Waters for International Rivers, usually known as "the Helsinki Rules". They deal with navigational as well as non-navigational uses of rivers. See International Law Association, 1967. See also Manner & Metsalampi (eds.), 1988; Bogdanovic, 2001 .

3. For the understanding of these principles prior to the adoption of the United Nations Watercourses Convention, see e.g., Caflisch, 1993 .

4. To name but a few, at the regional level: 1992 Helsinki Convention on the Protection and Use of Transboundary Watercourses and International Lakes, 1991 Espoo Convention on Environmental Impact Assessment in a Transboundary Context, 1999 London Protocol on Water and Health, 2003 Protocol on Civil Liability and Compensation for Damages Caused by the Transboundary Effects of Industrial Accidents on Transboundary Waters, 1995 Protocol on Shared Watercourse Systems in the Southern African Development Community and its 2000 Revised Protocol on Shared Watercourses in the Southern African Development Community; and, at a local or specific basin level: 1994 Danube Convention on Cooperation for the Protection and Sustainable Use of the Danube River, 1994 Meuse and Scheldt agreements, revised in 2002, 1998 Convention between Portugal and Spain on the Cooperation for the Protection and Sustainable Use of the Waters of the Luso-Spanish River Basins, as well as the 2008 Revised Protocol to the Convention, 1999 Convention on the Protection of the Rhine, 1995 Agreement on the Cooperation for the Sustainable Development of the Mekong River Basin, 2002 Tripartite Interim Agreement between Mozambique, South Africa and Swaziland for the Cooperation on the Protection and Sustainable Utilisation of the Water Resources of the Incomati and the Maputo Watercourses,

2002 Senegal River Water Charter, 2003 Protocol for Sustainable Development of the Lake Victoria Basin. On the interplay and interactions between universal, regional and local basin instruments, see Boisson de Chazournes, 2009; Boisson de Chazournes, 2015 .

5. In 2003, the International Law Commission considered the area of the law applicable to transboundary groundwater resources and, in 2008, it adopted the Draft Articles on the Law of Transboundary Aquifers: UN Doc A/CN.4/L.724 (29 May 2008). See International Law Commission, Report of the International Law Commission—Fifty-eighth session, UN Doc A/61/10 (11 August 2006), pp. 183-245; International Law Commission, Report of the International Law Commission—Sixtieth session, UN Doc A/63/10 (8 August 2008); McCaffrey, 2009; Mechlem, 2009. Following up on this input, the UN General Assembly, by Resolution 66/104 of 31 January 2012, captioned "The Law of transboundary aquifers", has also encouraged "the States concerned to make appropriate bilateral or regional arrangements for the proper management of their transboundary aquifers, taking into account the provisions of the Draft Articles annexed to its Resolution 63/124".

6. To name but a few, see, in the International Court of Justice: Gabcikovo-Nagymaros Project (Hungary v Slovakia), Judgment, ICJ Reports 1977; Kasikili/Sedudu Island (Botswana v Namibia), Judgment, ICJ Reports 1999; Land and Maritime Boundary between Cameroon and Nigeria (Cameroon v Nigeria: Equatorial Guinea intervening), Judgment, ICJ Reports 2002; Frontier Dispute (Benin/Niger), Judgment, ICJ Reports 2005; Pulp Mills on the River Uruguay (Argentina v Uruguay), Provisional Measures, Order of 13 July 2006, ICJ Reports 2006; Pulp Mills on the River Uruguay (Argentina v Uruguay), Provisional Measures, Order of 23 January 2007, ICJ Reports 2007; Dispute Regarding Navigational and Related Rights (Costa Rica v Nicaragua), Judgment, ICJ Reports 2009; Pulp Mills on the River Uruguay (Argentina v Uruguay), Judgment, ICJ Reports 2010; Certain Activities carried out in the Border Area (Costa Rica v Nicaragua), Provisional Measures, ICJ Order of 8 March 2011; Frontier Dispute (Burkina Faso/Niger), Judgment of 16 April 2013; in the Permanent Court of Arbitration: Case concerning the audit of accounts between the Netherlands and France in application of the Protocol of 25 September 1991 Additional to the Convention for the Protection of the Rhine from Pollution by Chlorides of 3 December 1976 (Netherlands/France), Arbitral Award 2004; Indus Waters Kishenganga Arbitration (Pakistan v India), Order on Interim Measures 2011; Indus Waters

Kishenganga Arbitration (Pakistan v India), Partial Award 2013; in the European Court of Justice. (a regional jurisprudence with international elements): Case 21/76 Handelskwekerij Bier v Mines de Potasse d'Alsace SA [1976] ECR 1735; Case C-36/98 Spain v Council of the European Union [2001] ECR I-00779; Case C-266/99 Commission of the European Communities v French Republic [2001] ECR I-2000; Case C-32/05 Commission of the European Communities v Grand Duchy of Luxembourg [2006] ECR I-11349.

7. We have been arguing this since Canelas de Castro, 2005. See also, Canelas de Castro, 2008.

8. The very notion of watercourse as well as other key notions of these regimes comprehend and integrate different types of waters as well as other elements. On the other hand, it excludes confined waters and other elements, which are better apprehended through the notion of "hydrographic basin" or alike. This leads several Authors to criticize the approach: see Salman, 2005, and Brown-Weiss, 2007, who proclaims that "The 1997 UN International Watercourses Convention has several deficiencies from the water science perspective".

9. For instance, in the United Nations Watercourses Convention, article 20

10. The notion of "hydrographic basin" apprehends better these interconnections. Whereas it is sometimes used in regional (e.g., African, see Kamto, 1990; see also the Water Framework Directive, in the European regional context) and local instruments, it was not retained in the UN Watercourses Convention, where the sovereignty sensitivities of States prevailed. See Paquerot, 2005; Sohnle, 2002; Coulée, 2011.

11. E.g., in the Watercourses Convention, article 23, which constitutes a recognition that land-based pollution is also a source of maritime pollution. See Canelas de Castro, 2003.

12. For instance, the 1998 Luso-Spanish Convention.

13. This is explicitly reflected, for instance, in the very designation of conventions like the 1994 Danube Convention, the 1998 Luso-Spanish Convention, the 2002 Tripartite Interim Agreement relating to the Incomati and Maputo watercourses. In a different normative strategy, in the 1997 UN Watercourses Convention, protection of the watercourse has been recognized as a component of equitable and reasonable utilization—hence, articles 5, 6 (a) and (f). In addition, the 1997 Convention codifies a number of cooperation obligations that help to prevent or mitigate

environmental damage. Moreover, its Part IV is dedicated to the protection, preservation and management of riverine ecosystems. Regionally, this is a marked difference between the Revised SADC Protocol, from 2000, and the first Protocol on Shared Watercourse Systems, adopted in 1995: e.g., the objectives listed in article 2 aim for sustainable, integrated and environmentally sound development and management.

14. This is even more so in Europe and North America, sometimes as a response to catastrophes deriving from industrial accidents. See Kiss, 1987.

15. E.g., Article 21 of the United Nations Watercourses Convention.

16. This is one of the triggers of precaution. See Boisson de Chazournes, 2007; and Martin, 1998 .

17. For instance, the threshold for the due diligence obligations to prevent, reduce and control pollution also existing in the Watercourses Convention, has been raised in the 2008 Draft Articles on the Law of Transboundary Aquifers through a provision, article 12, which requires States to take a precautionary approach. The precautionary principle also features highly in the Helsinki Convention (article 2 (5) (b)) and underlies the whole 1999 UNECE Protocol to the Helsinki Convention, on Water and Health. Locally, it may be traced in basin treaties, like the 1998 Luso-Spanish Convention and the revised 2002 Meuse and Scheldt Agreements. The principle has also been mentioned in Pulp Mills on the River Uruguay (Argentina v Uruguay), Judgment, ICJ Reports 2010, para 164.

18. See Part III of the United Nations Convention.

19. Both article 12 of the UN Watercourses Convention and article 15 of the Draft Articles on Transboundary Aquifers mention that the obligation of notification of planned measures should inter alia be accompanied by the results of environmental impact assessments. There is actually a linkage between the obligation to provide information and the impact assessments: this is demonstrated by the International Court of Justice's consideration in the Pulp Mills case that the information transmitted must include a complete environmental impact assessment in order to assess the effects of a planned measure on the environment and that the notification must "take place before the State concerned decides on the environmental viability of the plan, taking due account of the environmental impact assessment submitted to it", Pulp Mills on

the River Uruguay (Argentina v Uruguay), Judgment, ICJ Reports 2010, para 120.

20. This was indicated already in the Gabcikovo-Nagymaros case and explicitly spelled out in the Pulp Mills on the River Uruguay (Argentina v Uruguay), Judgment, ICJ Reports 2010, para 205: once operations of a project have started, continuous monitoring of its effects on the environment must be undertaken.

21. See, very appropriately, Brown-Weiss, 2013.

22. See Canelas de Castro, 2011.

23. Like adaptation strategies designed to face the impacts of climate change. See article 4 (1)(e) of the United Nations Framework Convention on Climate Change, of 9 May 1992, UNTS 1771 (1994).

24. See article 3 of the United Nations Convention.

25. See article 9(3) of the Helsinki Convention.

26. For an effort at designing a typology, see Caflisch, 1989; Boisson de Chazournes, 2003underlines the emergence of a trend towards their harmonization, though; one which is induced partially by global and regional conventions which themselves promote the creation of basin organizations and commissions.

27. Whereas the scope of cooperation in these organisations and commissions was narrow in the nineteenth century, it gradually broadened throughout the twentieth century in parallel with a movement of increased and more diversified use of the international rivers. The range of competencies of these organisations and commissions has equally become vaster. Whereas in the beginning their main task concerned navigation regulation, the scope was widened to cover activities like the production of energy, irrigation, recreational and environmental protection activities and include functions like those of information collection and dissemination, regulation by the adoption of standards and guidelines, the promotion and execution of joint operational activities, the brokering of discussions for the eventual development of other legal instruments. See exemplarily, the Luso-Spanish Convention, article 10.

28. For early institutional experiences, see Chamberlain, 1923; Blociszewski, 1926; Colliard, 1968;McCaffrey, 2007 .

29. Similarly, Pulp Mills on the River Uruguay (Argentina v Uruguay), Judgment, ICJ Reports 2010, para 81.

30. Their importance is stressed in the Pulp Mills on the River Uruguay (Argentina v Uruguay) Case, paras 115 and 119.

31. Also scientific associations called for such legal and institutional developments: see for instance, Institute of International Law, "Resolution on the International Regulations regarding the Use of International Watercourses" of 1911.

32. See article 3 (4) of the 2000 EU Water Framework Directive.

33. This function of platform for legal development and implementation is clearly spelled out in the designation of the Luso-Spanish commission established by the 1998 convention. See also article 10 of the Convention, devoting a particular attention to the law-making potential of the commission.

34. See Boisson de Chazournes, 2007and, specifically on water, Boisson de Chazournes, 2015.

35. The 1997 Convention on the Law of the Non-Navigational Uses of International Watercourses underlines such role in article 33(2). Different basin agreements, like the 1998 Luso-Spanish Convention and the 1909 Treaty on Boundary Waters, and Questions Arising between the United States and Canada (article IX) equally award this function to the corresponding commission, generally linking it to the object and purpose of the regime at stake.

36. For which, the international legal personality of a river commission may be added value, particularly in relations with third actors. See article 11 of the 1995 Agreement on the Cooperation for the Sustainable Development of the Mekong River Basin which expressly states: "The institutional framework for cooperation in the Mekong River Basin (...) shall (....) enjoy the status of an international body, including entering into agreements and obligations with the donor or international community".

37. With the "privatisation" of assistance ensuing from the 1992 Rio Conference, the Monterrey Conference, but especially the Johannesburg Summit, the private sector also helps in the financing of implementing projects and legal instruments—usually in partnerships between governments and civil society groups.

38. See Mekong River Commission for Sustainable Development, 2005.

39. A pivotal role is frequently played by these institutions' secretariats.

40. See e.g., Sand, 2003.

41. See McAllister, 1998.

42. See United Nations Economic Commission for Europe, 2000.

43. Similarly, in the African context, the African Convention on the Conservation of Nature and Natural Resources.

44. See Albuquerque, 2013.

45. The consideration of human needs in the development of international water law predates the recognition of the human right to water.

46. [46]It is important to realise that the human right to water and sanitation is linked to the satisfaction of personal and domestic needs, and thus to some privileged uses of water, in particular those related to household and personal uses. It therefore does not pertain to the whole spectrum of other usages, such as industrial, agricultural, fishing, navigation, hydroelectric uses or those related to the protection of the environment, irrespective of the close links existing among them. The fundamental rights nature of the right to water lends this right its objective priority status—as does the international law of watercourses with the provision of article 10 of the 1997 Watercourses Convention.

47. General Comment No. 15 (2002) of the Economic and Social Council, "The Right to Water", UN Doc E/C.12/2002/11 of 20 January 2010.

48. Other milestones in the process, even prior to General Comment No. 15, are the UN Mar del Plata Action Plan of 1977, the Dublin Statement on Water and Sustainable Development of 1992 and Agenda 21. Also international treaties contribute to defining aspects or beneficiaries of this right: in particular, the Convention on the Elimination of All forms of Discrimination Against Women (article 14 (2)), the Convention on the Rights of the Child (article 24 (2)), the Convention on the Rights of Disabled Persons (article 28 (2a)). Equally noteworthy are the Draft Guidelines for the Realization of the Right to Drinking Water Supply and Sanitation adopted by the Sub-Commission on the Promotion and Protection of Human Rights, in 2005. Besides human rights instruments, also those relating to the law of international watercourses contributed to the emergence of the right: particularly, the Protocol on Water and Health, the Charter of Water of the Senegal River, the Water Charter of the Niger Basin and the Charter of Water of Lake Chad.

49. Resolution 64/292 of the UN General Assembly, "The Human Right to water and sanitation", UN Doc A/Res/64/292, of 3 August 2010.

50. Resolution 15/L.14 of the Human Rights Council, "Human rights and access to safe drinking water and sanitation", UN Doc A/HRC/15/L. 14 of 24 September 2010.

51. Beyond the conceptual and even interpretative differences between the different normative instruments, as to the legal scope of the right, content, field of application and application (seeCaflisch, 2011), they all recognize the importance of this right and share a vision or general objective: the one of achieving access to safe drinking for the human beings and obtaining access to sanitation systems. This objective mobilized legally and politically different actors and set the framework for seeking effective implementation and realization of this right, a formidable endeavor in view of the realities in the field (see WHO and UNICEF, 2010). In this latter regard, certain initiatives stand out for their contribution to the advancement of the aforementioned general objective: namely, the decision of the Human Rights Council in 2008 (by Resolution 7/22) to appoint an Independent Expert on the issue of Human Rights relating to access to drinking water and sanitation , who became in 2011 (by Resolution 16/2) the Special Rapporteur on the Right to safe drinking water and sanitation—it established the right to water and the reports of the Special Rapporteur helped refine the contents thereof (see Albuquerque, 2012); also noteworthy are the calls by the Human Rights Council for States to implement this right.

52. Some instruments formulate this right as an autonomous right, while others link it to other rights and even make it derive therefrom: for instance, with the right to life and as a prerequisite for the realization of all human rights (e.g., Resolution 64/292 of the General Assembly), the right to an adequate standard of living and the right to the highest attainable standard of physical and mental health as well as the right to life and human dignity (Resolution 15/L.14 of the Human Rights Council). General Comment No. 15 also derives the human right to water from the right to an adequate standard of living and considers that it is "inextricably related to the right to the highest attainable standard of health and the rights to adequate housing and adequate food".

53. The notes of equitable access, quality, availability, affordability are usually invoked in this regard. See Coulée, 2011 and Albuquerque, 2010.

54. See article 2 (1) of the International Covenant on Economic, Social and Cultural Rights andSalman & McInerney-Lankford, 2004.

55. Idem, at pp. 67-68.

56. More broadly, drawing a connection between the fight for this right and the ascension of new actors in the international scene and their claim for treating water as a global public good and for a global governance of water, see Coulée, 2011.

57. Dealing with water as an economic good is one of the ways increasingly suggested in order to efficiently manage water. For instance, Dalhuisen, Groot, and Nijkamp, 2000 state that: "An economic approach to water supply and demand may contribute to a better management of water and to its sustainable use".

58. Idem, p. 3.

59. See Cossy, 2005a .

60. Carter et al. (eds.), 1994; Anderson (ed.), 1994; Libecap, 2005 .

61. Cossy, 2005a; Hildering, 2005; Caponera, 1992 .

62. See Haan, 1997; Hildering, 2005 .

63. Examples quoted or discussed include the tender between Turkey and Israel, the export of water from Canada to the USA, the transfers between Malaysia and Singapore, Lesotho and South Africa, Mainland China to Hong Kong and Macau. See Cossy, 2005a; Hildering, 2005; Little, 1996;Baumann, 2001 .

64. Brown-Weiss, 2005 .

65. Chapter 18, para. 18.8 alludes to water as a social and economic good, namely when it states that "integrated water resources management is based on the perception of water as an integral part of the ecosystem, a natural resource and a social and economic good".

66. Principle 4 of the Dublin Statement on Water and Sustainable Development states that "water has an economic value in all its competing uses and should be recognized as an economic good". On this, see Solanes, 1998.

67. See Cossy, 2005a.

68. See, in particular, Brown-Weiss, 2005; Cossy, 2005c; Tuerk, Ostrovsky, &, Speed, 2005; Boisson de Chazournes, 2015.

69. See the whole Chapter IV of Brown-Weiss, 2005; Boisson de Chazournes, Fresh Water in International Law, pp. 96-104; Bray, 2014.

70. This has to do with the fact that GATT applies to goods, a concept which is not defined but which seems to relate to a moveable thing which may be traded on a market.

71. Again this is an undefined operational concept determining the application of the GATT disciplines. It implies that something is produced as a result of a natural process or human operation, human intervention. Another element of the definition is the one of the attribution of a price. See Haan, 1997; Cossy, 2005b.

72. In a 2000 report on the Protection of Waters of the Great Lakes, the International Joint Commission between Canada and the United States stated expressly the view that water in its natural state is not a product or commodity. IJC, Final Report to the Government of Canada and the United States, Protection of the Waters of the Great Lakes, 2000. This view was reiterated in the 2004 report, where the International Joint Commission recommended that "both governments take steps to allay fears that Great Lakes water could be treated as a commodity" and again insisted on the idea that WTO rules do not affect the protection of water in its natural state. IJC, Review of the Recommendations in the February 2000 Report, Protection of the Waters of the Great Lakes, 2004.

73. The condition of natural resource and the fact that so many social expectations are attached thereto are considerable elements in such debate. As the WTO concluded in the World Trade Report 2010 on trade in natural resources, "WTO rules were not specifically drafted to regulate natural resources trade and may not always respond adequately to the specific features of this sector". WTO, World Trade Report: Trade in Natural Resources, p. 203.

74. The debate is particularly intense in regard to Canada. It explicitly involves the questioning whether the trade regimes of the WTO and in special the North American Free Trade Agreement (NAFTA) deny the right to limit water exports in respect of other members of the NAFTA and instead require the "water-rich State" to export its water as a tradable good, despite the risk that this poses to this State's control over the management and preservation of the water resources. SeeBaumann, 2001; Maravilla, 2001; Anderson, 1999 .

75. Canada, the United States and Mexico have expressly addressed the issue of the application of NAFTA to water, in 1993, by making a joint statement which reads: "The NAFTA creates no rights to the natural resources of any Party to the Agreement (...). Water in its natural state in lakes, rivers, reservoirs, aquifers, water basins and the like is not a good or product, is not traded, and therefore is not and has never been subject to the terms of any agreement".

Reprinted in Brown-Weiss, Boisson de Chazournes, & Bernasconi-Osterwalder (eds.), 2005 . On its one side, Canada insisted that water in the natural state should be excluded from the application of trade agreements, by having the Ministry of Foreign Affairs and International Trade, unilaterally declare that: "Water in its natural state can be equated with other natural resources, such as trees in the forest, fish in the sea, or minerals in the ground. While all of these things can be transformed into saleable commodities through harvesting or extraction, until that crucial step is taken they remain natural resources and outside the scope of the trade agreements". Department of Foreign Affairs and International Trade, "Paper on Bulk Water Removal and International Trade Considerations".

76. Brown-Weiss calls a particular attention to the interplay of this approach and the uncertain long-term effects of climate change. See Brown-Weiss, 2005 .

77. Particularly at stake seem to be articles I (a water-exporting State would have to extend its "benefits" to any other State, so as not to violate the principle of most-favoured-nation treatment); III (a State that would be engaged in transfers, concerning water within its borders, would have to treat national and foreign competitors alike, for the national treatment principle); XI (although the rules on measures of export tariffs are less detailed than those on exports, its paragraph 2, in particular, seems to allow State water exporters to establish prohibitions or restrictions on transfers of bulk water "to prevent or relieve critical shortages or foodstuffs or other products essential to the exporting contracting party", such as droughts, effects of industrial accidents, natural disasters or other emergencies, these measures have to be temporary and only to prevent a critical situation); XX (setting the conditions for allowing States to implement national measures which, under certain conditions, are inconsistent with other provisions of GATT).

78. In what concerns freshwater, the two openings or exceptions that seem to be relevant are those contained in sub-headings (b) and (g). Under the former, a State may maintain a measure otherwise inconsistent with other GATT provisions if that measure may be taken as "necessary to protect human, animal or plant life or health". In view of some case law concerning disputes before the Dispute Settlement Body of the WTO, it does not seem crucial that these actually versed on import restrictions on products—it seems possible for a State to argue for taking measures to restrict the export of water for environmental purposes and to protect the ecosystem of water resources: the State would thereby be seeking to protect human health and the preservation of flora and fauna.

Additionally, to determine that a measure is "necessary" to achieve a specific goal, recourse must be made to the WTO case law: it indicates that the term "necessary" is not limited to meaning "indispensable" but also encompasses "promote". Moreover, it equally implies that the "common interests" and "shared values" pursued by the measure must also be taken into account. The protection and conservation of water seem to be a good example of such vital common interests. Under the latter, a State may adopt measures "relating to the conservation of exhaustible natural resources if such measures are made effective in conjunction with restrictions on domestic production or consumption". Since WTO case law indicates that "renewable" resources may fall under the concept of "exhaustible natural resource", there would not be a problem, it seems, in applying the notion and the provision under article XX (g) to water. For a measure adopted by a State to be justified under Article XX, it is still necessary to meet the requirements of the "chapeau" of this provision. In particular, domestic measures must not constitute "a means of arbitrary or unjustifiable discrimination between countries where the same conditions prevail, or a disguised restriction on international trade". At stake, in the very clarification made by WTO case law, is "rather the manner in which the measure is applied" (US-Gasoline, Report of the Appellate Body, para. 22. On Article XX's "chapeau", see Gaines, 2001 .

79. It would appear that disputes about the allocation and use of water, as well as about the legitimacy to protect ecosystems and the ecology would be made by bodies more prepared for and attuned to trade considerations. Discussing this issue as other "reasons not to apply the GATT 1994 to water in its natural state or to bulk transfers", see Brown-Weiss, "Water Transfers and International Trade Law", in Brown-Weiss, 2005 .

80. Like the harmonized system of GATT relating to products, there is a classification list of services set by the WTO Secretariat, which is not mandatory but used by States to develop schedules of commitments in the liberalisation of markets. It does not contain any separate category for services related to water, but some of the sectors considered do contain references to activities related to water, like environmental services and sanitation, for instance.

81. The question is whether it is possible to argue that these water services fall under the provision of article I:3(b) which establishes that "services supplied in the exercise of governmental authority" are excluded from the scope of the GATS. These are defined as being supplied "neither on a commercial basis, nor in competition

with one or more suppliers". The thorny issue is the determination of the relationship between "public service" and "governmental authority": they can certainly not be interpreted as synonymous. It might equally be possible to argue that services of water distribution stand as a public monopoly. In such case, GATS would apply.

82. Cossy, 2005a .

83. Cossy, 2005b .

84. GATS does not mention privatization or demand that the water services suppliers are public or private—article XXVIII does not indicate any preference.

85. Namely, in the Aguas del Tunari v Bolivia ICSID Case No. ARB/02/3, in the Suez, Sociedad General de Aguas de Barcelona SA and Vivendi Universal SA v Argentine Republic ICSID Case No ARB/03/19, in the Biwater Gauff (Tanzania) Ltd v United Republic of Tanzania ICSID Case No ARB/05/22, and in the Azurix Corp v Argentine Republic, ICSID Case No ARB/01/12.

86. Bray, 2014 .

REFERENCES

1. Albuquerque, C. (2010). Water and Sanitation as Human Rights. In Conseil d'Etat, L'eau et son droit, Rapport publique. Paris: Conseil d'état.
2. Albuquerque, C. (2012). On the Right Track: Good Practices in Realising the Rights to Water and Sanitation. New York: The United Nations.
3. Albuquerque, C. (2013). Water and Sanitation Are Human Rights: Why Does It Matter? In L. Boisson de Chazournes, C. Leb, & M. Tignino, (Eds.). International Law and Freshwater: The Multiple Challenges. Cheltenham: Edward Elgar.http://dx.doi.org/10.4337/9781781005095.00013
4. Anderson, B. D. (1999). Selling Great Lakes Water to a Thirsty World: Legal, Policy and Trade Considerations. Buffalo Environmental Law Journal, 6, 219-220.
5. Anderson, T. L. Eds. (1994). Continental Water Marketing. San Francisco: Pacific Research Institute for Public Policy.

6. Baumann, C. (2001). Water Wars: Canada's Upstream Battle to Ban Bulk Water Export. Minnesota Journal of Global Trade, 10.

7. Blociszewski, J. (1926). Le régime international du Danube. Recueil des Cours de l'Académie de La Haye, 11, 253-340. http://dx.doi.org/10.1163/ej.9789028604827.253-340

8. Bogdanovic, S. (2001). International Law of Water Resources: Contribution of the ILA (1954-2000). London: Kluwer.

9. Boisson de Chazournes, L. (2003). The Role of Diplomatic Means of Solving Water Disputes: A Special Emphasis on Institutional Mechanisms. In The PCA/Peace Palace Papers. Resolution of International Water Disputes (Vol. 5, pp. 91-110). The Hague: Kluwer.

10. Boisson de Chazournes, L. (2007). Precaution in International Law: Reflection on its Composite Nature. In T. M. Ndlaye et al. (Eds.). Law of the Sea, Environmental Law and Settlement of Disputes: Liber Amicorum Judge Thomas A. Mensah (pp. 21-34). Leiden: M. Nijhoff. http://dx.doi.org/10.1163/ej.9789004161566.i-0.22

11. Boisson de Chazournes, L. (2007). Technical and Financial Assistance. In D. Bodansky, J. Brunnée, & E. Hey (Eds.), The Oxford Handbook of International Environmental Law (pp. 947-973). Oxford: Oxford University Press.

12. Boisson de Chazournes, L. (2009). Freshwater and International Law: The Interplay between Universal, Regional and Basin Perspectives. Paris: UNESCO, United Nations World Water Assessment Programme.

13. Boisson de Chazournes, L. (2015). Fresh Water in International Law. Oxford: Oxford University Press.

14. Bray, H. L. (2014). ICSID and the Right to Water: An Ingredient in the Stone Soup. ICSID Review, 1-10.

15. Brown-Weiss, E. (2005). Water Transfers and International Trade Law. In E. Brown-Weiss, L. Boisson de Chazournes, & N. Bernasconi-Osterwalder (Eds.), Fresh Water and International Economic Law (pp. 61-89). Oxford: Oxford University Press.

16. Brown-Weiss, E. (2007). The Evolution of International Water Law. Recueil des cours de l'académie de Droit international, 331, 222.

17. Brown-Weiss, E. (2013). International Law in a Water Scarce World. The Hague Academy of International Monographs, Volume 7, Leiden: Brill.

18. Brown-Weiss, E., Boisson de Chazournes, L., & Bernasconi-Osterwalder, N. (Eds.) (2005). Fresh Water and International Economic Law. Oxford: Oxford University Press.

19. Caflisch, L. (1993). Sic utere tuo ut alienum non laedas: Règle prioritaire ou élément servant à mesurer le droit de participation équitable et raisonnable à l'utilisation d'un coursd'eau international? In A. Ziegler (Ed.), Internationales Recht auf See und Binnengewaesser. Festschrift fuer Walter Mueller (pp. 27-47). Zuerich: Schulthess.

20. Caflisch, L. (2011). Le droit à l'eau—Un droit de l'homme internationalement protégé. In Société francaise pour le droit international, Colloque d'Orléans. L'eau en droit international (pp. 392-394). Paris: Pédone.

21. Caflisch. L. (1989). Règles générales du droit des cours d'eau internationaux. Recueil des Cours de l'Académie de La Haye, 219, 196-202. http://dx.doi.org/10.1163/ej.9780792321408.009-225

22. Canelas de Castro, P. (2003). Freshwaters-Sea Interface: Emerging International Legal Field? Boletim da Faculdade de Direito da Universidade de Macau, 16, 179-220.

23. Canelas de Castro, P. (2005). Recent Developments in International Law. Principles and Comparative Cases. Lisbon: Luso-American Foundation.

24. Canelas de Castro, P. (2008). The Global Challenge of Sustainable Water Management: International and European Union Law Responses. Temas de Integracao, 25, 95-133.

25. Canelas de Castro, P. (2011). Climate Change and Water Management: Is Water Law Adapted to Climate Change? In C. A. Brebbia, & V. Popov (Eds.), Water Resources Management VI (pp. 827-839). Southampton: WIT Press. http://dx.doi.org/10.2495/WRM110741

26. Caponera, D. (1992). Principles of Water Law and Administration. Rotterdam: A. A. Balkema.

27. Carter, H. O. (Ed.) (1994). Sharing Scarcity: Gainers and Losers in Water Marketing. Davis: University of California Agric. Issue Center.

28. Chamberlain, J. P. (1923). The Regime of the International River: Danube and Rhine. New York: Columbia University.

29. Colliard, C. A. (1968). Evolution et aspects actuels du régime juridique des fleuves internationaux. Recueil des Cours de

l'Académie de La Haye, 125, 417-431. http://dx.doi.org/10.1163/ej.9789028616226.337-442

30. Cossy, M. (2005a). Le statut de l'eau en droit international économique. Principaux aspects au regard des règles de l'Organisation mondiale du commerce, In L. Boisson de Chazournes, & S. M. A. Salman (Eds.), Les ressources en eau et le droit international (pp. 177-178). Leiden: Martinus Nijhoff.

31. Cossy, M. (2005b). Water Services and the GATS—Selected Legal Issues. In E. Brown-Weiss, L. Boisson de Chazournes, & N. Bernasconi-Osterwalder (Eds.), Fresh Water and International Economic Law (pp. 129). Oxford: Oxford University Press.

32. Cossy, M. (2005c). Water Services at the WTO—Selected Legal Issues. In E. Brown-Weiss, L. Boisson de Chazournes, & N. Bernasconi-Osterwalder (Eds.), Fresh Water and International Economic Law (pp. 117-141). Oxford: Oxford University Press.

33. Coulée, F. (2011). Rapport général—Du droit international de l'eau à la reconnaissance internationale d'un droit à l'eau: Les enjeux. In Société francaise pour le droit international, Colloque d'Orléans. L'eau en droit international (pp. 27-31). Paris: Pédone.

34. Dalhuisen, J. M., Groot, H. L. F., & Nijkamp, P. (2000). The Economics of Water: A Survey. International Journal of Development Planning Literature, 15, 4.

35. Franck, T. (1995). Fairness in International Law and Institutions. Oxford: Clarendon Press.

36. Gaines, S. (2001). The WTO's Reading of the GATT Article XX Chapeau: A Disguised Restriction on Environmental Measures. Journal of International Economic Law (University of Pacific), 22, 739.

37. Haan, E. (1997). Balancing Free Trade in Water and the Protection of Water Resources in GATT. In E. P. Brans et al. (Eds.), The Scarcity of Water—Emerging Legal and Policy Responses (pp. 246-247). The Hague: Kluwer.

38. Hildering, A. (2005). Water as an Economic Good. In L. Boisson de Chazournes, & S. M. A. Salman (Eds.), Les ressources en eau et le droit international (pp. 225-227). Leiden: Martinus Nijhoff. http://dx.doi.org/10.1163/ej.9789004137028.3-756.6

39. Kamto, M. (1990). Le droit international des ressources en eau continentales africaines. Annuaire francais de droit international, 36, 855-871.

40. Kiss, A. (1987). Tchernobale ou la pollution accidentelle du Rhin par des produits chimiques. Annuaire francais de droit international, 33, 719-727. http://dx.doi.org/10.3406/afdi.1987.2804

41. Kuhn, T. S. (1962). The Structure of Scientific Revolutions. Chicago: University of Chicago Press.

42. Libecap, G. D. (2005). Rescuing Water Markets: Lessons from Owens Valley. Bozeman: PERC.

43. Little, S. P. (1996). Canada's Capacity to Control the Flow: Water Export and the North American Free Trade Agreement. Pace International Law Review, 8, 127.

44. Manner, E., & Metsalampi, V. M. (Eds.) (1988). The Work of the International Law Association on the Law of International Water Resources. Helsinki: Finnish Branch of the International Law Association.

45. Maravilla, S. (2001). The Canadian Bulk Water Moratorium and Its Implications for NAFTA. Current International Trade Law Journal, 10, 31-35.

46. Martin, G. J. (1998). Le concept de risque et la protection de l'environnement: Evolution parallèle ou fertilization croisée? In M. Prieur (Ed.), Les hommes et l'environnement, en hommage à Alexandre Kiss (pp. 451-460). Paris: Frison-Roche.

47. McAllister, S. T. (1998). The Convention on Access to Information, Public Participation in Decision-Making, and Access to Justice in Environmental Matters. Colorado Journal of International Environmental Law and Policy, 9, 187.

48. McCaffrey, S. (2007). The Law of International Watercourses—Non-Navigational Uses (2nd ed.). Oxford: Oxford University Press.

49. McCaffrey, S. (2009). The International Law Commission Adopts Draft Articles on Transboundary Aquifers. American Journal of International Law, 103, 272. http://dx.doi.org/10.2307/20535150

50. Mechlem, K. (2009). Moving Ahead in Protecting Freshwater Resources: The International Law Commission's Draft Articles on Transboundary Aquifers. Leiden Journal of International Law, 22, 801. http://dx.doi.org/10.1017/S0922156509990239

51. Mekong River Commission for Sustainable Development (2005). Public Participation in the Lower Mekong Basin. Vientiane: Mekong River Commission for Sustainable Development.

52. Paquerot, S. (2005). Eau douce: La nécéssaire refondation du droit international. Sainte-Foy (Québec): Presses de l'Université du Québec.

53. Salman, S. M. A. (2005). Evolution and Context of International Water Resources Law. In S. M. A. Salman, & L. Boisson de Chazournes (Eds.), Les ressources en eau et le droit international (pp. 66-68). The Hague: Hague Academy of International Law. http://dx.doi.org/10.1163/ej.9789004137028.3-756.2

54. Salman, S. M. A., & Lankford, S. M. (2004). The Human Right to Water. Legal and Policy Dimensions. Washington DC: The World Bank. http://dx.doi.org/10.1596/0-8213-5922-3

55. Sand, P. H. (2003). Information Disclosure as an Instrument of Environmental Governance. Heidelberg Journal of International Law, 2, 487-502.

56. Sohnle, J. (2002). Le droit international des ressources en eau douce: Solidarité contre souveraineté. Paris: La documenta- tion francaise.

57. Solanes, M. (1998). Integrated Water Management from the Perspective of the Dublin Principles. CEPAL Review, 64, 165.

58. Tanzi, A., & Arcari, M. (2001). The United Nations Convention on the Law of International Watercourses: A Framework for Sharing. The Hague: Kluwer.

59. Tuerk, E., Ostrovsky, A., & Speed, R. (2005). GATS and Its Impact on Private Sector Participation in Water Services. In E. Brown-Weiss, L. Boisson de Chazournes, & N. Bernasconi-Osterwalder (Eds.), Fresh Water and International Economic Law (pp. 143-172). Oxford: Oxford University Press.

60. United Nations Economic Commission for Europe (2000). The Aarhus Convention: An Implementation Guide. New York: United Nations.

61. WHO and UNICEF (2010). Progress on Sanitation and Drinking Water: 2010 Update. Geneva: WHO and UNICEF.

62. Ziegler, A. (Ed.) (1993). Internationales Recht auf See und Binnengewaesser. Festschrift fuer Walter Mueller. Zuerich: Schulthess.

5

CHAPTER

The "Syria Traveller": Reintegration or Legal Sanctioning?

Katrine Fangen[a], Åshild Kolås[b]

[a] *Department of Sociology and Human Geography, University of Oslo, Oslo, Norway;*

[b] *Dimensions of Security, Peace Research Institute Oslo (PRIO), Oslo, Norway*

ABSTRACT

This article analyses discourses on Islamist radicalisation and threats of terrorism in Norway, with a focus on a new category of people known as "Syria travellers", i.e. young Norwegians who go to Syria to fight for the Islamic State. Our analysis of debates in the media, policy documents and parliamentary discussions revealed two main narratives regarding the authorities' response to Syria travellers: the first emphasises legal sanctions, and the second highlights the reintegration of returnees. We found that contentions about how to react to the new kind of people (the Syria travellers) are intertwined with the way these people are portrayed, understood or "made up". In the political realm, there is also a striking consensus on the need for both reintegrative and legislative responses.

Keywords: Foreign fighters, Syria, Islamic State, radicalisation, citizenship, Norway

INTRODUCTION

In Norway, the threat of terrorism was made painfully clear on 22 July 2011, with the horrific mass shooting at a Labour Party youth camp and concurrent bombing of the government complex in Oslo. Within a few years, however, the so-called "lone wolf" threat scenario and apprehensions about right-wing radicalisation were overshadowed by concerns about terrorism perpetrated by "Syria travellers", in other words, Norwegian foreign fighters recruited by Islamic State (IS) who might return with an aim to carry out terrorist attacks in Norway. The new threat was brought home to residents of Oslo in July 2014, when a terror alert warned of an imminent attack by foreign fighters returning from Syria. Authorities reportedly suspected an attack to coincide with the Eid celebration marking the end of the holy month of Ramadan. The alert was followed by days of heightened security, with an unprecedented number of armed security forces patrolling the streets of Oslo. The new threat perception has more recently been fuelled by media reports on the stories of the alleged perpetrators of terrorism in Paris and Brussels.

This article analyses contemporary discourse on radicalisation and the threat of terrorism in Norway, with a focus on the construction of a new category of people known as "Syria travellers", a term used to describe Norwegians who have travelled to Syria to fight for IS (aka ISIS). Our key concern is not to study Islamist or jihadist[1]radicalisation as such, but to investigate how Syria travellers are "made up" (Hacking 1986, 2006) in the particular context of Norway, a European country with a liberal democratic political culture and a deeply rooted welfare state model. We describe and analyse how such individuals are referred to by academics, journalists, politicians and bureaucrats (Wodak 2008, 302). We focus especially on how Norwegian elites refer to this category of people, and the measures they propose to deal with them. How people of power represent potential terrorists has important implications, not least for policymaking to counter radicalisation and address threats to public safety. Ultimately, it also affects the precarious balance between protection of civil liberties and counterterrorism. In our analysis of various types of textual data, we are thus interested in negotiations around issues such as whether or not Syria travellers represent a security threat, which measures are being proposed to deal with them, and how these measures are linked to the ways in which Syria travellers are described, or "made up".

An analysis of our data has revealed that there are (at least) two master narratives at work in the construction of the Syria traveller. One highlights the perceived differences between Syria travellers and the majority of Norwegians, and sees them as Muslim youth at odds with or voluntarily "outside" mainstream society. Proponents of this view draw on generalisations about the illiberal nature of Islam and the need to manage perceived cultural clashes. The other narrative views Syria travellers as young people who have grown up in Norway and become victims of exclusion, due to either socio-economic marginalisation or anti-Muslim prejudice among "ethnic Norwegians". In this view, we find an emphasis on the diverse backgrounds of Syria travellers and the fact that some of them are themselves "ethnically Norwegian", although they have converted to Islam as teenagers or young adults. These two narratives influence discussions about how to react to returning Syria travellers, how to prevent IS from mobilising in Norway and how to stop those who have been mobilised from leaving Norway to fight in Syria. According to one perspective, Syria travellers should be punished for their crimes and possibly deprived of their Norwegian citizenship, whereas the other narrative would stress the need to help those who return to reintegrate into society and deal with the trauma they have likely experienced.

THE LINK BETWEEN POLICY INTERVENTIONS AND RESEARCH

Since the turn of the century, a growing academic literature has emerged on the topic of Islamist radicalisation in general, and the Islamist or jihadist foreign fighter in particular (see, for example, Hegghammer 2010; Li 2010; Malet 2010; Borum 2011; Flyghed and Magnus 2012; Bakker, Paulussen, and Entenmann 2013; Al-Hashimi and Goerzig 2015). There is often a close link between research in this area and policy initiatives for countering radicalisation. After 11 September 2001, policymakers justified the Global War on Terror (GWOT) by portraying the Islamic brand of extremism as the greatest threat to Western liberal democracies (cf. Huntington 1993). A new political discourse emerged in which American, Australian and European Muslims were portrayed as the new "enemy within" or a "suspect community" (Pantazis and Pemberton 2009, 646). Meanwhile, much of the research on radicalisation turned its focus towards Muslims and Islamisation (Rahimullah, Larmar, and Abdalla 2013), with important implications for policymaking to counter radicalisation. As described by Heath-Kelly (2013), for instance, British research on "vulnerability indicators" for radicalisation has led to interventions in communities that are rendered suspicious, despite the fact that only a small minority are in danger of becoming radicalised.

Similarly, Li (2010, 356) criticises GWOT-driven interventions aiming to "separate foreign Muslim fighters – typically portrayed as Arab, rootless, fanatical, and brutal – from local Muslims whose potential for moderation must be nourished whenever possible". Li is sceptical of the identification of a section of enemy fighters as "foreign", and sees interventions such as extraordinary rendition, "black site" prisons and Guantánamo as the result of targeting "Muslims who are outside of their home countries". By equating the rootless and fanatical with the "foreign" Muslim, the threat of terrorism from groups such as al-Qa'ida or IS can "be used to justify any number of extraordinary measures, including human rights abuses and impunity for them" (Li 2010). Li here highlights the potential consequences of labelling and "making up" kinds of people as sources of insecurity, namely, the claim that the protection of society at large has to be prioritised over the rights of certain threatening individuals. As we will show, policymakers in Norway have raised similar arguments about Norwegian foreign fighters returning from (or preparing to join) the Syria conflict.

METHODOLOGY AND ANALYTICAL FRAMEWORK

The focus of this article is on the Norwegian debate on Syria travellers, particularly how they are described, the potential threat they represent and what measures are required to ameliorate this threat or otherwise deal with Norwegian returnees from the war in Syria. Our analysis is informed by Ian Hacking's (1986, 228–231) theorisation of how "kinds" of people "come into being" at the same time as the "kind itself" is invented, and that "if new models of description come into being, new possibilities for action come into being in consequence". We refer to Syria travellers as a "new" subject category because until 2011, the specific category of "people travelling to Syria to fight for the Islamic State" did not exist. We are of course aware that the category of "foreign fighters" existed, and that people also travelled to Syria before 2011. However, the combination of "foreign fighters" and "people joining IS" is, we argue, an entirely new category of people.

Hacking (2006, 10–12) describes seven "engines of discovery", namely, counting, quantifying, creating norms, correlating, medicalising, biologising and geneticising, that drive how people are made up within the human sciences. Hacking further identifies three engines at work outside of the scientific realm which also produce knowledge that makes up people. These are normalising (as an engine of organisation and control), bureaucratising (as an engine of administration) and resistance (by those who are "made up" or others speaking on their behalf). Our focus in this article is on the most basic engines of social scientific knowledge production (namely, counting and quantifying), as well as the engines at work outside the scientific realm (normalising, and bureaucratising). As will be discussed, however, it is often difficult to distinguish between knowledge production within and outside academia, as the line between them is porous.[2]

Document analysis for this study was carried out on data gathered for the NATION project.[3]The data comprised opinion pieces in Norwegian newspapers, minutes of parliamentary debates, interviews with bureaucrats and key policy documents. The parliamentary debates analysed here cover discussions about how to deal with Norwegians travelling to Syria to fight for IS, and are all from the current government's term of office (i.e. since September 2013).[4]We also analyse the main policy document related to this topic, namely, the Action Plan against Radicalisation and Violent Extremism (Norwegian Ministry of Justice and Public Security 2014). In addition, we draw on a subset of the NATION media dataset,[5]comprising 375 items based on various searches in the larger dataset, coded with the help of Nvivo™.

Our work on the media dataset confirms our assumption that the Syria traveller is a new kind of person in Norway. A text search with the keywords "radicalisation" or "extremism" in this dataset of opinion pieces gave the following results: 221 items in 2011, 192 items in 2012, 153 items in 2013 and 300 items in 2014. This indicates a continuous interest in radicalisation and extremism over the past years, with a significant increase in newspaper opinion pieces on these topics in 2014. However, when searching with the specific keyword "Syria traveller", we found 10 items using this term in 2014 and none in the preceding three years. A search with the keywords "foreign fighter" yielded the following results: none in 2011 and 2013, one in 2012 and 51 in 2014. About half of the items including the term "Syria traveller" were duplicated in this search. Another search was performed to include opinion pieces that focused on persons going to Syria, but without using the terms "Syria traveller" or "foreign fighter". The search words for this were "going to" and "Syria", in combination with either "radicalisation" or "extremism". This resulted in 303 newspaper articles. Based on these searches, we put together a subset comprising 375 items in total. The subset included 37 items published in 2011, 69 in 2012, 47 in 2013 and 223 in 2014. This suggests a sharp increase in references to persons travelling to Syria in newspaper opinion pieces in 2014.

HOW ACADEMIA "MAKES UP" FOREIGN FIGHTERS AND SYRIA TRAVELLERS

The scope of this article does not allow us to go through all the different strands of literature on relevant topics such as radicalisation or foreign fighters in Syria. We will nevertheless give a brief overview of how academia makes up (in the sense of defining and operationalising) the subjects in question. Here, we treat the academic definitions as data, in the sense that they can be seen as part of the making up of the category itself.

Defining

An oft-cited operationalisation of the concept "foreign fighter" is that given by Thomas Hegghammer (2010, 57–58), who describes him (or her) as an agent who (1) has joined and operates within the confines of an insurgency; (2) lacks citizenship of the conflict state or kinship links to its warring factions; (3) lacks affiliation to an official military organisation and (4) is unpaid. The last criterion suggests that joining a conflict in another country is not economically motivated. This is partly countered by Desai (2014) who claims that "some groups, like the Jabhat Al-Nusra and ISIS, provide modest stipends for their members". According to Hegghammer, however, the motivations of a foreign fighter are primarily nonmaterial, such as an idea of (expanded) nationhood, or other beliefs or ideologies. Rich and Conduit (2015) further distinguish between Sunni and Shi'a fighters, arguing that they are too different to be treated as a uniform group.

The term "radicalisation" is a broad concept, and there is an academic debate on how to define it, though it is commonly viewed as a "process of gradually subscribing to a violent ideology espousing terrorism" (Rahimullah, Larmar, and Abdalla 2013). A problem with this definition, which often spills over into counterterrorism policy, is that it builds on the assumption that there is a clear link between "extreme" attitudes and behaviour. By contrast, Tore Bjørgo and John Horgan (2009, 3–5) suggest a conceptual distinction between radicalisation and de-radicalisation on the one hand, and engagement and disengagement on the other. The latter describes changes in behaviour, for example, taking part in violent activities. Their definition is based on the belief that there is a loose connection, but no determination, between attitudinal and behavioural change.

Counting and quantifying

As described by Hacking (2006, 10), counting is an important engine of discovery of new categories of people. As for the Norwegian Syria traveller, after the 2011 outbreak of civil war in Syria, Norwegian authorities quickly started counting the number of people who travelled to Syria to take part in the war (see, for instance, Norwegian Police Security Service 2015). Researchers have subsequently used these figures to quantify the problem of jihadist radicalisation, particularly IS mobilisation. In addition to data from the Norwegian security service, another commonly used source of quantitative information is the International Centre for the Study of Radicalisation and Political Violence. According to their latest estimate, as many as 20,000 people worldwide have joined Sunni militant organisations involved in the Syria/Iraq conflict, of which nearly a fifth (4000) are residents or nationals of western European countries (Neumann 2015).

There is some disagreement regarding the number of individuals from Norway who have joined the war. According to some estimates, about 60 are from Norway, comprising approximately 12 per million inhabitants (Neumann 2015). This means that relative to population size, Norway is in the medium range: neither among the most heavily affected (for example, Belgium, Denmark, and Sweden, with up to 40, 27, and 19 per million respectively), nor among the least affected (for example, Italy, Spain, and Switzerland, with 1.5, 2, and 5 per million). The annual threat assessment by the Norwegian Police Security Service (PST) provides slightly higher figures, stating that more than 70 Norwegians have travelled to Syria to take part in the conflict (2015, 6). At least 10 of these have been killed in combat in Syria, while 20 have returned to Norway after having been involved in warlike actions in Syria. PST (7) maintains that the number of Norwegian foreign fighters in Syria is "among the highest in Europe", considering the size of the Norwegian population. In other words, although there is not much numerical discrepancy (60 vs. more than 70), it seems that Norwegian authorities perceive the threat to be comparatively more severe in Norway than in other European countries.

NORMALISATION: SITUATING SYRIA TRAVELLERS IN SPACE AND TIME

The making of Syria travellers coincides with the emergence in Syria of "the phenomenon of mujahidin foreign fighters ... after non-violent protest in March 2011 turned into a full-blown civil war" (Bakker, Paulussen, and Entenmann 2013, 2). This does not mean that no one went as a militant to Syria from Western countries before 2011. Rather, it means that the distinct meaning of a Syria traveller associated with Islamic radicalisation was non-existent in international discourse. As Hacking (2006, 11–12) points out, academic knowledge production in the form of counting and quantifying is invariably accompanied by knowledge production outside the sciences, seeking to make sense of the new "kind of person". One engine of discovery is normalisation, which requires situating the new "being" in space and time. Normalisation can also be a way "to make unfavourable deviants as close to normal as possible" (Hacking 1986).

Many of the Norwegians who have thus far travelled to Syria have their origins in Fredrikstad, a small town in eastern Norway, where they have grown up in what media has described as a multiethnic environment (see also Higgins 2015). This type of media coverage is also an example of Hacking's normalisation engine, since it highlights the fact that these individuals are Norwegian (just like us) and portrays "who they are" in the familiar terms of the social environment, especially close relations within the family, among circles of friends and other people in the neighbourhood. On the other hand, such cases can be seen as a variant of the "enemy within" narrative, suggesting that "evil is in our own neighbourhood, and you can never feel completely safe".

Another way of normalising is to compare the Syria travellers with foreign fighters known from history, who fought in other wars where they were not seen as terrorists or potential threats once they returned. Historical examples are numerous, though a common point of reference is the story of the socialists, anarchists and communists who joined international brigades in the Spanish Civil War (cf. Malet 2010). Similarly, as described by one of the bureaucrats, we interviewed on the Action Plan against Radicalisation and Violent Extremism:

During the work with the Action Plan, some have pointed out that we have seen this phenomenon earlier in history as well. As in the Civil War in Spain or the Winter War in Finland, people went to support different parties of the conflict back then as well.[6]

It is worth noting that participation in both the Spanish Civil War and the Finnish Winter War is commonly perceived as legitimate, if not commendable. Moreover, none of these foreign fighters have been associated in any way with terrorism. When foreign fighters in Syria are compared with foreign fighters in the Spanish Civil War, we see a clear example of normalisation.

Politicians draw on historical parallels to the Syria traveller phenomenon, both in parliamentary debates and in public documents, including the Action Plan against Radicalisation and Violent Extremism. Historical comparisons can be used as a way to normalise but also to highlight "foreignness". We see examples of both in the Norwegian debate, which we will return to later in this article.

BUREAUCRATISATION: DEALING WITH RADICALISATION

Modifying Hacking's (2006, 12) notion of bureaucratisation for our purposes would imply investigating how the bureaucracy defines the kind of person in question (in this case, foreign fighters in the context of the Syria conflict) and analysing governmental plans to deal with this kind of person (in other words, plans to prevent individuals from becoming foreign fighters and deal with their possible return). In Norway, the key policy document that describes these efforts is the 2014 Action Plan against Radicalisation and Violent Extremism (Norwegian Ministry of Justice and Public Security 2014), hereafter, the "Action Plan". In this section, we analyse the Action Plan's main arguments and definitions.

The Action Plan does not mention Syria travellers specifically, and according to our interviews with bureaucrats who took part in writing the Action Plan,[7]this is a conscious decision, since the plan is meant to be applicable more broadly and not only to one specific category of people. Nevertheless, the bureaucrats confirmed that a major concern when writing the plan was to prevent Norwegians from travelling to Syria to become foreign fighters. For the purpose of this article, the most relevant parts of the Action Plan are those that refer specifically to foreign fighters, who are defined as "individuals who have travelled to a conflict zone abroad and participated in hostilities without being part of the regular armed forces" (9). The Action Plan expresses a fear that the experiences of such foreign fighters may increase their violent intentions and give them "a lower threshold for supporting or utilizing violence as an instrument" (2). In short, the plan describes a concern that the experiences of foreign fighters may lead them (or "make it easier for them") to participate in planning and executing terrorist attacks in Norway. The Action Plan explicitly warns that individuals who perceive Norway as an enemy state may represent a threat to Norway and Norwegian interests.

Policymakers often use definitions proposed by researchers, and this is clearly the case with regard to Islamic or jihadist radicalisation. Similar to the previously mentioned definition by Rahimullah, Larmar, and Abdalla (2013), both the Action Plan and the security police (PST 2015) define radicalisation as a process where a person increasingly accepts the use of violence as a means to achieve political goals. The Action Plan further defines violent extremism as "activities of persons or groups who are willing to use violence to achieve their political, ideological or religious goals", while terror is defined as the "ultimate consequence of radicalisation and violent extremism". The plan states that preventive measures are central to safe-guarding fundamental values like democracy, human rights and security, and that "[a] fundamental aspect of a secure society is to be able to live without fear of becoming a target of hatred and violence". The following model illustrates the causal links described in the Action Plan:

Radicalisation → Terror

Preventive measures → Democracy, human rights, and security

A radicalisation process that leads to violent extremism is characterised by the Action Plan as a cognitive development towards an "increasingly biased or one-sided perception of reality" where there is no room for alternative perspectives, and subsequently, a further development in which this perception of reality is experienced as so acute and serious that acts of violence are necessary and just.

Critics have pointed out that a model that simply implies a causal link between radicalisation and terror risks confusing non-violent radicals with "real terrorists" (Bartolucci 2010, 128). As pointed out by Kühle and Lindekilde (2010, 25), the use of the adverb "increasingly" in the definition by Rahimullah, Larmar, and Abdalla (2013) gives the impression of a linear process. Moreover, the definition implies that radicalisation is an individual process, whereas the concept of radicalisation in its original form, as used in the 1980s and 1990s, understands it as a collective process (Kühle and Lindekilde 2010, 25). The problem with an individualised definition is that it obscures the fact that radicalisation often happens collectively in social networks or cults (Kühle and Lindekilde 2010, 96).

The Action Plan identifies two major extremist groups in Norway, both in strong opposition to each other: al-Qaida-inspired extremism, and anti-Islamic right-wing extremism. In the worst case, further polarisation among Norwegian extremists might lead to increased recruitment, radicalisation of existing groups and the emergence of new organisations on both sides. The Action Plan describes key actors in al-Qaida-inspired extremism as young individuals who have grown up in Norway. These individuals propagate hatred and violence against the West, specifically Norway and associated interests and symbols. According to the Action Plan, a violent attack by radical Islamists in Norway might contribute to mobilisation and greater coordination of Norwegian right-wing extremists. This is seen as paving the way for increased sympathy for, and association with, right-wing extremist ideology in the mainstream population. The plan identifies three challenges that make it difficult to prevent and counter radicalisation towards violent extremism. First is the emergence of the Internet and social media as a virtual arena for radicalisation. Second, international affairs have a much greater impact on the threat of radicalisation than earlier. Third, compared to the past, there is now a greater risk of increasing polarisation among different sections of society.

When the plan was launched, Prime Minister Erna Solberg (Conservative Party) stated that "[e]veryone must take their share of responsibility for creating an inclusive society", and pointed to the need for close follow-up to prevent radicalisation within local communities, schools, work places, and by authorities. In the parliamentary session on 14 January 2015, just after the armed attack against the headquarters of *Charlie Hebdo* in Paris, Prime Minister Solberg made another explicit reference to foreign fighters (Norwegian Parliament 2015). Answering a question posed by former Foreign Minister Jonas Gahr Støre (Labour Party) on the need for more stringent border controls, Solberg stated that "[w]e also have to work long-term to prevent the growth of extremism, prevent an increase in exchanges and movements of foreign fighters out of the country, while also managing to reintegrate them and limit the effects of what we have so far seen". Interestingly, Prime Minister Solberg left unstated the details of "what we have so far seen". On the other hand, her emphasis is clearly on the reintegration of foreign fighters when (or if) they return from Syria.

The Action Plan recommends a range of measures to combat radicalisation, such as support for dialogue arenas for young people, efforts to prevent hate speech on the Internet, training for teachers and information through schools, religious dialogue and related preventive measures against radicalisation, and research on radicalisation processes and motivational factors related to radical Islamism and foreign fighters. The stated purpose of the research is to fill a glaring knowledge gap and specifically to learn more about Norwegian foreign fighters who have travelled to Syria, to address concerns about their capacity and intention to use violence after they return to Norway. Other measures related directly to foreign fighters are to alert relevant authorities as soon as a foreign fighter returns to Norway, and to follow up on those who have already returned. Both the statements by the Prime Minister (cited above) and the Action Plan itself point to the need for sanctioning acts of violence, as well as the need for reintegration.

However, in Norway and in other countries, measures to prevent radicalisation have come under attack. In the United Kingdom, the government has since 2008 campaigned against radicalisation in schools, but as critics have pointed out, an estimated 400 British Muslims have joined IS in spite of these preventive measures (D'Souza 2015). Similarly, a wide range of de-radicalisation programmes in countries like Denmark, the Netherlands, Indonesia, Singapore, Malaysia, Saudi Arabia and Yemen have come under criticism for producing meagre or questionable results (D'Souza 2015, see also Rom 2013, Feldstein 2015). Against this backdrop, some countries have recently tried to limit the mobility of new recruits or block the return of foreign fighters. For instance, Malaysia has proposed to invalidate the passports of its citizens who join IS (D'Souza 2015). Australia initially banned its nationals from going to Raqqa, the location of the IS headquarters, and has since passed legislation that allows the government to revoke the Australian citizenship of dual nationals who affiliate with IS. We will discuss similar measures in the next section.

THE LEGAL SANCTIONS NARRATIVE

As argued in Norwegian parliamentary debates, as well as newspaper opinion pieces, some view Syria travellers primarily as criminals who should be met with legal sanctions. According to such a narrative, the problematics related to Syria travellers is above all a security issue and a task for the police. Among the strongest proponents of this view is the journalist Lars Akerhaug, author of two books on Norwegian "Muslim extremists" (Akerhaug 2013, 2015).As Akerhaug states in an op-ed in the tabloid daily newspaper, *Verdens Gang*:

The recruitment of young people growing up in Norway to Syria is an acute problem that cannot be solved solely by prevention. A dozen youths have acquired battle experience and contact with Islamist terror networks. This is an acute threat. Police and authorities need more tools [...] There is a lack of Norwegian research on effective preventive measures. Yet the government has shown a strong belief in the efficacy of such measures, often based on anecdotal examples from work against neo-Nazis and gangs in the 1990s. [...] The Minister of Justice and Public Security, Anders Anundsen [Progress Party], has largely used a single word, namely "prevention", to answer the question about what the government should do with the rise of extremist networks in Norway. The belief that preventive action can combat radicalization of young Muslims rests on the perception that there is a simple causation as regards who and why young people are extremists. [...] Today the PST [Police Security Service] stands watching while youth leave the country on their way to the battlefield. Surprisingly, unlike the previous government, this government has failed to prioritize legislative work. It's amazing that a Conservative-Progress Party coalition government increasingly seems to use words such as "prevention" as a resting pad, while society is faced with a threat. (Akerhaug 2014*)*

The arguments expressed here shed strong doubts about the use of preventive and reintegrative measures, favouring instead hard security and law-and-order measures. In response to this op-ed, Vidar Karlsen Brein (Progress Party), State Secretary of Justice and Public Security, defends his party's position:

To criminalize exiting, which Akerhaug in reality advocates, is probably a bit difficult. Many would travel to Syria via other countries without telling anyone in advance that they intend to go to Syria to fight. Moreover, it is difficult to prove that young people travelling for example to Turkey on the pretext of going for a vacation actually travel there to go ahead and fight in Syria. It is also strange that Akerhaug attempts to ridicule prevention against radicalization. If we succeed in the prevention work, there will be fewer people who pose a future threat to Norwegian interests. Simultaneously we will be tough against those who violate Norwegian law. Projecting prevention as "extreme paralysis" simply suggests a lack of situational awareness. As Akerhaug himself says, there is no prototype of who becomes radicalized. Therefore we need a comprehensive approach to prevention efforts involving parents, schools, municipalities, community child welfare services, and the police. If we focus less on prevention today, we will have to deal with more dangerous people tomorrow. (Karlsen 2014*).*

Interestingly, the State Secretary has no objections to Akerhaug's focus on new legislation in itself, but highlights the practical difficulties in stopping radicalised people from travelling to Syria to join the war. Many parliamentarians, even those representing the right-wing populist Progress Party, have similarly tended to emphasise prevention and reintegration above legislative measures, while most have tried to avoid the "legal sanction" narrative.

In Norway, a scheme to outlaw Syria travellers by withdrawing their citizenship was tabled in mid-2014. In July 2014, a month after the Action Plan's release, a terror alert warned of an imminent attack by foreign fighters returning from Syria. This resulted in several days of visibly heightened security, which directed considerable public attention to the threat of Syria travellers returning as terrorists. The following month, the Ministry of Children, Equality and Social Inclusion launched an evaluation of the feasibility of sanctioning foreign fighters by withdrawing their Norwegian citizenship. Professor Benedikte Moltumyr Høgberg was tasked with a preparatory study for the government, which entailed assessing the specific conditions that might lead to a foreign fighter's loss of Norwegian citizenship, or a "legal change of citizenship". The ministry's press release on the "rules for loss of citizenship" referred specifically to "Norwegian citizens who travel to Syria" and also mentioned "people who wish to participate in acts of terror and warfare". Minister Solveig Horne (Progress Party) emphasised that "no stone can be left unturned" in the search for effective measures against radicalisation and extremism. The press statement clarified that the new rules would apply to situations where a citizen "acts to strongly harm vital interests of the state or has voluntarily served in a foreign military service". Horne further explained the value of Norwegian citizenship: "It offers all rights in Norwegian society; to withdraw [Norwegian citizenship] can thus be a very strong signal" (Norwegian Parliament 2014a).

As a part of our study, we asked several bureaucrats about the logic behind the proposal to revoke the Norwegian citizenship of Syria travellers who return to Norway. In an interview with a bureaucrat from the Ministry of Justice and Public Security, the proposed measure was explained as follows[8]:

I believe that when you participate in a war which is led by someone other than the Norwegian state, then you defend values that we define as non-Norwegian, because they are partly a violation of our laws. And you conduct actions that are illegal. So in that respect, these are in a way nothing that we want to define as Norwegian. We do not want [those values and actions] to be a part of our society. We will sanction them, if this happens. [...] we think that Norwegians agree on what is permissible and acceptable and legal here, and those [values and actions] fall outside.

Interviewer: What do you think about the possible change of law proposed now, about depriving citizenship as a result of having participated in foreign fighting?

I think it may be fair to do that because citizenship is in a way like a mutual contract; you give your loyalty to the state and the state takes responsibility for you. Whereas if you actively and consciously choose another state, then you kind of stand by that choice. Then you must opt out of Norwegian citizenship.

Interviewer: So you think this can be understood as a real measure to counter radicalization and terror? Or is it mostly about giving some signals in relation to national identity?

I think that such a provision might not have a preventive effect, in the way that people would stop going and stop becoming foreign fighters because of the provision. Because I think that when you go to that step and you are so convinced, then it would not play such a big role. Plus, you probably identify yourself so little with the country you have citizenship in, so you might not care about it. But I think that it is not done only to create a signal either, because there's a sanction there. This is in a way to clean up in the aftermath of what happened.

This interviewee clearly emphasised the non-Norwegian identity of the foreign fighters in Syria who have travelled there from Norway. By underlining the importance of loyalty and belonging to the nation as a source of rights to citizenship, loss of citizenship is viewed as natural or given when someone shifts his or her loyalty to another state. However, the above-mentioned excerpt is a bit ambiguous as regards the purpose of revoking Norwegian citizenship, and whether there are punitive as well as preventive grounds for this measure. A similar ambivalence is seen among Norwegian politicians currently in the government, several of whom have supported the revocation of the Norwegian citizenship of returning IS fighters.

The current Norwegian government is a coalition made up of two parties: the more moderate Conservative Party and the right-wing populist Progress Party. They agree on the recent tightening of Norway's Penal Law § 147 on acts of terrorism, but not necessarily on the Act's suitability for preventing participation in war in a foreign country. As described by Michael Tetzschner (Conservative Party), an interpellant in the Norwegian parliament, "the actual security threat lies in the way in which the combat experience of foreign fighters in Syria may affect behaviour or provide weapons knowledge that can later be used in Norway" (Norwegian Parliament 2014b). The question raised is thus whether Penal Law § 147 is still sufficient to counteract the threat of terrorism in an adequate manner, or whether it is necessary to pass legislation that can more effectively prevent "war tourism".

In his reply, Minister of Justice and Public Security, Anders Anundsen (Progress Party), cites the PST's latest annual threat assessment, which concludes that the terror threat against Norway has increased. Anundsen argues that the rise of Syria travellers makes it necessary to re-examine the current legislation to find out whether it is adequate. This work should also assess possible new measures to prevent people from gaining war experience in countries that do not recognise international law. Anundsen agrees with the interpellant that joining the war in Syria potentially implies committing several crimes, such as murder, violent assault, sabotage and acts of terror, which are already illegal. The problem, as Anundsen explains, is to prove which crimes have been committed in another country. Therefore, it is of major concern "to prevent individuals from even going to these conflict areas to fight", Anundsen maintains. On the other hand, the minister also mentions softer preventive measures and reintegration. Here, he points to the Action Plan and the need to follow up on those returning from Syria, as well as information strategies for municipalities where the returning Syria travellers reside.

Despite considerable agreement between the interpellant and the minister on these matters, a key difference is that Tetzschner points to the problem of prohibiting individuals from going to Syria, since the law allows freedom of movement, and this is a right which is important in a free society. Anundsen agrees that this is problematic, also because some people go to Syria to do humanitarian work. He does not give a final conclusion to the issue of prohibiting individuals from going to Syria, but leaves open the question of how and whether this should be done.

THE REINTEGRATION NARRATIVE

The reintegration narrative can be seen as a technique of normalisation, using Hacking's terminology. As the term itself implies, integrative measures are given greater emphasis over legislative measures. This draws on the view that the Syria traveller phenomenon is related to difficulties in immigrants' assimilation and acceptance in their host countries. As described by Bass (2014), "[t]he reasons for ISIS's recruiting successes are likely as varied as the recruits themselves, including youth unemployment and globalization itself. But clearly many European recruits are pushed toward joining ISIS by their failure to be assimilated, accepted, and respected by their adoptive countries".

While politicians (for example, Anundsen) generally draw on both narratives, we see a remarkable degree of consensus on these narratives among the politicians taking part in parliamentary debates. Most of them point to the need for both legal sanctions and integrative measures. The same is true for our interviews with bureaucrats, who all hold quite nuanced views. Nevertheless, we find that most of the bureaucrats and politicians lean somewhat more strongly towards the reintegration narrative. This basically implies that the reason some young people go to Syria is that they have experienced marginalisation, and that returned Syria travellers need to be reintegrated. In this section, we will discuss the perspectives of some of the politicians and bureaucrats that argue more in line with such a narrative. Often, the emphasis on such measures is combined with a normalisation of those who travel to Syria. They may have been affiliated with criminal gangs, but they are not necessarily religious fanatics, as articulated in the following statement by one of the bureaucrats we interviewed[9]:

There are many different motives [for going] – everything from feeling the need to be part of a solution, that is, finding a solution, rescuing people, to more religious motives, which can be totally misunderstood [...]. Then there are also those who have underlined more the excitement. It is interesting too that there are many young men – practically a macho-culture. And you have a lot of access to weapons and can almost live out a video game in real life. What's interesting is that there are many who have a history of other types of criminality [...] since a young age, with youth criminality, youth gangs, established criminal gangs, and now into this field. And this can also support the argument that religion is not the most interesting aspect here; maybe there are other things, since this is like an offer, an offer of pride and belonging.

Many of the statements by politicians and bureaucrats underline the need for legislative measures, but regard integrative measures as somewhat more important. In a parliamentary debate, for example, Jorodd Asphjell (Labour Party) starts by expressing his approval of several of the measures discussed by the current government, and highlights that the previous government, of which he was a part, started revising the laws in order to prevent people from taking part in armed struggle. However, his main concern is that legislative measures are of less use when it comes to the traumas that the returned foreign fighters may have. He appreciates that the current Minister of Justice and Public Security (Anundsen) has a strategy for providing information to municipalities when individuals return, but he would like to know if he has plans for a template for the municipalities on how to deal with these persons. As of now, it is up to the individual municipality to figure out what to do, but this is not a satisfactory solution, he claims. He argues that Denmark has developed a work plan in prevention and follow-up of Syria travellers, where there is close cooperation between the police, the municipalities and groups of parents of the young people going to Syria. This also includes the use of mentors that can serve as positive role models for young people who are on their way to becoming radicalised.

Politicians across the political spectrum share similar views. For instance, Hårek Elvenes (Conservative Party), in the parliamentary debate (2014) cited earlier, calls for reintegrating foreign fighters into Norwegian society, in the labour market, and the education system, and treating them for the psychological scars they may have after experiencing trauma. Elvenes supports the need for role models and agrees to look to the programmes implemented in Denmark, concluding that the police (PST) should not have the main responsibility for reintegration. Elvenes' view is quite similar to that of Snorre Serigstad Valen, who belongs to a party on the opposite side of the political spectrum – the Socialist Left Party. When Valen (in the same debate) explains why young people join the battlefield in Syria, he normalises them by focusing on historical examples similar to that of the present-day Syria travellers. Valen also highlights the normality of youthful behaviour such as being rebellious and adventure-seeking. Valen further advises that people should be strongly warned against joining an extremist movement, stating that

we know there are fundamentalist ideologues who are actively recruiting fighters in Norway. This is dangerous and has to be stopped. In particular, groups like the Prophet's Ummah advocate religious dictatorship, glorify violence, and entice Norwegian youths to a terrible fate.

Valen further describes the foreign fighters as "young people who have so much to give and so much to live for, if they get a little help in choosing a different path". In this way, he points to the more collective aspect of radicalisation processes. Valen recommends acting tough on extremists and causes of extremism, as "we do not have a single Norwegian youth to lose to the ideology of hatred". Nevertheless, he concludes, it is important to remember the individual conditions and experiences of these youths. It is problematic to compartmentalise Syria travellers, and it is not easy to find a "one-size-fits-all solution" for how to treat people who have participated in "grave acts abroad", he states.

In the parliamentary debates we have analysed, the reintegration narrative is quite prominent, and there is little one-sided othering of the Syria travellers. Many politicians point to the diversity of motives for going to Syria, and emphasise that returned Syria travellers must be judged on an individual basis. By contrast, the Norwegian print media gives ample space for critics calling for more government action, as seen in the following editorial in the newspaper *Verdens Gang*:

It is therefore essential that you try to stop the flow of young Norwegians and other Europeans who travel to join the IS. [...] The government needs to speed this up. It does not make sense that we are now sending troops to Iraq, but fail to do enough to stop the Norwegian export of foreign fighters. (Editorial in Verdens Gang 2014*)*

Describing US news coverage of terrorism, Crenshaw (2014) states that "a news cycle that habitually others the attacker and obscures the related political and social issues creates a 'guilty of terror crimes until proven innocent' mindset". In Norwegian media, however, we find little evidence of the "outlaw" mode of othering, and a much greater focus on the radicalised jihadist as what could be called the "boy (or girl) next door". Linked mainly to the reintegration narrative, this portrayal of Syria travellers is relatively common in the media. For instance, the political scientist Kamil Azhar (2013) questions the othering of Syria travellers and the related perception of "threat" in the newspaper *Klassekampen*:

The two girls who are on their way to Syria are not only two Somali girls, rather they are our girls. What if Prime Minister Erna Solberg or Child and Inclusion Minister Solveig Horne had expressed concern for the safety of the young girls and boys, instead of only presenting them as a security threat for Norway when they return home?

A balance between (re)integrative and legislative measures is often emphasised in policymaking against the recruitment of Norwegians as foreign fighters. Many are sceptical of measures intended to stop people from travelling to Syria, such as confiscation of the passports of suspects. Furthermore, all politicians are in favour of reintegrative measures, though some want the police to take charge, whereas others want the municipalities to be responsible. There is also an overall consensus on the need to use legal sanctions when it is possible to prove that individuals have taken part in warlike actions in Syria, as well as the importance of reintegrating returnees. Yet, this might not be such a surprise. When it comes to sensitive topics, especially those concerning national security, a consensus is often emphasised by politicians across the political spectrum. In such situations, politicians in the opposition parties and the parties in government often close ranks.

MAKING UP THE SYRIA TRAVELLER: CATEGORIES AND THEIR IMPLICATIONS

In September 2014, Professor Benedikte Moltumyr Høgberg took on the task of assessing the specific conditions that might lead to a foreign fighter's loss of Norwegian citizenship. The practice of withdrawing the passports of nationals fighting with IS was then already implemented in the United Kingdom, Australia and France (Desai 2014). Several countries were also contemplating new legislation to allow the revocation of citizenship, among others Australia, Canada and Israel. In Høgberg's (2015) report to the Norwegian government, she concluded that three conditions need to be in place to allow withdrawal of Norwegian citizenship of persons joining wars abroad: (1) the individual in question must have dual citizenship, since nobody can be left stateless (which would constitute a breach of international conventions); (2) it must be proven in a Norwegian court that the individual has taken part in warlike actions (or similar crimes) and (3) the individual cannot have strong family ties in Norway (in line with the human rights paragraph concerning the right to family life).

Paradoxically, the proposed new citizenship legislation faces a major obstacle in the current Norwegian rules against dual citizenship. In principle, anyone who seeks Norwegian citizenship is required to renounce his or her previous citizenship. Norway is thus reluctant to accept dual citizenship, and equally disinclined to break international conventions against statelessness. It is therefore difficult to say whether Norway is actually taking a softer, more cautious approach than that of countries such as Israel, the United Kingdom or France. Nevertheless, the proposal to withdraw the Norwegian citizenship of foreign fighters has crucial implications for the debate about Norwegian nationhood and citizenship. Importantly, if the revocation of Norwegian citizenship were to be introduced as a measure against fighters in the war in Syria or elsewhere, loss of citizenship would have to be understood as an entirely new form of punishment.

As described by Hacking (1986, 228–231), whenever new "kinds" of people are invented and "new models of description come into being", we also see the emergence of "new possibilities for action". Our study shows that contentions about how to react to the new kind of people (the Syria travellers) are deeply intertwined with the way these people are portrayed, understood, or “made up”. Interestingly, the perception of returnees from the war in Syria as a new terror threat was not linked to any previous incident that had occurred in Norway (such as the 22 July 2011 events). Rather, it was founded on threat assessments made by the PST concerning the recruitment of Norwegians into IS, based on intelligence that was never actually disclosed to the public.

Contributors to the “making up” of Syria travellers have expressed different views about how to define and characterise the new “kind” of people, linked closely to proposals on how to deal with them. While views are complex and often ambiguous, two main narratives can be drawn from the debate, one emphasising similarities between Syria travellers and ordinary young Norwegians, and the other highlighting the exceptionality of the new kind of people, and the threat they pose to Norwegian society. Related to the way Syria travellers are understood, there is disagreement on policymaking between those who argue for sanctions against returning Syria travellers, versus those who call for more prevention and reintegration measures. At the same time, most politicians argue for both kinds of measures. As for legal sanctions, there is a debate on how stringent such measures should be, despite widespread agreement that returning fighters should be tried for participation in war or warlike actions in a Norwegian court.

Ultimately, it is difficult to see any clear differences between the “making up” or discovery (Hacking 2006, 10–12) that goes on “outside”, and that which occurs “inside” of the scientific realm. We find that the definitions and views of academics, government agencies and policymakers cut across the divides and disagreements on who the Syria travellers are, and how to respond to them. The security establishment draws extensively on the studies of academics, while terrorism researchers draw on intelligence gathered by the security establishment. In this situation, it is nearly impossible to distinguish between “realms” of discovery, or delineate the boundaries between the “making up” activities of researchers, authorities and policymakers.

ACKNOWLEDGMENTS

This study was carried out as a part of a project entitled, *Negotiating the nation: Implications of ethnic and religious diversity for national identity* (NATION), which explores the ways in which the nation is being negotiated in contemporary European societies, especially in Norway, France and the United Kingdom. The project revisits debates on nationalism and the nation state in view of both long-term societal changes and sudden events of particular impact. Mari Nielsen Vaage collected the data for this article. We would like to thank her and our other colleagues in the NATION project, as well as colleagues at the Department of Sociology and Human Geography, University of Oslo and at the Centre for the Study of Professions, Oslo University College of Applied Sciences, for fruitful discussions and constructive comments on earlier drafts of this article.

DISCLOSURE STATEMENT

No potential conflict of interest was reported by the authors.

NOTES

1. Jihad is here defined simply as a "struggle for the sake of Allah" (van Zuijdewijn and Bakker 2014, 1).
2. The "newness" of the Syria traveller might perhaps be regarded as different from that of Hacking's cases, such as people diagnosed with multiple personality disorder and autism. However, we still find Hacking's theorisation to be useful for our purposes.
3. The NATION project explores the ways in which the nation is being negotiated in contemporary Europe, revisiting long-running debates on nationalism, nation building and the nation state in view of both long-term societal changes and sudden events of particular impact.
4. The current government is a coalition between the Conservative Party (Norwegian: *Høyre*) and the right-wing populist Progress Party (*Fremskrittspartiet*), with support from two centre-right parties: The Liberal Party (*Venstre*) and the Christian Democrats (*Kristelig Folkeparti*).
5. The media data consist of opinion pieces published in Norwegian newspapers during the four-year period from 1 January 2011 to 31 December 2014. Covering a range of topics related to Norwegian identity and nationhood (immigration and integration, citizenship, multiculturalism, etc.), the dataset was compiled manually from the archives of five newspapers (three nation-wide and two regional) selected specifically to represent a cross section of political views and readerships across the country. These newspapers are *Aftenposten, Klassekampen, Verdens Gang, Bergens Tidende* and *Nordlys.*

6. Interview conducted on 11 March 2015 with two advisors in the Police Department of the Ministry of Justice and Public Security.
7. Interview conducted on 11 March 2015 with two advisors in the Police Department of the Ministry of Justice and Public Security.
8. Interview conducted on 11 March 2015 with advisor in the Migration Department of the Ministry of Justice and Public Security.
9. Interview conducted on 11 March 2015 with two advisors in the Police Department of the Ministry of Justice and Public Security.

ADDITIONAL AUTHOR INFORMATION

Katrine Fangen

Katrine Fangen is Professor of Sociology in the Department of Sociology and Human Geography at the University of Oslo, Norway. She has written extensively on migration, ethnicity, nationalism and right-wing extremism. She has conducted fieldwork in Eastern Germany in 1990, and in Norway in 1993, as well as several short-term fieldworks since then, and has authored three monographs, three co-edited books and numerous articles, in the areas of methodology, migrations studies, youth studies and studies on right-wing extremism. Her current research is on various expressions of national identity in Norway, as well as on counter-policies to radicalisation and hate speech.

Åshild Kolås

Åshild Kolås is a social anthropologist and Research Professor at the Peace Research Institute Oslo (PRIO). She has written extensively on the politics and representation of identity, ethnicity, nationhood and peacebuilding. She has conducted long-term fieldwork in Tibetan communities in India and China, and has authored two monographs and numerous articles, mainly on the politics and representation of identity in ethnically diverse areas of western China. Her current research is on gender, peacebuilding and conflict management in India, with a particular focus on insurgencies and ethnic movements in the hills of Northeast India.

REFERENCES

1. Akerhaug, L. 2013. Norsk jihad. Muslimske ekstremister blant oss [Norwegian Jihad: Muslim Extremists Among Us]. Oslo: Kagge Forlag.
2. Akerhaug, L. 2014. "Ekstrem handlingslammelse." [Extreme Paralysis.] Verdens Gang, January 1.
3. Akerhaug, L. 2015. En norsk terrorist. Portrett av den nye ekstremismen [A Norwegian Terrorist: Portrait of the New Extremism]. Oslo: Kagge Forlag.
4. Al-Hashimi, K., and C. Goerzig. 2015. Radicalization in Western Europe: Integration, Public Discourse, and Loss of Identity among Muslim Communities. London: Routledge.
5. Azhar, K. 2013. "Er de norske jihadistene bare en trussel for Norge?" [Are the Norwegian Jihadists Merely a Threat to Norway?] Klassekampen, October 24.
6. Bakker, E., C. Paulussen, and E. Entenmann. 2013. Dealing with European Foreign Fighters in Syria: Governance Challenges & Legal Implications. The Hague: The International Centre for CounterTerrorism (ICCT). ICCT Research Paper, December.
7. Bartolucci, V. 2010. "Analysing Elite Discourse on Terrorism and Its Implications: The Case of Morocco." Critical Studies on Terrorism 3 (1): 119–135. doi:10.1080/17539151003594269.
8. Bass, L. 2014. "What Motivates European Youth to Join ISIS?" Syria Comment, November 20. Accessed December 1, 2015. http://www.joshualandis.com/blog/push-factors-helping-isilrecruitment-loretta-bass/.
9. Bjørgo, T., and J. Horgan. 2009. "Introduction." In Leaving Terrorism Behind: Individual and Collective Disengagement, edited by T. Bjørgo and J. Horgan, 1–14. London: Routledge.
10. Borum, R. 2011. "Radicalization into Violent Extremism I: A Review of Social Science Theories." Journal of Strategic Security 4 (4): 7–36. doi:10.5038/1944-0472.
11. Crenshaw, E. 2014. "American and Foreign Terrorists: An Analysis of Divergent Portrayals in US Newspaper Coverage." Critical Studies on Terrorism 7 (3): 363–378. doi:10.1080/17539153.2014.953306.

12. D'Souza, S. M. 2015. "Online Radicalisation and the Specter of Extremist Violence in India." Mantraya Brief, no. 1. http://mantraya.org/onlineradicalisation-shanthie/.

13. Desai, S. 2014. "Syria: The Playground of Jihad – The Foreign Hand in Syrian War." Scholar Warrior Autumn: 76–96.

14. Feldstein, M. 2015. "Into the Fold: Evaluating Different Countries' Programs to De-Radicalize Islamist Extremists and Islamist Terrorists." Thesis submitted to Johns Hopkins University, Maryland, for a Master of Arts in Global Security Studies. https://jscholarship.library.jhu.edu/ handle/1774.2/38083

15. Flyghed, J., and H. Magnus. 2012. "Exclusion or Culture? The Rise and The Ambiguity of the Radicalisation Debate." Critical Studies on Terrorism 5 (3): 319–334. doi:10.1080/ 17539153.2012.717788.

16. Hacking, I. 1986. "Making Up People." In Reconstructing Individualism: Autonomy, Individuality, and the Self in Western Thought, edited by T. Heller, M. Sosna, and D. Wellbery, 161–171. Stanford, CA: Stanford University Press.

17. Hacking, I. 2006. "Kinds of People: Moving Targets." Proceedings of the British Academy 151: 285–318. doi:10.5871/bacad/9780197264249.003.0010.

18. Heath-Kelly, C. 2013. "Counter-terrorism and the Counterfactual: Producing the 'Radicalisation' Discourse and the UK PREVENT Strategy." The British Journal of Politics & International Relations 15 (3): 394–415. doi:10.1111/bjpi.2013.15.issue-3.

19. Hegghammer, T. 2010. "The Rise of Muslim Foreign Fighters: Islam and the Globalization of Jihad." International Security 35 (3): 53–94. doi:10.1162/ISEC_a_00023.

20. Higgins, A. 2015. "A Norway Town and Its Pipeline to Jihad in Syria." The New York Times, April 4. Accessed April 7, 2015. http://www.nytimes.com/2015/04/05/world/europe/a-norway-town-and -its-pipeline-to-jihad-in-syria.html?smid=fb-share&_r=1. Høgberg, B. M. 2015. "Tap av norsk statborgerskap." [Loss of Norwegian Citizenship.] NOU, 2015:4.

21. Huntington, S. 1993. "The Clash of Civilizations?" Foreign Affairs 72 (3): 22–49. doi:10.2307/ 20045621.

22. Karlsen, V. B. 2014. "To tanker i hodet, Akerhaug!" [Two Thoughts in Your Head, Akerhaug!] Verdens Gang, February 2.

23. Kühle, L., and L. Lindekilde. 2010. Radicalization among Young Muslims in Aarhus. Centre for Studies on Islamism and Radicalization (CIR) Research Report. Aarhus: Aarhus University. http://cir.au.dk/fileadmin/site_files/filer_statskundskab/subsites/cir/radicalization_aarhus_FINAL. pdf

24. Li, D. 2010. "A Universal Enemy? 'Foreign Fighters' and Legal Regimes of Exclusion and Exemption under the Global 'War on Terror'." Columbia Human Rights Review 41 (2): 355.

25. Malet, D. 2010. "Why Foreign Fighters? Historical Perspectives and Solutions." Orbis 54 (1): 97–114. doi:10.1016/j.orbis.2009.10.007.

26. Neumann, P. R. 2015. "Foreign Fighter Total in Syria/Iraq Now Exceeds 20,000; Surpasses Afghanistan Conflict in the 1980s." International Centre for the Study of Radicalisation and Political Violence, January 26. Accessed April 14, 2015. http://icsr.info/2015/01/foreign-fightertotal-syriairaq-now-exceeds-20000-surpasses-afghanistan-conflict-1980s/.

27. Norwegian Ministry of Justice and Public Security. 2014. "Action Plan against Radicalisation and Violent Extremism." Accessed April 7, 2015. https://www.regjeringen.no/contentassets/6d84d5d6c6df47b38f5e2b989347fc49/action-plan-against-radicalisation-and violent-extremism _2014.pdf.

28. Norwegian Parliament. 2014a. "Skal utrede lovendring om statsborgerskap." [Shall Assess Legal Change on Citizenship.] Accessed December 1, 2015. https://www.regjeringen.no/no/aktuelt/ Skal-utrede-lovendring-om-statsborgerskap/id2000217/.

29. Norwegian Parliament. 2014b. "Interpellasjon fra representanten Michael Tetzschner til Justis- og beredskapsministeren." [Interpellation from the Representative Michael Tetzschner to the Minister of Justice and Public Security.] April 24 (case 7). Accessed November 30, 2015. https://www.stortinget.no/no/Saker-og-publikasjoner/Publikasjoner/Referater/Stortinget/2013-2014/140424/7/.

30. Norwegian Parliament. 2015. "Muntlig Spørretime i Stortinget." [Questions to the Parliament.] January 14 (case 1). Accessed April 14, 2015. https://www.stortinget.no/no/Saker-ogpublikasjoner /Publikasjoner/Referater/Stortinget/2014-2015/150114 /muntligsporretime/. CRITICAL STUDIES ON TERRORISM 431 Norwegian Police Security Service. 2015. Annual Threat Assessment. Oslo: Politiets Sikkerhetstjeneste. Accessed April 7 2015. http://www.pst.no/media/75477/NTV_2015_engelsk.pdf.

31. Pantazis, C., and S. Pemberton. 2009. "From the 'Old' to the 'New' Suspect Community: Examining the Impacts of Recent UK Counter-Terrorist Legislation." British Journal of Criminology 49 (5): 646–666. doi:10.1093/bjc/azp031.

32. Rahimullah, R. H., S. Larmar, and M. Abdalla. 2013. "Radicalization and Terrorism: Research within the Australian Context." International Journal of Criminology and Sociology, no. 2: 180–185.

33. Rich, B., and D. Conduit. 2015. "The Impact of Jihadist Foreign Fighters on Indigenous Secular-Nationalist Causes: Contrasting Chechnya and Syria." Studies in Conflict & Terrorism 38 (2): 113–131. doi:10.1080/1057610X.2014.979605.

34. Rom, S. A. 2013. "'Extremist' Rehabilitation: A Fundamental Misunderstanding? Divergent Micro and Macro-level Narratives Regarding Motivations of Former Guantanamo Bay 'Extremists' Participating in the Saudi Arabian De-radicalization and Rehabilitation Program." Brussels Journal of International Studies 10 (2013): 144–186.

35. van Zuijdewijn, J. D. R., and E. Bakker. 2014. Returning Western Foreign Fighters: The Case of Afghanistan, Bosnia and Somalia. ICCT Background Note, June. The Hague: The International Centre for Counter-Terrorism (ICCT). Verdens Gang. 2014. "Kampen mot IS – ute og hjemme." [The Fight against IS – Abroad and at Home]. Verdens Gang, editorial, November 8. Accessed December 1, 2015. http://www.vg.no/ nyheter/meninger/is/vg-mener-kampen-mot-is-ute-og-hjemme/a/23331494/.

36. Wodak, R. 2008. "The Contribution of Critical Linguistic to the Analysis of Discriminatory Prejudices." In Handbook of Communication in the Public Sphere, edited by R. Wodak and V. Koller, 291–395. Berlin: Walter de Gruyter.

6

CHAPTER

Global Governance Principles for the Sustainable Development of Groundwater Resources

Kirstin I. Conti[1,2], Joyeeta Gupta[3,4]

[1] *Governance and Inclusive Development, Amsterdam Institute for Social Science Research (AISSR), University of Amsterdam, Nieuwe Actergracht 166, 1018 WV Amsterdam, The Netherlands*

[2] *International Groundwater Resources Assessment Centre (IGRAC), Westvest 7, 2611 AX Delft, The Netherlands*

[3] *UNESCO-IHE Institute for Water Education, Westvest 7, 2611 AX Delft, The Netherlands*

[4] *Department of Geography, Planology and International Development Studies, Faculty of Social and Behavioural Sciences, Amsterdam Institute of Social Science Research, University of Amsterdam, Room 2.12b, Plantage Muidergracht 14, 1018 TV Amsterdam, The Netherlands*

ABSTRACT

A normative framework for the governance of groundwater is emerging at the global level. However, existing analyses have not comprehensively covered all the governance texts that have a bearing on transboundary groundwater resources or looked at them from the perspective of sustainable groundwater governance. Therefore, this paper responds to the questions: What are the global governance texts (including international laws) applicable to groundwater resources; to which forms of the resource do they apply; which principles have been included over time; and what are the implications for sustainable development of groundwater resources now and in the future? The analysis highlights key groundwater concepts, discusses twelve global groundwater governance texts and the thirty principles therein, classifies the principles into ideal–typical categories based on the sustainable development concept; and assesses the gaps and conflicts between the principles and texts. The paper has three key findings. First, groundwater governance is rapidly evolving and there are a number of principles available to promote sustainable development. Second, however, these collective principles do not adequately address (a) the link with all water resources; (b) the potential impact of climate change on water resources; and (c) the impact of trade on equitable sharing of groundwater and protection of groundwater-related ecosystems. Third, to the extent that this collection of principles can contribute to sustainable development, they are inconsistently included in the legally binding groundwater governance texts. Therefore, much progress is needed to ensure a global normative framework that can guide the sustainable governance of groundwater resources.

Keywords: Groundwater governance, Transboundary aquifers, Sustainable development, Groundwater sustainability, International groundwater law, Law of transboundary aquifers, Principles for groundwater governance

ABBREVIATIONS

ECOSOC United Nations Economic and Social Council

HRC Human Rights Council

ICJ International Court of Justice

*ICWE*International Conference on Water and the Environment

*IGRAC*International Groundwater Resources Assessment Centre

*ILA*International Law Association

*ILC*International Law Commission

*IWRM*Integrated Water Resources Management

*PCA*Permanent Court of Arbitration

*SDGs*Sustainable Development Goals

*UN*United Nations

*UNCED*United Nations Conference on Environment and Development

*UNECE*United Nations Economic Commission for Europe

*UNESCO*United Nations Educational, Scientific and Cultural Organization

*UNGA*United Nations General Assembly

*WCED*World Commission on Environment and Development

1 INTRODUCTION

Groundwater constitutes 98–99 % of the world's available freshwater resources (Margat and van der Gun 2013: p. 5). Nearly 600 groundwater resources traverse political boundaries (International Groundwater Resources Assessment Centre (IGRAC) 2015a, b), and an unknown number solely reside within country borders. Approximately, 25 % of humans rely on groundwater for their domestic needs (Machard de Gramont et al. 2011) and 50 % use it for potable water supply (Mechlem 2003). Groundwater supplies over 40 % of irrigation needs globally (Döll and Hoffmann-Dobrev 2012; Siebert et al. 2010), partly due to increased reliability of individual irrigation wells over public surface water distribution schemes (Shah 2009a). Additionally, groundwater makes up 50 % of municipal and 40 % of industrial water withdrawals (Zektser and Everett 2004); thereby catalyzing growth, development and poverty alleviation (Shah 2009b; Wijnen et al. 2012). However, many aquifers are in jeopardy due to poor governance (Llamas and Martínez-Santos 2005) and insufficient legal frameworks that lack consideration for hydrogeological complexities and/or socio-political, environmental and economic aspects.

The literature has analyzed individual treaties (Eckstein 2007; McCaffrey 2011; McIntryre 2006; McIntyre 2011) or a combination thereof (Dellapenna 2011; Eckstein and Sindico 2014; Mechlem 2003). Several analyses relate to the six transboundary aquifers that have aquifer-specific legal mechanisms;[1] others to one or more of the 89 out of 196 countries that have groundwater regulations (IGRAC 2015a, b). However, no one has comprehensively assessed the norms in all relevant groundwater governance texts from the perspective of sustainable groundwater governance. Such an assessment becomes all the more relevant in the light of the recent entry into force of the United Nations Convention on the Law of the Non-Navigational Uses of International Watercourses (UN Watercourses Convention 1997); the opening of the United Nation Economic Commission for Europe Convention on the

Protection and Use of Transboundary Watercourses and International Lakes (UNECE Convention 1992) to accession by all UN member states (see Sect. 3); and the September 2015 adoption of the Sustainable Development Goals by 193 UN member states (UN SDGs 2015). Hence, this paper addresses the questions: What global governance texts apply to groundwater resources; to which types of groundwater resources do they apply; which principles have been included over time; and what are the implications for sustainable development of groundwater resources now and in the future?

This paper treats sustainable development and Integrated Water Resources Management (IWRM) as overarching concepts, rather than single principles; although they are mentioned as principles in several governance texts.[2] Sustainable development "aims to meet the needs of present generations without compromising on the ability of future generations to meet their own needs" (WCED 1987: 43) and can be operationalized through legal principles (Fuentes 2002; Rieu-Clarke 2000). Groundwater sustainability implies the development and use of groundwater without causing unacceptable long-term environmental, economic or social consequences through integrated, adaptive and inclusive governance (Custodio 2002; Gleeson et al. 2012; Gleeson and VanderSteen 2010; Llamas et al. 1992). IWRM calls for coordinated management of water-related resources (Biswas 2004; Global Water Partnership 2002: 22); adaptive governance for dealing with the inherent uncertainties of the system; and inclusive governance to focus on the socio-ecological dimensions.

This paper explains key groundwater concepts (see Sect. 2), global groundwater governance texts (see Sect. 3), and assesses the principles that emerge from these texts in terms of social, environmental and economic dimensions of sustainable development (see Sect. 4); before drawing conclusions (see Sect. 5).

2 GROUNDWATER: PHYSICAL AND POLITICAL TYPOLOGIES

Groundwater is water that fully saturates the pores and cracks of the earth's subsurface geology (Fitts 2002). It is primarily formed after percolating from the earth's surface through the soil and into the underlying geological formation, but it may have also been trapped during geologic processes, such as sedimentation or volcanic activity. Depending on the geology below (e.g., sand, clay, gravel, fractured rock), groundwater can accumulate into a distinct formation called an aquifer and often flows slowly through the subsurface.

An aquifer is a permeable layer of underground rock, which is saturated with and capable of yielding groundwater (Fetter 2001; Fitts 2002). Sometimes a groundwater resource is only defined as an aquifer when it has yield sufficient for human use. Aquifers can be unconfined, where the water table occurs within the aquifer layer and the groundwater is in direct contact with the atmosphere through soil pores, or confined, where it is over- and underlain by a semi-permeable or impermeable layer (Fitts 2002; Margat and van der Gun 2013). A non-recharging aquifer, containing "fossil" groundwater, does not receive meaningful recharge on a human timescale. Political typologies of aquifers include national aquifers completely contained within state boundaries; national aquifers hydrologically linked with international watercourses; and transboundary aquifers shared by two or more states.

3 EVOLUTION OF GROUNDWATER GOVERNANCE TEXTS AT THE GLOBAL LEVEL

This section discusses global groundwater governance texts (see Table 1) in terms of the political and hydro(geo)logical typologies mentioned above (see Table 2). Scholars within the International Law Association (ILA) codified the principles for governing international rivers in the non-binding Helsinki Rules on the Uses of the Waters of International Rivers (ILA Helsinki Rules 1966). In Article II, an International Drainage Basins is defined as a "geographical area extending over two or more States...including surface and underground waters flowing to a common terminus." This includes groundwater that is hydrologically connected to a transboundary surface water feature and flows toward a common point of discharge area.

In 1972, the world's first environmental conference adopted the Declaration of the United Nations Conference on the Human Environment which addressed human–environment interactions and water resources (UN Stockholm Declaration 1972, Preamble, Principle 2). The UN's first water conference adopted the Mar del Plata Action Plan and Recommendations (UN Mar del Plata Plan 1977) clarifying norms for water management and mentioning groundwater in relation to water supply for domestic and agricultural use.

In 1986, the ILA published its Seoul Rules on International Groundwaters (ILA Seoul Rules 1986), where these scholars already suggested focusing on aquifers, not groundwater. It went beyond the Helsinki Rules to include: "the waters of an aquifer that is intersected by the boundary between two or more States [...] *whether or not* the aquifer and its waters form surface waters part of a hydraulic system flowing into a common terminus" (Article I, emphasis added).

In 1992, at the second global environmental conference, the Brundtland Commission's exploration of sustainable development (WCED 1987) and the UN Stockholm Declaration (1972) influenced the Rio Declaration on Environment and Development (UN Rio Declaration 1992) and the accompanying non-binding action plan, Agenda 21 (1992) (Dellapenna and Gupta 2009). The Rio Declaration contains 27 environmental governance principles some of which are further assessed here; Agenda 21 is highlighted where relevant. That same year, many countries and NGOs adopted the ICWE Dublin Statement on Water and Sustainable Development (ICWE Dublin Statement 1992) at the International Conference on Water and the Environment with four principles recognizing the finite nature of water, the need for participatory processes, the role of women, and water as an economic good.

In the same year, the UN Economic Commission for Europe adopted the regional, Convention on the Protection and Use of Transboundary Watercourses and International Lakes (UNECE 1992). It covers "ground waters...which mark, cross or are located on boundaries between two or more States" (UNECE 1992: Art. 1.1). Its Protocol on Water and Health (UNECE 1999) focuses on protecting human health and well-being through water management. In 2013, amendments allowing all UN member states to accede to it entered into force (UNECE 2003)—making it global. In 2014, the UNECE adopted Model Provisions on Transboundary Groundwater Management, which "provide practical guidance" and "offer assistance" to the parties in creating agreements for the sustainable use, management and protection of groundwater (UNECE 2014: p. 3, para. 9). These Provisions apply both to groundwater and the geological formation containing the groundwater, subtly shifting from groundwater to aquifer.

In 1997, the UN member states adopted the UN Watercourses Convention (1997), culminating a 30-year process led by the UN's International Law Commission (ILC). It entered into force in 2014 and is binding for its parties. This Convention applies to international watercourses defined as a "system of surface waters and groundwaters constituting by virtue of their physical relationship a unitary whole and normally flowing into a common terminus [...] parts of which are situated in different States" (UN Watercourses Convention 1997, Article 2a). It focuses on surface water systems and some connected groundwater resources. There is debate as to whether it applies to two situations: first, where an aquifer hydrologically links two surface water bodies with different termini and second where a confined aquifer is linked to an unconfined aquifer or surface water body but would still constitute distinct systems rather than a "unitary whole" (Mechlem 2003). This issue is being gradually clarified by legal experts. However, the UN Watercourses Convention does not cover aquifers that lack hydrologic connection to surface water.

This gap was addressed in the ILA's non-binding Berlin Rules on Water Resources (ILA Berlin Rules 2004), which updated its Helsinki Rules. The ILA Berlin Rules proposes that states apply the rules to transboundary and national resources, "as appropriate" (ILA 2004b: Article 1.2; Dellapenna 2011) and are controversial as a result (Bogdanovic et al. 2004). Nevertheless, its contents contribute to normative developments in groundwater governance.

The UN ILC prepared the Draft Articles on the Law of Transboundary Aquifers (ILC Draft Articles 2008) in response to the gap in scope of the UN Watercourses Convention and the developments in the ILA Berlin Rules. The Draft Articles define an aquifer as "a permeable water-bearing geological formation underlain by a less permeable layer and the water contained in the saturated zone of the formation" and include all aquifers where its "parts ... are situated in different States" (ILC Draft Articles 2008: Art. 2a, 2c). Although thrice reviewed by UN member states, delegates still disagree about whether the Draft Articles should be a declaration of principles, an international framework convention, or remain a non-legally binding document. Consequently, it is a provisional agenda item for the UNGA's 71st session in September 2016.

The UN Human Rights Commission and UNGA adopted resolutions on the human right to water and sanitation in 2010, not only advancing rights-based approaches to (ground)water governance, but also having implications for the use and development of all groundwater resources (UN HRC 2010; UNGA 2010). In September 2015, the UN member states adopted the SDGs, which calls for the sustainable management of all fresh water resources. It implicitly includes groundwater, but does not apply any principles specifically to it.

Thus, the evolution of global groundwater governance texts has been nonlinear, influenced by developments in different fora, and is rapidly accelerating (see Table 1). This evolution has resulted in texts defining and including groundwater differently in their scopes (see Table 2). Only the Berlin Rules and Draft Articles explicitly define an aquifer and mention "layers of geological strata" (Article 3.2 in ILA 2004) and "aquifer systems" respectively (Eckstein 2007; ILC 2008). The Helsinki Rules and UN Watercourses Convention are ambiguous with respect to the types of links between ground and surface water, including multilayered aquifer systems.

Table 1 Status and ratifications of governance texts applicable to groundwater resources

Text	**Date**	**Legal status**	**Ratifying parties**
ILA Helsinki Rules	1966	Academic list of rules, non-binding	Not applicable
UN Stockholm Declaration	1972	Adopted by states, non-binding rules	Not applicable
UN Mar del Plata Action Plan	1977	Adopted by states, non-binding rules	Not applicable
ILA Seoul Rules	1986	Academic list of rules, non-binding	Not applicable
ICWE Dublin Statement	1992	Adopted, non-binding principl	Not applicable

Text	**Date**	**Legal status**	**Ratifying parties**		
		es			
UN Rio Declaration	1992	Adopted, non-binding declaration	Not applicable		
UNECE Convention	1992	Ratified, in-force treaty	Albania Austria Azerbaijan Belarus Belgium Bosnia and Herzegovina Bulgaria Croatia Czech Rep Denmark Estonia E.U. Finland Latvia	Liechtenstein Lithuania France Germany Greece Hungary Italy Kazakhstan Luxembourg Netherlands Norway Poland Portugal Republic of Moldova	Romania Russia Serbia Slovakia Slovenia Spain Sweden Switzerland Turkmenistan Ukraine U.K. Uzbekistan
UN Watercou	1997	Ratified, in-force	Benin Burkina	Italy	Paraguay

Text	Date	Legal status	Ratifying parties		
rses Convention		treaty	Faso Chad Côte d'Ivoire Denmark Finland France Germany Greece Guinea-Bissau Hungary Iraq Ireland	Jordan Lebanon Libya Luxembourg Montenegro Morocco Namibia Netherlands Niger Nigeria Norway Palestine	Portugal Qatar South Africa Spain Sweden Syria Tunisia U.K. Uzbekistan Venezuela Viet Nam Yemen
UNECE Protocol	1999	Ratified, in-force protocol to treaty	Albania Azerbaijan Belarus Belgium Bosnia and Herzegovina Croatia Czech Republic Estonia	France Germany Hungary Latvia Lithuania Luxembourg Netherlands Norway Moldova Portugal	Romania Russia Serbia Slovakia Spain Switzerland Ukraine

Text	**Dat e**	**Legal status**	**Ratifying parties**		
			Finland		
ILA Berlin Rules	20 04	Academ ic list of rules, non-binding	Not applicable		
ILC Draft Articles	20 08	Awaitin g adoptio n by states	Not applicable		
UN HRC; UNGA	20 10	Adopte d, non-binding resoluti ons	Not applicable		

Table 2 Governance texts and types of groundwater addressed

Text	**Scope/defini tion**	**Types(s) of groundwater**		
		Included	**Excluded**	**Ambiguo us**
ILA Helsinki Rules	International Drainage Basins: Watershed limits of system of waters, including	• Groundwat er from unconfined aquifers, recharging and discharging	• Groundw ater in unconfine d aquifers, only rechargin	• Groundw ater linking multiple surface water bodies

Text	Scope/definition	Types(s) of groundwater		
		Included	Excluded	Ambiguous
	surface and underground waters, flowing into a common terminus	in basin • Groundwater from unconfined aquifers, only discharging in basin • Groundwater in unconfined aquifers, which is the common terminus of a watercourse	g in basin • Groundwater in confined, non-recharging aquifers	with different termini • Distinct groundwater systems with links to surface water • Multilayer aquifer systems
UN Mar del Plata	Shared waters	Transboundary groundwater resources implicitly	–	–
ILA Seoul Rules	• An aquifer that contributes water to, or receives	All transboundary aquifers	Groundwater outside an aquifer	–

Text	Scope/definition	Types(s) of groundwater		
		Included	Excluded	Ambiguous
	water from, surface waters of an international basin that constitutes part of an international basin for the purposes of the Helsinki Rules • An aquifer intersected by the boundary between two or more States that does not contribute water to, or receive water from, surface waters of an International Drainage Basin constitutes an International Drainage Basin for the purposes of the Helsinki Rules			

Text	Scope/definition	Types(s) of groundwater		
		Included	Excluded	Ambiguous
ICWE Dublin Statement	All waters	All groundwater implicitly	–	–
UNECE Convention and Protocol	Transboundary Surface and Groundwater: Any surface or ground waters that mark, cross or are located on boundaries between two or more States	All transboundary groundwater[a]	–	–
UN Watercourses Convention	International Watercourses: A system of surface waters and groundwaters constituting by virtue of their physical relationship a unitary whole and	• Groundwater from unconfined aquifers, recharging and discharging in a basin • Groundwater from unconfined	• Groundwater in unconfined aquifers, only recharging in a basin • Groundwater in	• Groundwater linking multiple surface water bodies with different termini • Distinct groundwa

Text	Scope/definition	Types(s) of groundwater		
		Included	Excluded	Ambiguous
	normally flowing into a common terminus	aquifers, only discharging in a basin • Groundwater in unconfined aquifers, which is the common terminus of a watercourse	confined, non-recharging aquifers	ter systems with links to surface water • Multilayer aquifer systems
ILA Berlin Rules	Water of International Drainage Basins and all waters, including all aquifers where "aquifer" means a subsurface layer or layers of geological strata of sufficient porosity and permeability to allow	• All transboundary aquifers • National aquifers, as appropriate	–	–

Text	Scope/defini tion	Types(s) of groundwater		
		Included	Excluded	Ambiguo us
	either a flow of or the withdrawal of usable quantities of groundwater			
ILC Draft Articles	Transbounda ry aquifers and aquifer systems where: • “Aquifer” means a permeable water-bearing geological formation underlain by a less permeable layer and the water contained in the saturated zone of the formation; • “Aquifer system” means a series of two or more aquifers that are	All transbound ary aquifers and aquifer systems	Groundw ater outside an aquifer	–

Text	Scope/definition	Types(s) of groundwater		
		Included	Excluded	Ambiguous
	hydraulically connected			
UN HRC/UNGA	All waters	All groundwater implicitly	–	

The UN Stockholm Declaration and UN Rio Declaration are not included here because their scope is not specific to water

[a]The UNECE Model Provisions also include the geologic formation containing and allowing flow of groundwater

4 PRINCIPLES, RIGHTS AND MEASURES APPLICABLE TO GROUNDWATER

4.1 Principles applicable to groundwater and their classification

The twelve key groundwater governance texts discussed above include thirty principles, rights and measures (hereafter called "principles") as explained in Table 3. These principles are categorized into the environmental, social and economic dimensions of sustainable development with an additional general governance category. Although some principles cross multiple dimensions, each principle is given a primary designation. These principles have emerged from different historical stimuli and range in the degree to which they are considered legally binding or have attained customary status in international law. The analysis below focuses on the content of these principles, their inclusion in groundwater governance texts (illustrated in tables), and their ability to contribute to sustainable development. All tables in this paper list the principles in alphabetical order; there is no implicit prioritization in their listing.

Table 3 Simple explanations of principles/rights from groundwater governance texts

General: Riparian/aquifer states shall/should/must/may	
Exchange of information	Share relevant information with each other
Obligation to cooperate	Engage cooperatively with each other and act in good faith
Peaceful resolution of disputes	Settle disputes peacefully through negotiation, conciliation, mediation, consultation of good offices, arbitration and/or tribunal
Sovereignty	Do what they wish within their territories (within limits)
Primarily social	
Common but differentiated responsibilities and respective capabilities	Share obligations based on their responsibility for causing the problem and their ability to address the problem
Equitable and reasonable use	*Share transboundary waters based on each other's conditions and contexts*
Human right to sanitation[a]	*Ensure that all humans have a right to access improved and safe sanitation facilities*
Human right to water[a]	*Ensure that all humans have a right to access improved and clean water sources*
Prior informed consent	Inform and receive the consent of other states (or individuals) for activities that may

	affect them
No priority of use	*Recognize there is no inherent priority of uses for water; however, special attention may be given to vital human needs*
Public access to information	Provide the public access to information collected, procedures followed and decisions made by their governments
Public participation	Encourage the participation of the public or stakeholders in decision-making processes
Rights of women, youth and indigenous peoples	Account for the rights of individuals/groups in its decision-making process
Primarily environmental	
Basin as unit of management[b]	*Use the water basin or watercourse as unit for policy-making and implementation*
Best available technology/technique	Use the best technology/techniques available to reduce environmental harm
Conjunctive use and management	*Account for hydrological relationships between surface and groundwater resources in management and policy decisions*
Environmental Impact Assessment	Require project developers to assess potential (transboundary) impacts
Monitoring	Monitor groundwater quality and quantity
No significant harm	Not cause harm to other states; this limits the sovereign rights of a state

Notification of accidents	*Notify other potentially impacted states following an accident (e.g., industrial spills)*
Notification of emergency situations	*Notify other potentially impacted states during emergencies (e.g., droughts or floods)*
Notification of planned measures	*Notify other possibly impacted states of plans with potential (transboundary) impacts*
Pollution prevention	Take measures to prevent pollution
Precautionary principle	Take precautionary action to prevent irreversible harm even when there is inconclusive scientific evidence on cause and effect
Protection and preservation of ecosystems	Take measures to protect and preserve ecosystems
Protection of recharge and discharge zones[b]	*Take measures to protect groundwater discharge and recharge zones*
Subsidiarity	Take action at the lowest appropriate level of governance
Primarily economic	
Open international economic system	Not adopt actions that could affect the principles of international trade
Polluter pays	Require that polluters internalize the costs of pollution
Water as an economic good	*Recognize water has an economic value and should be considered an economic good*

Principles in italics are specifically applicable to water resources

[a]Although the human right to water and sanitation is a composite right in the UN General Assembly's text on the subject, it is separated here because most texts assessed do so

[b]Also included as principles here because they are strong starting points for water governance

Figure 1 shows that an increasing number of principles have been integrated into global groundwater governance texts over time. These texts have evolved from including an average of six legal principles prior to 1992, to more than twelve principles from 1992 onwards, indicating an increased sophistication in the global groundwater governance regime. Yet this progression has also led to gaps and conflicts in *how and when* these principles are included in governance texts.

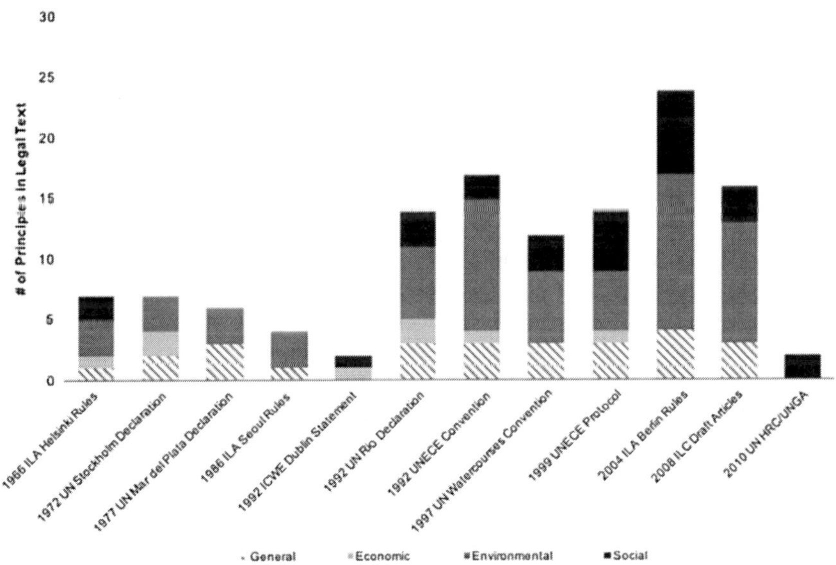

Fig. 1 Types of principles/rights in global governance texts

4.2 General principles applicable to groundwater

Table 4 shows which governance texts have adopted the general principles of transboundary governance. These principles support sustainable development of transboundary groundwater resources by providing a foundation for cooperative and peaceful interaction between states.

Table 4 General principles in global governance texts applicable to groundwater resources

	ILA Helsinki Rules	UN Stockholm Declaration	UN Mar del Plata Declaration	ILA Seoul Rules	ICWE Dublin Statement	UN Rio Declaration	UNECE Convention	UN Watercourses Convention	UNECE Protocol on Water and Health	ILA Berlin Rules	ILC Draft Articles	UNHCR/ UNGA
Year	1966	1972	1977	1986	1992	1992	1992	1997	1999	2004	2008	2010
Exchange of information	✓		✓	✓			✓	✓	✓	✓	✓	
Obligation to cooperate		✓	✓			✓	✓	✓	✓	✓	✓	
Peaceful resolution of disputes						✓	✓	✓		✓		
Sovereignty		✓	✓			✓			✓	✓[a]	✓	

[a] "State" means a sovereign state or a regional economic integration organization, there is no further reference to sovereignty with respect to water

The principles of cooperation, peaceful resolution of disputes and information exchange are also considered customary law (McCaffrey 1987)—i.e. "the collection of international behavioral regularities that nations over time come to view as binding on them as a matter of law" (Goldsmith and Posner 1998: 1116). Since 1972 most agreements require states to cooperate with respect to transboundary waters and to resolve disputes peacefully (PCA 1910), as codified in relation to water (ILA Helsinki Rules 1966: Art. II) and institutionalized in the UN Watercourses Convention (1997). Most agreements and codifications since 1977 call on riparian/aquifer states to exchange relevant water information and data (see UNECE 1992, Art. 11).

A fundamental principle of international law is state sovereignty (UN Charter 1945; UNGA 1963). Historically, states have claimed sovereignty (e.g., absolute territorial sovereignty and absolute integrity of state territory) over water resources within their territory and used it to opt in and out of international agreements, affecting interstate cooperation. Consequently, the applicability of the sovereignty principle to (ground)water resources has been the subject of debate (Dellapenna 2011; Eckstein and Sindico 2014; Eckstein 2007, 2011; McCaffrey 2009, 2011; Yamada 2011). Sovereign control over territorial resources, subject to not causing harm to others, was included in the Stockholm, Mar del Plata and Rio Declarations. However, it was excluded from all scholarly codifications and laws on international waters since then, until the 2008 ILC Draft Articles (see Article 3). Legal commentaries on the ILC Draft Articles indicate that countries wanted groundwater resources to be treated like other "similar" underground resources such as oil and gas (Eckstein 2007; ILC 2004). Some argue this reverses decades of progress in international water law (McCaffrey 2011; McIntyre 2011; Tanzi 2011). Others say sovereignty is "balanced" by the provisions on equitable and reasonable use of water, not causing significant harm to others, and the obligation to cooperate in managing transboundary aquifers (Eckstein 2007; Sindico 2011; Stephan 2011; Yamada 2011). Nevertheless, inclusion of the sovereignty principle could affect the achievement of sustainable development if used to avoid implementation of other groundwater governance principles.

4.3 Social principles applicable to groundwater

Table 5 shows the extent to which the nine identified social principles have been included in groundwater governance texts.

Table 5 Social principles in global governance texts applicable to groundwater resources

	ILA Helsinki Rules	ILA Stockholm Declaration	UN Mar del Plata Declaration	ILA Seoul Rules	ICWE Dublin Statement	UN Rio Declaration	UNECE Convention	UN Watercourses Convention	UNECE Protocol on Water and Health	ILA Berlin Rules	ILC Draft Articles	UNHRC/ UNGA
Year	1966	1972	1977	1986	1992	1992	1992	1997	1999	2004	2008	2010
Common but differentiated responsibilities and respective capabilities						✔						
Equitable and reasonable use	✔						✔	✔		✔	✔	
Human right to sanitation									✔[a]			✔
Human right to water									✔[a]	✔		✔
No priority of use	✔							✔[b]		✔[b]		
Prior informed consent								✔[c]		✔[d]	✔[c]	
Public access to information							✔		✔	✔		
Public participation					✔	✔			✔	✔[e]		
Rights of women, youth, and indigenous peoples										✔		

[a] Not framed as right, but as a state responsibility

[b] These documents adopt the principle of no priority of use, but give vital human needs attention

[c] Framed within procedures of notification of planned measures

[d] Called "expressed" consent

[e] Including that of women, youth and indigenous peoples

Internationally, there is no clear pattern of an increasing use of social principles or consistency between the applications of social principles in relation to groundwater governance, possibly because of tensions among the principles. While the principle of common but differentiated responsibility and respective capability of states is included in the Rio Declaration, this principle is not included in groundwater-specific texts. Doing so would mean that countries would also have to implement the other principles in accordance with their respective responsibilities and capabilities. This would have added additional factors to the existing list of factors included in the Watercourses Convention to determine how water can be shared equitably and reasonably.[3]

Similarly, the principle that there is no priority of use of water can potentially counter the human right to water and sanitation. With the exception of the ILA Berlin Rules (2004), agreements either choose the principle of no priority of use or the human right to water. The UN Watercourses Convention (1997: Art. 10) does not recognize a priority in water uses. The right to water and sanitation is included in UNHRC (2010) and UNGA (2010); the Berlin Rules (2004: Art 17) recognizes only the human right to water and the UNECE Protocol (1998: Art 6) implicitly recognizes state responsibility in this respect. This implies inconsistent rules (Obani and Gupta 2014), especially if the customary status of this right is contested (Bluemel 2004; UN ECOSOC 2003; Gleick 1998; Gupta et al. 2010; McCaffrey 1992; McIntyre 2012; Ziganshina 2008).

The remaining principles are interdependent and could collectively contribute to the social dimension of sustainable development. The rights of women, youth and indigenous peoples are elaborated in human rights law but not included in any legally binding groundwater governance text. The principle of prior informed consent supports the fulfillment of these rights and is framed as "express consent" in the governance texts. It is included in the ILA Berlin Rules (2004: Art 10) and placed within the context of notification of planned measures in the UN Watercourses Convention (1997: Art 3.4, 14(b)) and the ILC Draft Articles (2004: Art 9). The participation principle has been included in the UN Rio Declaration (1992: Principle 10), ICWE Dublin Statement (1992: Principle 2), UNECE Protocol (Arts. 5, 6, 16) and alluded to in the scholarly ILA Berlin Rules (2004: Arts. 4, 17, 20). Public access to information is only arranged in the UNECE Convention (1992: Art. 16) and Protocol (1997: Art 5(i)).

The combination of these social rights is critical for sustainable development. Yet, as can be seen, they have been included sporadically in the groundwater governance texts. In fulfilling these social principles, the potential impacts to the ecological sustainability of groundwater must also be considered.

Table 6 Environmental principles in global governance texts applicable to groundwater resources

	ILA Helsinki Rules	UN Stockholm Declaration	UN Mar del Plata Declaration	ILA Seoul Rules	ICWE Dublin Statement	UN Rio Declaration	UNECE Convention	UN Watercourses Convention	UNECE Protocol on Water and Health	ILA Berlin Rules	ILC Draft Articles	UNHRC/ UNGA
Year	1966	1972	1977	1986	1992	1992	1992	1997	1999	2004	2008	2010
Aquifer/Basin as management unit	✔			✔			✔	✔		✔	✔	
Best available technology/ techniques							✔			✔		
Conjunctive use and management				✔						✔		
Environmental impact assessment						✔	✔	✔[a]		✔	✔[a]	
Monitoring			✔	✔[c]			✔			✔[d]	✔	
No significant harm		✔				✔[e]	✔[f]	✔	✔	✔	✔	
Notification of accidents							✔[g]		✔[h]	✔		
Notification of emergency situations						✔	✔	✔		✔[b]	✔	
Notification of planned measures	✔					✔	✔	✔		✔	✔	
Pollution prevention	✔	✔	✔	✔			✔	✔		✔	✔	

	ILA Helsinki Rules	UN Stockholm Declaration	UN Mar del Plata Declaration	ILA Seoul Rules	ICWE Dublin Statement	UN Rio Declaration	UNECE Convention	UN Watercourses Convention	UNECE Protocol on Water and Health	ILA Berlin Rules	ILC Draft Articles	UNHRC/ UNGA
Year	1966	1972	1977	1986	1992	1992	1992	1997	1999	2004	2008	2010
Precautionary principle						✔	✔		✔	✔	✔i	
Protection and preservation of ecosystems		✔[j]				✔	✔	✔	✔	✔	✔	
Protection of recharge and discharge zones										✔	✔	
Subsidiarity									✔			

[a] Not obliged: can be requested
[b] Emergencies and accidents called "extreme conditions"
[c] "Data collection" and monitoring is done at the request of other watercourse states
[d] Framed as duty to acquire data
[e] Framed as not causing damage beyond harmful limits
[f] Falls under definition of "transboundary impact"
[g] Both emergencies and accidents called "critical situations"
[h] Specific to outbreaks of disease
[i] Only for pollution
[j] Uses "environment" not "ecosystem"

4.4 Environmental principles applicable groundwater

Table 6 illustrates how environmental principles are included in groundwater governance. These fourteen principles facilitate sustainable development through (a) resource-based management (b) principles on preventing harm (including over-exploitation and pollution prevention) and (c) notification procedures. The principle of basin management requires that hydrological rather than administrative units are used for groundwater management. Using this principle also facilitates subsidiarity (management at the lowest appropriate level) and conjunctive use and management when groundwater is appropriately included in the scope. However, these principles are hardly used. They are also limited because at the global level, groundwater resources outside of transboundary aquifers/basins are not fully included in the scope. This presents a practical challenge since politics is a function of administrative units not aquifers and river basins.

Several environmental principles depend on and/or support each other. The principle of no significant harm has been included in all global groundwater governance texts since the UN Watercourses Convention in 1997. This principle would prevent states from significantly impacting other aquifer states and would require them to implement pollution prevention principles to maintain groundwater quality and prevent over-abstraction throughout the transboundary aquifer. Use of best available technologies and resource monitoring would support these efforts. While technologies could reduce contaminant loads in water recharging to aquifers or remediate contaminated resources, the principle is only included in two texts—the UNECE Convention (1992: Art. 3) and the ILA Berlin Rules (2004: Art. 27)—as well as in the groundwater protection activities of Agenda 21 (1992). Monitoring, which is also critical to pollution prevention, has been included in half global groundwater governance texts since the 1977 Mar del Plata Declaration and pollution prevention in slightly more. However, in practice there is a lack of aquifer-specific data regarding the quality and quantity of groundwater. Thus, the precautionary principle is highly relevant and the legal approach to management should include measures that protect the resource from over-exploitation or irreparable contamination. Yet, it is not included in the UN Watercourses Convention (1997) and only included for pollution in the ILC Draft Articles (2008). Consequently, many aquifers/basin states may lack the practical and legal means to prevent significant harm to groundwater resources, especially because no environmental principles explicitly deal with over-abstraction.

Planned actions, such as diverting a watercourse that recharges an aquifer or abstracting groundwater during mining, may impact the state of the groundwater resource. The principle of notification of planned measures would require that states potentially affected by the projects receive advanced notification. States are also obliged to notify other aquifer states during emergencies such as droughts or accidents such as industrial spills. Each of these notification principles is included in most texts from 1992 onwards. Conducting environmental impact assessments, as included in the UNECE Convention (1992: Art. 3h) and ILA Berlin Rules (2004: Art 29) and suggested as a means of consultation in the UN Watercourses Convention (1997: Art. 12), and the ILC Draft Articles (2008: Art.15), would allow countries to account for any potentially significant harm that a project may cause to groundwater. The obligation to conduct environmental impact assessments might soon become a customary law obligation (ICJ Pulp Mills case 2010: para. 204; Eckstein and Sindico 2014). This indicates a convergence with regard to notification and impact assessment procedures in groundwater governance, which is further supported by the general principles of cooperation and information exchange. In general, the large number of environmental principles being discussed would suggest that if comprehensively adopted and implemented in legally binding agreements, the resource would be well-protected. However, true sustainability may be compromised by a lack of principles designed to cope with climate change.

4.5 Economic principles applicable to groundwater

Table 7 illustrates how the three identified economic principles are included in groundwater governance.

The polluter pays principle requires polluters to internalize the costs of pollution. It is the most-included economic principle, although still appearing sporadically in governance texts. Interestingly it is not always paired with principles for preventing pollution/harm or protecting ecosystems, principles which it supports. Since many products traded internationally use groundwater in their production processes, the principle of promoting an open international economic system is important in groundwater governance. It facilitates economic growth by ensuring that environmental trade policies are non-discriminatory and do not constitute a "disguised restriction on international trade" (Rio Declaration: Principle 12). The principle of water as an economic good was promoted by the ICWE Dublin Statement (1992: Principle 4) and is given significant attention within IWRM through water pricing and cost

Table 7 Economic principles in global governance texts applicable to groundwater resources

	ILA Helsinki Rules	UN Stockholm Declaration	UN Mar del Plata Declaration	ILA Seoul Rules	ICWE Dublin Statement	UN Rio Declaration	UNECE Convention	UN Watercourses Convention	UNECE Protocol on Water and Health	ILA Berlin Rules	ILC Draft Articles	UNHRC/ UNGA
Year	1966	1972	1977	1986	1992	1992	1992	1997	1999	2004	2008	2010
Open international economic system						✓						
Polluter pays[a]	✓					✓	✓		✓			
Water as an economic good					✓							

[a] Often expressed as "compensation" not payment

recovery mechanisms (Rogers et al. 1998; Savenije and van der Zaag 2002; Solanes et al. 1999) as applied by funding agencies.

Although water as an economic good and maintaining an open international system are not addressed in the global water governance texts (see Table 7), these principles are implemented *de facto* in trade regimes leading to increasing demand for water intensive products (Vörösmarty et al. 2015) and through "market environmentalism" which passes on economic and environmental costs to water users (Bakker 2007). In other words, the costs of these activities are simultaneously incorporated in water prices but excluded from prices of groundwater intensive products across the world, possibly shifting financial burdens to countries and affecting implementation of rights-based approaches and ecosystems protection.

5 CONCLUSIONS AND RECOMMENDATIONS

This paper assessed twelve key international groundwater governance texts (see Table 1) using a normative framework of thirty principles categorized according to the dimensions of sustainable development (Table 3). The assessment has shown that, for the most part, the principles necessary to achieve sustainable groundwater governance are present in the framework, but are not necessarily included in the formal legally binding documents applicable to groundwater. This leads us to three overarching conclusions.

First, groundwater governance has evolved rapidly in the last 25 years and includes an increasing number of principles (see Fig. 1). This is a positive trend in that collectively these principles could potentially promote sustainable development and use of groundwater resources.

Second, however, the framework of these collective principles does not adequately address (a) the link with all water resources including other groundwater resources; (b) the potential impact of climate change on water resources; and (c) the impact of trade on equitable sharing between regions and protection of groundwater-related ecosystems.

Third, to the extent that this collection of principles can contribute to sustainable development, they are inconsistently included in the legally binding groundwater governance texts (Tables 4, 5, 6, 7). Ideally, one would have expected that the legally binding texts would have included all the different relevant principles. However, (a) the scope and definitions of groundwater resources are inconsistently defined in the governance texts; (b) principles are inconsistently presented—for example using "expressed" consent rather than prior informed consent; or water as an economic good versus water as a human right; (c) critical principles such as the precautionary principle or protection of human rights are excluded from the legally binding texts; and last but not least (d) there is disagreement regarding how exactly sovereignty should be treated in groundwater governance texts. While limited sovereignty is more consistent with sustainable use of resources, where these resources are seen as limited in quantity and critical for state security, countries may use sovereignty to justify non-cooperation with others.

Hence, a normative framework for sustainable groundwater governance, which supports the global SDG agenda requires that groundwater governance texts (a) use a common terminology that is rooted either in the state-of-the art hydrogeology or legal norms, as appropriate; (b) include definitions and scope that recognize the duality of groundwater being both part of and apart from the contemporary hydrologic cycle, thus including aquifer of all types whether non-recharging, layered, or linked to surface water; (c) include norms presently underrepresented in legally binding texts; (d) reconcile tensions between principles; (e) elaborate best practices for well-accepted principles that are most challenging to implement; and (f) introduce principles or mechanisms to cope with the effects of trade and climate change. Further research on economic aspects of global groundwater governance and the relationship between the global framework and domestic rules and rights would greatly support such an endeavor.

FOOTNOTES

1. These agreements are listed in Eckstein and Sindico's (2014) publication. Since then, the Al-Sag/Al-Disi Aquifer Agreement (2015) was signed.

2. Sustainable development is included as a principle in the UN Rio Declaration (1992), UNECE Convention (1992) and Protocol (1999) as "sustainable use," ILA Berlin Rules (2004) as "sustainable use" and action agenda of the ICWE Dublin Statement (1992). IWRM is included in the ILA Seoul Rules (1986), UN Agenda 21 (1992), and ILA Berlin Rules (2004).

3. This principle is suggested in the scholarly Helsinki Rules and included in the Watercourses Convention (1997: Art. 5 and 6), the UNECE Convention (although not elaborated) and Draft Articles (2008: Art. 4, 5).

ACKNOWLEDGMENTS

This paper has been written as part of ongoing research being carried out collaboratively at the Amsterdam Institute for Social Science Research and the International Groundwater Resources Assessment Centre (IGRAC), Delft. Many thanks are owed to Dr. Neno Kukurić and Geert-Jan Nijsten of IGRAC for their support for this article. We would also like to thank three anonymous reviewers for their comments on an earlier version of this paper.

REFERENCES

1. Agenda 21. (1992). *Agenda 21.* In *Report of the United Nations Conference on Environment and Development.* Rio de Janeiro, Brazil: Annex II, UN Doc A/Conf. 151/26 (Vol. II).
2. Al-Sag/Al-Disi Aquifer Agreement (2015). *Agreement between the Government of the Hashemite Kingdom of Jordan and the Government of the Kingdom of Saudi Arabia for the Management and Utilization of the Ground Waters in the Al-Sag/Al-Disi Layer* (30 April 2015).
3. Bakker, K. (2007). The "Commons" versus the anti-privatization and the human right to water in the Global South. *Antipode, 39*(3), 430–455.
4. Biswas, A. K. (2004). Integrated water resources management: A reassessment. *Water International, 29*(2), 248–256.
5. Bluemel, E. B. (2004). The implications of formulating a human right to water. *Ecology Law Quarterly, 31*, 957–1006.
6. Bogdanovic, S., Bourne, C., Burchi, S., & Wouters, P. (2004). *ILA Berlin Conference 2004—Water resources committee report dissenting opinion.* Retrieved August 1, 2015, from http://www.internationalwaterlaw.org/documents/intldocs/ila_berlin_rules_dissent.html.

7. Custodio, E. (2002). Aquifer overexploitation: What does it mean? *Hydrogeology Journal,10*(2), 254–277.

8. Dellapenna, J. (2011). The customary law applicable to internationally shared groundwater. *Water International, 36*(5), 584–594.

9. Dellapenna, J., & Gupta, J. (Eds.). (2009). *The evolution of the law and politics of water*. Dordrecht: Springer.

10. Döll, P., & Hoffmann-Dobrev, H. (2012). Impact of water withdrawals from groundwater and surface water on continental water storage variations. *Journal of Geodynamics, 59–60*, 143–156.

11. Eckstein, G. E. (2007). Commentary on the UN International Law Commission's draft articles on the law of transboundary aquifers. *Colorado Journal of International Environmental Law and Policy, 18*(3), 537–610.

12. Eckstein, G. E. (2011). Managing buried treasure across frontiers: The international Law of Transboundary Aquifers. *Water International, 36*(5), 573–583.

13. Eckstein, G. E., & Sindico, F. (2014). The law of transboundary aquifers: Many ways of going forward, but only one way of standing still. *Review of European, Comparative and International Environmental Law, 23*(1), 32–42.

14. Fetter, C. W. (2001). *Applied hydrogeology* (Vol. 3). Upper Saddle River, NJ: Prentice Hall.

15. Fitts, C. R. (2002). *Groundwater science*. Boston, MA: Academic Press.

16. Fuentes, X. (2002). International law-making in the field of sustainable development: The unequal competition between development and the environment. *International Environmental Agreements, 2*(2), 109–133.

17. Gleeson, T., & VanderSteen, J. (2010). Groundwater sustainability strategies. *Nature Geoscience, 3*(6), 378–379.

18. Gleeson, T., Alley, W., & Allen, D. (2012). Towards sustainable groundwater use: Setting long-term goals, backcasting, and managing adaptively. *Ground Water, 50*(1), 19–26.

19. Gleick, P. (1998). The human right to water. *Water Policy, 10*(1), 487–503.

20. Global Water Partnership. (2002). *Integrated water resources management*. Sweden: Stockholm.

21. Goldsmith, J., & Posner, E. (1998). A theory of customary international law. *Chicago Law School, Journal of International Law, 66*, 1113–1178.

22. Gupta, J., Ahlers, R., & Ahmed, L. (2010). The human right to water: Moving towards consensus in a fragmented world. *Review of European Community and International Environmental Law, 19*(3), 294–305.

23. ICJ Case Concerning Pulp Mills on the River Uruguay (Argentina v. Uruguay) (2010).

24. ICWE Dublin Statement. (1992). The Dublin Statement and Report of the Conference. In *International conference on water and the environment: Development issues for the 21st century*. Dublin, Ireland.

25. International Groundwater Resources Assessment Centre (IGRAC). (2015a). *Global overview—Global Groundwater Information System (GGIS)*. Retrieved August 8, 2015, from https://ggis.un-igrac.org/ggis-viewer/viewer/go/public/default.

26. International Groundwater Resources Assessment Centre (IGRAC). (2015b). *Transboundary Aquifers of the World 2015*. Retrieved August 8, 2015 from http://tbamap.un-igrac.org.

27. ILA Berlin Rules. (2004). Berlin rules on water resources. In *Fourth report of the Berlin conference on water resources*. Berlin, Germany: Berlin Conference on Water Resources Law.

28. ILA Helsinki Rules. (1966). *Helsinki Rules on the Uses of the Water of International Rivers* (52nd Conf.). Helsinki, Finland: reprinted in Bogdanovic, S. (2001).

29. ILA Seoul Rules. (1986). *Seoul Rules on International Groundwaters*. Seoul, Korea: Report of the Sixty-Second Conference Held at Seoul.

30. Llamas, M. R., & Martínez-Santos, P. (2005). Intensive groundwater use: A silent revolution that cannot be ignored. *Water Science and Technology, 51*(8), 167–174.

31. Llamas, R., Back, W., & Margat, J. (1992). Groundwater use: Equilibrium between social benefits and potential environmental costs. *Hydrogeology Journal, 1*(2), 3–14.

32. Machard de Gramont, H., Noel, C., Oliver, J. L., Pennequin, D., Rama, M., & Stephan, R. M. (2011). *Towards a joint management of transboundary aquifer systems*. Paris, France: UNESCO.

33. Margat, J., & van der Gun, J. (2013). *Groundwater around the world: A geographic synopsis*. Leiden, Netherlands: CRC Press/Balkema.

34. McCaffrey, S. C. (1987). Third report on the law of the non-navigational uses of international watercourses. *Year Book of the International Law Commission, 2*(1), 16–36.

35. McCaffrey, S. C. (1992). Human right to water: Domestic and international implications, A. *Georgetown International Environmental Law Review, 5*(1), 1–24.

36. McCaffrey, S. C. (2009). The International Law Commission adopts draft articles on transboundary aquifers. *American Journal of International Law, 103*(2), 272–293.

37. McCaffrey, S. C. (2011). The International Law Commission's flawed draft articles on the law of transboundary aquifers: The way forward. *Water International, 36*(5), 566–572.

38. McIntryre, O. (2006). Role of customary rules and principles of international environmental law in the protection of shared international freshwater resources. *Natural Resources Journal,46*, 157–210.

39. McIntyre, O. (2011). International Water Resources Law and the International Law Commission Draft Articles on transboundary aquifers: A missed opportunity for cross-fertilisation? *International Community Law Review, 13*(3), 237–254.

40. McIntyre, O. (2012). The human right to water as a creature of global administrative law. *Water International, 37*(6), 654–669.

41. Mechlem, K. (2003). International groundwater law: Towards closing the gaps? *Yearbook of International Environmental Law, 14*, 47–80.

42. Obani, P., & Gupta, J. (2014). Legal pluralism in the area of human rights: Water and sanitation. *Current Opinion in Environmental Sustainability, 11*, 63–70.

43. PCA. (1910). *The Hague convention for the Pacific resolution of disputes.* (18 October 1907, entered into force 26 January 1910).

44. Rieu-Clarke, A. (2000). Reflections on the normative prescription of sustainable development in recent transboundary water treaty practice. *Water International, 25*(4), 572–579.

45. Rogers, P., Bhatia, R., & Huber, A. (1998). *Water as a social and economic good: How to put the principle into practice*. Sweden:

Global Water Partnership/Swedish International Development Cooperation Agency Stockholm.

46. Savenije, H. H. G., & van der Zaag, P. (2002). Water as an economic good and demand management paradigms with pitfalls. *Water International, 27*(1), 98–104.

47. Shah, T. (2009a). Climate change and groundwater: India's opportunities for mitigation and adaptation. *Environmental Research Letters, 4*(3), 035005.

48. Shah, T. (2009b). *Taming the anarchy: Groundwater governance in South Asia*. Washington, D.C.: Resources for the Future.

49. Siebert, S., Burke, J., Faures, J. M., Frenken, K., Hoogeveen, J., Döll, P., & Portmann, F. T. (2010). Groundwater use for irrigation—A global inventory. *Hydrology and Earth System Sciences Discussions, 7*(3), 3977–4021.

50. Sindico, F. (2011). The guarani aquifer system and the international law of transboundary aquifers. *International Community Law Review, 13*(3), 255–272.

51. Solanes, M., Gonzalez-Villarreal, F., and others. (1999). *The Dublin principles for water as reflected in a comparative assessment of institutional and legal arrangements for integrated water resources management.* Global Water Partnership Technical Advisory Committee.

52. Stephan, R. (2011). The Draft Articles on the law of Transboundary Aquifers: The process at the UN ILC. *International Community Law Review, 13*(3), 223–235.

53. Tanzi, A. (2011). Furthering international water law or making a new body of law on transboundary aquifers—An introduction. *International Community Law Review, 13*(3), 193–208.

54. UN Charter. (1945). *United Nations Charter.* 1 UNTS Xvi, (26 June 1945, entered into force 24 October 1945).

55. UN Stockholm Declaration. (1972). Declaration of the UN Conference on the Human Environment. In *Report of the United Nations Conference on the Human Environment* (5–16 June). Stockholm, Sweden.

56. UN ECOSOC. (2003). *General Comment No. 15: The Right to Water (Arts. 11 and 12 of the Covenant),* E/C.12/2002/11.

57. UN ILC. (2004). *Report of the 56th Session—Chapter VI Shared natural resources* (UN Doc A/59/10).

58. UN ILC Draft Articles. (2008). *Resolution on the law of transboundary aquifers.* A/RES/63/124.

59. UN Rio Declaration. (1992). Declaration of the UN Conference on Environment and Development. In *Report of the United Nations Conference on Environment and Development* (reprinted in 31 ILM 876). Rio de Janiero, Brazil: Annex 1, UN Doc A/Conf. 151/26 (Vol. I).

60. UN SDGs. (2015). Transforming our world: The 2030 Agenda for Sustainable Development. A/RES/70/1.

61. UN Mar del Plata Plan. (1977). *Report of the United Nations Water Conference.* UN Doc. E/CONF.70/29.

62. UN Watercourses Convention. (1997). *United Nations Convention on the Law of the Non-Navigational Uses of International Watercourses.* Reprinted in 36 ILM 700, (21 May 1997, entered into force 17 August 2014).

63. UNECE Convention. (1992). *United Nations Economic Commission for Europe Convention on the Protection and Use of Transboundary Watercourses and International Lakes.* 1936 UNTS 269, (17 March 1992, entered into force 6 October 1996) .

64. UNECE. (2003). *Amendments to Articles 25 and 26 of the Convention on the Protection and Use of Transboundary Watercourses and International Lakes.* Doc. ECE/MP.WAT/14, (28 November 2003, entered into force 6 February 2013).

65. UNECE. (2014). *Model Provisions on Transboundary Groundwaters.* ECE/MP.WAT/40.

66. UNECE Protocol on Water and Health. (1999). *Protocol on water and health to the 1992 convention on the protection and use of transboundary watercourses and international lakes.* 2331 UNTS 202, (17 June 1999, entered into force 4 August 2005).

67. UNGA. (1963). *Permanent Sovereignty over Natural Resources.* UN Doc A/5217.

68. UNGA. (2010). *The Human Right to Water and Sanitation.* A/Res/64/292.

69. UNHRC. (2010). *Human rights and access to safe drinking water and sanitation.* A/HRC/RES/15/9.

70. Vörösmarty, B. C. J., Hoekstra, A. Y., & Bunn, S. E. (2015). What scale for water governance? *Science, 349*(6247), 478–479.

71. WCED. (1987). *Our common future*. New York, NY: Oxford University Press.

72. Wijnen, M., Augeard, B., Hiller, B., Ward, C., & Huntjens, P. (2012). *Managing the invisible: Understanding and improving groundwater governance*. Washington, DC.

73. Yamada, C. (2011). Codification of the law of transboundary aquifers (groundwaters) by the United Nations. *Water International, 36*(5), 557–565.

74. Zektser, I., & Everett, L. (2004). *Groundwater resources of the world: And their use. IHP Series on Groundwater* (Vol. 6). Paris, France: UNESCO.

75. Ziganshina, D. (2008). Rethinking the concept of the human right to water. *Santa Clara Journal of International Law, 15*(15), 113–128.

7

CHAPTER

Trends of Development of International Water Law

Paulo Canelas de Castro

Faculty of Law, University of Macau, Macau, China

ABSTRACT

International water law has been witnessing profound changes in the latter twenty years. These changes denote certain cardinal options for new goals and values that the newer international water law is seeking to embrace. Amongst these new goals and values, the ones of environmentalization, humanisation, economicisation stand out as attempts at bringing efficient response to the challenges set by the current global water crisis and the more complex expectations of the international community. They amount to an innovative normative message and even true paradigm- shifts in the understanding of international water law. These trends of development of international water law set this legal field in line with other chapters of contemporary international law and derive in part from the cross-fertilisation of normative ideas and principles between these chapters of international law.

Keywords: Economicisation, Environmentalization, Global Water Crisis, Humanisation, Human Right to Water, International Water Law, Paradigm Changes, Trade in Water, Water Protection, Water Services

1. INTRODUCTION

After a few decades of a rather lethargic state, corresponding to the attempt at codifying it—undertaken, particularly, by the International Law Commission[1,2], and marked by a rather schizophrenic debate over the prevalence of two water sharing principles[3], simplistically seen as competing: those of the equitable and reasonable use of international watercourses and the obligation not to cause damage, also known as the no harm principle-International Water Law has been witnessing a considerable normative development in the latter two decades.

This normative development may be detected in multiple signs. Foremost, in the frantic law-making endeavors permeating international life: most noticeably, those translated in the adoption of numerous treaties at the different ambits of the international society[4]; but also in, the not less significant, soft law[5], undertaken in particular by manifold international organizations or conferences, which, in the period, have brought water issues to the forefront of the global international agenda. Additionally, also in the several international disputes where water is invoked as the main subject-matter and the unprecedented swathe of decisions which take water and international water law as their casus decidendi and rationale[6].

This hectic normative development is, moreover, of a much diversified character. Mirroring trends which had already been at the origin of the formidable development of International law at large, more broadly over the last seven decades, and which had led a leading scholar to adroitly proclaim the post-ontological hour of international law (Franck, 1995) , it seems arguable that this progress has in general been happening by cross-fertilizing the traditionally rather impermeable body of international water law with other fields of international law[7]. This global trend towards the corpus iuris of international water law building bridges with other fields of international law—and namely, international environmental law, international law of human rights and international economic law—may therefore be summarily apprehended in three main substantive "friendships" or "leanings" of international water law, its newer value or teleological choices: A choice towards "naturalizing", "environmentalising" or "greening" international water law; a trend towards "humanizing" international water law or, more broadly, rendering it more inclusive; and, more recently, a leaning towards looking more attentively at water, and the international law which is related to it, through a more consciously economic angle.

2. THE ENVIRONMENTALIZATION OF INTERNATIONAL WATER LAW

The environmentalization of International Water Law passes firstly through the normative apprehension of thereality of water bodies as it really happens: in its multiple interconnections and unitary complexity—of (non-confined) groundwater with surface water[8], of the watercourses with other biota and ecosystems[9], with the land mass[10] as well as with marine waters[11]. Several legal documents advocate that catchment areas or other analogous integrating concepts be used as the water management units[12]. This then permits and facilitates a more realistic or effective legal discipline: one where development of water is not any longer the sole goal pursued, but where instead development becomes integrated with the goal of protection of water[13]; one where, therefore, only sustainable development is lawful. Protecting the environment or ecosystems of watercourses, water quality, as well as the fight against diverse forms of pollution, thus become main concerns and normative areas of the newer international water legal disciplines[14]. Correspondingly, the scope of the obligations comprehended is equally enlarged: beyond obligations of mitigation and minimization or reduction and control of harm[15]—of risks[16], even—there are now obligations of prevention of impacts, of precaution[17] They all explain the consecration of procedural duties, ranging from notification of planned measures to consultations and negotiation[18], from simple obligations of access to information to a general duty to perform environmental[19] and strategic impact assessments, sometimes ex post even[20]. This wider approach becomes the more necessary as one acknowledges the crucial relevance of water in the ongoing conditions of scarcity[21]and climate change[22]. Both realisations call for actions and measures[23] that have a broader and cyclical time reference. These developments are in line with the concept of integrated water resources management as defined by the Global Water Partnership and based on the 1992 Dublin Statement on Water and Sustainable Development.

3. THE HUMANIZATION OF INTERNATIONAL WATER LAW

International Water Law has equally been witnessing a move towards including more legal personae within the remit of participating legal subjects.

This move concerns its traditional legal subjects, first: the States, the riparian States. Increasingly, the new international water law advocates that all those States, riparian to a particular shared watercourse, participate in the corresponding legal discipline[24], thus matching at this level an effort at ensuring that the said legal discipline corresponds to reality, and that it therefore may prove more efficient. Moreover, in a few instances, international law equally calls on the participation of coastal States adjacent to the riparian ones[25], in a legal development which again evidences an attention to natural reality and the real dynamics of impacts.

Secondly, the newer international water law equally concerns intergovernmental organizations and institutions of very different structures and functions[26,27]. Their establishment or revival[28] reflects the perceived need of States to enhance cooperation to manage shared water resources over several territories[29]. Their existence facilitates the recurring dialogue between the riparian States as to the activities that each of them purports to promote within its jurisdiction, particularly with regard to the sharing of rights and benefits deriving from the development of the waters as well as the prevention, reduction and control of risks of damages. They especially allow for an institutional process of communication, made of different procedural acts which permit the assessment of the effects of planned or existing measures or projects[30]. Finally, they also enable the carrying out of joint activities.

Most noticeably, different legal instruments[31] recommend that river/watercourse commissions be set up or that their experience is used[32] in the daily effort of implementing but also developing primary regimes[33]. In some cases, international organizations or international commissions are equally called to complement the action of the States (by providing financial and technical assistance[34], or working as instances for the prevention and settlement of disputes[35])[36].

Additionally, these organisations and institutions are sometimes also the platform for other non-governmental actors to intervene; like environmental, human rights' or governance NGOs, as well as epistemic communities, companies and individuals. All of them, thus thereby find their way to voice their concerns, grievances, interests, information, expertise[37]. Simultaneously, they obtain some legal status in the processes of decision-making or adjudicating the manifold issues of water management[38,39].

The whole movement reaches its climax once international law engages into its humanization—firstly, by recognizing procedural rights of access to information[40], participation in decision-making and in administrative decisions relating to the environment as well as the judicial appeal against such decisions, and rights of participation in impact assessments as well as in the aforementioned institutional water platforms. The 1998 Aarhus Convention on access to information, public participation in decision-making and access to justice in environmental matters[41], in the UNECE universe, stands out in such context as a prominent illustration[42,43].

The humanization of international water law is evidenced then, in the adoption of a human right to water and sanitation[44], which corresponds to the satisfaction of the most basic human needs[45,46] and overcomes a blatant *lacuna* of the International Bill of Human Rights. Initiated with General Comment n° 15 of the Economic and Social Council[47], the process of consolidation[48] of such double right gained momentum in 2010, by the adoption of corresponding resolutions by the General Assembly of the United Nations[49] and the Human Rights Council[50]. These documents[51] mainly anchor such right[52]of multifaceted content[53] in the remit of economic, social and cultural rights—a qualification, which renders these rights, ones of a progressive realization[54]. Be as it may, it equally implies a certain number of consequential obligations for the States, namely obligations to respect, protect and fulfill[55]. Amongst other duties, they call for the States' supplementary regulatory working. It is equally certain that the human right to water does not hinder the State to perceive payment for the services rendered. This applies, moreover, to not only the State but also other actors, which may, in particular, intervene in the provision of water services or waste treatment services[56]. This intervention seems justifiable not only because the right is neutral as to the economic model adopted by the State as to such vital public services, but also because momentous investments seem indeed to be in order for rendering this proclaimed right a true reality. In any event, the interface between this right and a kind of water management more economically-driven is, doubtlessly, one of the areas where international water law may need further development and clarification.

4. THE ECONOMICISATION OF INTERNATIONAL WATER LAW

The third vector of renewal of international water law contends with the integration of the economy and its international legal disciplines. The departing point is parallel to the ones seen in regard to the aforementioned strands of evolution of this body of rules: besides being taken as an environmental good, and a pole for legally empowering a diverse host of actors, and particularly for accrediting human rights, water is also more and more apprehended as a commodity, as an economic good[57].

This development is propitiated by several factors: the widespread awareness of water scarcity and unequal distribution[58], leading to a mounting demand for the resource as well as a rising capacity to dispose thereof over time and space[59].

Such developments then lead to elucubrations whether water or the service of its provision gains in being set in a market context[60], attached a "rationalizing" price tag[61]. It is equally questioned whether there is merit in trading bulk water[62] besides increasingly conveying it across space from "water-rich" to "water-poor" areas[63], as well as collecting it from the natural milieu, bottling it and selling it in a growing market of water "products"[64]. This approach is epitomized in some policy documents from the nineties of last century, like the Agenda 21[65], the Dublin Declaration[66] or the World Water Vision of the World Water Council[67].

Similarly, an apparently growing stream of legal thinking seems to be devoted to wondering whether there may be merit in applying international trade law (and the WTO agreements, GATT and GATS foremost)[68] as well as international investment law (the myriad of regional agreements and BITs)[69], as well as the corresponding institutions, to relevant water operations and what may be the consequences of such course of action.

More specifically, this rather creative or "outside-the-box" legal thinking is concerned, firstly, in regard to the trading of bulk water products, whether water may be treated as a "good"[70], a "product"[71,72]. It wonders, next, whether there is anything specific to water[73], justifying, if not imposing, that these principles governing international trade be derogated (the principles of most favored nation, of non-discrimination) or instead that it compels certain water-rich countries to envisage exporting water resources in abundance[74]. Were the GATT disciplines deemed to be applicable[75], another line of enquiry is what would the margin of maneuver for an exporting State mindful of the necessity to follow a precautionary approach in the management of its water resources be[76], so as to avoid violating GATT obligations aiming both at reducing tariff barriers and quantitative restrictions on trade as well as to remove any national measure that discriminates against domestic products vis-à-vis imported products[77]; whether in its managerial policies of environmental protection or driven by social considerations, such State could be comforted in the excepting clauses of Article XI. 2(a) and, particularly, Article XX of GATT[78]. Equally, it is asked whether it would be sensible to depend on the adjudicatory mechanisms of the WTO dispute settlement system for pursuing such policies[79].

In regard to water and wastewater services and the applicability of GATS, the main queries regard, besides classification issues[80], the possibility of carving out water public services in case of opening up the market to other foreign or domestic service providers[81]. Alternatively, it seems important to assess the usefulness of the reasons that article XIV of GATS provides, permitting derogations from the State's specific commitments, and, more largely, the extent of regulatory powers, which the host State may safeguard in the name of the pursuance of the public interest. Another provision with relevance is Article XIII of GATS, which sets out that the obligations of most favored nation treatment, market access and national treatment do not apply to "laws, regulations or requirements governing the procurement by governmental agencies of services purchased for governmental purposes and not with a view to commercial resale or with a view to use in the supply of services for commercial sale". If the contracts between public authorities and private water companies can be characterized as "government procurement", then the GATS regime (the obligations of most favored-nation, market access and national treatment) does not apply either[82]. It does not seem, however, that the concession contracts or build-operate-transfer contracts that are frequently used for ensuring water services should be considered public procurement[83].

In substantive connection to such debate, albeit not in terms of the legal instruments at stake, appear the discussions on investment solutions in the water sector. They derive from the apparent growing recognition of the financial crisis of the State. This financial crisis leads the State to rethink the priorities and engagement in the economic sector and, in particular, in the water area, towards catering technical expertise and financial assets through multiple forms of privatization of services which had previously axiomatically been seen as public— namely by engaging sometimes very powerful multinational enterprises willing to offer such services on an economic profit logics; as it drives the State to opening up to foreign direct investment, usually protected by the body of rules of international investment law and its mechanisms of dispute settlement, often relying on international arbitration. In spite of its close proximity, whereas the former debate on market liberalization systematically pertains to WTO law instruments and the GATS regime in particular[84], this latter one, for the lack of an investment dimension in the WTO agreements, rather has its systemic legal "seat" in the area related to the hundreds of regional and bilateral investment treaties.

The main issue debated relates to the host State's regulatory powers in view of the obligations to protect international investment and the mechanisms for the State to protect public interest in regard to private sector participation in the economic management of water. The effort is at striking the right balance between the powers seeking the protection of public interest and serving corresponding obligations like those correspective of a human right to water or those related to the protection of the environment, on the one hand, and those directed at the protection of international investments, on the other hand. A number of awards through ICSID dispute settlement[85] may be viewed as indicative of progress in such direction[86].

5. CONCLUDING REMARKS

The protrayed newer leanings or trends of development of international water law reveal an effort at holistically apprehending and giving normative response to a more complex reality of problems and social expectations than those that used to be addressed by the old international water law, centered on the pure regulation of the uses of water. The changes involved are diverse and numerous. It seems however possible to identify some common threads underlying all the changes and trends identified. A first one is the move towards establishing a creative interface between the traditional core of this body of principles and rules dedicated to water and those other disciplines of international law which more directly address the concerns with the protection of the environment, social equity, and a sensible weighing of the economic values. Internormativity is thus one of the keys for understanding the evolution of international water law and the vigor thereof; the normative dialogue generates cross-fertilisation and renovation of international water law. Another one is the implicit sense of urgency that these proposed changes and trends carry, corresponding only to the magnitude of the global water crisis. These changes are definitely momentous, as the newer law became much more complex in the normative responses pursued. They are not however deprived of an underlying vision: on the contrary, the newer international water law announces decisive cardinal options, pursues shared goals, honours certain values, follows principles which lend heuristic and interpretative sense to the reconstruction of this legal field. In the whole, the changes thus amount to true paradigm-shifts (Kuhn, 1962) . But this realisation also alerts us to the uncertainties that are still involved in the progress of international water law. It is of the very nature of paradigm-shifts themselves that they comprehend ambiguities and even elicit resistance. The uncertain harmonisation of the trends for environmentalisation and humanisation of water, on the one hand, and its economicisation, on the other, is in this regard telling. To this, one should add the realisation that these developments are an ongoing process: new problems seem already perceptible in the horizon—"climatising" international water law, adapting it to the challenges of climate change seems to be one of them. Another one is the struggle to render the whole movement of "legalisation" or more and newer law-making, a living reality: ensuring that the newer normative messages are complied with, should also become one of the major tenets of the evolution of international water law. Assessing the past but also looking ahead, one can not but be reminded of the works of Sisyphus.

NOTES

[1]See Tanzi & Arcari, 2001 , and McCaffrey, 2007 . The Law of International Watercourses—Non-navigational Uses, Oxford: Oxford University Press, 2nd ed., 2007.

[2]Prior to the International Law Commission's effort, the same concern had already led the International Law Association to adopt in 1966 the Rules on the Uses of the Waters for International Rivers, usually known as "the Helsinki Rules". They deal with navigational as well as non-navigational uses of rivers. See International Law Association, 1967. See also Manner & Metsalampi (eds.), 1988; Bogdanovic, 2001 .

[3]For the understanding of these principles prior to the adoption of the United Nations Watercourses Convention, see e.g., Caflisch, 1993 .

[4]To name but a few, at the regional level: 1992 Helsinki Convention on the Protection and Use of Transboundary Watercourses and International Lakes, 1991 Espoo Convention on Environmental Impact Assessment in a Transboundary Context, 1999 London Protocol on Water and Health, 2003 Protocol on Civil Liability and Compensation for Damages Caused by the Transboundary Effects of Industrial Accidents on Transboundary Waters, 1995 Protocol on Shared Watercourse Systems in the Southern African Development Community and its 2000 Revised Protocol on Shared Watercourses in the Southern African Development Community; and, at a local or specific basin level: 1994 Danube Convention on Cooperation for the Protection and Sustainable Use of the Danube River, 1994 Meuse and Scheldt agreements, revised in 2002, 1998 Convention between Portugal and Spain on the Cooperation for the Protection and Sustainable Use of the Waters of the Luso-Spanish River Basins, as well as the 2008 Revised Protocol to the Convention, 1999 Convention on the Protection of the Rhine, 1995 Agreement on the Cooperation for the Sustainable Development of the Mekong River Basin, 2002 Tripartite Interim Agreement between Mozambique, South Africa and Swaziland for the Cooperation on the Protection and Sustainable Utilisation of the Water Resources of the Incomati and the Maputo Watercourses, 2002 Senegal River Water Charter, 2003 Protocol for Sustainable Development of the Lake Victoria Basin. On the interplay and interactions between universal, regional and local basin instruments, see Boisson de Chazournes, 2009; Boisson de Chazournes, 2015 .

[5]In 2003, the International Law Commission considered the area of the law applicable to transboundary groundwater resources and, in 2008, it adopted the Draft Articles on the Law of Transboundary Aquifers: UN Doc A/CN.4/L.724 (29 May 2008). See International Law Commission, Report of the International Law Commission—Fifty-eighth session, UN Doc A/61/10 (11 August 2006), pp. 183-245; International Law Commission, Report of the International Law Commission—Sixtieth session, UN Doc A/63/10 (8 August 2008); McCaffrey, 2009; Mechlem, 2009. Following up on this input, the UN General Assembly, by Resolution 66/104 of 31 January 2012, captioned "The Law of transboundary aquifers", has also encouraged "the States concerned to make appropriate bilateral or regional arrangements for the proper management of their transboundary aquifers, taking into account the provisions of the Draft Articles annexed to its Resolution 63/124".

[6]To name but a few, see, in the International Court of Justice: Gabcikovo-Nagymaros Project (Hungary v Slovakia), Judgment, ICJ Reports 1977; Kasikili/Sedudu Island (Botswana v Namibia), Judgment, ICJ Reports 1999; Land and Maritime Boundary between Cameroon and Nigeria (Cameroon v Nigeria: Equatorial Guinea intervening), Judgment, ICJ Reports 2002; Frontier Dispute (Benin/Niger), Judgment, ICJ Reports 2005; Pulp Mills on the River Uruguay (Argentina v Uruguay), Provisional Measures, Order of 13 July 2006, ICJ Reports 2006; Pulp Mills on the River Uruguay (Argentina v Uruguay), Provisional Measures, Order of 23 January 2007, ICJ Reports 2007; Dispute Regarding Navigational and Related Rights (Costa Rica v Nicaragua), Judgment, ICJ Reports 2009; Pulp Mills on the River Uruguay (Argentina v Uruguay), Judgment, ICJ Reports 2010; Certain Activities carried out in the Border Area (Costa Rica v Nicaragua), Provisional Measures, ICJ Order of 8 March 2011; Frontier Dispute (Burkina Faso/Niger), Judgment of 16 April 2013; in the Permanent Court of Arbitration: Case concerning the audit of accounts between the Netherlands and France in application of the Protocol of 25 September 1991 Additional to the Convention for the Protection of the Rhine from Pollution by Chlorides of 3 December 1976 (Netherlands/France), Arbitral Award 2004; Indus Waters Kishenganga Arbitration (Pakistan v India), Order on Interim Measures 2011; Indus Waters Kishenganga Arbitration (Pakistan v India), Partial Award 2013; in the European Court of Justice. (a regional jurisprudence with international elements): Case 21/76 Handelskwekerij Bier v Mines de Potasse d'Alsace SA [1976] ECR 1735; Case C-36/98 Spain v Council of the European Union [2001] ECR I-00779; Case C-266/99 Commission of the European Communities v French Republic [2001] ECR I-2000; Case C-32/05 Commission of the European Communities v Grand Duchy of Luxembourg [2006] ECR I-11349.

[7]We have been arguing this since Canelas de Castro, 2005 . See also, Canelas de Castro, 2008 .

[8]The very notion of watercourse as well as other key notions of these regimes comprehend and integrate different types of waters as well as other elements. On the other hand, it excludes confined waters and other elements, which are better apprehended through the notion of "hydrographic basin" or alike. This leads several Authors to criticize the approach: see Salman, 2005, and Brown-Weiss, 2007 , who proclaims that "The 1997 UN International Watercourses Convention has several deficiencies from the water science perspective".

[9]For instance, in the United Nations Watercourses Convention, article 20.

[10]The notion of "hydrographic basin" apprehends better these interconnections. Whereas it is sometimes used in regional (e.g., African, see Kamto, 1990 ; see also the Water Framework Directive, in the European regional context) and local instruments, it was not retained in the UN Watercourses Convention, where the sovereignty sensitivities of States prevailed. See Paquerot, 2005; Sohnle, 2002; Coulée, 2011 .

[11]E.g., in the Watercourses Convention, article 23, which constitutes a recognition that land-based pollution is also a source of maritime pollution. See Canelas de Castro, 2003 .

[12]For instance, the 1998 Luso-Spanish Convention.

[13]This is explicitly reflected, for instance, in the very designation of conventions like the 1994 Danube Convention, the 1998 Luso-Spanish Convention, the 2002 Tripartite Interim Agreement relating to the Incomati and Maputo watercourses. In a different normative strategy, in the 1997 UN Watercourses Convention, protection of the watercourse has been recognized as a component of equitable and reasonable utilization—hence, articles 5, 6 (a) and (f). In addition, the 1997 Convention codifies a number of cooperation obligations that help to prevent or mitigate environmental damage. Moreover, its Part IV is dedicated to the protection, preservation and management of riverine ecosystems. Regionally, this is a marked difference between the Revised SADC Protocol, from 2000, and the first Protocol on Shared Watercourse Systems, adopted in 1995: e.g., the objectives listed in article 2 aim for sustainable, integrated and environmentally sound development and management.

[14]This is even more so in Europe and North America, sometimes as a response to catastrophes deriving from industrial accidents. See Kiss, 1987 .

[15]E.g., Article 21 of the United Nations Watercourses Convention.

[16]This is one of the triggers of precaution. See Boisson de Chazournes, 2007 ; and Martin, 1998 .

[17]For instance, the threshold for the due diligence obligations to prevent, reduce and control pollution also existing in the Watercourses Convention, has been raised in the 2008 Draft Articles on the Law of Transboundary Aquifers through a provision, article 12, which requires States to take a precautionary approach. The precautionary principle also features highly in the Helsinki Convention (article 2 (5) (b)) and underlies the whole 1999 UNECE Protocol to the Helsinki Convention, on Water and Health. Locally, it may be traced in basin treaties, like the 1998 Luso-Spanish Convention and the revised 2002 Meuse and Scheldt Agreements. The principle has also been mentioned in Pulp Mills on the River Uruguay (Argentina v Uruguay), Judgment, ICJ Reports 2010, para 164.

[18]See Part III of the United Nations Convention.

[19]Both article 12 of the UN Watercourses Convention and article 15 of the Draft Articles on Transboundary Aquifers mention that the obligation of notification of planned measures should inter alia be accompanied by the results of environmental impact assessments. There is actually a linkage between the obligation to provide information and the impact assessments: this is demonstrated by the International Court of Justice's consideration in the Pulp Mills case that the information transmitted must include a complete environmental impact assessment in order to assess the effects of a planned measure on the environment and that the notification must "take place before the State concerned decides on the environmental viability of the plan, taking due account of the environmental impact assessment submitted to it", Pulp Mills on the River Uruguay (Argentina v Uruguay), Judgment, ICJ Reports 2010, para 120.

[20]This was indicated already in the Gabcikovo-Nagymaros case and explicitly spelled out in the Pulp Mills on the River Uruguay (Argentina v Uruguay), Judgment, ICJ Reports 2010, para 205: once operations of a project have started, continuous monitoring of its effects on the environment must be undertaken.

[21]See, very appropriately, Brown-Weiss, 2013 .

[22]See Canelas de Castro, 2011 .

[23]Like adaptation strategies designed to face the impacts of climate change. See article 4 (1)(e) of the United Nations Framework Convention on Climate Change, of 9 May 1992, UNTS 1771 (1994).

[24]See article 3 of the United Nations Convention.

[25]See article 9(3) of the Helsinki Convention.

[26]For an effort at designing a typology, see Caflisch, 1989 ; Boisson de Chazournes, 2003underlines the emergence of a trend towards their harmonization, though; one which is induced partially by global and

regional conventions which themselves promote the creation of basin organizations and commissions.

[27]Whereas the scope of cooperation in these organisations and commissions was narrow in the nineteenth century, it gradually broadened throughout the twentieth century in parallel with a movement of increased and more diversified use of the international rivers. The range of competencies of these organisations and commissions has equally become vaster. Whereas in the beginning their main task concerned navigation regulation, the scope was widened to cover activities like the production of energy, irrigation, recreational and environmental protection activities and include functions like those of information collection and dissemination, regulation by the adoption of standards and guidelines, the promotion and execution of joint operational activities, the brokering of discussions for the eventual development of other legal instruments. See exemplarily, the Luso-Spanish Convention, article 10.

[28]For early institutional experiences, see Chamberlain, 1923; Blociszewski, 1926; Colliard, 1968;McCaffrey, 2007 .

[29]Similarly, Pulp Mills on the River Uruguay (Argentina v Uruguay), Judgment, ICJ Reports 2010, para 81.

[30]Their importance is stressed in the Pulp Mills on the River Uruguay (Argentina v Uruguay) Case, paras 115 and 119.

[31]Also scientific associations called for such legal and institutional developments: see for instance, Institute of International Law, "Resolution on the International Regulations regarding the Use of International Watercourses" of 1911.

[32]See article 3 (4) of the 2000 EU Water Framework Directive.

[33]This function of platform for legal development and implementation is clearly spelled out in the designation of the Luso-Spanish commission established by the 1998 convention. See also article 10 of the Convention, devoting a particular attention to the law-making potential of the commission.

[34]See Boisson de Chazournes, 2007 and, specifically on water, Boisson de Chazournes, 2015 .

[35]The 1997 Convention on the Law of the Non-Navigational Uses of International Watercourses underlines such role in article 33(2). Different basin agreements, like the 1998 Luso-Spanish Convention and the 1909 Treaty on Boundary Waters, and Questions Arising between the United States and Canada (article IX) equally award this function to the corresponding commission, generally linking it to the object and purpose of the regime at stake.

[36]For which, the international legal personality of a river commission may be added value, particularly in relations with third actors. See article 11 of the 1995 Agreement on the Cooperation for the Sustainable Development of the Mekong River Basin which expressly states: "The institutional framework for cooperation in the Mekong River Basin (...) shall (....) enjoy the status of an international body, including entering into agreements and obligations with the donor or international community".

[37]With the "privatisation" of assistance ensuing from the 1992 Rio Conference, the Monterrey Conference, but especially the Johannesburg Summit, the private sector also helps in the financing of implementing projects and legal instruments—usually in partnerships between governments and civil society groups.

[38]See Mekong River Commission for Sustainable Development, 2005 .

[39]A pivotal role is frequently played by these institutions' secretariats.

[40]See e.g., Sand, 2003 .

[41]See McAllister, 1998 .

[42]See United Nations Economic Commission for Europe, 2000 .

[43]Similarly, in the African context, the African Convention on the Conservation of Nature and Natural Resources.

[44]See Albuquerque, 2013 .

[45]The consideration of human needs in the development of international water law predates the recognition of the human right to water.

[46]It is important to realise that the human right to water and sanitation is linked to the satisfaction of personal and domestic needs, and thus to some privileged uses of water, in particular those related to household and personal uses. It therefore does not pertain to the whole spectrum of other usages, such as industrial, agricultural, fishing, navigation, hydroelectric uses or those related to the protection of the environment, irrespective of the close links existing among them. The fundamental rights nature of the right to water lends this right its objective priority status—as does the international law of watercourses with the provision of article 10 of the 1997 Watercourses Convention.

[47]General Comment No. 15 (2002) of the Economic and Social Council, "The Right to Water", UN Doc E/C.12/2002/11 of 20 January 2010.

[48]Other milestones in the process, even prior to General Comment No. 15, are the UN Mar del Plata Action Plan of 1977, the Dublin Statement on Water and Sustainable Development of 1992 and Agenda 21. Also international treaties contribute to defining aspects or beneficiaries of this

right: in particular, the Convention on the Elimination of All forms of Discrimination Against Women (article 14 (2)), the Convention on the Rights of the Child (article 24 (2)), the Convention on the Rights of Disabled Persons (article 28 (2a)). Equally noteworthy are the Draft Guidelines for the Realization of the Right to Drinking Water Supply and Sanitation adopted by the Sub-Commission on the Promotion and Protection of Human Rights, in 2005. Besides human rights instruments, also those relating to the law of international watercourses contributed to the emergence of the right: particularly, the Protocol on Water and Health, the Charter of Water of the Senegal River, the Water Charter of the Niger Basin and the Charter of Water of Lake Chad.

[49]Resolution 64/292 of the UN General Assembly, "The Human Right to water and sanitation", UN Doc A/Res/64/292, of 3 August 2010.

[50]Resolution 15/L.14 of the Human Rights Council, "Human rights and access to safe drinking water and sanitation", UN Doc A/HRC/15/L. 14 of 24 September 2010.

[51]Beyond the conceptual and even interpretative differences between the different normative instruments, as to the legal scope of the right, content, field of application and application (see Caflisch, 2011), they all recognize the importance of this right and share a vision or general objective: the one of achieving access to safe drinking for the human beings and obtaining access to sanitation systems. This objective mobilized legally and politically different actors and set the framework for seeking effective implementation and realization of this right, a formidable endeavor in view of the realities in the field (see WHO and UNICEF, 2010). In this latter regard, certain initiatives stand out for their contribution to the advancement of the aforementioned general objective: namely, the decision of the Human Rights Council in 2008 (by Resolution 7/22) to appoint an Independent Expert on the issue of Human Rights relating to access to drinking water and sanitation , who became in 2011 (by Resolution 16/2) the Special Rapporteur on the Right to safe drinking water and sanitation—it established the right to water and the reports of the Special Rapporteur helped refine the contents thereof (see Albuquerque, 2012); also noteworthy are the calls by the Human Rights Council for States to implement this right.

[52]Some instruments formulate this right as an autonomous right, while others link it to other rights and even make it derive therefrom: for instance, with the right to life and as a prerequisite for the realization of all human rights (e.g., Resolution 64/292 of the General Assembly), the right to an adequate standard of living and the right to the highest attainable standard of physical and mental health as well as the right to life and human dignity (Resolution 15/L.14 of the Human Rights Council). General

Comment No. 15 also derives the human right to water from the right to an adequate standard of living and considers that it is "inextricably related to the right to the highest attainable standard of health and the rights to adequate housing and adequate food".

[53]The notes of equitable access, quality, availability, affordability are usually invoked in this regard. See Coulée, 2011 and Albuquerque, 2010 .

[54]See article 2 (1) of the International Covenant on Economic, Social and Cultural Rights and Salman & McInerney-Lankford, 2004 .

[55]Idem, at pp. 67-68.

[56]More broadly, drawing a connection between the fight for this right and the ascension of new actors in the international scene and their claim for treating water as a global public good and for a global governance of water, see Coulée, 2011 .

[57]Dealing with water as an economic good is one of the ways increasingly suggested in order to efficiently manage water. For instance, Dalhuisen, Groot, and Nijkamp, 2000 state that: "An economic approach to water supply and demand may contribute to a better management of water and to its sustainable use".

[58]Idem, p. 3.

[59]See Cossy, 2005a .

[60] Carter et al. (eds.), 1994; Anderson (ed.), 1994; Libecap, 2005 .

[61] Cossy, 2005a; Hildering, 2005; Caponera, 1992 .

[62]See Haan, 1997; Hildering, 2005 .

[63]Examples quoted or discussed include the tender between Turkey and Israel, the export of water from Canada to the USA, the transfers between Malaysia and Singapore, Lesotho and South Africa, Mainland China to Hong Kong and Macau. See Cossy, 2005a; Hildering, 2005; Little, 1996;Baumann, 2001 .

[64] Brown-Weiss, 2005 .

[65]Chapter 18, para. 18.8 alludes to water as a social and economic good, namely when it states that "integrated water resources management is based on the perception of water as an integral part of the ecosystem, a natural resource and a social and economic good".

[66]Principle 4 of the Dublin Statement on Water and Sustainable Development states that "water has an economic value in all its competing uses and should be recognized as an economic good". On this, see Solanes, 1998 .

[67]See Cossy, 2005a .

[68]See, in particular, Brown-Weiss, 2005; Cossy, 2005c; Tuerk, Ostrovsky, &, Speed, 2005; Boisson de Chazournes, 2015 .

[69]See the whole Chapter IV of Brown-Weiss, 2005 ; Boisson de Chazournes, Fresh Water in International Law, pp. 96-104; Bray, 2014 .

[70]This has to do with the fact that GATT applies to goods, a concept which is not defined but which seems to relate to a moveable thing which may be traded on a market.

[71]Again this is an undefined operational concept determining the application of the GATT disciplines. It implies that something is produced as a result of a natural process or human operation, human intervention. Another element of the definition is the one of the attribution of a price. See Haan, 1997; Cossy, 2005b .

[72]In a 2000 report on the Protection of Waters of the Great Lakes, the International Joint Commission between Canada and the United States stated expressly the view that water in its natural state is not a product or commodity. IJC, Final Report to the Government of Canada and the United States, Protection of the Waters of the Great Lakes, 2000. This view was reiterated in the 2004 report, where the International Joint Commission recommended that "both governments take steps to allay fears that Great Lakes water could be treated as a commodity" and again insisted on the idea that WTO rules do not affect the protection of water in its natural state. IJC, Review of the Recommendations in the February 2000 Report, Protection of the Waters of the Great Lakes, 2004.

[73]The condition of natural resource and the fact that so many social expectations are attached thereto are considerable elements in such debate. As the WTO concluded in the World Trade Report 2010 on trade in natural resources, "WTO rules were not specifically drafted to regulate natural resources trade and may not always respond adequately to the specific features of this sector". WTO, World Trade Report: Trade in Natural Resources, p. 203.

[74]The debate is particularly intense in regard to Canada. It explicitly involves the questioning whether the trade regimes of the WTO and in special the North American Free Trade Agreement (NAFTA) deny the right to limit water exports in respect of other members of the NAFTA and instead require the "water-rich State" to export its water as a tradable good, despite the risk that this poses to this State's control over the management and preservation of the water resources. See Baumann, 2001; Maravilla, 2001; Anderson, 1999 .

[75]Canada, the United States and Mexico have expressly addressed the issue of the application of NAFTA to water, in 1993, by making a joint statement which reads: "The NAFTA creates no rights to the natural resources of any Party to the Agreement (...). Water in its natural state in lakes, rivers, reservoirs, aquifers, water basins and the like is not a good or product, is not traded, and therefore is not and has never been subject to the terms of any agreement". Reprinted in Brown-Weiss, Boisson de Chazournes, &Bernasconi-Osterwalder (eds.), 2005 . On its one side, Canada insisted that water in the natural state should be excluded from the application of trade agreements, by having the Ministry of Foreign Affairs and International Trade, unilaterally declare that: "Water in its natural state can be equated with other natural resources, such as trees in the forest, fish in the sea, or minerals in the ground. While all of these things can be transformed into saleable commodities through harvesting or extraction, until that crucial step is taken they remain natural resources and outside the scope of the trade agreements". Department of Foreign Affairs and International Trade, "Paper on Bulk Water Removal and International Trade Considerations".

[76]Brown-Weiss calls a particular attention to the interplay of this approach and the uncertain long-term effects of climate change. See Brown-Weiss, 2005 .

[77]Particularly at stake seem to be articles I (a water-exporting State would have to extend its "benefits" to any other State, so as not to violate the principle of most-favoured-nation treatment); III (a State that would be engaged in transfers, concerning water within its borders, would have to treat national and foreign competitors alike, for the national treatment principle); XI (although the rules on measures of export tariffs are less detailed than those on exports, its paragraph 2, in particular, seems to allow State water exporters to establish prohibitions or restrictions on transfers of bulk water "to prevent or relieve critical shortages or foodstuffs or other products essential to the exporting contracting party", such as droughts, effects of industrial accidents, natural disasters or other emergencies, these measures have to be temporary and only to prevent a critical situation); XX (setting the conditions for allowing States to implement national measures which, under certain conditions, are inconsistent with other provisions of GATT).

[78]In what concerns freshwater, the two openings or exceptions that seem to be relevant are those contained in sub-headings (b) and (g). Under the former, a State may maintain a measure otherwise inconsistent with other GATT provisions if that measure may be taken as "necessary to protect human, animal or plant life or health". In view of some case law concerning disputes before the Dispute Settlement Body of the WTO, it does not seem crucial that these actually versed on import restrictions on products—it seems possible for a State to argue for taking measures to restrict the

export of water for environmental purposes and to protect the ecosystem of water resources: the State would thereby be seeking to protect human health and the preservation of flora and fauna. Additionally, to determine that a measure is "necessary" to achieve a specific goal, recourse must be made to the WTO case law: it indicates that the term "necessary" is not limited to meaning "indispensable" but also encompasses "promote". Moreover, it equally implies that the "common interests" and "shared values" pursued by the measure must also be taken into account. The protection and conservation of water seem to be a good example of such vital common interests. Under the latter, a State may adopt measures "relating to the conservation of exhaustible natural resources if such measures are made effective in conjunction with restrictions on domestic production or consumption". Since WTO case law indicates that "renewable" resources may fall under the concept of "exhaustible natural resource", there would not be a problem, it seems, in applying the notion and the provision under article XX (g) to water. For a measure adopted by a State to be justified under Article XX, it is still necessary to meet the requirements of the "chapeau" of this provision. In particular, domestic measures must not constitute "a means of arbitrary or unjustifiable discrimination between countries where the same conditions prevail, or a disguised restriction on international trade". At stake, in the very clarification made by WTO case law, is "rather the manner in which the measure is applied" (US-Gasoline, Report of the Appellate Body, para. 22. On Article XX's "chapeau", see Gaines, 2001 .

[79]It would appear that disputes about the allocation and use of water, as well as about the legitimacy to protect ecosystems and the ecology would be made by bodies more prepared for and attuned to trade considerations. Discussing this issue as other "reasons not to apply the GATT 1994 to water in its natural state or to bulk transfers", see Brown-Weiss, "Water Transfers and International Trade Law", in Brown-Weiss, 2005 .

[80]Like the harmonized system of GATT relating to products, there is a classification list of services set by the WTO Secretariat, which is not mandatory but used by States to develop schedules of commitments in the liberalisation of markets. It does not contain any separate category for services related to water, but some of the sectors considered do contain references to activities related to water, like environmental services and sanitation, for instance.

[81]The question is whether it is possible to argue that these water services fall under the provision of article I:3(b) which establishes that "services supplied in the exercise of governmental authority" are excluded from the scope of the GATS. These are defined as being supplied "neither on a commercial basis, nor in competition with one or more suppliers". The thorny issue is the determination of the relationship between "public

service" and "governmental authority": they can certainly not be interpreted as synonymous. It might equally be possible to argue that services of water distribution stand as a public monopoly. In such case, GATS would apply.

[82] Cossy, 2005a .

[83] Cossy, 2005b .

[84]GATS does not mention privatization or demand that the water services suppliers are public or private—article XXVIII does not indicate any preference.

[85]Namely, in the Aguas del Tunari v Bolivia ICSID Case No. ARB/02/3, in the Suez, Sociedad General de Aguas de Barcelona SA and Vivendi Universal SA v Argentine Republic ICSID Case No ARB/03/19, in the Biwater Gauff (Tanzania) Ltd v United Republic of Tanzania ICSID Case No ARB/05/22, and in the Azurix Corp v Argentine Republic, ICSID Case No ARB/01/12.

REFERENCES

1. Albuquerque, C. (2010). Water and Sanitation as Human Rights. In Conseil d'Etat, L'eau et son droit, Rapport publique. Paris: Conseil d'état.
2. Albuquerque, C. (2012). On the Right Track: Good Practices in Realising the Rights to Water and Sanitation. New York: The United Nations.
3. Albuquerque, C. (2013). Water and Sanitation Are Human Rights: Why Does It Matter? In L. Boisson de Chazournes, C. Leb, & M. Tignino, (Eds.). International Law and Freshwater: The Multiple Challenges. Cheltenham: Edward Elgar. http://dx.doi.org/10.4337/9781781005095.00013Anderson, B. D. (1999). Selling Great Lakes Water to a Thirsty World: Legal, Policy and Trade Considerations. Buffalo Environmental Law Journal, 6, 219-220.
4. Anderson, T. L. Eds. (1994). Continental Water Marketing. San Francisco: Pacific Research Institute for Public Policy.
5. Baumann, C. (2001). Water Wars: Canada's Upstream Battle to Ban Bulk Water Export. Minnesota Journal of Global Trade, 10.
6. Blociszewski, J. (1926). Le régime international du Danube. Recueil des Cours de l'Académie de La Haye, 11, 253-340. http://dx.doi.org/10.1163/ej.9789028604827.253-340

7. Bogdanovic, S. (2001). International Law of Water Resources: Contribution of the ILA (1954-2000). London: Kluwer.

8. Boisson de Chazournes, L. (2003). The Role of Diplomatic Means of Solving Water Disputes: A Special Emphasis on Institutional Mechanisms. In The PCA/Peace Palace Papers. Resolution of International Water Disputes (Vol. 5, pp. 91-110). The Hague: Kluwer.

9. Boisson de Chazournes, L. (2007). Precaution in International Law: Reflection on its Composite Nature. In T. M. Ndlaye et al. (Eds.). Law of the Sea, Environmental Law and Settlement of Disputes: Liber Amicorum Judge Thomas A. Mensah (pp. 21-34). Leiden: M. Nijhoff. http://dx.doi.org/10.1163/ej.9789004161566.i-0.22

10. Boisson de Chazournes, L. (2007). Technical and Financial Assistance. In D. Bodansky, J. Brunnée, & E. Hey (Eds.), The Oxford Handbook of International Environmental Law (pp. 947-973). Oxford: Oxford University Press.

11. Boisson de Chazournes, L. (2009). Freshwater and International Law: The Interplay between Universal, Regional and Basin Perspectives. Paris: UNESCO, United Nations World Water Assessment Programme.

12. Boisson de Chazournes, L. (2015). Fresh Water in International Law. Oxford: Oxford University Press.

13. Bray, H. L. (2014). ICSID and the Right to Water: An Ingredient in the Stone Soup. ICSID Review, 1-10.

14. Brown-Weiss, E. (2005). Water Transfers and International Trade Law. In E. Brown-Weiss, L. Boisson de Chazournes, & N. Bernasconi-Osterwalder (Eds.), Fresh Water and International Economic Law (pp. 61-89). Oxford: Oxford University Press.

15. Brown-Weiss, E. (2007). The Evolution of International Water Law. Recueil des cours de l'académie de Droit international, 331, 222.

16. Brown-Weiss, E. (2013). International Law in a Water Scarce World. The Hague Academy of International Monographs, Volume 7, Leiden: Brill.

17. Brown-Weiss, E., Boisson de Chazournes, L., & Bernasconi-Osterwalder, N. (Eds.) (2005). Fresh Water and International Economic Law. Oxford: Oxford University Press.

18. Caflisch, L. (1993). Sic utere tuo ut alienum non laedas: Règle prioritaire ou élément servant à mesurer le droit de participation équitable et raisonnable à l'utilisation d'un coursd'eau

international? In A. Ziegler (Ed.), Internationales Recht auf See und Binnengewaesser. Festschrift fuer Walter Mueller (pp. 27-47). Zuerich: Schulthess.

19. Caflisch, L. (2011). Le droit à l'eau—Un droit de l'homme internationalement protégé. In Société francaise pour le droit international, Colloque d'Orléans. L'eau en droit international (pp. 392-394). Paris: Pédone.

20. Caflisch. L. (1989). Règles générales du droit des cours d'eau internationaux. Recueil des Cours de l'Académie de La Haye, 219, 196-202. http://dx.doi.org/10.1163/ej.9780792321408.009-225

21. Canelas de Castro, P. (2003). Freshwaters-Sea Interface: Emerging International Legal Field? Boletim da Faculdade de Direito da Universidade de Macau, 16, 179-220.

22. Canelas de Castro, P. (2005). Recent Developments in International Law. Principles and Comparative Cases. Lisbon: Luso-American Foundation.

23. Canelas de Castro, P. (2008). The Global Challenge of Sustainable Water Management: International and European Union Law Responses. Temas de Integracao, 25, 95-133.

24. Canelas de Castro, P. (2011). Climate Change and Water Management: Is Water Law Adapted to Climate Change? In C. A. Brebbia, & V. Popov (Eds.), Water Resources Management VI (pp. 827-839). Southampton: WIT Press. http://dx.doi.org/10.2495/WRM110741

25. Caponera, D. (1992). Principles of Water Law and Administration. Rotterdam: A. A. Balkema.

26. Carter, H. O. (Ed.) (1994). Sharing Scarcity: Gainers and Losers in Water Marketing. Davis: University of California Agric. Issue Center.

27. Chamberlain, J. P. (1923). The Regime of the International River: Danube and Rhine. New York: Columbia University.

28. Colliard, C. A. (1968). Evolution et aspects actuels du régime juridique des fleuves internationaux. Recueil des Cours de l'Académie de La Haye, 125, 417-431.

29. Cossy, M. (2005a). Le statut de l'eau en droit international économique. Principaux aspects au regard des règles de l'Organisation mondiale du commerce, In L. Boisson de Chazournes, & S. M. A. Salman (Eds.), Les ressources en eau et le droit international (pp. 177-178). Leiden: Martinus Nijhoff.

30. Cossy, M. (2005b). Water Services and the GATS—Selected Legal Issues. In E. Brown-Weiss, L. Boisson de Chazournes, & N. Bernasconi-Osterwalder (Eds.), Fresh Water and International Economic Law (pp. 129). Oxford: Oxford University Press.

31. Cossy, M. (2005c). Water Services at the WTO—Selected Legal Issues. In E. Brown-Weiss, L. Boisson de Chazournes, & N. Bernasconi-Osterwalder (Eds.), Fresh Water and International Economic Law (pp. 117-141). Oxford: Oxford University Press.

32. Coulée, F. (2011). Rapport général—Du droit international de l'eau à la reconnaissance internationale d'un droit à l'eau: Les enjeux. In Société francaise pour le droit international, Colloque d'Orléans. L'eau en droit international (pp. 27-31). Paris: Pédone.

33. Dalhuisen, J. M., Groot, H. L. F., & Nijkamp, P. (2000). The Economics of Water: A Survey. International Journal of Development Planning Literature, 15, 4.

34. Franck, T. (1995). Fairness in International Law and Institutions. Oxford: Clarendon Press.

35. Gaines, S. (2001). The WTO's Reading of the GATT Article XX Chapeau: A Disguised Restriction on Environmental Measures. Journal of International Economic Law (University of Pacific), 22, 739.

36. Haan, E. (1997). Balancing Free Trade in Water and the Protection of Water Resources in GATT. In E. P. Brans et al. (Eds.), The Scarcity of Water—Emerging Legal and Policy Responses (pp. 246-247). The Hague: Kluwer.

37. Hildering, A. (2005). Water as an Economic Good. In L. Boisson de Chazournes, & S. M. A. Salman (Eds.), Les ressources en eau et le droit international (pp. 225-227). Leiden: Martinus Nijhoff. http://dx.doi.org/10.1163/ej.9789004137028.3-756.6

38. Kamto, M. (1990). Le droit international des ressources en eau continentales africaines. Annuaire francais de droit international, 36, 855-871.

39. Kiss, A. (1987). Tchernobale ou la pollution accidentelle du Rhin par des produits chimiques. Annuaire francais de droit international, 33, 719-727. http://dx.doi.org/10.3406/afdi.1987.2804

40. Kuhn, T. S. (1962). The Structure of Scientific Revolutions. Chicago: University of Chicago Press.

41. Libecap, G. D. (2005). Rescuing Water Markets: Lessons from Owens Valley. Bozeman: PERC.

42. Little, S. P. (1996). Canada's Capacity to Control the Flow: Water Export and the North American Free Trade Agreement. Pace International Law Review, 8, 127.

43. Manner, E., & Metsalampi, V. M. (Eds.) (1988). The Work of the International Law Association on the Law of International Water Resources. Helsinki: Finnish Branch of the International Law Association.

44. Maravilla, S. (2001). The Canadian Bulk Water Moratorium and Its Implications for NAFTA. Current International Trade Law Journal, 10, 31-35.

45. Martin, G. J. (1998). Le concept de risque et la protection de l'environnement: Evolution parallèle ou fertilization croisée? In M. Prieur (Ed.), Les hommes et l'environnement, en hommage à Alexandre Kiss (pp. 451-460). Paris: Frison-Roche.

46. McAllister, S. T. (1998). The Convention on Access to Information, Public Participation in Decision-Making, and Access to Justice in Environmental Matters. Colorado Journal of International Environmental Law and Policy, 9, 187.

47. McCaffrey, S. (2007). The Law of International Watercourses—Non-Navigational Uses (2nd ed.). Oxford: Oxford University Press.

48. McCaffrey, S. (2009). The International Law Commission Adopts Draft Articles on Transboundary Aquifers. American Journal of International Law, 103, 272. http://dx.doi.org/10.2307/20535150

49. Mechlem, K. (2009). Moving Ahead in Protecting Freshwater Resources: The International Law Commission's Draft Articles on Transboundary Aquifers. Leiden Journal of International Law, 22, 801. http://dx.doi.org/10.1017/S0922156509990239

50. Mekong River Commission for Sustainable Development (2005). Public Participation in the Lower Mekong Basin. Vientiane: Mekong River Commission for Sustainable Development.

51. Paquerot, S. (2005). Eau douce: La nécéssaire refondation du droit international. Sainte-Foy (Québec): Presses de l'Université du Québec.

52. Salman, S. M. A. (2005). Evolution and Context of International Water Resources Law. In S. M. A. Salman, & L. Boisson de Chazournes (Eds.), Les ressources en eau et le droit international

(pp. 66-68). The Hague: Hague Academy of International Law. http://dx.doi.org/10.1163/ej.9789004137028.3-756.2

53. Salman, S. M. A., & Lankford, S. M. (2004). The Human Right to Water. Legal and Policy Dimensions. Washington DC: The World Bank. http://dx.doi.org/10.1596/0-8213-5922-3

54. Sand, P. H. (2003). Information Disclosure as an Instrument of Environmental Governance. Heidelberg Journal of International Law, 2, 487-502.

55. Sohnle, J. (2002). Le droit international des ressources en eau douce: Solidarité contre souveraineté. Paris: La documenta- tion francaise.

56. Solanes, M. (1998). Integrated Water Management from the Perspective of the Dublin Principles. CEPAL Review, 64, 165.

57. Tanzi, A., & Arcari, M. (2001). The United Nations Convention on the Law of International Watercourses: A Framework for Sharing. The Hague: Kluwer.

58. Tuerk, E., Ostrovsky, A., & Speed, R. (2005). GATS and Its Impact on Private Sector Participation in Water Services. In E. Brown-Weiss, L. Boisson de Chazournes, & N. Bernasconi-Osterwalder (Eds.), Fresh Water and International Economic Law (pp. 143-172). Oxford: Oxford University Press.

59. United Nations Economic Commission for Europe (2000). The Aarhus Convention: An Implementation Guide. New York: United Nations.

60. WHO and UNICEF (2010). Progress on Sanitation and Drinking Water: 2010 Update. Geneva: WHO and UNICEF.

61. Ziegler, A. (Ed.) (1993). Internationales Recht auf See und Binnengewaesser. Festschrift fuer Walter Mueller. Zuerich: Schulthess.

8

CHAPTER

Trying to End the War on the World: The Campaign to Proscribe Military Ecocide

Peter Hough

Department of Law & Politics, Middlesex University, London, UK

ABSTRACT

Military ecocide, the destruction of the natural environment in the course of fighting or preparing for war, has a long history and remains a regular feature of contemporary conflicts. Efforts to prohibit this in international law were initiated after the US' notorious defoliation campaign in the Vietnam War in the 1960s and have advanced since then. Legal ambiguities and the defence of military necessity have limited the application of this body of law but the proscription of ecocide has, nonetheless, progressed and looks set to develop further. Normative change driven by scientists, environmentalists and legal experts has raised awareness of and stigmatised such practises to the extent that recourse to the worst excesses of ecocide now appears to have lessened and some recompense for past crimes has been made. Military activities, though, still inflict a heavy cost on the environment.

Keywords: Ecocide, scorched earth, Agent Orange

1. INTRODUCTION

This article provides an historical overview of the progression of international legal efforts to prohibit military ecocide, the deliberate or inadvertent destruction of the natural environment in the course of fighting or preparing for war. Ecocide is a term that has also come to be applied in reference to the criminal and industrial destruction of the environment – such as in illegal deforestation or dumping of toxic waste at sea – but this review will confine itself to militarily induced degradation. There is a long history of military-induced environmental degradation and it is a facet of warfare that has, in general, worsened over time with the advent of more devastating and poisonous forms of weaponry. In stark illustration of how both the politics of international security and industrialisation have traditionally been played out, such devastation has often been justified on the grounds of military necessity in ways that could not so readily be done if the casualties were human, where a large body of international law offers some restraint. The perennial problem of the natural environment being valued only instrumentally – for its human utility – rather than intrinsically, has been apparent in the recourse to military strategies such as scorching the earth, altering freshwater supplies or chemical deforestation throughout history.

However, many and an increasing number of people do value the environment for its own sake, as evidenced by the rise of ecocentric domestic policy since the 1960s. In particular, many people have come to be convinced of the need for ecocentric restraints on human behaviour through scientific evidence. Despite the popular imagery of mystic, tree-hugging hippies, it should not be forgotten that the green movement in the 1960s was kick-started by the emergence of ground-breaking, rational and convincing scientific evidence. In particular, U.S. marine biologist Rachel Carson's *magnum opus Silent Spring*proved that the widespread use of organochlorine pesticides in the fight against disease-carrying and crop-consuming insects, following their discovery in the 1940s, was also polluting streams and killing wildlife (Carson, 1962). As a consequence of this, these activities, though serving human interests, began to be constrained in the U.S. and then elsewhere. Whilst military ecocide continues to feature in military campaigns, the legal and normative prohibition of such practices has advanced, in roughly the same timescale as the advance of ecologism, again largely due to the efforts of scientists and campaigners in highlighting the issue to a horrified public.

2. THE HISTORY OF MILITARILY INDUCED ENVIRONMENTAL DAMAGE

The wilful destruction of nature in the course of war can occur both as an offensive or defensive strategy.

2.1. Offensive ecocide

The 'scorched earth' destruction of the crops and livestock of an enemy is a strategy that has been deployed in wars since ancient times. It is a method that has formed part of many international conquests, such as in the Roman sacking of Carthage, and also in the course of domestic counter-insurgency campaigns, such as in the Norman's 'Harrying of the North' after annexing England in the eleventh century. In the modern era, similar methods were still being employed by U.S. in the Philippines from 1898 to 1902 to undermine nationalist resistance, much of which was from jungle-based guerrilla units, after having seized the islands from the Spanish. Domestic alarm at how an intervention, initially sold to the American public as liberating the Filipinos from Spanish tyranny, had become a typically brutal colonisation prompted criticism from prominent quarters, with the likes of former President Grover Cleveland, business tycoon Andrew Carnegie and literary great Mark Twain expressing outrage at Roosevelt's war as part of the American Anti-Imperialist League established in 1898. Twain articulated his horror in the form of a mock prayer, calling on God to 'help us to turn them out roofless with little children to wander unfriended the wastes of their desolated lands in hunger and thirst' (Twain, 2016).

With the advent of synthetic organochlorine pesticides, offensive ecocide was able to move beyond the razing of food sources to include the tactical destruction of tree cover utilised by insurgent guerrilla forces. The British were the first to undertake a strategy of 'industrialised chemical defoliation' in wartime in the early 1950s during the 'Malayan Emergency'. The acidic herbicide formulations 2,4,5-T and 2,4-D (later combined in *Agent Orange* used by the U.S. in Vietnam) were used to clear lines of communication and wipe out food crops in the struggle against communist insurgents. With Imperial Chemical Industries (ICI) providing the technical advice, British and Malayan troops in 1952 despatched fire engines spraying mixtures of these herbicides along a number of key roads. The strategy was not successful and after seven months, it proved more effective, both economically and practically, to remove vegetation by hand and the spraying was stopped. The following year, though, saw the use of herbicides as an aid to fighting the guerrillas restarted with the more traditional goal of destroying food crops grown by the communist forces in jungle clearings (Connor & Thomas, 1984). The environmental costs of this British ecocide are unclear. Since this episode predated *Silent Spring* and the environmental era, the sorts of scientific studies which later highlighted the environmental and health damage resulting from similar spraying operations 10 years later in Vietnam, never took place.

The application of herbicides was far more widespread in the Vietnam War, with an estimated 80 million litres of 2,4,5-T (2,4,5-trichlorophenoxyacetic acid), 2,4-D (2,4-dichlorophenoxyacetic acid), picloram and cacodylate blended in a variety of mixtures – including the notorious *Agent Orange* – and sprayed on jungle foliage from military aircraft between 1962 and 1971 in the most infamous ever systematic military assault on the environment. American scientists have estimated that 10% of Vietnam's inland forests, 36% of her mangrove forests and 3% of cultivated land were affected by the programme codenamed 'Operation Ranch Hand' (NAS, 1974, pp. 5, 6). This scale of ecological damage indirectly affected the health of millions of Vietnamese by reducing the quality of their nutritional intake and creating internally displaced persons susceptible to disease. More clearly deadly were the cases of direct poisoning by herbicides. In particular dioxin, which arises as a by-product in the manufacture of 2,4,5-T, is one of the most toxic chemicals known, an estimated 170 kg of which was sprayed over Vietnam and the neighbouring countries of Laos and Cambodia (NAS, 1974, pp. vii–9). Dioxin is severely toxic in several dimensions. It is teratogenic (causes birth defects), hepatotoxic, mutagenic, carcinogenic, a skin irritant and known to increase cholesterol levels in blood. Many studies have linked instances of such symptoms amongst South Vietnamese residents and their offspring with the sprayings between 1962 and 1971 (Franklin, 2003). As is in the nature of toxicology, and particularly carcinogenicity and teratogenicity, proving causal factors is difficult but myriad cases have documented spontaneous abortions and infant deformities. The evidence, though, is completely unambiguous with regard to liver damage due to dioxin exposure. A study led by Do Thuc Trinh found that 'chronic hepatitis was more than ten times as prevalent among those subjects who had been directly exposed to military herbicides (more than a decade previously) than amongst those who had not' (Westing, 1984, p. 166).

Despite some initial uncertainties in the scientific data relating to dioxin exposure, the US's defoliation campaign in Vietnam, Cambodia and Laos was quickly and roundly condemned by the American scientific community and many international statesmen. The American Association for the Advancement of Science in 1969 set up a Herbicide Assessment Commission to investigate the effects of Operation Ranch Hand made up of four leading domestic scientists, of whom the most prominent voice to emerge was Arthur Westing. Westing's background was as a Botanist and Forest Ecologist but the fact that he had also served in the U.S. military, seeing action as an artillery officer in the Korean War, equipped him with insights into both sides of the military-environment equation. Westing became the best known academic critic of the U.S. defoliation campaign in Vietnam which he described as causing 'widespread, long-lasting and severe disruptions of perennial croplands, and of farmlands – that is to say of millions of hectares or the natural resource base essential to an agrarian society' (Westing, 1989, p. 337). Westing's writings also advocated the need to criminalise and prosecute such acts, notably highlighted in the 1974 article, 'Proscription of Ecocide':

... what is urgently required at this time is the establishment of the concept that widespread and serious ecological debilitation – so called ecocide – cannot be condoned. (Westing, 1974, *p.* 26*)*

Westing here utilised the term 'ecocide' probably first employed by fellow U.S. scientist Arthur Galston in 1970. Galston was a biologist central to the discovery of the defoliant qualities of 2,4,5-T who became alarmed at how his work had come to be put into practice and wrote critically about how Operation Ranch Hand was destroying Vietnamese river ecosystems (Cook, Heseltine, & Galston 1970). Continued pressure by the Herbicide Assessment Commission, including a petition signed by 5000 scientists (of whom 17 were holders of Nobel prizes), led to the termination of the campaign in 1971, fuelled in particular by public horror at evidence of appalling birth defects occurring in the South Vietnamese population (Hay, 1982, p. 151).

Criticism of U.S. ecocide, though, did not end with the termination of Operation Ranch Hand. In particular, high-profile international political expression was given to the crime of military ecocide when Swedish Prime Minister Olaf Palme, after meeting Westing for a briefing on the subject, used this term to denounce the Vietnam defoliation programme, indirectly at the 1972 United Nations Conference on the Human Environment (UNCHE) at Stockholm. Palme did not explicitly cite the U.S. in condemning environmental warfare at UNCHE, but then did so overtly in several speeches in the following months (Hay, 1982, p. 165). The U.S. administration managed to use the threat of pulling out of UNCHE to avert any direct reference to Operation Ranch Hand in the official principles and paperwork that came out of the conference, but Palme's continued criticism prompted Nixon to suspend full diplomatic relations with Stockholm for several months, an extraordinary situation for two Western democracies to find themselves in.

No compensation has ever been forthcoming for any of the Vietnamese, Cambodian or Laotian victims of birth deformities, liver damage or other ailments attributable to Operation Ranch Hand. The Cambodian Government attempted to claim compensation for damage done in

Kompong Cham province but the case dissolved when that regime was overthrown in 1970. The only victims compensated for illnesses attributable to 'Operation Ranch Hand', are soldiers who fought on the side responsible. War veterans from the U.S., Australia and New Zealand, who have suffered subsequent skin and liver disorders or birth defects in their offspring, won a long battle for compensation in 1979, when a U.S. Federal Judge ruled that they could sue the companies responsible for manufacturing Agent Orange. Over 45,000 people have since claimed a share of the $180 million in damages from Dow and six other chemical firms. Dow agreed to the settlement in the face of public pressure and mounting legal costs, but have always denied that the various illnesses incurred by the veterans were directly related to Agent Orange and other herbicide mixtures sprayed in Vietnam.

Despite the controversy of Operation Ranch Hand, U.S. ecocide in Vietnam also served to inspire other governments and armed groups engaged in conflicts in woodland or arid terrain susceptible to tactical manipulation. Mimicking the tactics used in Vietnam, the Indonesian Government in the late 1960s conducted what has been asserted to be the biggest deforestation in history to quell insurgencies in Borneo and West Kalimantan (Peluso & Vandergeest, 2011). Similarly, the 1980s civil war in El Salvador saw the government bomb agricultural lands and forests in seeking to deny guerrilla forces a base and sustenance. Partly as a consequence of this, El Salvador today is virtually deforested. In a different form of domestic ecocide, Saddam added to his long list of environmental and human crimes deliberate desertification in diverting the courses of the rivers Tigris and Euphrates in order to drain marshland areas that were home to the Shia 'Marsh Arabs', after they had initiated an uprising against his rule after the Gulf War in 1991. This act of ecological ethnic cleansing drained around 90% of the region's marshes and also depleted its population from 250,000 to around 40,000 (Weinstein, 2005, p. 715). Saddam's 'hydro-terrorism' doubtless served as an inspiration to ISIS who, in 2015, dammed sections of the Euphrates in order to dehydrate opponents in the Syrian Civil War.

2.2. Defensive ecocide

The 'backs to the wall' tactic of destroying your own resources to prevent an invading enemy making use of them is also a well-established military strategy. Perhaps most famously, Russian forces in 1812 retreated from the invading French army whilst destroying their own arable lands in an ultimately successful strategy that paved the way for Napoleon's disastrous 'retreat from Moscow', which sowed the seeds of his downfall. The Russian strategy was learned from British military leader Wellington who two years earlier, in alliance with Portuguese guerrilla forces, had resisted a French invasion in the Peninsular War in a similar manner. French military power was build on its arable supremacy, allowing her to feed the biggest army in Europe, and this had come to be realised by those on the receiving end of her autarky.

Whilst, by the twentieth century, industrial rather than arable might had become the main determinant of military power, scorching the earth could still serve its purpose. During the Second World War, the British took responsibility for rendering uninhabitable the islands of Norway's Svalbard archipelago (Spitsbergen) in order to limit German interest in its coalfields (despite Norwegian opposition). Consequently, the German presence on the Arctic islands was limited to the manning of some weather stations. In a different and more dramatic form of defensive ecocide, the Yellow River was deliberately flooded in 1938 by the Chiang Kai-shek government in resisting the Japanese invasion of Manchuria. In doing so, the Chinese succeeded in slowing down the invaders by creating a bigger barrier and destroying potential food supplies but achieved this at the cost of the lives of hundreds of thousands of their own citizens and the homes of millions more. More recently, defensive ecocide, more spiteful than strategic, featured in the Gulf War when Saddam's forces set fire to several oil wells whilst retreating from Kuwait in 1991, some of which continued to burn for several months. Oil was also deliberately leaked into the Persian Gulf by the Iraqi troops.

3. COLLATERAL DAMAGE: INDIRECT MILITARY ENVIRONMENTAL DEGRADATION

Environmental degradation due to war can also occur more indirectly as a result of the general destruction of battle. The aforementioned 1938 Manchurian war was, in fact, a multi-faceted environmental (and human) horror show. The Japanese used chemical and biological weaponry in a brutal invasion and then, once their defeat in the Second World War became apparent, abandoned much of the remaining munitions across north-eastern China to prevent them falling into allied hands. Shells containing chemicals such as mustard gas and phosgene were dumped in fields, lakes and streams prompting a slow-burning public health disaster in which thousands of Chinese people have subsequently died or been disabled in the decades that have since passed.

Elsewhere during World War Two, 'total war' bombings were of such a scale and nature that environmental catastrophes were, of course, inevitable. However, in spite of the revival of limited and just war principles since then, 'collateral ecocide' has still been apparent in the supposedly more strategic strikes of recent conflicts. In 2006, for example, between 20 and 30,000 tonnes of oil polluted a large stretch of the Eastern Mediterranean Sea and coastline after Israel bombed the Jiyeh Power Station during the Lebanon War (CoE, 2011). Similarly, in the 1999 Kosovan War, NATO included amongst its strategic bombing targets several chemical plants and fossil fuel facilities which would inevitably pollute waterways and cause other forms of environmental damage. The campaign led to the significant pollution of the Danube and also released toxic and carcinogenic chemicals into the ground and air. Most notorious was the targeting of the major Serbian petrochemical and fertiliser plants at Pancevo. NATO acknowledged the environmental consequences of the strikes but asserted that military necessity justified some collateral fallout since the plants were a key source of the Serb regime's power. Longer lasting forms of environmental and human damage from the Kosovan War bombings and other recent campaigns such as in Iraq have come from contamination resulting from the U.S. and U.K. use of the radioactive and highly persistent chemical 'depleted uranium' to coat munitions shells. Greenhouse gasses, CFCs, mercury, sulphur dioxide and nitrous oxide emissions are also now part of the common collateral damage of contemporary bombing campaigns (Sanders, 2009, pp. 71, 72).

Battlefield destruction can also render arable land and other natural resources useless to humanity and other life forms. In addition to the pollution and defoliation, millions of craters today mark the agricultural belts of Vietnam and Laos as a consequence of a combination of deliberate and collateral military actions by the U.S. in the 1960s. Many French and Belgian World War One battlefields remain barren today nearly a century on. Resource depletion through over-utilisation is another typical consequence of war. The appropriation of food and fuel by invading troops is the most predictable form of this phenomenon, but too much strain can also be put on the home resources of the invading forces. Environmental degradation can also occur more indirectly as a result of sudden influxes of refugees fleeing war. For example, 38 sq km of forest in Kivu Province of Congo DR were lost within three weeks of the arrival of Rwandan refugees fleeing genocide in the mid-1990s (UNEP, 2002). As well as being worsened deliberately, deforestation can be accelerated as a consequence of countries trying literally to rebuild their country after a conflict. Many Iraqi city trees were felled for fuel in the aftermath of the US-led invasion of 2003 and it is also known that Afghan water supplies and vegetation were seriously damaged and depleted following the onset of war in 2001 (CoE, 2011; Sheehan, 2003). Animals, of course, are frequent casualties of war. Gorilla numbers in the Democratic Republic of Congo are known to have fallen as a consequence of that country's persistent civil conflict, both through direct killings and more indirectly as a result of the destruction of their habitat through deforestation (Kalpers, 2001). Collateral killings of wildlife can also occur in the context of military preparation. Peacetime NATO naval exercises off the south coast of Spain, for instance, are known to have killed at least 15 beached whales in 2002 (CoE, 2011CoE. (2011). *Armed conflicts and the environment* (Report of the Committee on the Environment, Agriculture and Local and Regional Affairs, Doc 12744, October 17th). Strasbourg: Parliamentary Assembly of the Council of Europe.)(Figure 1).

514-512 BC Scythians defending against invading Persians (Darius)
146 BC 3rd Punic Wars: Romans on Carthage, to subjugate after military defeat
52 BC Gallic Wars: Gauls (Vercingetorix) defending against invading Romans
1069-70 'Harrying of the North': Normans (William) against English uprising
1414 'Hunger Wars': Teutonic Knights (Germanic crusaders) invading Poland-Lithuania
1565 Great Siege of Malta: Crusaders resisting Turkish invasion
1581 2nd Desmond Rebellion: English settlers suppressing Irish rebellion in Munster
1644 30 Years War: Swedes (Torstensson) in invading Denmark
1679 Mughal-Maratha Wars: Marathas of India (Shivaji) against Mughal Empire
1708-09 Great Northern War: Russians defending against invading Swedes (Charles XII)
1810 Peninsular War: British and Portuguese in defending against French invasion
1812 'Retreat from Moscow': Russians defending against French invasion
1812-13 South American War of Independence: Argentine patriots defending against Spanish / Royalists
1817-18 Sri Lankan Great Rebellion- British colonial suppression of uprising
1864 'March to the Sea': US Unionists (Sherman) against Confederates in the Civil War.
1867-69 US (Sherman) extermination of the Buffalo to subjugate native Americans
1898-1902 US-Philippine War: US colonial suppression of uprising
1900 2nd Boer War: British against Boers in power struggle over South Africa
1922 Greco-Turk War: Greeks in Western Anatolia in retreat
1938 Manchurian War: Chinese flooding in defending against Japanese invasion
1938 Manchurian War: Japanese dumping of chemical weapons
1941 World War Two: Soviets in defending against German invasion
1941 World War Two: British in Spitsbergen to render useless to German invasion
1944-5 World War Two: Germans in retreat from Soviets in Northern Norway and Finland
1952 'Malayan Emergency': British and Malayan government suppressing leftist insurgency
1962-69 Vietnam War: US intervention against leftist insurgency
1967 Indonesia government suppression of insurgencies in Borneo and West Kalimantan
1980-90 Salvadoran Civil War: government suppression of leftist insurgency
1981-2 Guatemalan Civil War: government suppression of leftist insurgency
1990 Gulf War: Iraq (Saddam) in retreat from Kuwait
1991 Iraqi government (Saddam) suppression of uprising by 'Marsh Arabs'
1999 East Timorese secession from Indonesia: pro-government militia in retreat
1999 Kosovan War: pollution from NATO bombing of Serbia
1999-2009 Chechen Wars- pollution from Russian bombing
2003-08 Darfur Crisis: Sudanese government and Janjaweed militia against Darfurians
2006 Lebanon War: pollution from Israeli bombing
2006-09 Sri Lankan Civil War: government suppression of Tamil insurgency
2011 Libyan Civil War: Government (Gadaffi) suppression of rebels in Benghazi.
2014-15 Syrian Civil War: Insurgents (ISIS) river diversion against government and slashed earth v Kurds.

Figure 1. Timeline of some major incidences of environmental damage in war.

4. THE MILITARISATION OF THE ENVIRONMENT

As the case of the whale fatalities in the NATO exercise case illustrates, it is not just actual war which can prompt environmental damage but the whole phenomenon of defence and military preparation. The scale and nature of the cold war defence greatly intensified the traditional ecological side effects associated with this. The rise of nuclear weapons testing, mass military exercises and the global proliferation of military bases came with significant costs, many of which are continuing to be counted. The Soviet testing of nuclear weapons and dumping of the waste from this was particularly extensive in its peripheral regions such as the northern reaches of Siberia. At least 130 tests were carried out in the Soviet Arctic between 1955 and 1970, prompting landslides as well as depositing radioactive material in the soil, water, ice and air (Glasby & Voytekhovsky, 2010, p. 20). Environmental damage was also inflicted on parts of the Soviet empire during the cold war. For example, Soviet military camps occupied nearly 2% of Estonia and left behind significant pollution in that country on their withdrawal in 1994. No compensation for water and soil pollution by oil, cadmium, lead, uranium and general waste was ever paid in a clean-up that the Estonian Government claimed cost them $4 billion (Auer, 2004, pp. 119–121).

U.S. militarism at home and particularly in its overseas outposts has also carried significant environmental costs. Again in the Philippines, realpolitik and imperial neglect saw the Subic Bay naval base become the scene of a notorious ecological disaster which included the wilful pollution of side-stepping sewage treatment and allowing human waste to be dumped directly into the sea. The Philippine Government claimed compensation for such pollution but the Americans never paid and abandoned the base in 1991 whilst pointing to the 1947 Military Bases Agreement between the two countries absolving them of any legal responsibility. In domestic politics, American military exceptionalism is also apparent with the Pentagon exempted from being reported on by the Environmental Protection Agency and, hence, never having been held accountable for known instances of pollution by solvents, fuels and munitions near military bases well above state limits (Schettler, 1995).

In a different facet of ecocide, the military securitisation of the environment can sometimes take the form of a kind of 'nationalisation of nature' with wild badlands forcibly tamed. Tropical woodlands have regularly featured in security politics as both the arenas and symbols of resistance. Much of the resistance to the Japanese invasions in South-East Asia during the Second World War was jungle-based and this also came to be the stage for resisting European colonial rule after 1945. Hence, as well as carrying out deforestation for tactical reasons, many governments consciously came to construct their woodland as 'jungle' so as to invoke notions of lawlessness, danger and insecurity that required the assertion of sovereign control through enforced land purchases, coerced population movements and the establishment of permanent military bases (Peluso & Vandegeest, 2011). This was very much the case with the aforementioned governmental deforestations in Indonesian and El Salvadoran.

In a more general sense, it should always be remembered that there is a significant ecological side effect to the sheer existence of the military-industrial complex. A study in the 1990s found that the military accounted for around a quarter of the world's jet fuel, 9% of its iron and steel consumption and employed 20% of its scientists (Ostling, 1992, p. 8). Given that, two decades on, global military expenditure has significantly increased, it must be assumed that this ecological footprint is now even greater.

5. HISTORY OF INTERNATIONAL TREATIES AND LAWS TO ADDRESS MILITARY ECOCIDE

A body of international law proscribing military ecocide has steadily advanced since the 1970s; but in a predictable illustration of traditional national security trumping environmental concerns, there is little precedent for enforcing this legislation. Explicit references to the 'environment' were not made in the war laws of the Geneva or Hague Conventions prior to the 1970s, despite their extensive evolution since the nineteenth century (Figure 2). The second Hague Convention of 1907 though does declare illegal military methods which 'destroy or seize the enemy's property, unless such destruction or seizure be imperatively demanded by the necessities of war'. In more general terms, the centuries old tradition of Just War, upon which the Geneva and Hague Conventions are built, can be seen as helping safeguard the environment since the notion of 'limited war', which proscribes the escalation of conflicts beyond their specific purposes and acts of pure retribution and spite, logically must also apply to the destruction of nature beyond military necessity. International arms control law can similarly be suggested to proscribe ecocide, in principle at least. The 1925 Geneva Protocol on Chemical Weapons (and its effective contemporary successor the 1993 Chemical Weapons Convention), whilst driven by humanitarian rather than environmental concerns, by outlawing the military use of toxins, inherently makes wilful pollution illegitimate.

C3rd – C13th:	Evolution of Just War principles within Christianity and Islam proscribe excessive military damage
1868:	Declaration of St Petersburg by European powers outlawing explosive bullets includes agreed principle that only military targets should be considered legitimate.
1899:	First Hague Convention on Laws of War- article IV (ii) outlaws use of poison gas by great powers (except US)
1907:	Second Hague Convention- article 23(g) outlaws wanton destruction
1925:	Geneva Protocol to Hague Convention outlaws chemical weapons
1948:	Nuremburg War Trials establish scorched earth tactics without clear military purpose are illegal.
1969:	General Assembly Resolution 2603 states that all military applications of chemicals (including defoliants) is contrary to the 1925 Geneva Protocol.
1976:	Convention on the Prohibition of Military or any Hostile Use of Environmental Modification Techniques (ENMOD)
1977:	Geneva Conventions on War Protocol I Articles 35 and 55 outlaw widespread, long-term and severe military damage to the environment
1981:	UN General Assembly Resolution 36/150 condemns Israeli canal plan because of its implications for Jordan in the context of their dispute.
1990:	Cairo Declaration on Human Rights in Islam Resolution Article 3b outlaws military destruction of crops or livestock
1991:	UN Security Council Resolutions 687 and 692 prosecute Iraq government for environmental destruction in invasion of Kuwait.
1992:	UN General Assembly Resolution 47/37 states that military ecocide is contrary to International Law
1992:	UN Conference on Environment & Development- Rio Declaration Principle 24 affirms that the environment should be respected in warfare.
1993:	Chemical Weapons Convention outlaws use and possession of chemical weapons
1995:	Organization of African Union Conference of Ministers of Health Resolution 14(5) outlaws destruction of crops in war.
1999:	International Criminal Court Statute 8(2) b (iv) lists excessive damage to the environment as a war crime

Figure 2. Timeline of international law and military ecocide.

That the wanton destruction of buildings and land is contrary to international law was confirmed at the Nuremberg war trials at the close of the Second World War. German General Lothar Rendulic was prosecuted by the International Military Tribunal for his command of scorched earth raids in Finnmark, Norway when in retreat from the Russian army. Rendulic was actually acquitted, as the Tribunal accepted that he genuinely believed the destruction to be militarily justified, but a precedent that such acts could amount to an international crime was, nonetheless, established. (Boas & Schabas, 2003, p. 293) Another German General, Alfred Jodl, was convicted and hanged for several war crimes amongst which was culpability for scorched earth in Finnmark for which no military justification could be found. The UN War Crimes Commission at Nuremberg also confirmed that German plundering of Polish forestry constituted a war crime (case 7150). Military ecocide was more acute in the War in the East but national interest and an early manifestation of cold war realpolitik ultimately trumped humanitarian concerns when it came to prosecuting Japanese war crimes. The Tokyo War Crimes Trials did not properly address the Japanese deployment and dumping of chemical and biological weapons in Manchuria, largely due to the US's desire to keep such knowledge to themselves and out of the hands of the Soviet Union.

Japan's actions in Manchuria were clearly counter to the Geneva Protocol and Hague Convention, but the will to implement these instruments was not apparent, as it had not been a few years earlier when appeasement saw Mussolini's chemical assault on Abyssinia overlooked by the League of Nations in 1935. The effective death knell of the Geneva Protocol came when it became apparent that the huge advances in chemical synthesis in the 1940s and 1950s had rendered it redundant by the time an attempt came to prosecute the U.S. for Operation Ranch Hand on the basis of a 1969 General Assembly request. In response to this, U.S. Secretary of State Rogers stated that 'the 1925 Geneva Protocol does *not* cover chemical herbicides', on the grounds that the chemicals used were not known in 1925 and that their intention was to kill plants not humans.

The simultaneous rise of environmentalism and the Vietnam War, however, did prove twin catalysts for the emergence of international law specifically dealing with military ecocide. In the spirit of detente, the Americans and Soviets actually cooperated in formulating a draft for what would become the 1976 Convention on the Prohibition of Military or any Hostile Use of Environmental Modification Techniques (ENMOD Convention). Moscow, able to capitalise on the controversy that had emanated from Operation Ranch Hand, initiated the idea of an 'ecocide convention' and Washington, having terminated the strategy in 1971 and then the whole war in 1975, had no strategic need to risk the reputational loss of allowing the Soviets to claim the moral high ground. ENMOD was adopted by Resolution 31/72 of the United Nations General Assembly in 1976 and opened for signature the following year.

Simultaneous to the negotiation of ENMOD a Protocol to the Geneva War Conventions (1977) dealing with ecocide was also agreed. Protocol I additional to the Geneva Conventions, added in 1977, includes two Articles dealing directly with the dangers that modern warfare poses for the environment.

Article 35 – Basic rules

3. It is prohibited to employ methods or means of warfare which are intended, or may be expected, to cause widespread, long-term and severe damage to the natural environment.

Article 55 – Protection of the natural environment

1. Care shall be taken in warfare to protect the natural environment against widespread, long-term and severe damage. This protection includes a prohibition of the use of methods or means of warfare

which are intended or may be expected to cause such damage to the natural environment and thereby to prejudice the health or survival of the population.

2. Attacks against the natural environment by way of reprisals are prohibited.

By 2016, Protocol I had been ratified by some 174 states but notable amongst the non-parties were the U.S., India, Israel, Iran, Pakistan, Turkey and Libya. Parties to the ENMOD Convention similarly undertake not to use environmental manipulation that would have 'widespread, long-lasting or severe effects as the means of destruction, damage or injury to any other State Party' (Article I). Far less universal than Protocol I, ENMOD had, by 2016, 77 parties (though this does include the United States).

Taken together, parties to the twin ecocide instruments are prohibited from attacking, destroying, removing or rendering useless objects indispensable to the survival of the civilian population, such as foodstuffs, agricultural areas and drinking water supplies. Protocol I is the more ecological of the twin instruments since its aim is to protect the environment from war, whilst ENMOD is really humanitarian as is seeks to prohibit the use of the environment (land, sea, atmosphere or space) as a weapon in war. ENMOD is limited by the stipulation that such manipulation of the environment must be 'widespread, long-lasting or severe' ('WLS') to be deemed illegal but, nevertheless, has the advantage of being worded in such a way that gives it the potential to outlaw war-making methods not yet devised (Roberts & Guelff, 2000, pp. 407–418). Hence the sort of defence used by the U.S. against prosecution for Operation Ranch Hand under the Geneva Protocol would not stand up in the event of a country being prosecuted under ENMOD (although this could not happen to the U.S. as the Convention does not permit retrospective jurisdiction). Indeed, it was international concern that the U.S. strategy in Vietnam could evolve to include tactics such as deliberate flooding and the manipulation of the weather that did much to inspire ENMOD.

Moving on to the early 1990s, the oil and ordnance pollution that marked the Gulf War along with the general multilateral optimism that permeated international relations in the aftermath of the cold war reinvigorated international efforts to prevent ecocide. Hence, in 1991, the Security Council held Iraq liable for ecocide in their Kuwaiti invasion through the adoption of Resolution 687, confirming that they were:

liable under international law for any direct loss, damage, including environmental damage and the depletion of natural resources, or injury to foreign Governments, nationals and corporations, as a result of Iraq's unlawful invasion and occupation of Kuwait. (S/RES/687 (1991) 8 April)

On the basis of this, the Kuwaiti Government filed claims against Iraq for damages to its natural resources and related public health concerns. The UN Compensation Commission (UNCC) was subsequently established by Security Council Resolution 692 in May 1991 to adjudicate the amount of damages and its Governing Council then approved, in December 1996, an award of $610 million to Kuwait. Hence, the Saddam government became the first and, to date, only international entity to be charged for military ecocide.

As a corollary of this Iraqi prosecution, the UN General Assembly in November 1992 adopted a resolution on 'the protection of the environment in time of conflict', which stated that the 'destruction of the environment not justified by military necessity and carried out wantonly, is clearly contrary to international law' (A/RES/47/37). In further developments, in 1992 and 1993, the UN Secretary General submitted two reports on the protection of the environment which paved the way for a General Assembly resolution (A/RES/49/50) mandating the International Committee of the Red Cross (ICRC) to encourage the inclusion of their guidelines on the protection of the environment during conflict in military manuals. Consequently, many countries have adapted ICRC-drafted principles into the rules of engagement they provide for their armed forces.

A further legal milestone for ecocide came with the adoption of Article 8(2)(b)(iv) in the statutes of the International Criminal Court, which lists as a war crime the launching of an attack that may cause excessive damage to the natural environment. However, whilst this makes individual criminal responsibility for ecocide clearly established under an international treaty, the statute suffers from the same lack of precision as the Geneva Protocol and ENMOD in terms of determining what constitutes 'excessive damage' (Peterson, 2009). Hence, to date, no individual or government has been prosecuted specifically for military ecocide under the Hague Convention, ENMOD or through the ICC. A case was presented to the International Criminal Tribunal for Yugoslavia (ICTY) (a special ad hoc UN court set up to try crimes committed in the wars of the Yugoslav secession) by the Serbian Government against NATO bombing raids in the Kosovan War but was dismissed by the ICTY committee on the basis that it did not exceed the WLS threshold.

In some other areas of international laws that could potentially limit ecocide, military necessity is explicitly cited as an exemption. The 1993 Prevention of Major Industrial Accidents Convention, for example, does not apply to military installations. The Arctic Council, an intergovernmental organisation that has produced a range of soft and hard laws on environmental and shipping issues covering the region since the mid-1990s, has it written into its rules of procedure that military matters are off the table.

Reflecting international relations as a whole, early 1990s international solidarity against Saddam has proved to be something of a false dawn for prosecuting military ecocide and the efforts of campaigners and UN experts have since then have, instead, focussed on improving the implementation of existing legislation and developing new instruments. Through its Environmental Cooperation for Peacebuilding programme, UNEP has worked with the International Committee of the Red Cross in seeking to strengthen international laws protecting the environment during times of conflict. This work came together and was showcased in 2009 in an International Day for Preventing the Exploitation of the Environment in War and Armed Conflict on 6 November. The event emphasised the need to clarify and enforce existing laws and made some particular recommendations including the following: (1) give greater clarity to the 'widespread, long-term and severe' (WLS) threshold; *severe* should be taken to mean environmental impacts over several hundred square kilometres and *long term* should be considered to be a period of several months or over a season; (2) establish new laws to demilitarise important ecosystems, which should be determined at the outset of conflict; (3) laws should deal with civil as well as inter-state wars; (4) environmental crimes should be referable to The Permanent Court of Arbitration and be considered for inclusion in the ICC Statutes.

At the same time, a campaign for a more comprehensive and unambiguous UN treaty on ecocide, picking up the mantle from Westing and Falk in the early 1970s, has gathered momentum over recent years, led by British lawyer Polly Higgins. The campaign, launched in 2008, seeks to end the ambiguities around military (and industrial) necessity by establishing ecocide as a crime under customary international law (like genocide and torture) and opening it up to ICC prosecution. Celebrities, politicians and the Morales government of Bolivia are amongst those who have pledged their support to this cause which has set a deadline of 2020 for the codification of a new treaty (Higgins, 2010). Higgins was also instrumental in the setting up of the 'End Ecocide in Europe' campaign in 2012 seeking to get the EU Commission to draft a directive criminalising corporate and military damage to the environment. The movement was the first to take advantage of a new EU participatory democracy scheme, the European Citizens Initiative, under which signatures can be gathered to trigger new policies to be considered for proposal by the Commission in Brussels.

6. NORMATIVE PROGRESS IN CURBING MILITARY ECOCIDE

A UN Treaty on ecocide by 2020 seems like an ambition unlikely to be achieved, but the popular support and attention gathered by the campaign is probably as important as establishing a clear legal platform for prosecution. The precedent for enforcing the conventions on genocide, torture and (anthropocentric) war crimes is pretty limited, but the (fairly) unambiguous universal acknowledgement of these crimes has still made them less likely to occur than in the 'total war' era of the twentieth century. Implementing moral international laws is inherently difficult in a sovereign state system, but few could deny that overall progress has been made in advancing human rights and environmental principles over recent decades. Huge gaps and problems with implementation remain, but sovereign states have come to be restrained on the basis of humanitarian and ecological values as they have crystallised in the form of laws and in the rules of looser international regimes. The principle that military ecocide is unacceptable has, in line with this, come to be much better acknowledged. This has been reaffirmed at several high-profile intergovernmental forums, including at UNCED in 1992, where Principle 24 of the Rio Declaration unambiguously states that 'warfare is inherently destructive of sustainable development. States shall therefore respect international law providing protection for the environment in times of armed conflict and cooperate in its further development, as necessary'.

This normative evolution of proscribing ecocide can actually be traced back to the late cold war era once detente had seen humanitarian law advanced and the backlash against Operation Ranch Hand had occurred, particularly in the context of the Arab–Israeli dispute. Long before New World Order optimism had come to inform international relations, General Assembly Resolution 36/150 in 1981 condemned Israeli plans to construct a canal linking the Mediterranean to the Dead Sea, because of its environmental impact on Jordan (as well as the political ramifications for Palestinian independence), with only the U.S. and Israel voting against. On the basis of this, UNEP's Governing Council adopted several decisions condemning Israeli actions that had led to environmental damage against the Palestinians and their Arab neighbours including reaffirming the General Assembly position on the canal in 1983. UNEP have also contributed to this normative wave by advancing the *idea* of environmental protection in war. The Disasters and Conflicts Programme offers services and advice on: post-crisis environmental assessment, post-crisis environmental recovery, environmental cooperation for peacebuilding and disaster risk reduction which have been utilised in Afghanistan, Democratic Republic of the Congo and Sierra Leone. UNEP also lead the initiative ENVSEC, linking it with the

United Nations Development Programme, Organization for Security and Cooperation in Europe and other intergovernmental organisations in researching the environmental impacts of war. In 2006, ENVSEC carried out a scientific assessment of the environmental impact of the Israeli invasion of Lebanon in 2006, submitting a detailed report just four months after the ceasefire.

Intergovernmental forums outside of the UN system have also taken up the cause of exposing and stigmatising military ecocide. The Parliamentary Assembly of the Council of Europe have called for the environment to be more explicitly cited in Geneva Protocol I and argued that conflicts in Bosnia-Herzegovina and Chechnya should have seen prosecutions mounted on the basis of that legal instrument (CoE, 2011). This body, representing all of Europe bar the dictatorship of Belarus, have also called for the strengthening of existing international legislation and for greater funding for UNEP and ENVSEC for carrying out of environmental impact assessments on conflict zones.

Whilst there has only been the one clear legal ecocide case (against Iraq), we can see some small steps being taken by other culpable but unprosecuted governments to make amends for historical environmental war crimes. The Japanese Government, having denied knowledge of the chemical weapons used in Manchuria for over half a century, in 1997 finally entered into talks with the Chinese Government over how to remedy the damage. This led to a 1999 memorandum committing Tokyo to a plan to locate and destroy some 700,000 abandoned weapons at a cost of over $500 million (BBC, 2004). Whilst accepting no international legal liability for Operation Ranch Hand, President Ford in 1975 ratified the Geneva Protocol and issued Executive Order 11850, renouncing the military use of herbicides 'as a matter of national policy'. Thirty year on the U.S. position, articulated in response to a persistent campaign by Vietnam War victims by Judge Weinstein, was that 'there is no basis for any of the claims of plaintiffs under the domestic law of any nation or state or under any form of international law' (USDC, 2015, p. 233). However, the fact that U.S. war veterans suffering from dioxin exposure have received compensation from the chemical manufacturers for injuries inflicted and international support for the Vietnamese victims made this a difficult position to sustain and maintained pressure on Washington. Hence in 2012, whilst still not accepting liability, the U.S. initiated a clean-up of ecological damage by dioxin in Vietnam. Washington gave $43 million to two American firms working in conjunction with the Vietnamese Defence Ministry in an operation Hanoi hope to complete by 2020. Partial atonement was also apparent in 2012 when the U.S. returned to Subic Bay in the Philippines in preparation for the reopening of the naval base in 2015. In re-establishing military relations with their former colony, the Americans were now cooperating with a government party to MARPOL and not having to accept being literally 'crapped on' as a price of their protection. The Subic Bay Metropolitan Authority now provides Philippine oversight of the U.S. naval presence and has helped highlight concerns at the dumping of waste and even hosted maritime pollution conferences.

Realpolitik could still be said to underpin these cases of atonement since twenty-first-century U.S. foreign policy still values South-East Asian influence and a flat-lining Japanese economy cannot ignore the resuscitating possibilities offered by its growing neighbour, but moral pressure has undoubtedly played a part. Global civil society has been highly vocal with groups like the Alliance for Bases Clean Up (ABC) (formerly known as the People's Task Force for Bases Clean Up (PTFBC)) and the Vietnamese Association of Victims of Agent Orange (who have led the legal campaign) presenting the U.S. with a reputational incentive to act. The Manchuria case presents a clear illustration of how normative forces can influence governments both by shaming and encouragement. The Chinese came to throw their weight behind the Chemical Weapons Convention by recognising that abandoning their own stockpile (a condition of ratification) would be a price worth paying in order to secure a moral victory over their old adversary and remedy a festering environmental and health sore. At the same time, the Japanese, as champions of arms control on the international stage, felt compelled to confront their past demons and make reparation for the sins of their grandparents (Frieman, 2004).

It is no coincidence that political ecology rose to prominence at the same time as the backlash against the U.S. intervention in Vietnam and the rise and persistence of the powerful green social movement since then has given impetus to the anti-ecocide campaign. However, the green wave has not always advanced the proscription of ecocide. The mainstreaming of the ecological agenda has sometimes served to weaken its tradition of pacifism and even advance the military–industrial complex. The controversy stoked by German Green Foreign Minister Joschka Fischer's backing for NATO in the Kosovan War is a case in point. Assigning increased political significance to the environment through 'securitisation' by governments has enhanced the profile of issues like climate change on the international political stage but often in profoundly anthropocentric, state-centric and militaristic ways. Since the 1990s, environmental security has featured in the stated foreign policy aims of countries like the U.S., U.K. and Russia, IGOs like NATO and been debated at the UN Security Council. This, though, has actually been a very traditional security discourse driven by the 'resource wars' thesis that environmental changes, such as increased droughts, will trigger political tensions and make wars more likely. For these reasons, many ecologists remain sceptical about securitisation in spite of the advance of the ontological challenges presented by critical and human security perspectives in advocating urgent political action on environmental issues on the basis of the threats posed not to national interests but to people in general or even non-human life forms.

However, not all environmental securitisation has been of the state-centric and militaristic form and a 'green tide' continues to advance ecocentric norms in other situations. The Netherlands' 2006 Foreign Policy Agenda acknowledges the potential role that environmental degradation plays in triggering conflicts but notably goes on to declare as one of eight goals a commitment 'to protect and improve the environment', without the addition of any clause indicating that this is another case of valuing the environment for instrumental rather than intrinsic reasons (Netherlands, 2006). This ecocentric turn of making the environment the referent object of security has also been advanced in a different political form in recent years outside of the Western World as part of the 'new left' wave in Latin America from the late 2000s. One expression of the critical stance on Western capitalism and focus on indigenous people that marks this political movement has been the empowerment of nature. In 2008, Ecuador's new constitution declared that nature had the 'right to exist, persist, maintain and regenerate its vital cycles, structure, functions and its processes in evolution' and mandates the government to take 'precaution and restriction measures in all the activities that can lead to the extinction of species, the destruction of the ecosystems or the permanent alteration of the natural cycles' (Ecuador, 2008). Whilst many countries have cited environmental protection in their constitutions, none have done so in such unambiguously ecocentric terms. This 'rights of nature' approach has also been followed by the Morales government in Bolivia where the 'Law of Mother Earth' has defended the right of nature 'to not be affected by mega-infrastructure and development projects that affect the balance of ecosystems and the local inhabitant communities' (Bolivia, 2011). For both of these Andean countries, this idea of environmental rights comes from the twin impact of indigenous people's empowerment and a legacy of particularly dire environmental pollution. The rights of long-marginalised indigenous Americans (of which Morales is one) have become an important domestic political concern aided by greater international discourse promoted within the UN system by the Trustee Council, Working Group on Indigenous Populations, Human Rights Council, Human Rights Council and the International Labour Organization. In addition, the long-standing problem of 'industrial ecocide' from pollution by oil in Ecuador and tin in Bolivia has heightened environmental concerns beyond that witnessed in most developing countries.

Protecting the environment has sustained itself as a populist political strategy in the West since the 1960s and continues to attract activists around the world. As Sen's 'entitlements thesis' convincingly argues, the empowerment of people through democratisation or self-determination leads to the establishment of a right to food or health (Sen, 1981). Democratic governments are compelled to be responsive to the needs of ordinary people whose security is imperilled, either directly or indirectly due to the pressure of the media or other concerned citizens, for reasons of their own self-preservation if nothing else. Hence, today health and safety standards, welfarism and the notion of 'social security' are accepted as integral to the governance of most developed democracies. Increasingly, this thesis is coming to have applicability in non-democratic settings also with a clear example being the implementation of a range of anti-pollution measures by the Chinese Government over recent years in the face of public protest at the levels of smog in many cities. We can also see evidence from political evolution in many developed, democratic states that public demands on government are not always self-serving and anthropocentric. Ecocentrism has been apparent in much domestic policy on the environment since the U.S. responded to Rachel Carson's critique and restricted the use of DDT in the 1960s, even though the use of the organochlorine as a pesticide had been successful in increasing food yields. Human co-responsibility and a respect for non-human life sometimes supersede economic and government self-interest in democratic domestic governance, because people demand that to be the case. In several countries, rights comparable to those enshrined for humans have been granted to other species, such as with apes (in New Zealand and Spain) or dolphins (in India). New Zealand has also seen this status granted to inanimate elements of nature with the Wanganui River in 2014 granted legal personality in the culmination of a campaign by the Iwi Maori dating back to the nineteenth century.

The maturation of politics in this way can also be observed at the global level as the globalisation of ideas and ethics advances, aided in particular by global civil society and global epistemic communities of transnational experts usually working within the UN system. Sociologists Inoue and Drori, in an empirical analysis of global health policy, observe that this political arena has evolved in a process of 'discursive sedimentation' in which a 'right to health' for all has gradually begun to emerge after centuries of international policy driven by self-interest or charity (Inoue & Drori, 2006, p. 211). Charity, fear and commercialism persist as values underpinning the motivations of actors in the global health world, but a rights-based approach has gradually been built on top of this and is now the foremost culture evident in the discourse of the WHO and NGOs like MedAct and Medecins Sans Frontier. In general, the existence of 'global ethics' can be seen in the development of human rights law and in many other dimensions of global law and policy. The reform of the World Bank, from being an advocate of 'unreconstructed liberalism' into a more socially oriented set of institutions, is a clear example of such normative change. The World Bank now routinely considers the environmental or social cost of any development project, as well as its economic viability, before granting it its seal of approval. This metamorphosis occurred through the development of a different epistemic community working within the system of organisations making up the 'bank', largely in response to pressure group and academic criticism. Similar change has occurred in the UNDP as the normative shift from advocating 'pure' economic growth to more human-centred development has occurred amongst experts in the field. An emergent global discourse has promoted the normative change that has seen principles like a right to health and concrete aims such as the Millennium Development Goals become established on the international stage not directly equitable with national interests. Promoted by an epistemic community of scientists, lawyers and expert campaigners, respected as acting outside of parochial interests by an ever more enlightened global public, environmental rights can be understood as part of this progression. Whilst it is hardly likely to be eradicated, it is difficult to imagine anything other than there coming to be increased international awareness of and an increased desire to restrict military ecocide.

7. CONCLUSIONS

Military necessity will probably always be argued to trump environmental concerns at times of crisis, as is still regularly seen in the enactment of emergency measures which compromise democracy and human rights on the grounds of national interest, but this is not to say that moral restraints cannot advance. Just War principles continue to be sidestepped in contemporary conflicts but they have, nevertheless, greatly advanced in the years since the end of the cold war. Globalisation makes national reputations more important than ever and exposes illegality and immorality more easily than ever. In this way, moral laws and norms tend not to unravel once established. The recent U.S. and Japanese ecocide clean-up operations show that the passage of time, both in terms of the building up of moral pressure in support of victims and in creating 'distance' for the perpetrator, can permit small, initial steps to be taken in making amends for historical crimes. Doubtless governments will continue to carry out acts of ecocide if they feel they can get away with it, but they are increasingly unlikely to get away with it, even if only reputationally rather than legally.

However, as is the case in many facets of environmental politics and the politics of securitisation, the high-profile catastrophes are but the tip of the iceberg. We may be unlikely to witness again anything comparable to Operation Ranch Hand or the burning oilfields of the Persian Gulf, but beneath the surface of international political attention lies a huge military–

industrial complex eating up the earth's resources and spitting and belching what it does not need back out. As with security politics in general, the instinctive treatment of international military matters as more important than environmental concerns covers a multitude of sins and human insecurities.

DISCLOSURE STATEMENT

No potential conflict of interest was reported by the author.

NOTES ON CONTRIBUTOR

Peter Hough is an associate professor in International Politics at Middlesex University. Hough is the author of *Understanding Global Security* (3rd ed. Routledge 2013) and *Environmental Security. An Introduction* (Routledge 2014).

REFERENCES

1. Auer, M. (2004). Restoring cursed Earth: Appraising environmental policy reforms in East Europe and Russia. Oxford: Rowman & Littlefield.
2. Boas, G., & Schabas, W. (2003). International criminal law. Developments in the case law of the ICTY. Lieden: Martinus Nijhoff.
3. Bolivia. (2011). Law of mother Earth. Law 071. BBC. (2004). WW2 bombs unearthed in China June 19. Retrieved January 31, 2016, from http://news.bbc.co.uk/1/ hi/world/asia-pacific/3822007.stm
4. Carson, R. (1962). Silent spring. Harmondsworth: Penguin. Connor, S., & Thomas, A. (1984). 'How Britain sprayed Malaya with Dioxin' in Sahabat Alam Malaysia, pesticide dilemma in the Third World. A case study of Malaysia.
5. Penang: Sahabat Alam Cook, R.E., Haseltine, W., & Galston, A.W. (1970). What have we done to Vietnam? In B. Weisberg (Ed.), Ecocide in Indochina: The ecology of war (pp. 89–94).

6. San Francisco, CA: Canfield Press. CoE. (2011). Armed conflicts and the environment (Report of the Committee on the Environment, Agriculture and Local and Regional Affairs, Doc 12744, October 17th).

7. Strasbourg: Parliamentary Assembly of the Council of Europe. Ecuador. (2008). Rights for nature. Constitution, adopted September 28th.

8. Franklin, H. (2003). Agent Orange and cancer. An overview for clinicians. Environmental Carcinogens 53, 245–255.

9. Frieman, W. (2004). China, arms control and non-proliferation. London: Routledge. Geneva. (1977). Protocol additional to the Geneva conventions of 12 August 1949, and relating to the protection of victims of international armed conflicts (protocol I), 8 June 1977.

10. Glasby, G., & Voytekhovsky, Y. (2010). Arctic Russia: Minerals and resources. Geoscientist, 8, 16–21.

11. Hay, A. (1982). The chemical scythe – Lessons of 2,4,5, T and Dioxin. New York, NY: Plenum Press.

12. Higgins, P. (2010). Eradicating ecocide: Laws and governance to prevent the destruction of our planet. London: ShepheardWalwyn.

13. Inoue, K., & Drori, G. (2006). The global institutionalization of health as a social concern: Organizational and discursive trends. International Sociology, 21, 199–219.

14. Kalpers, J. (2001). Armed conflict and biodiversity in SubSaharan Africa: Impacts, mechanisms and responses. In Armed conflict and biodiversity in Sub-Saharan Africa. Washington, DC: Biodiversity Support Program.

15. National Academy of Sciences. (1974). The effects of herbicide in South Vietnam, part a summary and conclusion. Washington, DC: Author.

16. Netherlands. (2006). Policy agenda 2006. The Hague: Ministry of Foreign Affairs. Peluso, N., & Vandergeest, P. (2011). Taking the jungle out of the forest. In R. Peat, P. Robbins, & M. Watts (Eds.), Global political ecology (pp. 252–284). London: Routledge.

17. Peterson, I. (2009). The natural environment in times of armed conflict: A concern for international war crimes law? Leiden Journal of International Law, 22, 325–343.

18. Ostling, K. (1992, May/June). The impact of militarism on the environment. Peace Magazine, 8–9.

19. Roberts, A., & Guelff, R. (2000). Documents on the laws of war. (3rd ed.). Oxford: Oxford University Press.

20. Sanders, B. (2009). The green zone. Oakland, CA: AK Press.

21. Schettler, T. (1995). Reverberations of militarism: Toxic contamination, the environment, and health. Medicine and Global Survival, 2(1), 7–18.

22. Sen, A. (1981). Poverty and famines: An essay on entitlement and deprivation. Oxford: Clarendon Press.

23. Sheehan, N. (2003, May 1). The aftermath of an invasion: A field report from Nasiriyah. Warchild.

24. Twain, M. (2016). War prayer. Retrieved January 13, 2016, from http://warprayer.org/ UNEP. (2002). GEO-3: Global environment outlook 3. London: Earthscan.

25. USDC. (2005). 'Agent Orange' product liability litigation (Memorandum Order and Judgement, MDL No. 381 March 10th). New York, NY: United States District Court.

26. Weinstein, T. (2005). Prosecuting acts that destroy the environment: Environmental crimes or humanitarian atrocities? Georgetown International Law Review, 17, 607–722.

27. Westing, A. (1974). Proscription of ecocide. Science and Public Affairs, 26, 24–27.

28. Westing, A. (1984). Herbicides in war–the long term ecological and human consequences. London: Taylor & Francis.

29. Westing, A. (1989). Herbicides in warfare: The case of Indochina. In P. Bourdeau, J.A. Haines, W. Klein, & C. R. Krishna (Eds.), Ecotoxicology and climate (pp. 337–357). Chichester, IL: Wiley

9

CHAPTER

The Evolution of the Concept of International Peace and Security in light of UN Security Council Practice (End of the Cold War-Until Now)

Rasool Soltani, Maryam Moradi

Department of Law, Qeshm International Branch, Islamic Azad University, Qeshm, Iran

ABSTRACT

With the start of globalization and the third millennium, international peace and security have gradually lost their traditional westphalian notion and have become complicated. The nature of threats against international peace and security has also spread to political, economical, social and environmental aspects as well as military ones. Therefore, it is not just governments who are responsible for establishing international peace and security; rather all the actors of the international system including individuals and major international bodies have their own share in bringing about peace and security. In this regard, UN Security Council, which is the most significant pillar of UN and guardian of international peace and security, has faced multiple challenges during its lifetime. During the Cold War and due to the competition between west and east superpowers, this council has proved principally impotent in encountering international crises. When the Cold War came to an end and the Soviet Union collapsed, there had been offered a great chance to the council to analyze international affairs with a new approach. The evolution of international peace and security notion and new interpretations of threats are the most manifested matters of the council in the post-Cold War era. This has proceeded to an extend that sometimes finding a legal status for the measures of the UN Security Council is difficult and the council has become sort of a legislator in the world. The most important issues that were addressed in the Council regarding international peace and security in post-Cold War era have been human rights violations, humanitarian law, terrorism, proliferation of mass destruction weapons and environmental problems. Expanding the Council's authorities should be based on a clear and general interpretation of them in the framework of the principles of the UN Charter. Consequently, the Security Council is not legally capable of doing arbitrary and limitless actions.

Keywords: International Peace and Security, Security Council, Human Rights, Humanitarian Law, Terrorism, Weapons of Mass Destruction

1. INTRODUCTION

The ultimate goal of human during history in all societies is to achieve such peace and security that as a result violence of human life disappeared, and the dignity of man restores its place. From a long time ago, the thought of freedom from strife and war has been equaled to peace. However, war as a country foreign policy tool has formed part of human existence and simultaneously, most is looking for ways to save mankind from this disaster.

According to the United Nations Charter UN began with the decision to protect future generations from the war disasters. Meanwhile, maintaining international peace and security were considered as the first target. According to Article 24 of the Charter, United Nations members gave it to Security Council and agreed that the Security Council perform its duties behalf of members (Malone, 2008) . UN Security Council as the custodian of international peace and security during its life witnessed numerous developments in the international system that naturally have been effective in this important international body functioning, so this study was to investigate the role of the security Council in the unofficial fundamental change in the concept of international peace and security beyond the traditional concept of political and economic measures which is stipulated in the Charter (Tsagourias, 2011) .

2. THE NEW DEFINITION OF PEACE

Perhaps the most serious and the most important part in peace operations is linked to the definition of peace. In other words, assessment and analysis in the peace context of the operational require the understanding approaches related to definition and explanation of this universal value content. Because of the diverse and different definitions and explanations of this value, has become a category for the processes, security and political legal doctrines, and discourse deployment of them against each other as well. This notion not only shows the freshened substrates of anti-peace phenomena, but determines the measures and requirements which are worthy of support in peace refuge and as well as many other concepts there is no general agreement about it. Thus knowing peace is related to precondition of any curiosity about finding good peace and distinguishing it from a bad peace and other concepts. Due to the different position of Peace in various fields is, different concepts depending on each of these has been mentioned. It is thought the most important thing is that whether peace should simply be defined as the absence of war and direct violence (negative peace), or whether it involves both mean of absence of war and direct violence in the presence of social justice (positive peace) (Kurtz, 1999). In the second sense, peace is political conditions that guarantee social justice and stability through institutions, procedures and the formal and non-formal norms (Miller, 2005). In the etymological meaning, peace means are as follows:

- State which is prevailing in the absence of a war,
- Treaty after the war,
- State of harmony and balance (Free Collins Dictionaries) ,
- The silence and calmness state.

Traditional thinking to peace was directed only to avoid the war and because of being unaware of the peace removing ongoing process based on social and economic inequalities, it was never successful. Traditional Peace is not only compelled to maintain the status quo , but counts on same goal and it is natural that such a view to the preservation of unequal conditions, will not make peace universal and will not share to everyone. It can not be expected from the traditional peace instead of calming down inflamed condition. Although with the conceptual frameworks are called as comprehensive peace, Sustainable situation will not exist, although it is called eternal peace.

By the traditional thinking receding, new thinking experts know peace as repre- senting situation in which all human beings are endowed with real human dignity and human life. This means that people, regardless of creed, race and etc. be able to live with having relative prosperity, education, health, employment, equality before the law, free elections and etc. and be safe to speak their minds without. In this context, any agent or biological factors expose these components to damage, are threatening to peace (Vankovska & Wiberg, 2002).

3. THE STATUS OF INTERNATIONAL PEACE AND SECURITY IN THE CHARTER OF THE UNITED NATIONS

The failure of the League of Nations in the prevention of World War II, in the belief that the creation of an efficient system of international cooperation can be effective in protecting the world against the war did not create doubt. U.N in accordance with the Charter of the United Nations, began with decision to protect future generations from the ravages of war. The maintenance of peace and international security was considered as the first target. Although the peace is one of the oldest human aspirations, human history is full of conflicts, contradictions and collisions. Two devastating and damaging wars in the short distance of each other, in the first half of the twentieth century, shook the international community and public opinion and caused politicians and lawyers attempted to find a way to reduce the threats to peace in the international community. Earlier it was mentioned that the peace in Classic concept is a condition where there is no war. Before the founding of the United Nations Peace in the international system had the same concept but UN Charter has broadens its concept and considered as "an international order institution based on justice". So in the current perspective, no longer merely lack of war does not mean peace establishment and Continuity, but anything that conflicts with justice, may be threatening for the peace and violate it (Ashra'fi, 2015).

In 1945, when world leaders gathered in San Francisco to form the United Nations, their minds was mainly on international peace and security. In fact, the first line of the introduction of the Charter points out the need to preserve future generations from the dangers of war. To achieve this goal, the founders of the organization, awarded the power of collective security system to maintain peace and international security to U.N. In this system, aggression against a member state is seen as aggression against all. These executive powers are concentrated in the Security Council. The most important reason of forming, the existence purpose and goal of United Nations, to maintain international peace and security. This purpose is stated in paragraph 1 of Article 1. Of course outlined goals in 2, 3 and 4 paragraphs are also somehow related to international peace and security and their realization is supplies this goal. The goal of the Charter clearly was to prevent war and maintain peace in the negative sense. For this purpose, 2 (4) Article of the Charter prohibits the threat of force or use of force and has been entrusted collective security organization to the Security Council. It should be noted that The Charter contains seemingly conflicting and contradictory articles. On the one hand in the first part of Article (1) and in a predicted manner in Chapter VII, knows his mission to preserve the status quo. On the other hand, in 2 and 3 paragraphs of Article 1 and Article 55 of the Charter and some other articles, world desirable change through the development of friendly relations among nations and international cooperation in the economic, social, humanitarian and etc. has been considered. According to the UN Charter the use of force is possible only in two ways: one on the implementation of the collective security system in cases that peace is threatened, or aggression action has been done and the other in self-defense. In this way government individual resort of force is only possible in self-defense, not to prosecute or justice concept (Shaygan, 2002).

United nations charter article 10, paragraphs 3, 2 states strengthen international peace through development of friendly relations that reduce the underlying causes of war and world peace Consolidation. As the provisions of Articles 33, 34, 36, 39 and 50 Article of the Charter, the goal is attainment of these objectives through peaceful means. According to Article 24 of the Charter, the United Nations members handed international peace and security over to the Security Council and agreed that the Security Council takes action that is responsible for behalf of members. UN Security Council as the custodian of international peace and security during his lifetime has seen several developments in the international system that has naturally been effective in functioning of this important international institution. Security Council was largely powerless in the international crisis during the Cold War and rivalry between the two superpowers of East and West and for multiple use of the veto and thus this increase the activities of the General Assembly and the typical case was United resolution approval for Peace in the field of international peace and security maintaining under which the General Assembly is empowered to convene within 24 hours and apply measures to deal with violations (Soltani, 2005).

4. THE DEFINITION OF PEACE, THREATEN OR VIOLATION IN THE CHARTER

With a view to the UN Charter, we find that nowhere in the Charter, there is not any definition of peace or breach of the peace or a threat to international peace and security[1]. Is this lack of definition and presentation of objective criteria associated with peace and international security maintaining in terms of the nature of international peace and security and or the main reason should be found in the context of the international community. It seems that the main reason of lack of determination of the boundaries of the concept of international peace and security should be searched in the structure of the international community (Henderson & Lubell, 2013). The structure of the United Nations, especially the Security Council reflects the international structure and power relationship during the foundation of the organization and the years following it. In fact, fear that the two world wars had created in the world public opinion; put the need to maintain international peace and security in head of other international needs. So that San Francisco conference participants are forced to accept broad powers of Security Council in Authentication of a threat to peace and its permanent member special privilege and veto right in a way that was outlined in the Dumbarton proposals.

So it seems the lack of definition for the concepts of peace, or threatens or peace breach in the Charter of the United Nations was deliberate and the founders of the Charter have given judging the occurrence or the amplitude of each of these concepts to the Security Council. This technique allows flexibility on the one hand and adapt to changing conditions when the international organization provides and on the other to allow the Security Council is due to new developments in the world, the sense of peace and international security (Bruno, 2012) .

5. NEW THREATS AND CHALLENGES CONFRONTING INTERNATIONAL PEACE AND SECURITY

Since the beginning of the United Nations was with the aim of preventing ruinous wars like World Wars I and II, the governments understating of breach of peace and international security can be known as emergence of a situation that the world will be facing similar events. Hence the most effort of origination to end the 80s was to prevent the development of disputes between states, limiting the scope of the war and the threat of weapons of mass destruction. But after the collapse of the Soviet Union and the perspective transformation of this imperial heirs to international system and the gradual transformation in some of the concepts related to peace and security and members collaboration enhancement, the United Nations focused on the more general field of governments direct war (Williams, 2008). According tasks that United Nations Charter considered for each of the pillars of the United Nations, primary responsibility for maintaining international peace and security is entrusted to Security Council which in this case has general jurisdiction. UN Security Council for doing its tasks requires tools that were put at the disposal of the Council in the sixth and seventh seasons Charter of the United Nations (Mousazadeh, 2012).

By studying the performance of the Security Council as custodian of international peace and security in recent years suggest a broad interpretation of this pillar of concept of international peace and security or peace threatening. The UN Security Council adopted a statement on 31 January 1992 and reiterated in the statement that a lack of inter-state conflict alone is not peace, but economic, social, humanitarian and environmental instability is a threat to peace and security[2]. The Declaration was the origin of the evolution of the concept of peace in the Security Council. What in The new era and the beginning of the third millennium is different from the past, first is the change in threshold of threat and breach of the peace. That is, peace is not necessarily opposed to the war but its realization requires a set of conditions associated with a healthy, quiet, safe and excellent lifestyle for human beings. Secondly subject area of benefited and committed has expanded in peace area that is the peace is not just an intergovernmental phenomenon but is inter-human and inter-group as well (Vakil, 2013) .

Also international peace and security Threats and challenges texture is got out from traditional mode which was more military and in addition to it, political, economic, social and environmental threats caused international peace and security hazard (Ashra'fi, 2015) . Civil War, violation of human rights, weapons of mass destruction development, organized crime, international terrorism, lack of democracy and government instability and poverty and underdevelopment, are included in the challenges and threats that have strong potential for growth and negatively affecting peace and international security. In the following we study some of international events and the Security Council performance according to the new concept of international peace and security (High-Level Panel, 2004) .

6. THE EVENTS OF 11 SEPTEMBER, THE MILESTONE OF TERRORISM CONSIDERATION AS A THREAT TO INTERNATIONAL PEACE AND SECURITY

Early morning hours Disaster of September 11 led to the collapse of two skyscrapers of the World Trade Center in New York and the destruction of Pentagon building in Washington, impressed global geopolitical gradual formation trend in 2001 wonderfully. Nearly 4000 persons of various nationalities died in the harmful crash and thousands of innocent and helpless were wounded and have been reintegrated. However, from the perspective of economic damages were estimated at $50 billion, but also hundreds of billions of dollars consequential commercial bankruptcy should be added to this figure. From moral and psychological perspective, United States of America for the first time was met with apprehension and bitterness of war.

General Assembly one day after the September 11 terrorist attacks ,on September 12, 2001 a resolution condemning the terrorist attacks on America called for international cooperation for the arrest and punishment of the organizers of the attacks on America and also to prevent terrorist acts and terrorism Eradication globally. The Security Council has issued two resolutions on the events that are significant in terms of innovation:

6.1. 1368 Resolution[3]

The resolution was issued on 12 September 2001 by the Security Council. In this unanimously resolution the Council condemned the terrorist attacks on America and sympathized with the victims, it considered the attack as a threat to international peace and security and recognizes the rejoin individual or collective for America (Resolution Introduction).

The second paragraph of the resolution wants all States to cooperate with each other to give perpetrators, organizers and sponsors of these attacks to justice. In the fourth paragraph of the resolution also asked the international community to increase efforts to prevent and prohibit acts of terrorism with the cooperation and full implementation of international anti-terrorist conventions and Security Council resolutions, and finally the fifth paragraph the Council has announced readiness to take the necessary steps in response to these attacks and to combat all forms of terrorism in accordance with its responsibilities under the United Nations.

6.2. 1373 Resolution[4]

This resolution issued by the Security Council on 28 September 2001 that was second resolution on terrorism, following the events of September eleventh. The council by issuing the resolution constructed international anti-terrorist infrastructure along with some basic obligations on governments. This resolution that is the most important counter-terrorism resolution particularly in connection with the financing of terrorism has a great importance. So that the foundation of the next Security Council counter- terrorism resolutions are adjusted based on this resolution and has always emphasized the implementation of the resolution. In the preface of the second resolution, this really is an extension of the first resolution, in addition to addressing these things as threatening for international peace and security and recognition of the right of individual or collective self-defense in accordance with the Charter, containing substantial tips, including:

- Stressed the need to combat terrorist acts that endanger international peace and security.
- Expressing concern about the spread of terrorist acts that are caused by intolerance or extremism in various regions of the world.
- Wants all governments to immediately cooperate to ban and prevent terrorist acts.

In connection with the above analysis we can say 1373 resolution actually completes 1378 Resolution and several points are noteworthy:

1) Terrorism has been considered as a phenomenon threatening international peace and security.
2) It considered individual or collective self-defense for governments.
3) Governments are required to cooperate and to monitor this cooperation a committee is formed and wants government to report their performance on the implementation of this resolution to committee.
4) Council puts an emphasis to take the next steps if necessary (Under article 41 and 42 of the Charter) (Nielsen, 2010) .

Considering the above, it can be said that the two resolutions and especially 1373 Resolution, are most complete and comprehensive resolution which has been issued in relation to terrorism by the United Nations Security Council (Brown, 2003) .

7. THE CONVERGENCE OF INTERNATIONAL PEACE AND SECURITY AND THE PROLIFERATION OF WEAPONS OF MASS DESTRUCTION

The spread of nuclear weapons, unconventional, mass murder on the eve of the third millennium, has faced the international community with serious concerns. Concern of spreading of these weapons, has raised fears of another world war that if occurs will not be comparable with previous wars. Especially in recent years increasing terrorist attacks around the world and concern of access of terrorists to such weapons and endanger the security of the people Even inside their homes has caused The international community becomes sensitive about monitoring and safety mechanisms toward the prevalence of these weapons and their controls (Laqueut, 1996) .

Washington and New York cities Terrorist attacks put some of the topics including the prohibition and control of weapons of mass destruction, including chemical weapons, biological, nuclear and biological in top of the agenda of the international community program and put it as one of the serious, outstanding and significant international, regional and national contemporary concerns (Oostithuzen & Wimshurts, 2004) . Examples of the use of weapons of mass destruction against innocent people, including atomic bomb on Hiroshima and Nagasaki in 1945, use of weapons of mass destruction against civilians in Japan, the use of chemical weapons by Iraq in its war with Iran, Halabja civilians killing by the regime And reported 124 cases of nuclear smuggling in 1994 that has doubled compared to a year earlier, indicates that these weapons can be considered as a threat to international peace and security[5]. By the end of the Cold War, important developments in the field of disarmament and control of Arms control were done by the United Nations. This evolution is more as a result of the security environment after the Cold War and the extended interpretation of United Nations Charter in relation to peace and international security. Beginning of such a change was the Kuwait crisis in 1990. With Iraq's invasion to Kuwait and occupation of this country by Iraqi forces shortly Security Council condemned the Iraqi action and issued a resolution Successive calling for the withdrawal of Iraq from Kuwait. Following Iraq's refusal to comply with Security Council resolutions this council issued 678 Resolution and permitted military attack on the country and by attacking coalition forces, Kuwait became Free and country occupation was ended. .In the crisis over Kuwait, it became apparent that Iraq had a wide range of programs to develop weapons of mass destruction, especially nuclear weapons and has provided considerable success in this area. Meanwhile, the Iraqi was a member of Treaty and the International Atomic Energy Agency (IAEA) has overseen the activities of the country. The inability of IAEA inspection of all nuclear activities in Iraq, led the Security Council should itself took action, Therefore 687 Resolution passed in April 1991[6]. Actually the Security Council under resolution which issued for Chapter VII of the Charter of the United Nations moved in the direction of the Iraq disarmament. In 1993, in the wake of North Korea's threat to leave the nuclear Non-proliferation treaty, passed 825 resolutions[7]. Following the nuclear tests by India and Pakistan in May 1998 by the 1172 resolution condemned[8] these experiments and in 8 Nov of the 2002 issued 1441 resolution on Iraq[9].

8. IRAN'S NUCLEAR ISSUE AND THE APPROACH OF THE SECURITY COUNCIL

Board of Governors of the International Atomic Energy Agency on February 4, 2006 decided to send the case report nuclear activities of the Islamic Republic of Iran to the Security Council[10]. This action was performed after the March forum by the agency general secretary (IAEA, 2006) . From then, along the International Atomic Energy Agency which already had monitor on Iran's nuclear program, The UN Security Council adopted decisions in this regard which in many aspects from the perspective of international law, is noticeable. After reception of IAEA Director, the Security Council put issue in its agenda and in the first step issued a presidential statement quickly. Argentinean Director of the Security Council announced reference position in relation to Iran's nuclear program in a statement on March 29, 2006[11]. In this statement despite emphasizing the right of States Parties to the Non Proliferation Treaty (NPT) to use nuclear energy for peaceful purposes without discrimination, the Council expressed serious concern, asked Iran to take steps for requirements of Board of Governors in particular full and stable suspension of enrichment. Subsequently, according to lack of acceptance of Council demands contained in Security Council presidential statement by Iran, after the publication of the Council demanded report requested from the international atomic energy agency Director General, Security Council was adopted 1696 resolution on 31 July 2006 in accordance with Article 40 of the Charter. In this resolution, the Council stressed on agency previous resolutions and its former statements, along with a series of demands, notably asked from Iran to suspend all activities related to enrichment and Reprocessing. Council introduced this request with reference to 40 Article of the Charter of the United Nations with the goal to non-binding suspension. Failure to comply with resolutions 1737, 1747, 1803 and 1929 requests followed under article 41 that asked from Iran and other members of the United Nations to enforce certain sanctions And in fact Iran's nuclear activities was considered by the Council as a threat to international peace and security.

Legal Review of Security Council Entering to Iran's Nuclear Program

It is believed that generally sending Iran issue to the Security Council was too hasty because still peaceful means, such as conciliation, commission of inquiry, mediation, good offices and legal remedies such as arbitration and the International Court of Justice which is predicted in Charter of the United Nations have not been used (Kosha & Eskandari, 2012) . Some lawyers believe that on the basis of the Charter, the Security Council in its primary task to maintain international peace and security, has unlimited jurisdiction and could eventually ignore international law. Others believe that the Security Council is bounded based on the final part of a charter practice based on the principles of justice and international law. What is not disputed, there is specific responsibilities in relation to the powers of the Council which must comply with the fundamental principles of international law and the international. In other words, if the Security Council decision is inconsistent with the international principles and rules, it is discredited and the government can object to it.

However, in accordance with Article 24 of the Charter of the United Nations UN member are required to comply with the resolutions and decisions of the Security Council under Chapter VII of the Charter, According to Article 25 of the Charter states commitment to this depends on the Security Council action based on the principles of the Charter that in The view of number of lawyers According to the description, the principles of the Charter are not included about Security Council decisions on Iran (Kosha & Eskandari, 2012) .

9. CRISIS IN LIBYA, THE SECURITY COUNCIL AND THE RESPONSIBILITY TO PROTECT

With the start of the uprising against authoritarian regimes in North Africa and the Arab world unrest spread from Tunisia and Egypt to Libya in February 2011, the government of Muammar Gaddafi responsed violently and did brutal crackdown (Bellamy & Williams, 2011) . The severity of violence committed by the Gaddafi regime in the face of protesters and civilians have been attracted international attention (Reuters, 22 Feb,

2011) and finally by the rapid intervention of the Security Council in relation to the same crises, led to the collapse of Gaddafi's 42-year rule. The importance of this issue is that Libya case is the first critical that the Security Council based on the doctrine of responsibility to protect every government is responsible to protect their populations against war crimes, genocide, ethnic cleansing and crimes against humanity (Thakur, 2011). The Sovereignty essential nature has changed from the regime privileges and immunities of the responsibility to protect people against brutal crimes; so if the government fails in its responsibility, the responsibility of the international community will be achieved through UN structures and procedures (Bellamy & Williams, 2011).

The Security Council in The first step in 1970 consensus resolution[12] in 26 February 2011 explicitly emphasize on the "responsibility to protect" the Libyan government about its population and adopt a series of civilian actions and of course Punitive. Diplomatic measures, asset freezes, travel bans, arms embargo, suspending Libya's membership in some international and regional institutions and referral of Libya to the International Criminal Court, were Among these proceedings. This process leads to resolution 1973 (with 10 votes in favor and 5 abstentions) of Security Council based on no- fly zone on March 17, 2011, which led to the use of military force to protect the civilian population in Libya[13]. The resolution condemning violence in Libya again and explicitly emphasized on the "responsibility" of the government of Libya in "support" of its population. operations in Libya In addition to running no-fly zone, was to protect civilian population and also threatened areas and while the participants with justification for this purpose, have targeted pro-Gaddafi forces in the numerous air strikes Which eventually led to the fall of the Gaddafi regime and the revolution in Libya.

Libya crisis that triggered international intervention in the country based on the doctrine of responsibility to protect, Showed that in case of a consensus, or at least lack of opposition to international human rights norms Not only an international context exists to support people in situations where the government is not able to fulfill their responsibility to the people, but U.N and at the head of the it the security Council can act effectively in this regard (Bellamy & Williams, 2011). The Libyan crisis practically highlighted the importance of the responsibility to protect doctrine and predisposing to turn it into an international norm. Genesis of the doctrine of responsibility to protect could underlie international peace and security with respect for human rights and international humanitarian law. The application of this doctrine in Darfur and Libya with a focus on the Security Council and with other international and regional bodies cooperation All suggest increasing the credibility, legitimacy of responsibility to protect and a basis for consolidation it as a international norm.

10. CONCLUSION

In this study, the expression of the traditional concept of peace as well as peace in the modern sense of the international community, the role and actions of the Security Council in the evolution of this concept are studied. The council during cold war due to the competition between two East and West superpowers has shown largely powerless in the face of international crises. The end of the Cold War and the collapse of East Camp Council have provided a new opportunity for Security Council to take a new approach to the analysis of international events and take action. It is said that the traditional concept of peace, which is solely confined to the absence of conflict between the parties extended interoperation by the Security Council has changed to the today sense that even contains bad economic situation and environmental risks. In this way, resolutions and actions of the Security Council under the Charter of the United Nations that occurred by recognizing the events issued as a threat to the peace and security situation, Have a significant impact on the evolution of the concept. To prove this, the present study explores some events, such as the events of September eleven, referring the Iranian nuclear issue to the security Council as well as the performance of the Council in the cases of Iraq and Bosnia that develop decisions of the council on the crisis and recognize them as a threat to international peace and security the same measures in same events of peace concept to what is today among jurists. This has gone so far that in some cases of problem a proper legal status can be found for Security Council action based on the provisions of the Charter and somehow has become a legislator on a world stage. The most important areas that the Security Council develop international peace and security during the Cold War and the beginning of the millennium was Human rights and humanitarian violations, terrorism, proliferation of weapons of mass destruction and environmental issues. In any case, the development of Authority of the Security Council should be based on the Authority explicit and general interpretation of that pillar and in the framework of Charter principles. As a result, the Council is not legally able to do arbitrary and without any kind of restriction.

NOTES

[1]Of course, secretary general supreme board report under the title of "A more secure world, our shared responsibility" that was awarded to the secretary general on Sept. 22, 2004, has offered a definition against international security that according to it threatening against international security or out of border threatening , there are threatening connected to each other that attacking to one, is considered, the attack to all thus the base of threaten against international security expends the danger of other threats: A More Secure World: Our Shared Responsibility: The Report is Available: http://www.un.org/secureworld/report.pdf.

[2]S/PV 46, 31Jnuary, 1992.

[3]SC/Res/1363/2001/30, July.

[4]SC/Res/1373/2001/28, September.

[5]A Report of the United Nations Association of the United States of American the Security Council and Non-proliferation, comforting the proliferation Danger: The Rule of the U.N Security Council, 22 may 1995.

[6]Sc/Res/687/1991/3April.

[7]Sc/Res/825/1993/11 may.

[8]Sc/Res/1172/1998/6 Jun.

[9]Sc/Res/1441/2002/8 Nov.

[10]IAEA Doc. Resolution of Board of Governors, GOV/2006/14, 4 February 2006. Available at:http://www.iaea.org

[11]UN Doc. Statement by the President of the Security Council, S/PRST/2006/15, 29 March 2006.

[12]Sc/Res/1970/2011/26 Feb.

[13]Sc/Res/1973/2011/17 March.

REFERENCES

1. Ashra'fi, D. (2015). International Organizations and the Conceptual Evolution of National Sovereignty. Tehran: Khorsandy Pub.

2. Bellamy, A. J., & Williams, P. D. (2011). The New Politics of Protection? Cote d'Ivoire, Libya and Responsibility to Protect.

International Affairs, 87, 825-850. https://doi.org/10.1111/j.1468-2346.2011.01006.x

3. Brown, D. (2003). Use of Force against Terrorism after September 11: State Responsibility, Self-Defence and Other Responses. Cardozo Journal of International and Comperative Law, 11.

4. Bruno, S. (2012). The Charter of United Nations: A Commentary. Oxford, New York: Oxford University Press.

5. Free Collins Dictionaries Online.http://www.collinslanguage.com

6. Henderson, C., & Lubell, N. (2013). The Contemporary Legal Nature of UN Security Council Ceasefire Resolutions. Leiden Journal of International Law, 26, 369-397. https://doi.org/10.1017/S0922156513000083

7. High-Level Panel on Threats (2004). Challenges and Change, A More Secure World: Our Shared Responsibility. New York, Part B, Synopsis. http://www.un.org/en/peacebuilding/pdf/historical/hlp_more_secure_world.pdf

8. IAEA Doc. Resolution of Board of Governors, GOV/2006/14, 4 February 2006 http://www.iaea.org/Publication/Documents/board/ 2006/gov2006-14.pdf

9. Kosha, S., & Eskandari, M. A. (2012). Legal Challenges of the Referral of Iran's Nuclear File to the Security Council and sanction Resolutions, Tehran. Journal of Foreign Policy, 26, No. 2.

10. Kurtz, R. L. (1999). Encyclopedia of Violence, Peace, & Conflict. San Diego, CA: Academic Press.

11. Laqueut, W. (1996). Postmodern Terrorism. Foreign Affairs, 75, No. 50 Sep/Oct.

12. Malone, D. M. (2008). Security Council, in the Oxford Handbook on the United Nations, Ed.

13. Miller, C. A. (2005). A Glossary of terms and Concepts in Peace and Conflict Studies. Ciudad Colón: University for Peace.

14. Mousazadeh, R. (2012). The Law of International Organizations: The Security Council Law. Tehran: Mizan Legal Foundation.

15. Nielsen, E. (2010). State Responsibility for Terrorist Groups. Davis Journal International Law, 17.

16. Oostithuzen, G., & Willmshorts, E. (2004). Terrorism and Weapons of Mass Destrruction: United Nations Security Council Resolution 1540, Chatham House BP 04/01, September, 2.http://www.riia.org

17. Shaygan, F. (2002). The United Nations Security Council and Concept of International Peace and Security. Tehran: Tehran University Pub.

18. Soltani, R. (2005). Security Council in the Beginning of Third Millennium (pp. 2-20). M.A. Thesis on International Law, Iran: Razavi University.

19. Thakur, R. (2011). Libya and Responsibility to Protect: Between Opportunistic Humanitarianism and Value-free Pragmatism. Security Challenges, 7, 13-25.

20. Tsagourias, N. (2011). Security Council Legislation Article 2(7) of the UN Charter and the Principle of Subsidiarity. Working Papers Series 05. Glasgow: Adam Smith Research Foundation

21. Vakil, A. S. (2013). Human Rights: International Peace and Security. Tehran: Majd Pub.

22. Vankovska, B., & Wiberg, H. (2002). Between Past and Future: Civil-Military Relations in Post-Communist Balkan States (p. 17). I.B. Tauris.

23. Williams, J. (2008). New Approaches in Changing World: The Human Security Agenda. In: Banning Landmines (p. 284). UK: Roman and Littlefield Publisher, INC.

10

CHAPTER

Probing the Relationship between Ecosystem Perceptions and Approaches to Environmental Governance: An Exploratory Content Analysis of Seven Water Dilemmas

Ryan Plummer, Julia Baird, Ryan Bullock, Diane Dupont and Steven Renzetti

a Environmental Sustainability Research Centre, Brock University, St. Catharines, Canada;

b Stockholm Resilience Centre, Stockholm University, Stockholm, Sweden;

c Environmental Sustainability Research Centre, Brock University, St. Catharines, Canada;

d Department of Environmental Studies and Sciences, The University of Winnipeg, Winnipeg, Canada;

e Environmental Sustainability Research Centre, Brock University, St. Catharines, Canada; f Department of Economics, Brock University, St. Catharines, Canada

ABSTRACT

Addressing wicked 'water dilemmas' requires an understanding of the context within which they are embedded. This study explored perceptions of the ecosystem in terms of resilience and the governance approaches employed through a content analysis of documents from seven case studies across the globe. Analytical constructs developed for resilience and governance approaches guided the exploration. Multiple resilience types were present in documents for each case, but few patterns emerged across cases. Governance approaches were strongly focused on state approaches in most cases. A relationship between resilience type and governance approach was not clear; however, a pattern emerged between the presence of the social–ecological resilience type and non-state-centred governance forms. The type of author (government, non-government) or the type of document (research and advisory, descriptive) were not found to mediate the findings as resilience framings varied considerably and state governance approaches were emphasised throughout. As the findings stand in contrast to contemporary scholarship on understanding ecosystems and environmental governance they raise important issues to which individuals must be cognizant when accessing documents for guidance. They also open avenues for future investigation of water dilemmas at the nexus of theory, policy and practice.

Keywords: Content analysis, perceptions, resilience, water dilemmas, water governance

INTRODUCTION

Water dilemmas are situations involving the biophysical world and humans where difficult choices are required among contested alternatives. These dilemmas are often described as wicked problems (e.g. FitzGibbon & Mensah, 2012; Head, 2010; Hearnshaw, Tompkins, & Cullen, 2011; Reed & Kasprzyk, 2009). While the definition of precisely what constitutes a wicked problem varies, it generally refers to a class of challenges characterised by extreme complexity (high risk, scientific uncertainty, ecological and social interdependencies, large scope and scale) and 'the absence of a clear public consensus on value, the nature of the problem, or acceptable solutions' (Balint, Stewart, Desai, & Walters, 2011, p. 9; see also Batie, 2008; Lazarus, 2009; Rittel & Webber, 1973).

Addressing water dilemmas is imperative and connected to how people see these wicked problems. Who should make decisions in water dilemmas and how should interventions occur? A vast discussion is underway about who should intervene in society and how it should take place; thus, governance has emerged as an integral concern in rethinking approaches to planning and managing water resources (de Loë & Kreutzwiser, 2007; Galaz, 2007; Pahl-Wostl et al., 2013; Plummer, de Grosbois, Velaniskis, & de Loë, 2011; Rogers & Hall, 2003).

As wicked problems are inherently embedded in a social context and involve multiple actors, attention is directed to diversity in terms of values, views/perceptions and problem framings (Balint et al., 2011; Batie, 2008; Rittel & Webber, 1973). Attention to diversity is necessary for understanding and navigating wicked problems as they are inherently embedded in a social context and involve multiple actors (Balint et al., 2011; Batie, 2008; Rittel & Webber, 1973). The question of how individuals perceive the environment has been explored in relation to geography, complex and synergistic causes, and complicated and contested solutions (Dunlap, Van Liere, Mertig, & Jones, 2000; Holling, Gunderson, &Ludwig, 2002; Stern, 1993). Stern, Dietz, and Guagnano (1995, p. 740) argue that: 'Given the ongoing debates about public understanding of science, and especially of risk, we need to understand the way values and worldview are implicated in the framing of public debate and the construction of public opinion ... – how the general influences the specific.' Exploring this connection has firmly taken hold within research examining the contingency of action for climate change (i.e. mitigation and adaptation) as related to endogenous societal factors such as perception and attitude of risk, knowledge, ethics and culture (e.g. Adger et al., 2009; Leiserowitz, 2007). It also extends into research on risk relating to water resources (e.g. Pahl-Wostl, 2007; Stenekes, Colebatch, Waite, & Ashbolt, 2006; Wolsink, 2006). Resilience has been an increasingly common framing in the context of wicked problems (e.g. Goldstein, 2011; Martin-Breen & Anderies, 2011; Powell, Larsen, & van Bommel, 2014; Termeer, Dewulf, & Breeman, 2013; Waddock, 2013).

This article explores the relationship between ecosystem perceptions in terms of resilience and the approaches to governance in a series of water dilemmas as described in documents arising from the cases. In line with the purpose of this research, the following four questions were explored:

1) How are ecosystems perceived in terms of resilience?
2) What governance approaches are taken to address the water dilemmas and how are they expressed?
3) Is there a relationship between perceptions of the ecosystem and governance approaches in these water dilemmas (and if yes, what is it)?
4) How does the relationship between ecosystem perceptions and governance approaches vary across document type?

Unpacking the constructs of resilience and environmental governance in the following section illuminates different ways of understanding the natural world and approaches for intervening. It also sets out important implications of resilience framing for environmental interventions that have been established with the scholarly evolution of these constructs. The main premise underpinning this study is that resilience framing relates to the approach for intervention in the seven water dilemmas from around the world.

Unpacking resilience and environmental governance: background and theory

The natural world is understood in many different ways and the historical assumptions underpinning the views people hold of it have implications for policy and action (Holling et al., 2002). Resilience entered the academic lexicon in the 1970s and developed rapidly in the disciplines of psychology and ecology along parallel tracks (Lundholm & Plummer, 2010). Several thorough reviews have traced the historical and conceptual development of the resilience construct in these disciplines as well as its more contemporary integrative usage (see Folke, 2006; Martin-Breen & Anderies, 2011; Masten, 2007). More recently, resilience is increasingly identified in association with understanding and responding to wicked problems in the scholarly literature (e.g. Goldstein, 2011; Martin-Breen & Anderies, 2011; Termeer et al., 2013; Waddock, 2013) and has been extended to popular news sources such as the *New York Times* (Zolli, 2012).

While several entry points are possible to consider how people perceive the environment, we draw upon the construct of resilience and employ it as a lens in this research for several reasons. First, types of resilience have been traced to differences in world views held by people (Holling et al., 2002) and these have important implications as set out in the introductory section of this paper. Second, notwithstanding duly noted difficult normative issues, resilience has spurred conversation about governance in relation to contemporary conditions of complexity and change (Brown, 2014; Duit, Galaz, Eckerberg, & Ebbesson, 2010; Nelson, Adger, & Brown, 2007). Third, recent approaches of using resilience as an optic to usefully explore different subjects with characteristics of wicked problems have been established, such as rural studies (Scott, 2013) and ecosystem services in cities (Barthel, Parker, & Ernstson, 2013). In developing a resilience lens to meet the needs of our inquiry we direct attention to a descriptive aspect by drawing upon work by Cumming et al. (2005), as well as an interpretive aspect by developing a typology of resilience perspectives.

Resilience is thus understood in several ways and tensions are evident among interpretations (e.g. Brand & Jax, 2007; Brown, 2014; Hornborg, 2009, 2013; Leech, 2008; Strunz, 2012). Categorising types of resilience is essential to its use as a lens to illuminate how actors perceive the ecosystem in water dilemmas. A resilience typology, using four 'types' of resilience (engineering, ecological, social-ecological and epistemic) was developed in 2012 based on a thorough review of the literature (see

Table 1. A typology of ecosystem perception in terms of resilience.

	Dimensions			
Type of resilience	System boundary	Desirable system attributes	Relationships among elements	Proxies/measures of resilience
Engineering	Ecological boundaries, typically at the level of populations and communities	Efficiency of function	Linear	Maximum sustained yield
		Constancy and predictability	Behaviour around a single equilibrium	Carrying capacity
		Ability to resist disturbance and change		speed of return to equilibrium
		Far from instability		
Ecological	Ecological boundaries	Persistent	Non-linear dynamics	Adaptive capacity
		Able to withstand disturbances and maintain function	Multiple stability domains	Size of stability domains
		Adaptive	Thresholds	Magnitude of disturbance tolerated before structural changes in controlling variables and processes
			Limited predictability	
			Systems go through adaptive cycle and are part of panarchy	
Social-ecological	Boundaries may be bio-physical, ecological, social and/or a combination	Capacity to absorb shocks and still maintain function	Interconnectedness between social and ecological systems	Adaptive capacity – learning, innovation, flexibility
		Capacity for renewal, re-organisation and development	Multiple thresholds	Capacities for self-organisation, adaptation and learning
		Responsiveness between ecosystem dynamics and management/governance which is flexible and adaptive	Uncertainty and nonlinearity	Resilience surrogates
			Panarchy	
Epistemic	Contested (soft) boundaries	Negotiable and flexible	Nonlinear and dynamic	Adaptive capacity
	Stakeholder/purpose defined systems	Plasticity	Inherently unstable	Collective action
		Learning oriented	People and their environment are structurally coupled and co-specify	Ability to generate scenarios and options
				Capacity of the coupled system to learn co-dependently

Source: adapted from Plummer et al. (2012).

Plummer, Baird, Dupont, & Renzetti, 2012). It was subsequently operationalised for use in content analysis by identifying corresponding word and phrase indicators for each type. Table 1 provides an overview of the resilience typology and for each type sets out its boundaries, desirable attributes, relationships among system elements described and proxies/measures. While considerable efforts were made to clearly distinguish between the types, it is important to recognise that they are not mutually exclusive and a degree of overlap exists between some of the boundaries due to the nature of development of resilience types over time by diverse disciplinary perspectives (see e.g. Folke, 2006).

Governance, in the broadest sense, is deliberate intervention in society that is goal oriented (Kooiman, 1993). As set forth by the Global Water Partnership, water governance refers to 'the range of political, social, economic and administrative systems that are in place to develop and manage water resources, and the delivery of water services, at different levels of society' (Rogers & Hall, 2003, p. 16). Water is one of many resources about which attendant concerns about governance are growing. For example, the World Water Assessment Programme (2003) diagnoses the present dilemma concerning water as a crisis of governance, brought about by the mismanagement of water by humans. Ideas of environmental governance are being taken up in specific relation to water.

Questions of governance are often expressed or represented as models. These models reflect underlying positions about who should make decisions, the manner in which decisions should be made, and how societal change should occur (Glasbergen, 1998). A reconfiguration of environmental governance is underway in which the state or government is no longer seen as the sole decision-making authority (Armitage, de Loë, & Plummer, 2012; Bryant & Wilson, 1998). Attention is thus being directed to a broader array of governance models that highlight the particular roles of markets, civil society, self-regulation and co-operation (Glasbergen, 1998). Moreover, a growing emphasis is being placed on the way these models hybridise (see Armitage et al., 2012; Lemos & Agrawal, 2006) and combine to influence outcomes (Duit & Galaz, 2008) in light of the complex and multi-scale nature of contemporary environmental challenges. Table 2 summarises four of the more common models of environmental governance and unpacks each in terms of who is involved, how decisions are made and the anticipated outcomes of change.

Table 2. Environmental governance models and key analytical considerations (Glasbergen, 1998; Lemos & Agrawal, 2006).

	Considerations		
Model	Who is primarily involved in governance?	How are decisions made?	What are the outcomes (how does change occur)?
State	Government (state, agencies, legislators, centralised, bureaucracy, regulators, administrators) is the main entity	Decision are made through 'formal' policy processes with an emphasis on legal/regulatory aspect	Change takes place through regulations, rules, prescriptions, proscriptions, legislations, acts, standards, policies, plans, procedures Bureaucratic administration and enforcement
Market	State (government) facilitates market processes to varying degrees which mediate the interactions of corporations, private businesses and citizens	Consumers and industries make choices with the environmental costs of production incorporated	Price or allocation mechanisms account for environmental costs and/ or considerations (e.g. taxes, fees, tradable permits, market exchanges, certification)
Civil society	Citizens, non-governmental organisations (NGO), community, stakeholders	Determinations achieved through democracy ('participatory ideal' and 'rejectionist approach'), with emphasis placed on broad participation, deliberation, consensus, public debate, civil opposition	Interventions occur at small scales (involving resource users) and through decentralisation Informal institutions are emphasized where authority and legitimacy is connected to community based processes
Hybridised forms	Governance is a shared endeavour	Decisions are made in a myriad of ways (e.g. problem-solving process, deliberation, negotiation, joint policy practices), but some degree of power sharing is present	The following outcomes are examples from some popular hybrid environmental governance forms Co-management: cooperative agreements, joint-management boards, voluntary/ negotiated agreements Public-private: concessionary arrangements, self-regulation Private-social: payments for ecosystem services, carbon sequestration

As set out in the introduction, the intent of this study is to explore the relationship between how a system of interest is understood in terms of resilience and the governance approach(es) to the water dilemma. Resilience framing has important implications for environmental interventions. An exclusive emphasis on engineering resilience is associated with the pervasive application of top-down command and control management (Folke et al., 2004; Holling & Gunderson, 2002; Holling & Meffe, 1996; Plummer, 2010). Government is the main entity in this model of intervention and control occurs through regulations (Glasbergen, 1998).

The fundamental distinction in framing resilience away from an equilibrium steady state (i.e. ecological resilience) connotes the need for adaptive management (e.g. Gunderson, 2000; Holling & Meffe, 1996). The social–ecological framing of resilience broadens the context to linked systems of humans and nature (Folke, 2006) and correspondingly emphasises adaptive and collaborative approaches (e.g. Folke, Hahn, Olsson, & Norberg, 2005; Olsson, Folke, & Berkes, 2004; Walker, Holling, Carpenter, & Kinzig, 2004). Finally, the epistemic framing of resilience is rooted in social constructivism epistemology and draws attention to the contested boundaries defining systems with the implied requirement of participation in collective action with the hallmarks of agency, negotiation and co-dependence (Powell & Jiggins, 2003; Powell et al., 2014).

METHODS

A multiple case study design was used to explore the relationship between ecosystem perceptions and the approaches to governance in a series of water dilemmas. In line with direction from Kuzel (1999) and Shakir (2002), the selection of cases fulfilled the objectives of appropriateness and adequacy. Specifically, each exhibited a water dilemma (the unit of analysis) and was located in a different geographic location, and the boundary of the location was defined by the water dilemma. The opportunity to engage with these cases was made possible through a broader research consortium, of which all the case studies were part, entitled 'Climate Adaptation and Water Governance' (CADWAGO). The locations of each case study and a brief description of the water dilemma are shown in Figure 1.

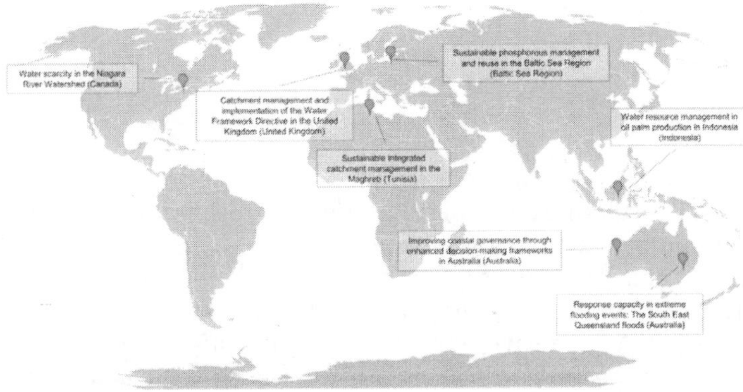

Figure 1. Geographic location of cases.

Analysis of documents is often undertaken in association with case study research (Stake, 1995; Yin, 2003) as well as policy relevant questions in the environmental domain (e.g. Berke & Conroy, 2000; Gupta et al., 2010; Plummer et al., 2011). A request was made via e-mail to each case study leader (a person in each case with extensive knowledge of the water dilemma and who had undertaken primary research in the case) for three key documents that addressed the water dilemma (e.g. management plans, research reports, policy documents). Each document was scrutinised to ensure it encompassed the elements of a water dilemma and that it was directly relevant to the case. Where a portion of a document was not directly relevant to the water dilemma or was clearly redundant it was excluded from the analysis.

The data collection protocol resulted in three documents for each case (21 documents in total) with an average length of 65 pages (see Appendix 1 for the list of documents). Content analysis was guided by analytical constructs in the literature – specifically, the resilience typology and governance approaches identified in Tables 1 and 2. A comprehensive codebook was prepared which elaborates upon each aspect of these constructs by providing definitions, keywords, phrases and examples (as suggested by Creswell, 2009; Krippendorff, 2013). Coding was performed in two stages using NVivo 10 (QSR International). Text queries were initially used to identify all relevant passages related to ecosystems and/or governance. A subsequent round of deductive coding, using the codebook as a guide, assigned all relevant codes to passages identified via the text query (Creswell, 2009; Krippendorff, 2013).

In coding for the analytical construct of 'resilience typology', codes were assigned by resilience type (i.e. engineering, ecological, social–ecological and epistemic) and by consideration (i.e. system boundary, desirable system attributes, relationships and functions, and/or proxies/measures of resilience) that were exhibited in the passage. The proportion of all codes assigned for each consideration within each resilience type was calculated. From these data, a simple mean value for each resilience paradigm was calculated to identify relationships in the cross-case analysis. Codes for the analytical construct 'governance approaches' were assigned for: (1) the governance approach (i.e. state, market regulation, civil society and hybrid forms); (2) considerations for governance approaches (i.e. actors, processes and outcomes); (3) the tone of the language used within each passage (positive, negative or neutral); and, (4) the magnitude, or intent, of the language used within the passage. Tone and magnitude provide a means to gauge the governance approach and associated considerations in terms of the nature and strength of expression. Magnitude was assigned using three categories (i.e. explicit, implicit and empty) described in detail in Plummer et al. (2011). The number of codes assigned to a single magnitude was divided by the total number of magnitude codes assigned and a proportion value was identified for each tone type for each document and combined for cases.

Cross-case analysis was subsequently undertaken to probe patterns among the water dilemmas that related to the four research questions guiding the study. 'Fingerprints' were created to visualise how resilience and governance was expressed across the cases by plotting the proportion of coded passages using a radar graph, where each axis represents a resilience consideration or governance dimension. All points on each axis sum to one (100% of codes assigned to that axis) and the resulting 'shape' shows how strongly it is expressed within each case (i.e. shapes with greater area indicate a stronger expression of the resilience type/governance approach). Relational patterns between how the ecosystem was perceived in terms of resilience and governance of the water dilemma were then explored through the use of scatterplots.

A limitation to the methods and study relates to the documents used for the analysis. Each case study leader was asked for three key documents that addressed the water dilemma. We relied upon the case study leaders to identify 'key' documents that address the water dilemma because it was beyond the scope of this research to investigate the extent to which the documents accurately reflected perspectives of actors in each case. While the wording of the request was intended to enable flexibility in the provision of documents based on a high degree of familiarity with the case, their selection has acknowledged implications. These include a different mix of document types between cases document as well as preparation by a variety of organisations (governmental and non-governmental) and the perceptions presented therein are reflective of author(s)/organisations. To explore the influence(s) of different types of documents, each document was classified into one of three categories: research and advisory documents authored by government agencies ($n = 8$); research and advisory documents written by non-governmental groups ($n = 6$); and descriptive documents authored by any source ($n = 7$). This categorisation was used to understand the differences between the two main types of documents provided by case study leaders, as well as potential differences between author types for research and advisory documents as this category was broad.

FINDINGS

How are ecosystems perceived in terms of resilience?

A 'resilience fingerprint' using the resilience typology was generated for each case and is illustrated in Figure 2. Multiple resilience types were represented in each case (albeit to varying extents). The fingerprints highlighted the similarity of the UK, AUS coastal, AUS floods, Indonesia and Tunisian case in the dominance of ecological resilience framings of proxies/measures of resilience. It also showed a relatively similar 'fingerprint' for Niagara and Tunisian cases. The associated water dilemmas in these similar cases showed little similarity. For example, the Niagara and Indonesian cases focus on water quality and transboundary issues, the Tunisian case focuses on water quantity variability, the UK case deals with institutional constraints to integrated water resource management and the AUS coastal case deals with diverse development pressures on protection of marine ecosystems. In addition, the types of stakeholders and governance structures in these cases vary substantially. This supports the assertion that diverse actors from different places can still commonly frame issues because they are connected to a larger environmental discourse ('resilience' and 'climate change' being prime current examples) (Dryzek, 2005; Forsyth, 2003). As Forsyth (2003, p. 226) observes: 'all forms of environmental explanation reflect a wider social framing and solidarity such as a network or community…'.

Some discernible patterns appeared with regards to perception of the ecosystem across cases. First, multiple resilience framings occurred in each of the cases. Engineering and ecological resilience framings tended to occur most strongly in different axes in the resilience fingerprint (i.e. for different considerations) and often in isolation of other resilience framings (Figure 2). Social–ecological resilience often co-occurred with other types and also tended to more frequently be oriented towards 'system boundary' and 'relationships and functions' considerations. Expressions of these multiple types may reflect evolution, uptake and overlapping boundaries associated with resilience as an analytical construct, which has evolved and been shaped by various disciplines in the social and natural sciences. Epistemic resilience was not identified in key documents in a proportion large enough to be exhibited in the fingerprints. This finding is unsurprising given the relatively recent advent of epistemic resilience and the formative nature associated with its scholarship.

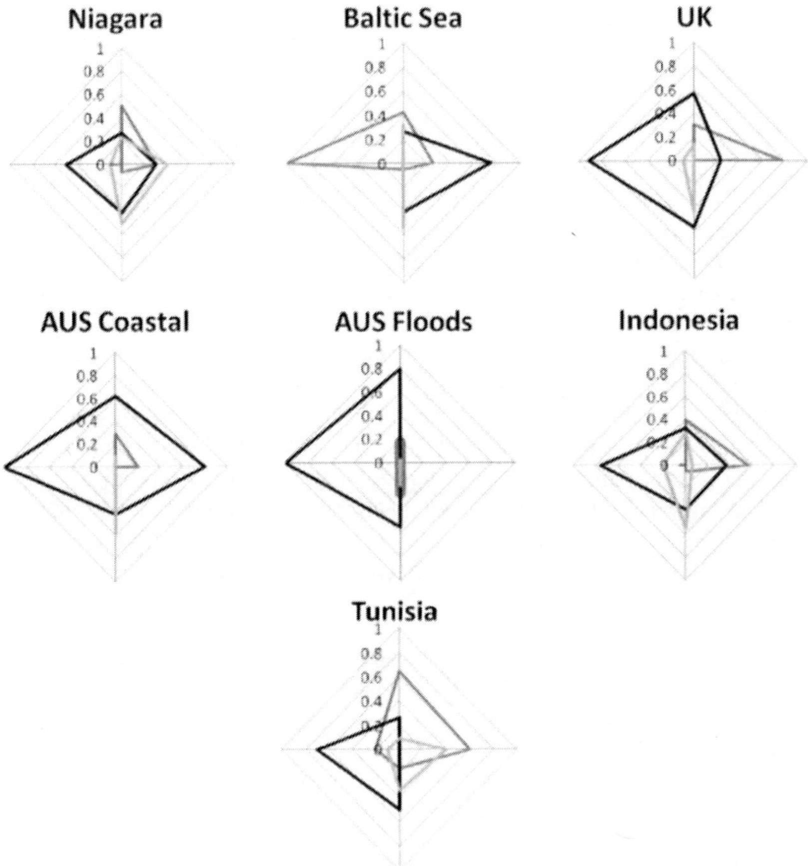

Figure 2. Resilience fingerprints for each case. Notes: axes of the radar graph correspond to the four considerations of resilience paradigms: top = system boundary, right = system attributes, lower = relationships and functions, and left = proxies/measures of resilience. Line colours correspond to resilience types: blue = engineering, black = ecological, orange = social-ecological, and purple = epistemic.

What governance approaches are taken to address these water dilemmas and how are they expressed?

The second analytical construct concerned approaches to water governance and was unpacked using the fingerprint technique in terms of actors, processes and outcomes (Figure 3). A clear pattern emerged across cases with state governance approaches most common across all governance considerations. State approaches were particularly strongly represented in the consideration of outcomes across cases, while non-state approaches (market regulation, civil society and hybrid forms) appeared more often for the considerations of actors and processes. This finding was unsurprising as government regulatory control forms the basis of environmental policy (Glasbergen, 1998; Kettl, 2002) and thus is likely to be closely aligned with governance outcomes.

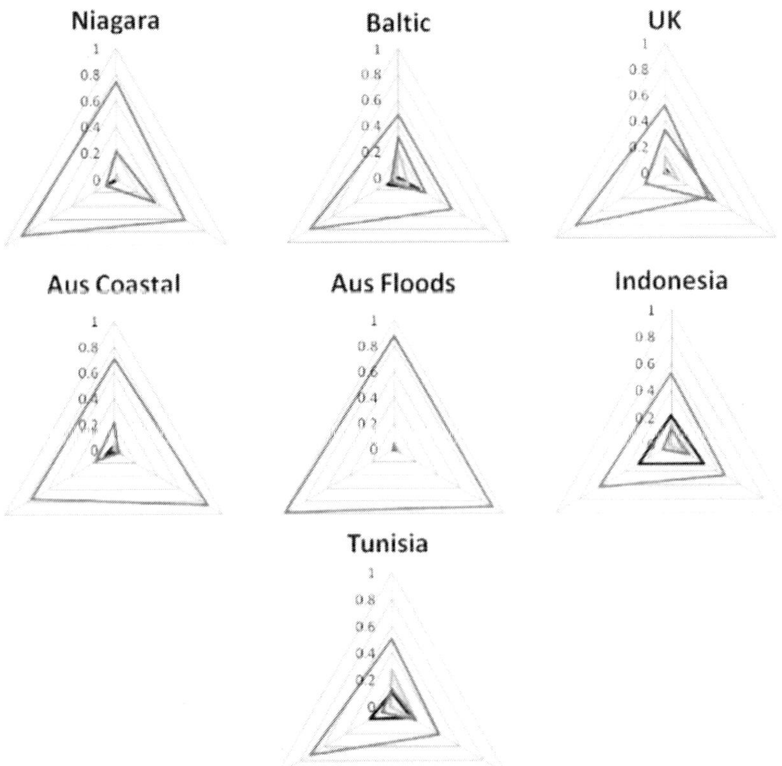

Figure 3. Governance fingerprints for each case. Notes: axes of the radar graph correspond to the three considerations of governance approaches: top = actors, lower right = processes and lower left = outcomes. Line colours correspond to governance approaches: blue = state, black = market, orange = civil society and purple = hybrid forms.

Metrics of magnitude and tone were analysed to gauge strength and direction of the governance approaches to each water dilemma. Three distinguishable patterns emerged from the cross-case analysis. First, magnitude types were distributed among governance approaches and considerations, but passages mentioning state approaches tended to be explicit or empty, market approaches tended to be implicit or empty, and no clear patterns emerged for civil society and hybrid approaches. Second, as the proportion of state governance approaches increased, the proportion of passages with a neutral tone also increased, indicating a positive relationship between them. This is indicative of a descriptive tone (i.e. statements of what 'is') in reference to state governance approaches and is consistent with the findings about regarding the prevalence of this type of approach in most cases. Third, as the proportion of hybrid governance approaches increased, the proportion of passages with a positive tone increased, and those with a negative tone decreased, indicating that hybrid governance approaches are positively related to a positive tone and negatively related to a negative tone. While all magnitude types occur for all governance approaches, the proportions of passages mentioning market regulation, civil society and hybrid governance approaches are much lower than for state approaches. This highlights the explicit (directive) and empty (descriptive) nature of many of the passages that address state governance approaches and the implicit (advisory) and empty nature of passages for other governance approaches. This finding may be a signal of change in terms of water governance (while acknowledging the study limitation identified above), and coincides with growing emphasis for transformation of water governance beyond state approaches (e.g. Pahl-Wostl, 2009; Rogers & Hall, 2003; Tropp, 2007). A case study example of this can be drawn from the United Kingdom where non-governmental organisations legally challenged the existing approach to water management in the 1990s and fundamentally changed the way water resources were managed (Melo Zurita et al., 2013). The Department for Environment Food and Rural Affairs' (Department for Environment Food & Rural Affairs (DEFRA), 2013, p. 3) most recent policy framework for an integrated catchment approach states: 'We firmly believe that better coordinated action is desirable at the catchment level by all those who use water or influence land management and that this requires greater engagement and delivery by stakeholders'.

Is there a relationship between perceptions of the ecosystem and governance approaches in these water dilemmas (and if yes, what is it)?

This question brings together the previous analyses and informs the overarching intent of the research. The relationship(s) between perception of the ecosystem and governance approaches across cases were probed using a scatterplot to identify patterns (data not shown), however, a clear relational pattern did not appear from this exercise. The lack of clear patterns between resilience paradigms and governance approaches was surprising given the inherent associations in the literature, as set out in second section of the paper. Our findings stand in contrast to the literature (e.g. Folke et al., 2004; Holling & Gunderson, 2002; Holling & Meffe, 1996;

Plummer, 2010) in which the engineering framing of resilience corresponds to intervention via government regulation. Specifically, resilience was framed in a variety of ways in the cases whereas an emphasis on intervention by government approaches was found consistently. The absence of relationship between resilience framing and governance intervention in the cases contradicts the main premise with which the research was undertaken. However, previous content analyses of discourse illustrate how contradictions and tensions can and do often exist both within and among framings of complex problems (Creed, Langstraat, & Scully, 2002). This may well be the situation in regard to the multiple framings of resilience and the implications for governance.

Two tendencies were observable in the relationship between resilience types and governance approaches. When social-ecological resilience was present in cases, the proportion of codes assigned for state governance approaches tended to decrease, indicating that state governance approaches were mentioned in a lesser proportion to other approaches when a social-ecological paradigm was expressed. This may indicate the possibility of an emphasis on non-state agents, processes and outcomes occurs in texts exhibiting this resilience type. Moreover, weak positive relationships between the social–ecological resilience type and market, civil society and hybrid governance approaches were also evident, indicating an increase in the presence of these approaches as the social–ecological resilience type was expressed. These findings are generally consistent with the transition underway in natural resources management and environmental governance scholarship where the limitations of command and control approaches are being acknowledged (e.g. Holling & Meffe, 1996; Ludwig, 2001) and novel governance arrangements are being explored (e.g. Armitage et al., 2012; Folke et al., 2005). Further, it appears that the social-ecological resilience perspective is most congruent with the promotion of this transition.

How does the type and source of document influence the findings?

Finding relatively few patterns among cases in the above question prompted further investigation into the influence(s) documents themselves may be having in mediating the findings. The presence of patterns within and across document types was explored spanning all cases in regard to each of the aforementioned queries. In terms of perceptions of the ecosystem, engineering resilience was more consistently present (in boundary and attributes considerations) in research and advisory documents authored by government agencies than for the non-government documents of the same type, or the descriptive documents. This may reflect the historically dominant role played by engineers and engineering consulting firms in water resource management. The perceptions of the ecosystem also were highly variable within each document type. Patterns within and across document type in reference to governance approach revealed that: state approaches were highly dominant in passages for all three document types for all considerations; for research and advisory documents authored by non-governmental groups, there was some mention of civil society actors and market outcomes; for research and advisory documents authored by government agencies and for descriptive documents, hybrid actors and processes were sometimes mentioned; and in terms of outcomes, research and advisory documents authored by government agencies were highly focused on state outcomes. While it was anticipated that documents authored by government would emphasise state governance approaches, the dominance of these approaches within and across document types was unexpected. Again, a clear relationship between resilience framing and governance approach was not evident. Moreover, the findings also suggest little uptake of non-state governance approaches as has been argued for in the scholarly literature over the past 15 years (e.g. Armitage et al., 2012; Folke et al., 2005; Glasbergen, 1998) and as required for second or next generation environmental policy (Durant, Chun, Kim, & Lee, 2004; Kettl, 2002). Thus, agents directly participating in these cases and drawing upon these texts for information and guidance may find that the documents reflect resilience perspectives not entirely congruent with their own or other agents participating in the same cases.

In considering magnitude, research and advisory documents authored by non-governmental groups exhibited mostly empty and implicit language for market, civil society and hybrid approaches, whereas state-based approaches were associated with a higher proportion of explicit passages (mean of 25% of all passages). Research and advisory documents authored by government agencies were written using mostly explicit and empty language for all governance types, and descriptive documents exhibited a mix of magnitude types for all governance approaches with no clear pattern. For all three document types, tone was most often neutral; however, a pattern was evident in tone between document types with research and advisory documents authored by both governments and non-governmental groups being more negative (approximately 30 and 20% of passages coded, respectively) as compared to descriptive documents (approximately 30% of passages coded were positive and only 10–16% negative). It is possible that certain document types could have been written to support a political position on an issue or set of issues or written by individuals that have a conceptual or professional stake in advancing the material and knowledge presented. As Bullock, Armitage, and Mitchell (2012, p. 317) observe with respect to dominant framings of resilience and non-resilience in natural resource dilemmas:

Experts cannot and should not be viewed as neutral consultants and objectives technicians employed to advise their client social groups in situations of learning – because they bring their own disciplinary assumptions, tools and reputations to a problem domain, based on certain cultures of learning.

Robust relational patterns between ecosystem perceptions and governance approaches were not evident within document types; however, a trend emerged in government authored research in advisory reports and descriptive documents where a strong focus on state-based governance approaches was consistent despite the resilience perspectives expressed. This finding, again, stands in opposition to the anticipated relationship, informed by the literature, in which government regulatory intervention is associated with engineering framing of resilience. It also contradicts the tendencies outlined above between social–ecological resilience framing and governance approaches across the cases investigated. Consequently, evidence from the document analysis suggests relatively little reflection or uptake of the widespread calls for new and different approaches to intervening. For example, the need for new approaches for management and governance that correspond or 'fit' with complex adaptive systems perspective of resilience has been argued strongly (e.g. Boyd & Folke, 2012; Folke et al., 2004; Holling & Meffe, 1996). Attention to shifting paradigms and cultivating corresponding governance approaches is similarly present in water resource scholarship (e.g. Ison, Röling, & Watson, 2007; Pahl-Wostl, 2007; Scholz & Stifel, 2005). Inroads into wicked problems (e.g. water dilemmas) require processes and tools that are different from those contributing to their creation (Brown, Harris, & Russel, 2010; FitzGibbon & Mensah, 2012).

CONCLUSION

Ecosystem perceptions, governance approaches and the relationships among these were explored in a document analysis of seven water dilemmas across the globe. In drawing upon conceptual developments of resilience in relation to ecosystems and environmental governance, relationships were anticipated between resilience framing and approaches for intervening in the cases. However, these patterns did not clearly emerge from the analysis. In particular, the relationship between engineering framing of resilience and regulatory intervention via government was absent. A pattern across cases linked the presence of the social–ecological resilience framing and non-state-centred governance approaches. This trend appeared most strongly in references to governance actors and processes, and less so in governance outcomes which is consistent with a transition in governance from command and control to other forms (Armitage et al., 2012; Folke et al., 2005). However, the findings from these cases indicate that transition may be occurring slowly and in an incomplete way, and that a transfer of authority from state to non-state actors may not have accompanied this shift. The persistent expression of state governance approaches found in documents authored by governments, regardless of the resilience perspective taken, raises important questions about the limited uptake as called for above as well as the entrenchment pathology within resource agencies (cf. Holling & Meffe, 1996).

While this research was initiated with expectations of finding congruence between resilience framings and governance approaches, the discordance found reveals important cautions when considering documents as well as opens directions for future research. Reflections on the process of using documents in this research highlight the influence of author type and messaging (language and tone) in the analysis. Results indicating the occurrence of negative content emanating from government and non-government authors serve as a reminder that while documents are stable sources of data, they must not be viewed as apolitical or neutral data sources. Instead, they are imbued with the political meanings of their authors, explicit and implicit, whether intentional and unintentional. This is a noteworthy challenge for actors who are addressing local water issues and perhaps participating in governance that in their efforts to gain information and guidance from available texts, may confront resilience perspectives in these texts that do not reflect the most recent conceptualisations of the wicked water dilemmas being addressed.

The findings from this study also highlight several important directions for future research. The (mis)alignment of perceptions and beliefs about ecosystems and governance by stakeholders in the water dilemmas with the anticipated relationships from the literature is extremely perplexing and requires further investigation. Grounded speculation from this research suggests that resilience may be a challenging lens to capture framing because of the multi-faceted nature of the construct, incremental manner in which it has evolved and issues of mutual exclusivity. The pervasiveness of the government regulatory approach to address the water dilemmas studied requires concerted investigation. Why is the transition underway in water scholarship and policy regarding the inclusion of non-state actors in contemporary water governance not reflected in documents associated with water dilemmas? Is the emphasis on government regulation manifest in documents reflective of how water dilemmas are being addressed in practice? Another question called up by this study is how individuals (stakeholders) in water dilemmas perceive ecosystems and prefer governance to be approached. Comparisons could then be made among those conceptually advanced by scholars, manifest in documents and held by individuals. These future avenues of research are essential next steps to sort out inconsistencies in addressing water dilemmas among theory, policy and practice.

NOTES ON CONTRIBUTORS

Ryan Plummer holds a PhD in Rural Studies (University of Guelph). He is a professor in the Environmental Sustainability Research Centre at Brock University where he held a Chancellor's Chair for Research Excellence from 2008–2011. He is also a senior research Fellow at the Stockholm Resilience Centre (Sweden) and a faculty investigator with Water Policy and Governance Group (Canada). His multi-faceted programme of research broadly concerns resilience and governance of social–ecological systems. Water resources are the context in which his research mainly occurs.

Julia Baird holds a PhD in Environment and Sustainability and a MSc in Soil Science (University of Saskatchewan). At present, she is a research associate at Brock University. Her current research focuses on collaborative and adaptive environmental governance within the contexts of water resources and climate change. Within this area, she has a strong interest in resilience, learning and social networks.

Ryan Bullock holds a PhD in Geography and Environmental Management (Waterloo). He is an assistant professor with The University of Winnipeg's Department of Environmental Studies and Sciences and he is the director of the Centre for Forest Interdisciplinary Research (C-FIR). His research addresses the human dimensions of environmental resource management, northern governance and development, and community-based research approaches.

Diane Dupont holds a PhD in Economics (University of British Columbia). She is a professor in the Economics Department and associate dean, Graduate Studies and Research, Faculty of Social Sciences at Brock University. Her current research programme concentrates upon examining ways to encourage more efficient and sustainable use of water resources both on the supply and demand side. On the supply side, she is looking at factors that help to identify which water utilities operate most efficiently and sustainably. On the demand side, she has undertaken a number of non-market valuation studies to determine the value of good quality water as it relates to individuals' perceptions of the health effects of tap water.

Steven Renzetti holds a PhD in Economics (University of British Columbia). He is a professor in the Department of Economics and associate vice president, Research for Humanities and Social Sciences at Brock University. His current research interest is in the economics of water resources. He is particularly interested in understanding the factors influence households' and businesses' water use and employing that information to design incentives (such as water prices) that will promote efficient and sustainable water use.

DISCLOSURE STATEMENT

No potential conflict of interest was reported by the authors.

FUNDING

Funding for this work, as part of the CADWAGO project, was provided by Riksbankens Jubileumsfond, the Volkswagen Stiftung and Compagnia di San Paolo through the Europe and Global Challenges programme.

ACKNOWLEDGEMENTS

We wish to thank Samantha Morris, Katrina Krievins and Julia Lawler for their research assistance. Our appreciation is also extended to the case study leaders in the CADWAGO project for their generous assistance in identifying and providing key documents.

APPENDIX 1

Table A1. Documents used for content analysis of water dilemmas.

Case	Document (citation)
Australia coastal management	Natural Resource Management Ministerial Council. (2006). *National cooperative approach to integrated coastal zone management. Framework and implementation plan.* Canberra, Australia: Australian Government. Retrieved from http://www.environment.gov.au/resource/national-cooperative-approach-integrated-coastal-zone-management-framework-and
	O'Toole, K., Haward, M., Coffey, B., Leith, P., Rees, C., Quinn, G., Wescott, G., Scarborough, H., Wallis, A., Keneley, M., Macgarvey, A., Miller, K., Baxter, T., Kriwoken, L., Mount, R., Nursey-Bray, M., & Vince, J. (2013). *Knowledge systems theme. Final report.* CSIRO.
	Stocker, L., Bruekers, G., Danese, C., Hofmeester, C., Shaw, J., Petrova, S., Middle, G., Pokrant, B., & Zafrin, S. (n.d.). *Final report: Governance theme.* CSIRO.
Australia flooding	Brisbane City Council. (2012). *Brisbane City Council disaster management plan.* Retrieved from http://www.brisbane.qld.gov.au/downloads/community/community_safety/Section%201%20-%20Disaster%20Management%20Plan%20-%20no%20signature%20copy.pdf
	Queensland Floods Commission of Inquiry. (2012). *Final report of the Queensland Floods Commission of Inquiry.* Retrieved from http://www.floodcommission.qld.gov.au/__data/assets/pdf_file/0007/11,698/QFCI-Final-Report-March-2012.pdf
	Wenger, C., Hussey, K., & Pittock, J. (2013). *Living with floods: Key lessons from Australia and abroad.* Gold Coast, Australia: National Climate Change Adaptation Research Facility.
Baltic	Heeb, A. (2012). *Constructed wetlands and flood control a synthesis of four Baltic COMPASS case studies. Part I: Background report – September 2012.* Retrieved from http://www.balticcompass.org/PDF/Reports/WetlandsFloods-synthesis-AH-final.pdf
	Larsen, R.K. (2012). *Governance innovations for improved phosphorus management and reuse – voices from the Baltic Sea Region.* Retrieved from http://www.sei-international.org/mediamanager/documents/Publications/SEI-BalticCOMPASS-GovernanceInnovationsForImprovedPhosphorusManagementAndReuse-2012.pdf
	Stockholm Environment Institute (SEI). (2013). *The common agricultural policy post-2013: Could reforms make Baltic Sea Region farms more sustainable?* Stockholm, Sweden: Stockholm Environment Institute
Indonesia	Ancestral Land/Domain Watch (ADLAW). 2013. The Palawan Oil Palm Geotagged Report 2013. 94 pp.
	Meijaard, E., Stanley, S.A., Pollard, E.H.B., Gouyon, A., & Paoli, G. (2006). *Practitioners guide to managing High Conservation Value Forest in Indonesia: A case study from East Kalimantan.* Samarinda, Indonesia: The Nature Conservancy. Retrieved from http://www.hcvnetwork.org/resources/assessments/Practitioners%20Guide%20to%20HCVF%20in%20Indonesia%20_Kalimantan.pdf
	Larsen, R.K., Osbeck, M., Jiwan, N., Rompas, A., Nito, J., & Tangan, A. (2012). *Competing water claims in biofuel feedstock operations in Central Kalimantan.* Stockholm, Sweden: Stockholm Environment Institute. Retrieved from http://www.sei-international.org/mediamanager/documents/Publications/SEI-WorkingPaper-Larsen-CompetingWaterClaimsInBiofuel-2012.pdf
Niagara	Environmental Sustainability Research Centre (ESRC). 2013. Liquid Assets: Assessing Water's Contribution to Niagara. WaterSmart Niagara, Niagara Region. 80 pp.
	International Joint Commission (IJC). (2011). *15th biennial report on Great Lakes water quality.* Retrieved from http://www.ijc.org/files/tinymce/uploaded/15biennial_report_web-final.pdf
	Niagara Peninsula Conservation Authority (NPCA). (2011). *Assessment report – Niagara peninsula source protection area.* Retrieved from http://www.sourceprotection-niagara.ca/assess_report.html
UK	Department for Environment Food and Rural Affairs (DEFRA). (2011). *Defra statement on the principles of River Basin Planning Guidance and the future direction of Water Framework Directive implementation.* Retrieved from http://assets.wwf.org.uk/downloads/defra_sop_2011.pdf
	Department for Environment Food and Rural Affairs (DEFRA). (2013). *Catchment based approach: Improving the quality of our water environment.* Retrieved from https://www.gov.uk/government/uploads/system/uploads/attachment_data/file/204,231/pb13934-water-environment-catchment-based-approach.pdf
	Tweed Forum. (2010). *Tweed catchment management plan.* Tweed Forum: Roxburgshire, Scotland. Retrieved from http://www.tweedforum.org/catchment-management-planning/catchment-management-plan
Tunisia	El Hedi Louati, M. & Bucknall, J. (2010). *Tunisia's experience in water resource mobilization and management.* Retrieved from http://siteresources.worldbank.org/INTWDR2010/Resources/5,287,678-1,255,547,194,560/WDR2010_BG_Note_Louati.pdf
	Sghaier, M., Ouessar, M., Catacutan, D.C., & Briki, M. (n.d.). *Context of Oum Zessar Watershed Tunisia.* Retrieved from http://www.oss-online.org/sites/default/files/projet/contexte_oum_zessar.pdf
	Tunis International Center for Environmental Technologies. 2009. *Institutional framework and decision-making practices for water management in Tunisia: Toward the development of a strategy for improved groundwater management.* Retrieved from http://environ.chemeng.ntua.gr/ineco/UserFiles/File/Deliverables/Publishable%20Report%20-%20Tunisia.pdf

REFERENCES

1. Adger, N. W., Dessai, S., Goulden, M., Hulme, M., Lorenzoni, I., Nelson, L., ... Wreford, A. (2009). Are there social limits to adaptation to climate change? Climatic Change, 93, 335–354.
2. Armitage, D., de Loë, R., & Plummer, R. (2012). Environmental governance and its implications for conservation practice. Conservation Letters, 5, 245–255.
3. Balint, P. J., Stewart, R. E., Desai, A., & Walters, L. W. (2011). Wicked environmental problems. Washington, DC: Island Press.
4. Barthel, S., Parker, J., & Ernstson, H. (2013). Food and green space in cities: A resilience lens on gardens and urban environmental movements. Urban Studies, 52(7), 1–18.
5. Batie, S. S. (2008). Wicked problems and applied economics. American Journal of Agricultural Economics, 90, 1176–1191.
6. Berke, P., & Conroy, M. M. (2000). Are we planning for sustainable development?. Journal of the American Planning Association, 66, 21–33.
7. Boyd, E., & Folke, C. (2012). Adapting institutions, adaptive governance and complexity: An introduction. In E. Boyd & C. Folke (Eds.), Adapting institutions: Governance, complexity and social-ecological resilience (pp. 1–8). Cambridge: Cambridge University Press.
8. Brand, F. S., & Jax, K. (2007). Focusing the meaning(s) of resilience: Resilience as a descriptive concept and a boundary object. Ecology and Society, 12, 23. Retrieved from http://www.ecologyandsociety.org/vol12/iss1/art23/
9. Brown, K. (2014). Global environmental change I: A social turn for resilience? Progress in Human Geography, 38, 107–117.
10. Brown, V. A., Harris, J. A., & Russel, J. (2010). Tackling wicked problems: Through the transdisciplinary imagination. New York, NY: Earthscan.
11. Bryant, R., & Wilson, G. (1998). Rethinking environmental management. Progress in Human Geography, 22, 321–343.
12. Bullock, R., Armitage, D., & Mitchell, B. (2012). Shadow networks, social learning, and collaborating through crisis: Building resilient forest-based communities in northern Ontario, Canada. In B.

Goldstein (Ed.), Collaborative resilience: Moving through crisis to opportunity (pp. 309–337).

13. Boston, MA: The MIT Press. Creed, W., Langstraat, J., & Scully, M. (2002). A picture of the frame: Frame analysis as technique and as politics. Organizational Research Methods, 5, 34–55.

14. Creswell, J. W. (2009). Research design: Qualitative, quantitative, and mixed methods approaches. Thousand Oaks, CA: Sage.

15. Cumming, G. S., Barnes, G., Perz, S., Schmink, M., Sieving, K. E., Southworth, J., ... Van Holt, T. (2005). An exploratory framework for the empirical measurement of resilience. Ecosystems, 8, 975–987.

16. de Loë, R., & Kreutzwiser, R. (2007). Challenging the status quo: The evolution of water governance in Canada. In K. Bakker (Ed.), Eau Canada: The future of Canada's water (pp. 85–103). Vancouver: UBC Press.

17. Department for Environment Food and Rural Affairs (DEFRA). (2013). Catchment based approach: Improving the quality of our water environment – A policy framework to encourage the wider adoption of an integrated catchment based approach to improving the quality of our water environment. London: Author. Retrieved from https://www.gov.uk/government/uploads/system /uploads/attachment_ data/file/204231/pb13934-water-environment-catchment-based-approach.pdf

18. Dryzek, J. (2005). The politics of the earth: Environmental discourses (3rd ed.). New York, NY: Oxford University Press.

19. Duit, A., & Galaz, V. (2008). Governance and complexityemerging issues for governance theory. Governance, 21, 311–335.

20. Duit, A., Galaz, V., Eckerberg, K., & Ebbesson, J. (2010). Governance, complexity, and resilience. Global Environmental Change, 20, 363–368. Dunlap, R. E., Van Liere, K. D., Mertig, A. G., & Jones, R. E. (2000). New trends in measuring environmental attitudes: Measuring endorsement of the new ecological paradigm: A revised NEP scale. Journal of Social Issues, 56, 425–442.

21. Durant, R. F., Chun, Y.-P., Kim, B., & Lee, S. (2004). Toward a new governance paradigm for environmental and natural resources management in the 21st century? Administration and Society, 35, 643–682.

22. FitzGibbon, J., & Mensah, K. O. (2012). Climate change as a wicked problem: An evaluation of the institutional context for rural water management in Ghana. Sage Open, 1–14.

23. Folke, C. (2006). Resilience: The emergence of a perspective for social–ecological systems analyses. Global Environmental Change, 16, 253–267.

24. Folke, C., Carpenter, S., Walker, B., Scheffer, M., Elmqvist, T., Gunderson, L., & Holling, C. S. (2004). Regime shifts, resilience, and biodiversity in ecosystem management. Annual Review of Ecology, Evolution, and Systematics, 35, 557–581.

25. Folke, C., Hahn, T., Olsson, P., & Norberg, J. (2005). Adaptive governance of social-ecological systems. Annual Review of Environment and Resources, 30, 441–473.

26. Forsyth, T. (2003). Critical political ecology: The politics of environmental science. New York, NY: Routledge.

27. Galaz, V. (2007). Water governance, resilience and global environmental change – A reassessment of integrated water resources management (IWRM). Water Science & Technology, 56(4), 1–9.

28. Glasbergen, P. (1998). The question of environmental governance. In P. Glasbergen (Ed.), Co-operative environmental governance: Public-private agreements as a policy strategy (pp.1–18). Dordrecht: Kluwer Academic.

29. Goldstein, B. E. (2011). Collaborative resilience: Moving through crisis to opportunity. Boston, MA: MIT Press.

30. Gunderson, L. H. (2000). Ecological resilience – In theory and application. Annual Review of Ecology and Systematics, 31, 425–439.

31. Gupta, J., Termeer, C., Klostermann, J., Meijerink, S., van de Brink, M., Jong, P., ... Bergsma, E. (2010). The adaptive capacity wheel: A method to assess the inherent characteristics of institutions to enable the adaptive capacity of society. Environmental Science and Policy, 13, 459–471.

32. Head, B. W. (2010). Water policy: Evidence, learning and the governance of uncertainty. Policy and Society, 29, 171–180.

33. Hearnshaw, E. J., Tompkins, J. M., & Cullen, R. (2011, February). Addressing the wicked problem of water resource management: An ecosystem services approach. Paper presented at Australian Agricultural and Resource Economics Society 2011 Conference

(55th), Melbourne, Australia. Retrieved from http://ageconsearch.umn.edu/handle/100556

34. Holling, C. S., & Gunderson, L. H. (2002). Resilience and adaptive cycles. In L. H. Gunderson & C. S. Holling (Eds.), Panarchy: Understanding transformations in human and natural systems (pp. 25–62). Washington, DC: Island Press.

35. Holling, C. S., Gunderson, L. H., & Ludwig, D. (2002). In quest of a theory of adaptive change. In L. H. Gunderson & C. S. Holling (Eds.), Panarchy: Understanding transformations in human and natural systems (pp. 3–24). Washington, DC: Island Press.

36. Holling, C. S., & Meffe, G. K. (1996). Command and control and the pathology of natural resource management. Conservation Biology, 10, 328–337.

37. Hornborg, A. (2009). Zero-sum world: Challenges in conceptualizing environmental load displacement and ecologically unequal exchange in the world-system. International Journal of Comparative Sociology, 50, 237–262.

38. Hornborg, A. (2013). Revelations of resilience: From the ideological disarmament of disaster to the revolutionary implications of (p)anarchy. Resilience, 1, 116–129.

39. Ison, R., Röling, N., & Watson, D. (2007). Challenges to science and society in the sustainable management and use of water: Investigating the role of social learning. Environmental Science and Policy, 10, 499–511.

40. Kettl, D. F. (2002). Environmental governance: A report on the next generation of environmental policy. Harrisonburg: Brookings Institution Press.

41. Kooiman, J. (Ed.). (1993). Modern governance: New government–society interactions. Thousand Oaks, CA: Sage.

42. Krippendorff, K. H. (2013). Content analysis: An introduction to its methodology. Thousand Oaks, CA: Sage.

43. Kuzel, A. J. (1999). Sampling in qualitative inquiry. In B. F. Crabtree & W. L. Miller (Eds.), Doing qualitative research (pp. 33–45). Thousand Oaks, CA: Sage.

44. Lazarus, R. (2009). Super wicked problems and climate change: Restraining the present to liberate the future. Cornell Law Review, 94, 1153–1234. Retrieved from http://cornelllawreview.org/files/2013/02/LazarusSuperWickedProblems.pdf

45. Leech, M. (Ed.). (2008). Re-framing resilience: A symposium report (STEPS Working Paper 14). Brighton: STEPS Centre. Retrieved from http://opendocs.ids.ac.uk/opendocs/bitstream /handle/123456789/2315/Reframing%20Resilience.pdf?sequenc e=1

46. Leiserowitz, A. (2007). International public opinion, perception, and understanding of global climate change. New York, NY: UNDP. Retrieved from http://environment.yale.edu/climate-communication/ article/international-public-opinion-perception-and-understanding-of-global-cl

47. Lemos, M. C., & Agrawal, A. (2006). Environmental governance. Annual Review of Environment and Resources, 31, 297–325.

48. Ludwig, D. (2001). The era of management is over. Ecosystems, 4, 758–764.

49. Lundholm, C., & Plummer, R. (2010). Resilience and learning: A conspectus for environmental education. Environmental Education Research, 16, 475–491.

50. Martin-Breen, P., & Anderies, J. M. (2011). Resilience: A literature review. New York, NY: The Rockefeller Foundation.

51. Masten, A. S. (2007). Resilience in developing systems: Progress and promise as the fourth wave rises. Development and Psychopathology, 19(3), 921–930.

52. Melo Zurita, M. L., Smith, T., Thomsen, D., Lyth, A., Baum, S., & Preston, B. (2013). CADWAGO work package two: First phase case study report (Climate Adaptation and Water Governance (CADWAGO) Project Report). Sippy Downs: University of the Sunshine Coast.

53. Nelson, D. R., Adger, W. N., & Brown, K. (2007). Adaptation to environmental change: Contributions of a resilience framework. Annual Review of Environment and Resources, 32, 395–419.

54. Olsson, P., Folke, C., & Berkes, F. (2004). Adaptive comanagement for building resilience in socialecological systems. Environmental Management, 34, 75–90.

55. Pahl-Wostl, C. (2007). Transition towards adaptive management of water facing climate and global change. Water Resources Management, 21, 49–62.

56. Pahl-Wostl, C. (2009). A conceptual framework for analysing adaptive capacity and multi-level learning processes in resource governance regimes. Global Environmental Change, 19, 354–365.

57. Pahl-Wostl, C., Arthington, A., Bogardi, J., Bunn, S. E., Hoff, H., Lebel, L., ... Tsegai, D. (2013). Environmental flows and water governance: Managing sustainable water uses. Current Opinion in Environmental Sustainability, 5, 341–351.

58. Plummer, R. (2010). Social-ecological resilience and environmental education: Synopsis, application, implications. Environmental Education Research, 16, 493–509.

59. Plummer, R., Baird, J., Dupont, D., & Renzetti, S. (2012). Work package one: Ecological components of ecosystems (Climate Adaptation and Water Governance (CADWAGO) Project Meeting Presentation). Sippy Downs: University of the Sunshine Coast. Resilience 19

60. Plummer, R., de Grosbois, D., Velaniskis, J., & de Loë, R. (2011). Probing the integration of land use and watershed planning in a shifting governance regime. Water Resources Research, 47, W09502.

61. Powell, N., & Jiggins, J. (2003). Learning from participatory land management. In H. A. Becker & F. Vanclay (Eds.), The international handbook of social impact assessment: Conceptual and methodological advances (pp. 42–55). Cheltenham: Edward Elgar Press.

62. Powell, N. S., Larsen, R. K., & van Bommel, S. (2014). Meeting the 'Anthropocene' in the context of intractability and complexity: Infusing resilience narratives with intersubjectivity. Resilience, 2, 135–150.

63. Reed, P. M., & Kasprzyk, J. R. (2009). Water resources management: The myth, the wicked, and the future. Journal of Water Resources Planning and Management, 135, 411–413.

64. Rittel, H. W. J., & Webber, M. M. (1973). Dilemmas in a general theory of planning. Policy Sciences, 4(2), 155–169.

65. Rogers, P., & Hall, A. W. (2003). Effective water governance (TEC Background Papers 7).

66. Stockholm: Global Water Partnership. Retrieved from http://www.gwp.org/Global/GWP-CACENA_Files/en/pdf/tec04.pdf

67. Scholz, J. T., & Stifel, B. (2005). Adaptive governance and water conflict: New institutions for collaborative planning. Washington, DC: Resources for the Future Press.

68. Scott, M. (2013). Resilience: A conceptual lens for rural studies? Geography Compass, 7, 597–610.

69. Shakir, M. (2002). The selection of case studies: Strategies and their applications to IS implementation cases studies. Research Letters in the Information and Mathematical Sciences, 3, 191–198. Retrieved from http://mro.massey.ac.nz/handle/10179/4332

70. Stake, R. (1995). The art of case research. Newbury Park, CA: Sage. Stenekes, N., Colebatch, H. K., Waite, T. D., & Ashbolt, N. J. (2006). Risk and governance in water recycling: Public acceptance revisited. Science, Technology and Human Values, 31, 107–134.

71. Stern, P. C. (1993). A second environmental science: Human–environment interactions. Science, 260, 1897–1899.

72. Stern, P. C., Dietz, T., & Guagnano, G. A. (1995). The new ecological paradigm in social-psychological context. Environment and Behavior, 27, 723–743.

73. Strunz, S. (2012). Is conceptual vagueness an asset? Arguments from philosophy of science applied to the concept of resilience. Ecological Economics, 76, 112–118.

74. Termeer, C., Dewulf, A., & Breeman, G. (2013). Governance of wicked climate adaptation problems. In J. Knieling & W. Leal Filho (Eds.), Climate change governance (pp. 27–39). New York, NY: Springer.

75. Tropp, H. (2007). Water governance: Trends and needs for new capacity development. Water Policy, 9, 19–30.

76. Waddock, S. (2013). The wicked problems of global sustainability need wicked (good) leaders and wicked (good) collaborative solutions. Journal of Management for Global Sustainability, 1, 91–111.

77. Walker, B. H., Holling, C. S., Carpenter, S. R., & Kinzig, A. (2004). Resilience, adaptability and transformability in social–ecological systems. Ecology and Society, 9, 5. Retrieved from http://www.ecologyandsociety. org/vol9/iss2/art5/

78. Wolsink, M. (2006). River basin approach and integrated water management: Governance pitfalls for the Dutch Space-Water-Adjustment Management Principle. Geoforum, 37, 473–487.

79. World Water Assessment Programme. (2003). Water for people water for life (The United Nations World Water Development Report). UNESCO. Retrieved from http://unesdoc.unesco.org/images/0012/001295/129556e.pdf

80. Yin, R. K. (2003). Case study research (Vol. 5). Thousand Oaks, CA: Sage.

81. Zolli, A. (2012, November 2). Learning to bounce back. The New York Times. Retrieved from http://www.nytimes.com/2012/11/03/opinion/forget-sustainability-its-about-resilience.html?pagewanted=all&_r=2

11 CHAPTER

Sustainable Development Goals and Inclusive Development

Joyeeta Gupta [1,2], Courtney Vegelin [3]

[1] *Governance and Inclusive Development Programme Group, Amsterdam Institute for Social Science Research, University of Amsterdam, Amsterdam, The Netherlands*

[2] *UNESCO-IHE Institute for Water Management, Delft, The Netherlands*

[3] *International Development Studies, University of Amsterdam, Amsterdam, The Netherlands*

ABSTRACT

Achieving sustainable development has been hampered by trade-offs in favour of economic growth over social well-being and ecological viability, which may also affect the sustainable development goals (SDGs) adopted by the member states of the United Nations. In contrast, the concept of inclusive development emphasizes the social, ecological and political dimensions of development. In this context, this paper addresses the question: What does inclusive development mean and to what extent is it taken into account in the framing of the SDGs? It presents inclusive development as having three key dimensions (social, ecological, and relational inclusiveness) with five principles each. This is applied to the 17 SDGs and their targets. The paper concludes that while the text on the SDGs fares quite well on social inclusiveness, it fares less well in respect to ecological and relational inclusiveness. This implies that there is a risk that implementation processes also focus more on social inclusiveness rather than on ecological and relational inclusiveness. Moreover, in order to de facto achieve social inclusiveness in the Anthropocene, it is critical that the latter two are given equal weight in the actual implementation process.

Keywords: Sustainable development goals, Inclusive development, Anthropocene, Growth

ABBREVIATIONS

MDGs Millennium development goals

SDGs Sustainable development goals

UN United Nations

UNDP United Nations Development Programme

UNEP United Nations Environment Programme

DDT Dichlorodiphenyltrichloroethane

WCED World Commission on Environment and Development

WHO World Health Organization

UNGA United Nations General Assembly

1 INTRODUCTION

The literature on, and politics of, sustainable development shows that achieving *strong* sustainability, which implies no trade-offs between the economic, social and ecological goals, is rare; politics tend to make trade-offs in favour of the economy at the cost of social and ecological issues (Lorek and Spangenberg 2014). Furthermore, autonomous processes of globalization allocate resources through a poorly regulated market, resulting in a 'one dollar one vote' approach, rather than a 'one person one vote' system at the national level, or a 'one country one vote' system at the global level (Karabarbounis 2011; Stiglitz 2015; Piketty 2014). Without strong countervailing power, this might concentrate resources in the hands of the few, as is already happening (Oxfam 2014, 2015).

The millennium development goals (MDGs) of 2000 aimed to compensate for this autonomous concentration of wealth by focusing on ensuring dignity for the very poorest people. It mobilized people in different parts of the world and in different capacities to implement the MDGs, even though the end results have been uneven. Negotiations on the follow-up to the now expired MDGs have expanded the scope of discussion to include ecological issues. They have led to the adoption of a document entitled 'Transforming our World: The 2030 Agenda for Sustainable Development' which includes the sustainable development goals (UNGA 2014) under the auspices of the United Nations General Assembly (for background see Chasek and Wagner and Gellers in this issue). The sustainable development goals (SDGs) set goals to ensure a 'social floor' á la Raworth (2012), and 'planetary boundaries' á la Rockström et al. (2009) and suggest some of the means that should help in achieving these goals.

This paper analyses whether the SDG text prioritizes the poor and (their) ecological concerns or whether the SDG agenda runs the risk of being hijacked by the ecological and developmental interests of the rich and focus on economic growth at the cost of the other aspects. It does so by exploring the concept of inclusive development (Sect. 2) and applying it to the SDGs (Sect. 3) in order to highlight likely problems in the successful interpretation and operationalization of the SDGs. Its key question is: What does inclusive development mean and to what extent is it taken into account in the framing of the SDGs? Its central argument is that without a deep commitment to inclusive development, the SDGs run the risk of not directing the substantive transformation needed to achieve strong sustainable development. Its key motivation rests in the spirit of optimists like Jeffrey Sachs and realists like Fukuda-Parr who hope that the SDGs will help bring change at multiple levels of governance; it is less in line with sceptics like Clemens and Easterly, or critics like Saith and Pogge, who see the SDGs as poorly defined and a red herring (Hulme 2009).

2 INCLUSIVE DEVELOPMENT

2.1 Introduction

While sustainable development has ecological, social and economic aspects, the difficulties in optimizing all three aspects for present and future generations has led to the rise of concepts that embody dualities of this trinity—green economy/growth (which combines the environment with the economy, UNEP 2011; World Bank 2012), green society (which combines the environment with social goals), inclusive growth (which combines growth with social aspects) and inclusive development (which focuses on social and ecological aspects) (Gupta and Baud 2015). Green growth and inclusive growth are the two most dominant dualities and both have neo-liberal roots but take on an additional dimension—either environmental issues or the need to share economic growth with the poorest. As Fig. 1 shows, interpretation of these dualities can take place anywhere along the spectrum and at the extremes it highlights one aspect more than the other. In contrast, inclusive development questions the need for continuous economic growth in a business-as-usual paradigm (Sect. 2.2). If the global community is willing to develop legally binding rules within which such growth is achieved, then the growth paradigm may also contribute to sustainable development. Until this happens, however, an inclusive development approach is necessary to balance the dominance of the growth approach, especially in the context of global recession.

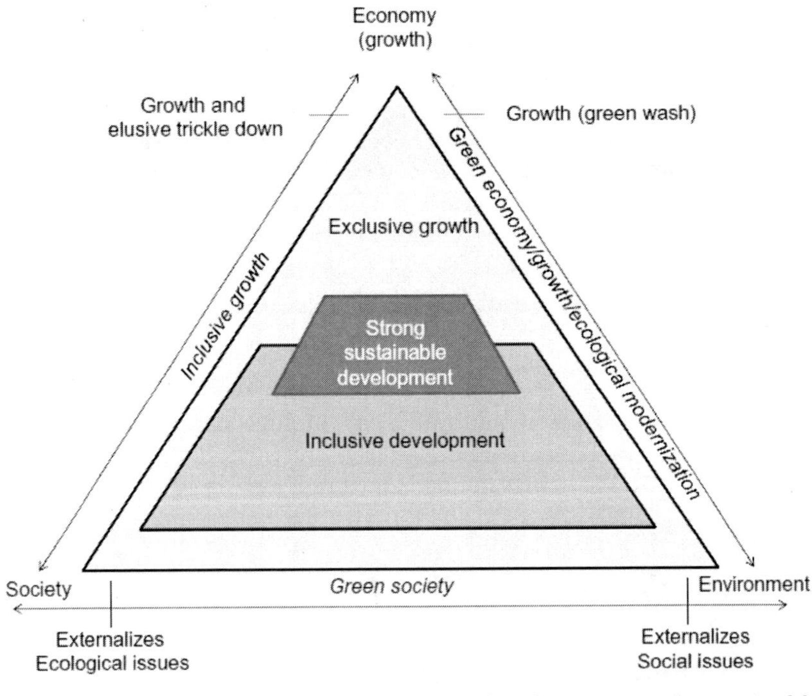

Fig. 1 The relationship between inclusive development and sustainable development

This section draws on the theoretical work on inclusive development which builds on the following intellectual roots (Gupta et al. 2015a, b, c): social roots which lead to the articulation of social inclusiveness (Sect. 2.2); ecological roots which leads to the articulation of ecological inclusiveness (Sect. 2.3); and political geography roots which argue that power politics need to be addressed to protect social and ecological goals (e.g.

Mosse 2010), which leads to the articulation of relational inclusiveness (Sect. 2.4). After explaining these aspects of inclusiveness, we derive five principles for each (see Table 1).

Table 1 The proposed SDGs and inclusive development

Principles	**Which goals**	**Achievements and limitations**
Social inclusiveness		
Ensure equity principles to share the opportunities for development; Include the knowledge of all; Build targeted capacity building to enable effective participation; Enhance protection for the poorest; Engage all in the politics of development	Goal 1: end poverty everywhere; Goal 2: end hunger/ malnutrition; Goal 3: enhance well-being and healthy lives; Goal 4: inclusive and equitable education; Goal 5: end inequality between sexes; Goal 6: universal access to water and sanitation; Goal 7: universal access to energy; Goal 8: employment for all; Goal 9: inclusive industrialization; Goal 10: reduce inequalities; Goal 11: inclusive cities; Goal 15: sustainable livelihoods; Goal 16: inclusive institutions	These goals (a) enhance the level of protection for the poor and the small-scale sector, and (b) to a limited extent include all in the opportunities for development. However, there is little on including the knowledge of all, engaging all in the politics of development, or effective capacity building to enable better participation
Ecological inclusiveness		
Adopt ecocentric limits from local to global level; Equitably share rights, responsibilities	Goal 1: Resilience to disasters and land ownership; Goal 2: Sustainable agriculture; Goal 6: Sustainable water management; Goal 7: Sustainable	Some goals (a) establish some ecocentric targets; (b) focus on building resilience and adaptive capacity; and (c) regulating financial

Principles	Which goals	Achievements and limitations
and risks; Build resilience and adaptive capacity; 'Green' international cooperative instruments; Involve all stakeholders	energy; Goal 8: Enhance resource efficiency, decouple growth from degradation; Goal 9: Sustainable industrialization; Goal 11: sustainable cities; Goal 12: Sustainable consumption and production patterns; Goal 13: Combat climate change; Goal 14: Sustainably use marine resources; Goal 15: Promote sustainable ecosystems and halt land degradation	institutions. However, there are no measures for how rights, responsibilities and risks are to be shared between different groups; international cooperation is mentioned but not in how it needs to be reformed; and there is not enough guarantee of the participation of all stakeholders
Relational inclusiveness		
Ensure that public goods and merit goods do not become privatized or securitized; Address all drivers and actors; and combat offshoring, tax havens, and other instruments that lead to concentration of wealth and ecospace; Address	Goal 3: refers to Tobacco Convention—with strong relational approach; Goal 4: gender equality; Goal 10: reduce inequality; Goal 11: urban rural interface; Goal 12: control private ownership; Goals 13 and 14: encourages developed countries to take responsibilities on climate change and biodiversity; Goal 16: promote peaceful and inclusive societies, access to justice; Goal 17: Revitalize global	These goals aim to (a) promote rule of law and equality of access; (b) address issues of bribery and corruption, illicit financial flows; (c) end inequality in terms of enhancing voice. However, they do not address the logic of market-based economic growth, safeguard public goods from privatization and securitization, or ensure downward

Principles	Which goals	Achievements and limitations
discourses that concentrate wealth to ensure that markets and growth takes place within inclusive development paradigm; Test instruments for inclusiveness and ensure downward accountability; Ensure global rule of law and constitutionalism	partnership	accountability

2.2 Social inclusiveness

Social inclusiveness has its roots in human rights, inequality, redistribution, rural development, entitlements and capabilities concepts (cf. Meier 2001; Thorbecke 2006; Easterly 2007; Sen 1999; Gupta and Thomson 2010) and has been expressed in the Millennium Development Goals (Collier 2007). Social inclusiveness is a multi-level challenge: at the global level, it implies accounting for the least developed and developing countries and post-conflict societies (see e.g. Third World Approaches to International Law (TWAIL) papers such as Okafor 2008). This can be done by encouraging meaningful participation in UN processes, adopting equity principles, capacity building, technology transfer, and financial support. At the regional level, it implies taking the issues of the more vulnerable countries into account and equitable sharing of transboundary resources. At the national level, it implies taking account of marginalized sectors, places, and communities. At the local level, it would imply accounting for specific individuals and groups.

There are seven reasons that justify social inclusiveness (cf. Gupta 2014): humanitarian and normative concerns for the most vulnerable (Sachs 2004a); legal reasons call for the protection of the dignity and human rights of people; economic reasons aim to promote social well-being and participation of the poor in labour and consumption markets (Pouw and McGregor 2014); national security reasons justify meeting the needs of humans (e.g. UNDP 1994); democratic and communist discourses require sharing the results of prosperity with all; public health reasons require investing in the conditions in which the poor live to prevent the spread of poverty related diseases such as cholera, typhoid and others; and international reasons to ensure sustainable societies both within and across borders (where investing in crises affected countries, not only ensures sustainable societies in situ, but can also pre-empt the mass exodus of refugees for ex situ rehabilitation).

Social inclusiveness aims at empowering the poorest through investing in human capital and enhancing the opportunities for participation. It is non-discriminatory and is age, gender, caste, sect and creed sensitive in terms of income, assets and the opportunities for employment (Huang and Quibria 2013). It aims to reduce the exposure to risks such as natural disasters and civil conflict that exacerbate vulnerability (Rauniyar and Kanbur 2010). In doing so, inclusive development policies focus attention on the places (e.g. rural, peri-urban), sectors (e.g. small-scale farming, fishing and community forestry), and arenas (home-based activities, street vendors) of high vulnerability to enhance well-being, including material (i.e. living conditions through access to infrastructure and amenities such as drinking water and sanitation services, education and transport services), social-relational (i.e. in terms of human relations), and cognitive well-being (i.e. taking people's knowledge, experiences and aspirations into account) (Gough and McGregor 2007; Fritz et al. 2009; Narayan et al. 2009; Borel-Saladin and Turok 2013; Arthurson 2002; Mansuri and Rao 2004). These policy processes need to be contextually sensitive (Fritz et al. 2009; Borel-Saladin and Turok 2013), and encourage participatory governance and capacity building to enhance such participation (Sachs 2004a, b; Lawson 2010).

Drawing on the above, this paper suggests that social inclusiveness implies applying five principles (Gupta et al. 2014). These are (a) adopting equity principles to share in development opportunities and benefits; (b) including the knowledge of the marginalized in defining development processes and goals; (c) ensuring a social minimum through a higher level of protection for the most marginalized; (d) targeted capacity building to help the poor benefit from opportunities since they may not be able to otherwise use such opportunities; and (e) engaging the marginalized in the politics of development governance.

2.3 Environmental inclusiveness

Historically, environmental issues focused on single issues like the protection of endangered species. Over time, ecological issues were seen less as single one-off incidents and more as interlocked with development issues (WCED 1987). The knowledge that resource exploitation has experienced 'the great acceleration' (Steffen et al. 2007) such that we are living beyond our ecological means (WWF 2012), confirms that the Earth has entered the geological era of the Anthropocene (Crutzen 2006; see also Boas et al. in this issue).

In scalar terms, ecological inclusiveness at the local level focuses on protecting local access to and ownership of resources as well as protecting local ecosystems. At the national level, it requires that resources are well managed and the sustainability of ecosystem services are ensured. At the transboundary and global level, it implies not causing harm to other countries and using common but differentiated responsibilities for dealing with global problems.

Environmental inclusiveness, or the relation between environmental issues and the marginalized, emerges from three different strands. First, the livelihoods argument has been that the poor depend on their local ecosystem for their survival (e.g. Chambers and Conway 1991). Second, the vulnerability argument focuses on how the vulnerability of the poor may be exacerbated by the effects of climate change (Paavola and Adger 2006) and thus calls for enhancing adaptive capacity and resilience (Nelson et al. 2007). Third, the Anthropocene argument is that the great acceleration in the demand for limited land, water, and other resources and sinks may lead to ecospace grabbing or the large-scale transfer of these resources from local communities to governments, large corporations and the private sector by changing the rules of access to these resources (cf. Zoomers 2010; Fairhead et al. 2012; Leach et al. 2012) which may further exacerbate the vulnerability of the poor (Gupta 2014). Limited sinks refers to the amount of greenhouse gases that we may emit into the atmosphere if we wish to address the problem of climate change; or the carrying capacity of our ecosystems if we wish them to continue to provide us the supporting (e.g. nutrient cycling), regulating (e.g. climate regulation), provisioning (e.g. fish), and cultural services they have always provided us (Chopra et al. 2005). Living and progressing within these limits requires a different vision regarding prosperity and well-being. It challenges the need for continuous growth (Lorek and Spangenberg 2014) with its perverse incentives for a throwaway materialistic society. It calls for equitably allocating rights (i.e. who has the right to access these resources and when can these rights be curtailed), responsibilities (i.e. who has relevant responsibilities and how can such responsibilities be monitored and implemented) and risks (i.e. who faces the risks caused by abuse of the rights and responsibilities and who compensates for these risks) associated with such ecocentric limits for all peoples and countries (Gupta and Lebel 2010). It also calls for greening the financial, aid and trade institutions (e.g. Hicks et al. 2008).

This translates into five principles. These include (a) the adoption of multiple sets of internally consistent, contextually relevant, but not necessarily identical ecocentric limits from the local to the global level to maintain ecosystem capital and services (e.g. the 2 degree target for climate change); (b) developing equitably shared rights, responsibilities and risks; (c) ensuring adequate legal protection and building the adaptive capacity of the most vulnerable to cope with resource conflicts and the impacts of climate change; (d) greening existing international instruments on trade, investment and development assistance; and (e) engaging relevant stakeholders in defining and implementing the above instruments.

2.4 Relational inclusiveness

Relational inclusiveness recognizes that poverty and ecological degradation are often the result of actions taken by others (Harriss-White 2006; Mosse 2010) because of increasing inequality in society (Piketty 2014; Stiglitz 2015) and the substance and process of politics (e.g. Okafor 2008). A scalar perspective requires understanding and addressing the multi-level drivers of inequality, exclusion and vulnerability (see e.g. Laven 2010; Ros-Tonen et al. 2015).

Social inequality refers to the difference in income, wealth, opportunity and access between the rich and the poor. Currently, an astounding 85 individuals possess more wealth than the bottom half of the global population (Oxfam 2014). By 2016, the richest 1 % is expected to own more than the remaining 99 %, rising from 44 % in 2009 (Oxfam 2015). Although historical inequalities were reduced in the twentieth century, the trend is towards rising inequality today (Piketty 2014; Stiglitz 2015; Ortiz and Cummins 2011; Milanovic 2011). The rich have become richer through the historical accumulation of wealth that is unevenly taxed, exploitation of capital markets (which may or may not create bubbles such as the housing bubble—where investors were bailed out by tax-payers at the cost of home-owners), and the development of intellectual property rights that protect medical patents, among others.

Given the importance of natural resources and sinks for economic growth, the rich invest heavily in these resources (land rights, water rights, minerals and metals, the electromagnetic spectrum) and sinks (e.g. by purchasing emission rights) leading also to ecological inequality. By not accepting their responsibility for environmental pollution (e.g. the USA has not ratified the Law of the Seas, the Kyoto Protocol, the Biodiversity Convention), the rich can also avoid their responsibility with impunity by influencing the rules of governance at the national and international level.

Thus, the concentration of wealth leads to inequality through direct and indirect resource expropriation. It also increases the ability of the rich to lobby for a certain kind of politics such as calling for small government and deregulation. Countering the cause and effect of structural inequalities caused by the political relations that keep them intact requires both scholarly engagements on inclusive development through multi-scalar, geographically and sectorally diverse analyses, and social movements to bring attention to them (Townsend 1993; Hickey et al. 2015; Hickey 2005).

A relational approach first requires a rethinking of how merit and public goods are managed (Kaul et al. 2003) and whether the privatization and securitization of these by state entities compromises human security or not. Second, the direct and indirect drivers of poverty, exclusion, and environmental degradation operate from the local to the global level, involving marginal to extremely powerful actors. This calls for policies that deal with all actors as opposed to policies that only deal with empowering the poorest (cf. Harriss-White 2006; Mosse 2010). This would counter the tendency to offshore economic activities and offload governance activities (deregulation) as a way to bypass rules. Third, it recognizes that the roots of the direct and indirect drivers of inequality may lie in the ideological foundations of society calling for the questioning of dominant discourses and vested interests. Fourth, it sees the normative, legal, and instrumental interventions (Cook 2006; Rappaport 1987: 122) as not value-neutral. For example, when states make trade-offs between economic growth for all (i.e. collective well-being) and individual well-being, this can lead to marginalization of the latter (Pouw and McGregor 2014) and adverse inclusion. This calls for the downward accountability of institutions (Narayan 2002). Finally, an inclusive relational approach calls for global constitutionalism and rule of law to ensure that powerful actors like governments, entities, banks, and tax havens are subject to common rules (cf. Koskenniemi 2009; Gupta 2014).

This translates into the following principles: (a) develop specific rules on public and merit goods and ensure that these do not become privatized or securitized directly or indirectly; (b) address all drivers at all levels, and combat 'offshoring' and 'virtualization' of the economy by large corporations and the wealthy to bypass tax and other rules; tax the accumulation of wealth and check when deregulation affects the rights of the poorest; (c) question the discourses that lead to exclusive growth and ensure that markets function within the constraints of inclusive development rules and that these rules are made legally binding; (d) test instruments for inclusiveness and ensure downward accountability; and (e) promote the rule of law and constitutionalism at the global and national levels as a way to combat power politics at both the global and national level to ensure that no country or powerful entity is above the law.

3 APPLYING ID TO THE SDGS

3.1 Introduction

The UN document, 'Transforming our World: The 2030 Agenda for Sustainable Development' includes a declaration of the 17 SDGs and their respective targets along with follow-up and review measures (for other approaches to these 17 Goals, see Chasek and Wagner and Boas et al. in this issue). The document has a rhetorical commitment to 'sustainable development' (mentioning it 85 times). It does not mention 'inclusive development'. It has 41 references to the term 'inclusive' including six references to 'inclusive societies' and 'inclusive and sustainable economic growth' respectively and one to 'inclusive growth'. It focuses strongly on 'growth' which is repeated 16 times (which is occasionally qualified by adjectives such as inclusive or sustainable). Target 8.4 aims at decoupling growth from environmental degradation. However, this does not reflect that a true decoupling will require drastic redefinition of what constitutes growth. Theoretically, sustainable growth implies growth that takes social, economic and ecological aspects into account, but 'sustained growth'—the term used nine times in the document, often in relation to inclusiveness and sustainability—has a different meaning. This reflects the view of some development economists that growth is needed to reduce inequality, a vision we contest. In Goal 9, 'sustainable industrialization' and increased resource use efficiency recognize the concept of limited ecospace by encouraging sustainable use of resources for economic growth. Even so, the emphasis on economic growth reflects the type of dualities mentioned above and undermines more ecocentric goals.

This confirms our fear that there is a risk that the SDGs will go the way of the sustainable development discourse and make trade-offs in favour of growth over social and ecological issues. Business-as-usual growth is justified as necessary for reducing social inequalities and for addressing ecological issues instead of making clear commitments to redefine the development process. This would be to live within ecological constraints for the well-being of society, even if it is at the cost of sustained growth. Beyond the use of terms, we now assess whether the SDG document is truly transformative by assessing it in relation to our inclusive development principles (see Table 1).

3.2 SDGs and social inclusiveness

Of the 17 Goals, 13 focus on social inclusiveness, but also take some ecological or relational aspects into account. Goal 1 aims to end all forms of poverty everywhere, recognizes that poverty is not simply measured in income per capita and that it is also not exclusively located in poor countries. It specifies targets for eradicating extreme poverty, ensuring social protection systems including floors, and ensuring access to basic resources. These social floors are further elaborated in Goal 2 which aims to end hunger and malnutrition by 2030, while doubling the productivity and incomes of small-scale food producers; and in Goal 3 which aims at enhancing well-being and healthy lives through targets on reducing maternal mortality, preventable deaths of children, and major epidemics, managing substance abuse and traffic related deaths, and universal access to sexual and reproductive health care services and health coverage by 2030. Social floors also include Goal 4's focus on inclusive and equitable education through universal completion of primary and secondary education, access to pre-primary education, and opportunities to enhance vocational and lifelong learning by 2030. Similarly, Goal 6 aims to ensure universal access to water and sanitation. Goal 7 ensures universal access to affordable, reliable, sustainable and modern energy, while Goal 8 promotes universal employment opportunities. Goal 9 focuses on resilient and sustainable infrastructure with affordable and equitable access for all and inclusive and sustainable industrialization. It aims to integrate small-scale enterprises into value chains.

Goal 5 focuses on gender equality by eliminating discrimination, violence, harmful social practices, recognizing the value of unpaid care, promoting participation, and promoting access to sexual and reproductive health rights. Goal 10 aims at reducing inequalities within and among countries to achieve social, economic and political inclusion. Goal 11 is likewise defined by inclusive aspirations in cities and human settlements to make them safe and resilient. It guarantees access to housing, basic services, and transportation, but with special attention for women, children, people with disabilities and older persons. Goal 15 refers also to sustainable livelihoods for local communities so that they can avoid relying on poaching and trafficking of protected species for income. Finally, Goal 16 promotes inclusive societies and institutions aiming to reduce violence and death, abuse, trafficking and torture of children, provide legal identity and birth certificates to all, ensure participatory decision-making, guarantee access to information, and protect fundamental freedoms.

Most targets are national-level targets with primarily national-level responsibilities. Goal 10 has very specific global (target 10.5, 10.6, 10.a, 10.b), transnational or non-territorial (target 10.7, 10.c), and national (10.1, 10.2, 10.3, 10.4) aspects while also incorporating global (migrant) and national populations.

While these goals clearly meet two of the five principles—namely that of (a) enhancing the level of protection for the poor/marginalized and small-scale sector; and (b) enhancing development opportunities for all to a limited extent—there is little emphasis on including the knowledge of all, or engaging all, or promoting effective capacity building to enable better participation.

3.3 SDGs and ecological inclusiveness

Eleven goals focus on ecological inclusiveness, marking a shift away from the MDG targets and towards recognizing the interrelationships between exclusion, marginalization and an overburdened environment. They set targets on production and consumption patterns (Goal 12) including sustainable and resilient agricultural practices, maintaining ecosystem services and adaptation to climate change, genetic diversity and securing seed and plant banks (Goal 2), demand side management through energy efficiency and supply side management through promoting renewable energy (Goal 7), resource efficiency, decoupling growth from pollution (Goal 8) and sustainable industrialization (Goal 9); and on enhancing the quality of life by providing access to open and green spaces for all, sustainable transport systems, sustainable urbanization, sustainable human settlement planning, and improving air quality and waste management within sustainable and resilient cities (Goal 11). These targets also focus on sustainable water management from local to global levels (Goal 6 and 14), mitigating climate change (Goal 13), and protecting ecosystems and forests (Goal 15). Perhaps most significant for the prospects of ensuring ecological inclusiveness is target 15.9 which calls for mainstreaming the principle of ecosystem protection into international, national, and local development agendas. In terms of building resilience, Goals 11 and 13 call to minimize exposure to disasters and enhance resilience and adaptive capacity, not least through emphasizing the importance of land and resource ownership of the poorest (Goal 1).

Different levels are addressed in the need to adopt sustainable practices including the state, the private sector, local economies depending on tourism, and populations. Key to these steps is also the effective mobilization of financial resources and the role of international law.

Thus some of these goals (a) establish ecocentric targets, if vague in qualitative and quantitative terms; (b) focus on building resilience and adaptive capacity; and (c) regulate financial institutions. However, few if any deal with the other principles of allocating rights, responsibilities and risks between countries, or how to 'green' international cooperation institutions. There is also not enough guarantee of the participation of all stakeholders.

3.4 SDGs and relational inclusiveness

Three of the 17 SDGs take an explicitly relational approach (Goals 10, 16 and 17), while others are more implicit. It is remarkable, relative to the MDGs, that the proposed SDGs made a clear relational goal on reducing inequality within and among countries. Goal 10 provides guards against exclusion at different levels and recognizes the overlap between multiple forms of exclusion and marginalization. Inclusion refers to closing the income gap between the rich and poor, eliminating discriminatory laws and implementing social protection to enhance equality. This goes beyond social protection purely to prevent people from falling below the absolute poverty line. Furthermore, inclusion is facilitated by monitoring global financial markets, and by enhancing representation and conditions for developing countries in global decision-making fora. It tries to tackle structural inequality through changing decision-making processes, aid, investment, and trade agreements.

Goal 16 goes a step further to call for the rule of law and equal access to justice for all, which is critical for addressing structural issues. It also focuses on reducing illicit financial and arms flows, reducing corruption and bribery and ensuring responsive participatory institutions. Goal 17 addresses structural issues by focusing on enhancing tax imposition on the rich, reiterating the 0.7 % official development assistance commitment of rich countries and addressing structural international debt issues. It includes the usual clauses on technology transfer and capacity building, the promotion of policy coherence, multi-stakeholder partnerships and monitoring and accountability.

Additional targets embracing relational aspects focus on enhancing opportunities for the poor and managing migration possibilities, as well as progressive taxation, monitoring of global institutions and financial markets, and giving more voice to developing countries in global financial and economic policy. Goal 3 includes a reference to WHO's Framework Convention on Tobacco Control, an instrument with a relational approach since it not only focuses on rules to reduce demand, but also on rules to control supply by producers. It also recommends that there should be access to medicines in developing countries using the flexibilities of intellectual property rights laws in order to promote public health. Goal 4 on gender equality tries to address the complex issue of ownership rights, but otherwise is not really dramatic in its relational approach.

Goal 11 encourages positive links between urban, peri-urban and rural areas to promote mutually inclusive instead of exclusive development. Goal 12 includes targets which address the threat of private ownership of resources and aims to regulate private actors and their reporting practices. Goal 13 emphasizes the need for national ratification of climate change measures, and the responsibility that developed countries have to developing countries to help them act in accordance with them. Goal 15 reiterates the need for developed countries to raise financial resources to protect biodiversity and other ecological goals.

The SDGs (a) promote the rule of law and equality of access to justice; (b) attempt at addressing issues of bribery, corruption, illicit financial flows, tax evasion, unfair subsidies, and debt forgiveness; and (c) deal with ending inequality by enhancing fair participation within domestic and international institutions. However, they do not address the logic of market-based economic growth, safeguard public goods from privatization and securitization, nor ensure downward accountability. Furthermore, the lack of clear quantitatively defined targets and timetables for some of these issues may run the risk that they pacify critics without actually delivering on the goals.

3.5 SDGs and implementation

This section explores what the document says about SDG implementation. While Goal 17 on implementation highlights the importance of finance, technology, capacity building, trade, and systemic issues, other goals also include some aspects of implementation. On social inclusiveness, Goals 1 and 17 seek better domestic financial resource mobilization; Goals 9 and 17 promote cooperation on science, technology, innovation and ICT; Goals 4 and 8 promote capacity building of teachers, scholarships for higher education in other countries, and a global strategy for youth employment.

On ecological inclusiveness, Goals 7, 11, 14, and 17 emphasize raising financial resources and cooperating on environmentally sound technologies between states and recommend multilateral negotiations within the UN calling, inter alia, for the full implementation of international law on climate change and water (Goals 6, 17).

Relational inclusiveness is more complex as it challenges the existing status quo and is expressly developed in Goal 10. It calls on the powerful countries to meet their ODA commitments, debt restructuring to help developing countries, and to deal with tax evasion. Goal 17 calls on powerful institutions such as the trading regime to promote more balanced trading and to implement the principle of special and differential treatments for developing countries, in accordance with long-standing WTO agreements. Beyond this, implementation also means doubling the share of global exports of LDCs by 2020 and using international forums to give special attention to rural infrastructure and agricultural research and to managing food price volatility. Goal 8, which focuses on aid for trade, may counter the relational approach if carried to its logical conclusion.

Some goals call on all countries to enhance tax collection capacities to generate revenue which may also force multinational corporations to reduce their own tax avoidance practices. There is also a focus on reducing unfair subsidies. Technology transfer to developing countries is required to take place on terms favourable to them, including concessional and preferential terms. Importantly, in Goal 17, capacity building is meant to come from support from developed countries. In terms of social aspects, pro-poor and gender-sensitive policies are to be included from the national to the international level.

The targets in Goal 17 addressing policy coherence are implicitly relational in nature. Aiming for macroeconomic stability without undermining the national integrity of developing countries implicitly restricts developed countries from being too invasive and setting their economic conditions. Likewise, the target to enhance global access to data and information means that—with equal understanding and knowledge about any issue area—there will be a more level playing field between developed and developing countries in negotiating all forms of development interventions.

Thus these targets reflect relational criteria by putting pressure on developed countries to take their responsibilities seriously and to work through multilateral institutions. More radically (though extremely limited), they hint at reducing the opportunities for tax breaks and evasion by multinationals. Nonetheless, they do not collectively represent a powerful enough relational text that challenges status quo politics and existing power relations to create more conducive conditions for enhancing inclusive development.

4 CONCLUSION

This paper argues that an inclusive development analysis of the SDGs may help to assess whether the textual design truly aims at ensuring that development focuses both on social and ecological issues, as well as on the political tools for achieving the transformation to which it aims. Recognizing the risk that the SDG agenda may go the same route as the sustainable development discourse—that priority will go to economic growth over social and economic goals—this paper has surveyed the 17 SDGs to assess how well they represent inclusive development. We conclude first that the SDG document continues to emphasize the growth component in its interpretation of sustainable development. Second, the SDG text scores well on the articulation of social inclusiveness—as 11 of the 17 goals focus on issues concerning the most marginalized. Third, its commitment to addressing ecological inclusiveness is significantly lower. Although eleven goals deal with ecological issues, the actual quantitative and qualitative commitment is lower. They are largely focused on technology transfer and scientific solutions and not enough on the need to redefine the growth concept based on the availability of limited ecospace and the need to enhance human welfare. Fourth, while relational politics generally received low attention, the SDGs do groundbreaking work by at least mentioning global inequalities, and the need to tax the rich and reform global institutions to create a level playing field. However, in contrast to the other two aspects of inclusive development, relational politics has received the least amount of attention, though the unexpected mention of private sector responsibility and focus on multi-scalar decision-making bodies represents the potential for important changes.

Fifth, what is however remarkable is that there are few goals that either only focus on social issues or only focus on ecological or relational issues. All focus quite substantively on the nexus between two of three criteria, except SDG 11 which straddles all three elements, and SDG 17 which takes relational issues to an operational level (see Fig. 2).

The foregoing content analysis leads us to some points for reflection. First, from the perspective of inclusive development, successful implementation of the SDGs would not only mean that poverty and marginalization are reduced, ecological sustainability is enhanced, and the gap between the powerful and less powerful is minimized. Rather, it also means recognizing a powerful ends-means connection between the goals and the ways in which they are integrated into global society. This requires conceptual coherence between the SDGs themselves and how they are applied. Thus, the methods for implementation would need to embrace the principles of inclusive development in themselves to overcome unequal power relations in order to genuinely address the goals.

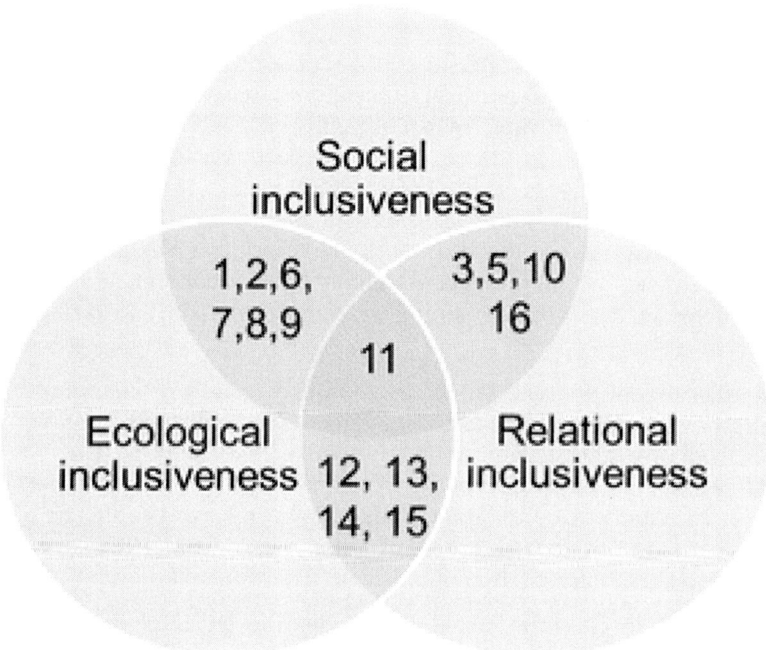

Fig. 2 Applying the inclusive development concept to the SDGs

Second, the implementation of the SDGs would need to challenge the business-as-usual approach to growth. Seeking to promote the rule of law at the national and international levels, upward and downward accountability in institutions, enhanced participation, freedoms and capabilities at all levels, the SDGs clearly aim to bring up the baseline for developing countries and poorer global populations. The articulation of these goals focuses a good deal on what the developed world should do to help achieve them. While this is a crucial component, this may problematically assume a full commitment to equality, sustainable development, and ecological protection on the part of the developed countries as well as large corporations. The scholarly community and NGOs will need to monitor this commitment. The risk of undermining the relational approach can only be avoided by setting the terms for truly equal and participatory interactions between developed and developing countries.

Third, as a corollary to this, the inclusive approach to the SDGs requires developed countries to give something up. This might be done by establishing implementation goals for enhanced democratic and multi-scalar decision-making frameworks which include clear stipulations for how richer participants must change their own behaviour and adjust their own interests as well as ensure that there are resources for financing the implementation of the goals. Additionally, social movements may need to put more pressure on the political or economic powers-that-be to level out the playing field by their own volition, beyond providing required financing or creating conditions for more participation (for example through crowdsourcing as highlighted in Gellers this issue). This might mean that the content of the SDGs would have been stronger with a mention of the UN Global Compact with corporations given that several other frameworks are mentioned to enhance policy coherence. In short, goals to bring up the 'bottom' should be complemented by lowering the 'top'.

There is potential for the SDGs to mobilize scholarly communities, communities of practice and social movements around them to demand relational change and accountability by those implementing the SDGs. This effort can be enhanced with a commitment to the principles of inclusive development by all stakeholders. Even where the current SDG text falls short in this regard, it has provided a more comprehensive and holistic context in which such a commitment has room to flourish.

REFERENCES

1. Arthurson, K. (2002). Creating inclusive communities through balancing social mix: A critical relationship or tenuous link? *Urban Policy and Research, 20*(3), 245–261.

2. Borel-Saladin, J. M., & Turok, I. N. (2013). The green economy: Incremental change or transformation? *Environmental Policy and Governance, 23*(4), 209–220.

3. Chambers, R., & Conway, G. R. (1991). *Sustainable rural livelihoods: Practical concepts for the 21st century*. Institute of Development Studies DP.

4. Chopra, K., Lemans, R., Kumar, P., & Simons, H. (Eds.). (2005). *Ecosystem services and human well-being: Policy responses. Findings of the responses working group of the millennium ecosystem assessment. The millennium ecosystem assessment series* (Vol. 3, pp. 489–523). Washington, DC: Island Press.

5. Collier, P. (2007). *The bottom billion. Why the poorest countries are failing and what can be done about it.* Oxford: Oxford University Press.

6. Cook, S. (2006). Structural change, growth and poverty reduction in Asia: Pathways to inclusive development. *Development Policy Review, 24*(1), 51–80.

7. Crutzen, P. J. (2006). The anthropocene. In E. Ehlers & T. Kraft (Eds.), *Earth system science in the anthropocene* (pp. 13–18). Berlin: Springer.

8. Easterly, W. (2007). Was development assistance a mistake? *American Economic Review,97*(2), 328–332.

9. Fairhead, J., Leach, M., & Scoones, I. (2012). Green grabbing: A new appropriation of nature? *Journal of Peasant Studies, 39*(2), 237–261.

10. Fritz, D., Miller, U., Gude, A., Pruisken, A., & Rischewski, D. (2009). Making poverty reduction inclusive: Experiences from Cambodia, Tanzania and Vietnam. *Journal of International Development, 21*(5), 673–684.

11. Gough, I., & McGregor, J. A. (Eds.). (2007). *Wellbeing in developing countries. From theory to research.* Cambridge: Cambridge University Press.

12. Gupta, J., & Lebel, L. (2010). Access and allocation in earth system governance: Water and climate change compared. *International Environmental Agreements: Politics, Law and Economics, 10*(4), 377–395.

13. Gupta, J., & Thompson, M. (2010). Development and development cooperation theory. In J. Gupta & N. van de Grijp (Eds.), *Mainstreaming climate change in development cooperation: Theory, practice and implications for the European Union* (pp. 33–66). Cambridge: Cambridge University Press.

14. Gupta, J. (2014). *Sharing our Earth.* Inaugural address as professor of environment and development in the global south, University of Amsterdam, 5 June 2014. http://www.oratiereeks.nl/upload/pdf/PDF-3450weboratie_Gupta.pdf. Retrieved 7 Oct 2015.

15. Gupta, J., Baud, I., Bekkers, R., Bernstein, S., Boas, I., Cornelissen, V., et al. (2014). *Sustainable development goals and inclusive development,* Post 2015/UNU-IAS Policy Brief #4. http://sdg.earthsystemgovernance.org/sdg/publications/sustainable-development-goals-and-inclusive-development. Retrieved 7 Oct 2015.

16. Gupta, J., & Baud, I. S. A. (2015). Sustainable development. In P. Pattberg & F. Zelli (Eds.), *Encyclopedia of global environmental politics and governance* (pp. 61–72). Cheltenham: Edward Elgar.

17. Gupta, J., Cornellissen, V., & Ros-Tonen, M. A. F. (2015a). Inclusive development. In P. Pattberg & F. Zelli (Eds.), *Encyclopedia of global environmental politics and governance* (pp. 35–44). Cheltenham: Edward Elgar.

18. Gupta, J., Pouw, N., & Ros-Tonen, M. (2015b). Towards an elaborated theory of inclusive development. *European Journal of Development Research, 27,* 541–559.

19. Harriss-White, B. (2006). Poverty and capitalism. *Economic and Political Weekly,* 1–7.

20. Hickey, S. (2005). Capturing the political? The role of political analysis in the multi-disciplining of development studies. Working Paper. GPRG (Global Poverty Research Group).

21. Hickey, S., Sen, K., & Bukenya, B. (Eds.). (2015). *The politics of inclusive development: Interrogating the evidence.* Oxford: Oxford University Press.

22. Hicks, R. L., Parks, B. C., Timmons Roberts, J., & Tierney, M. J. (2008). *Greening aid: Understanding the environmental impact of development aid.* Oxford: Oxford University Press.

23. Huang, Y. & Quibria, M. G. (2013). The global partnership for inclusive growth. UNU-WIDER Working Paper No. 2013/059.

24. Hulme, D. (2009). The millennium development goals (MDGs): A short history of the world's biggest promise (September 30, 2009). BWPI Working Paper No. 100.

25. Karabarbounis, L. (2011). One dollar, one vote. *The Economic Journal, 121,* 621–651. doi:10.1111/j.1468-0297.2010.02406.

26. Kaul, I., Conceicao, P., Le Goulven, K., & Mendoza, R. U. (Eds.). (2003). *Providing global public goods: Managing globalization.* Oxford: Oxford University Press.

27. Koskenniemi, M. (2009). The politics of international law—20 years later. *The European Journal of International Law, 20*, 7–19.

28. Laven, A. C. (2010). *The risks of inclusion: Shifts in governance processes and upgrading opportunities for Cocoa farmers in Ghana*. Amsterdam: KIT publishers.

29. Lawson, V. (2010). Reshaping economic geography? Producing spaces of inclusive development. *Economic Geography, 86*(4), 351–360.

30. Leach, M., Fairhead, J., & Fraser, J. (2012). Green grabs and biochar: Revaluing African soils and farming in the new carbon economy. *Journal of Peasant Studies, 39*(2), 285–307.

31. Lorek, S., & Spangenberg, J. H. (2014). Sustainable consumption within a sustainable economy: Beyond green growth and green economies. *Journal of Cleaner Production, 62*, 33–44.

32. Mansuri, G., & Rao, V. (2004). Community-based and -driven development. A critical review. *The World Bank Research Observer, 19*(1), 1–39.

33. Meier, G. M. (2001). Ideas for development. In G. M. Meier & J. E. Stiglitz (Eds.), *Frontiers of development economics: The future in perspective* (pp. 1–12). Oxford, DC: Oxford University Press and World Bank.

34. Milanovic, B. (2011). *The haves and the have-nots*. New York: Basic Books.

35. Mosse, D. (2010). A relational approach to durable poverty, inequality and power. *The Journal of Development Studies, 46*(7), 1156–1178.

36. Narayan, D. (2002). *Empowerment and poverty reduction: A sourcebook*. Washington, DC: The World Bank.

37. Narayan, D., Pritchett, L., & Kapoor, S. (2009). *Moving out of poverty: Success from the bottom up* (Vol. 2). Washington, DC: World Bank.

38. Nelson, D. R., Adger, W. N., & Brown, K. (2007). Adaptation to environmental change: Contributions of a resilience framework. *Annual Review of Environment and Resources, 32*(1), 395–419.

39. Okafor, O. C. (2008). Situating third world approaches to international law (TWAIL): Inspirations, challenges and possibilities. *International Community Law Review, 10*, 371–378.

40. Ortiz, I., & Cummins, M. (2011). *Global inequality: Beyond the bottom billion—a rapid review of income distribution in 141 countries.* New York: UNICEF.

41. Oxfam, (2014). *Even it up: Time to end extreme inequality.* Great Britain: Oxfam.

42. Oxfam, (2015). *Wealth: Having it all and wanting more.* Great Britain: Oxfam.

43. Paavolaa, J., & Adger, W. N. (2006). Fair adaptation to climate change. *Ecological Economics,56*, 594–609.

44. Piketty, T. (2014). *Capital in the twenty-first century.* Cambridge MA: Harvard University Press.

45. Pouw, N. R. M. & McGregor, J. A. (2014). An economics of wellbeing. How would economics look like if it were focused on human wellbeing? IDS Working Paper 436. Brighton: Institute of Development Studies, Sussex University.

46. Rappaport, J. (1987). Terms of empowerment/exemplars of prevention: Toward a theory for community psychology. *American Journal of Community Psychology, 15*(2), 21–148.

47. Rauniyar, G., & Kanbur, R. (2010). Inclusive growth and inclusive development: A review and synthesis of Asian Development Bank literature. *Journal of the Asia Pacific Economy, 15*, 455–469.

48. Raworth, K. (2012). A safe and just space for humanity: Can we live within the doughnut. *Oxfam Policy and Practice: Climate Change and Resilience, 8*(1), 1–26.

49. Rockström, J., Steffen, W., Noone, K., Persson, Å., Chapin, F. S., Lambin, E. F., et al. (2009). A safe operating space for humanity. *Nature, 461*, 472–475.

50. Ros-Tonen, M. A. F., Van Leynseele, Y., Laven, A., & Sunderland, T. (2015). Landscapes of social inclusion: Inclusive value-chain collaboration through the lenses of food sovereignty and landscape governance. *European Journal of Development Research, 27*, 523–540.

51. Sachs, I. (2004a). From poverty trap to inclusive development in LDCs. *Economic and Political Weekly, 39*(18), 1802–1811.

52. Sachs, I. (2004b). Inclusive development strategy in an era of globalization. International Labour Office working paper No. 35. Geneva: International Labour Organization.

53. Sen, A. K. (1999). *Development as freedom*. Oxford: Oxford University Press.

54. Steffen, W., Crutzen, P. J., & McNeill, J. R. (2007). The anthropocene: Are humans now overwhelming the great forces of nature. *Ambio: A Journal of the Human Environment, 36*(8), 614–621.

55. Stiglitz, J. E. (2015). *The great divide: Unequal societies and what we can do about them*. New York: WW Norton and Company.

56. Thorbecke, E. (2006). The evolution of the development doctrine: 1950–2005. UNU-WIDER Discussion Paper 2006/155. Helsinki: World Institute for Development Economics Research of the United Nations University.

57. Townsend, P. (1993). *The international analysis of poverty*. New York: Harvester Wheatsheaf.

58. UNDP (United Nations Development Programme). (1994). *New dimensions of human security human development report*. New York: UNEP.

59. UNEP (United Nations Environmental Programme). (2011). *Towards a green economy: Pathways to sustainable development and poverty*. Nairobi: UNEP.

60. UNGA (United Nations General Assembly). (2014). Report of the Open Working Group of the General Assembly on Sustainable Development Goals, UNGA a/68/970.

61. UNGA (United Nations General Assembly) (2015). *Transforming Our World: The 2030 Agenda for sustainable development*. Draft resolution referred to the United Nations summit for the adoption of the post-2015 development agenda by the General Assembly at its sixty-ninth session. UN Doc. A/70/L.1 of 18 September.

62. WCED (World Commission on Environment and Development). (1987). *Our common future*. Oxford: Oxford University Press.

63. World Bank. (2012). *Inclusive green growth. The pathway to sustainable development*. Washington, DC: The World Bank.

64. WWF. (2012). *Living planet report*. World Wide Fund for Nature.

65. Zoomers, A. (2010). Globalisation and the foreignisation of space: Seven processes driving the current global land grab. *The Journal of Peasant Studies, 37*(2), 429–447.

Index